FUNCTIONAL ASSESSMENT-BASED INTERVENTION

Also Available

Developing a Schoolwide Framework to Prevent and Manage Learning and Behavior Problems, Second Edition

Kathleen Lynne Lane, Holly Mariah Menzies,
Wendy Peia Oakes, and Jemma Robertson Kalberg

*Managing Challenging Behaviors in Schools:
Research-Based Strategies That Work*

Kathleen Lynne Lane, Holly Mariah Menzies,
Allison L. Bruhn, and Mary Crnobori

*Supporting Behavior for School Success:
A Step-by-Step Guide to Key Strategies*

Kathleen Lynne Lane, Holly Mariah Menzies,
Robin Parks Ennis, and Wendy Peia Oakes

*Systematic Screenings of Behavior to Support Instruction:
From Preschool to High School*

Kathleen Lynne Lane, Holly Mariah Menzies,
Wendy Peia Oakes, and Jemma Robertson Kalberg

Functional Assessment-Based Intervention

Effective Individualized Support
for Students

John Umbreit
Jolenea B. Ferro
Kathleen Lynne Lane
Carl J. Liaupsin

THE GUILFORD PRESS
New York   London

Copyright © 2024 The Guilford Press
A Division of Guilford Publications, Inc.
370 Seventh Avenue, Suite 1200, New York, NY 10001
www.guilford.com

Portions of this work are based on Umbreit, J., Ferro, J. B., Liaupsin, C. J., & Lane, K. L. (2007). *Functional Behavioral Assessment and Function-Based Intervention: An Effective, Practical Approach*. Pearson.

All rights reserved

Except as noted, no part of this book may be reproduced, translated, stored in a retrieval system, or transmitted, in any form or by any means, electronic, mechanical, photocopying, microfilming, recording, or otherwise, without written permission from the publisher.

Printed in the United States of America

This book is printed on acid-free paper.

Last digit is print number: 9 8 7 6 5 4 3 2 1

LIMITED DUPLICATION LICENSE

These materials are intended for use only by qualified professionals.

The publisher grants to individual purchasers of this book nonassignable permission to reproduce all materials for which photocopying permission is specifically granted in a footnote. This license is limited to you, the individual purchaser, for personal use or use with students. This license does not grant the right to reproduce these materials for resale, redistribution, electronic display, or any other purposes (including but not limited to books, pamphlets, articles, video or audio recordings, blogs, file-sharing sites, internet or intranet sites, and handouts or slides for lectures, workshops, or webinars, whether or not a fee is charged). Permission to reproduce these materials for these and any other purposes must be obtained in writing from the Permissions Department of Guilford Publications.

The authors have checked with sources believed to be reliable in their efforts to provide information that is complete and generally in accord with the standards of practice that are accepted at the time of publication. However, in view of the possibility of human error or changes in behavioral, mental health, or medical sciences, neither the authors, nor the editors and publisher, nor any other party who has been involved in the preparation or publication of this work warrants that the information contained herein is in every respect accurate or complete, and they are not responsible for any errors or omissions or the results obtained from the use of such information. Readers are encouraged to confirm the information contained in this book with other sources.

Library of Congress Cataloging-in-Publication Data
Names: Umbreit, John, author. | Ferro, Jolenea, author. | Lane, Kathleen L., author. | Liaupsin, Carl, author.
Title: Functional assessment-based intervention : effective individualized support for students / John Umbreit, Jolenea B. Ferro, Kathleen Lynne Lane, Carl J. Liaupsin.
Description: New York : The Guilford Press, 2024. | Includes bibliographical references and index. |
Identifiers: LCCN 2023035207 | ISBN 9781462553815 (paperback) | ISBN 9781462553822 (cloth)
Subjects: LCSH: Multi-tiered systems of support (Education) | Problem children—Functional assessment. | At-risk youth—Functional assessment. | Problem children—Education. | At-risk youth—Education. | Behavior modification. | Behavioral assessment. | BISAC: EDUCATION / Special Education / Behavioral, Emotional & Social Disabilities | PSYCHOLOGY / Assessment, Testing & Measurement
Classification: LCC LB1029.M85 U63 2024 | DDC 371.93—dc23/eng/20230920
LC record available at *https://lccn.loc.gov/2023035207*

For all the students who have taught us, and for Sid Bijou, who started it all.
—JU

To the students, teachers, families, and colleagues who have contributed so much to my knowledge and understanding of behavior.

To my mother, who instilled in me the value and love of education, and to my children, who have supported me throughout.

To John, Kathleen, and Carl—working with you always makes me think my best thoughts, and your friendships are cherished.

Thank you all for your part in making this book a reality.
—JBF

To my father, whom I lost while writing this book, and my grandfather, whose portrait and memories keep me company. . . . I miss you both every day.

To husband, Craig; my son, Nathan; and my daughter, Katie—The years have flown by, and I treasure the time with you all. I love you beyond measure (despite what it says in Step 3 of this book) and wish you good health and the time and resources to pursue that which inspires you. Please stay close in the years ahead.

To my students and colleagues who have learned the FABI process and the educators and families who have supported their work—It has been gift to be a small part of your partnerships. I appreciate and admire the work you are doing to create a place where all students have what they need to enjoy positive, productive learning environments, with a process that also prioritizes teacher well-being.

To John, Jolenea, and Carl—Through all the seasons, thank you for your time and commitment to this work and our friendships. I am so thankful our paths crossed at the University of Arizona so many years ago.
—KLL

To my wife, Patty, and my son.—Thanks for making our family life full and rich, while including time for me to pursue my personal and professional passions.

To the teachers, other professionals, and students I've worked with over the years—I've learned so much from you all about where to focus my energy to make a difference that matters.

To John, Jolenea, and Kathleen—You've been gracious colleagues and mentors who've enriched my professional life in countless ways.
—CJL

About the Authors

John Umbreit, PhD, is Professor Emeritus of Special Education at the University of Arizona, where he previously served as Professor of Special Education in the College of Education and as Professor of Family and Community Medicine in the College of Medicine. Dr. Umbreit specializes in the areas of behavioral analysis and positive behavioral supports. His research focuses on functional assessment-based intervention and positive behavioral interventions and supports (PBIS) in natural environments such as schools, homes, and the workplace. He has been a visiting professor in special education at the University of Washington, an editorial board member or manuscript reviewer for 17 professional journals, a frequent reviewer of grant proposals for the U.S. Department of Education, and Principal Investigator for 18 research and personnel preparation grants.

Jolenea B. Ferro, PhD, BCBA-D, is Research Associate Professor in the Department of Child and Family Studies at the University of South Florida and Training Director for the Florida Center for Inclusive Communities, the University's Center for Excellence in Developmental Disabilities. Dr. Ferro has developed interventions and supports for learners with severe behavior problems and has extensive experience in inservice and preservice education. Her research focuses on functional assessment and implementation of PBIS in natural settings. Dr. Ferro is the author of many journal articles and chapters related to functional behavioral assessment, treatment integrity, and PBIS leadership training.

Kathleen Lynne Lane, PhD, BCBA-D, is a Roy A. Roberts Distinguished Professor in the Department of Special Education and Associate Vice Chancellor for Research at the University of Kansas. Dr. Lane's research interests focus on designing, implementing, and evaluating comprehensive, integrated, three-tiered (Ci3T) models of prevention to prevent the development of learning and behavior challenges and to respond to existing instances, with an emphasis on systematic screening. She is coeditor of *Remedial and Special Education* and has published 14 books, more than 240 refereed journal articles, and 55 book chapters.

Carl J. Liaupsin, EdD, is Professor and Department Head of the Department of Disability and Psychoeducational Studies at the University of Arizona. Dr. Liaupsin has worked as a teacher of students with emotional and behavioral disorders, as a full-time behavior specialist for a midwestern school district, and as a research associate for the National Center on Positive Behavioral Interventions and Supports and the National Center on Education, Disability, and Juvenile Justice. His research interests include the validation of function-based behavior intervention methods, development and evaluation of effective training in intervention practices, and use of technology-based tools to support teachers who work with students who exhibit challenging behavior. He is the author or coauthor of numerous peer-reviewed publications and media-based professional development products, and has served as the coordinator and editor for leading journals in his field.

Contents

PART I. Introduction and Overview — 1

1. **An Introduction to Functional Assessment-Based Interventions** — 3
   Functional Assessment-Based Interventions Defined 4
   FABIs in Tiered Systems 6
   Considering the Cultural Context 8
   An Overview of This Book 9
   Summary 13

2. **Primer on Behavior Analysis** — 14
   Behavior 16
   Antecedents 17
   Reinforcement 18
   Extinction 20
   Punishment 22
   Summary 24

PART II. Step 1: Identifying Students Who May Need a Functional Assessment-Based Intervention — 27

3. **Working in Tiered Systems of Support: A Focus on Tier 3 Considerations** — 29
   Ci3T: An Overview 30
   Creating Transparency at Tier 3: Tertiary (Tier 3) Intervention Grids 36
   A Closer Look at Tier 3 in Ci3T: FABIs 37
   Summary 37

4. **Identifying Students Who May Benefit from a Functional Assessment-Based Intervention** — 38
   Identifying Students in Need of Intensive Intervention Efforts 39
   Summary 44
   FORM 4.1. Referral Checklist: Functional Assessment-Based Interventions 45

PART III. Step 2: Conducting the Functional Assessment   47

5. Getting Started: Understanding the Context   49
Conducting Informal Observations: Learning about the School and Classroom Setting   50
Learning about the Student's History: Reviewing Cumulative Files   53
Summary   54
FORM 5.1. Universal Checklist   55

6. Functional Assessment Interviews: Identifying the Problem and Establishing the Target Behaviors   57
Defining and Prioritizing Problem Behaviors   60
Recommendations for the FABI Interview   63
Summary   66
FORM 6.1. Target Behavior Template   67
APPENDIX 6.1. Preliminary Functional Assessment Survey (PFAS)   68
APPENDIX 6.2. Student-Assisted Functional Assessment Interview (SAFAI)   71

7. Functional Assessment: Direct Observation   73
The Antecedent–Behavior–Consequence Model   75
How to Collect A-B-C Data   76
Summary   82
FORM 7.1. A-B-C Data Collection Form   83

8. Determining the Function of the Behavior: The Function Matrix   85
The Function Matrix   87
Writing a Statement of Function   93
Selecting the Replacement Behavior   95
Summary   98

PART IV. Step 3: Collecting Baseline Data   101

9. Identifying the Dimension of Interest and Selecting an Appropriate Measurement System   103
Why Measure Behavior?   105
Dimensions of Behavior   106
Measuring Behavior   107
How to Collect Data: Methods and Considerations   112
Summary   116

10. Getting Started: Collecting Baseline Data   117
Baseline Data   117
Baseline Data Collection Procedures   119
Interobserver Agreement   123
Factors Affecting Data Reliability   126
Summary   128

PART V. Step 4: Designing the Functional Assessment-Based Intervention   129

11. Designing and Testing the Intervention   131
Purpose   133
Designing the Intervention: An Overview   133

Using the Function-Based Intervention Decision Model to Select an Intervention Method 134
Testing the Intervention: An Overview 141
Summary 143
FORM 11.1. Functional Assessment and Behavior Intervention Plan: Planning Form 145

12. Intervention Method 1: Teach the Replacement Behavior   155

Can the Student Perform the Replacement Behavior? 157
The A-R-E Components for Method 1 161
Calli and Her Teachers 162
Summary 167
FORM 12.1. Functional Assessment and Behavior Intervention Plan: Planning Form for Calli 168

13. Intervention Method 2: Adjust the Environment   175

Understanding the Current Environment 175
Method 2: Adjust the Environment 180
At the Elementary Level: David and Ms. Jones 182
Summary 189
FORM 13.1. Functional Assessment and Behavior Intervention Plan: Planning Form for David 190

14. Intervention Method 3: Shift the Contingencies   198

Method 3: Shift the Contingencies 198
At the Early Elementary Level: Claire 199
Summary 207
FORM 14.1. Functional Assessment and Behavior Intervention Plan: Planning Form for Claire 208

15. Intervention Methods 1 and 2: Teach the Replacement Behavior and Adjust the Environment   215

Saida and Her Social Studies Teacher 216
Summary 220
FORM 15.1. Functional Assessment and Behavior Intervention Plan: Planning Form for Saida 221

16. Treatment Integrity   228

Treatment Integrity Defined 229
The Importance of Treatment Integrity Data 230
Collecting and Using Treatment Integrity Data 230
Summary 234

17. Social Validity   235

Social Validity Defined 237
The Importance of Social Validity 237
Collecting and Using Social Validity Data 237
Summary 242

18. Generalization and Maintenance   243

Generalization and Maintenance Defined 244
Strategies to Explore 246
Collecting and Using Generalization and Maintenance Data 249
Summary 252

19. Designing Your Intervention   254

Drafting A-R-E Components: Linking to Hypothesized Functions 255
Preparing for Intervention Implementation: Checking for Understanding 260
Summary 262

PART VI. Step 5: Testing the Intervention — 263

20. Determining Intervention Outcomes — 265
Treatment Integrity: Is the Intervention Happening as Planned? 267
Student Performance: How Well Is the FABI Working? 267
Social Validity: What Do Stakeholders Think about the Goals, Procedures, and Outcomes? 268
The Logistics of Testing the FABI 268
Summary 269

21. Wrapping It Up: Ending with a Defensible Functional Assessment-Based Intervention — 270
The Process 271
Summary 272
FORM 21.1. Behavior Intervention Plan 273

PART VII. Getting Started in Your Own Context — 279

22. Implementation Considerations — 281
Working Individually or as Part of a Team 282
Summary 285

23. A Step-by-Step Training Model: One Approach to Building Capacity — 286
Lessons Learned with Inservice Educators 287
Suggested Pacing for Teaching FABI at the University Level 288
Summary 288

APPENDIX. Published Research on the Functional Assessment-Based Intervention Model — 293

FABI Completion Checklists — 295
Step 1: Identifying Students Who May Need a Functional Assessment-Based Intervention 297
Step 2: Conducting the Functional Assessment 299
Step 3: Collecting Baseline Data 301
Step 4: Designing the Intervention 303
Step 5: Testing the Intervention 305

References — 307

Index — 317

Purchasers of this book can download and print copies
of the reproducible forms and checklists
at *www.guilford.com/umbreit-forms* for personal use
or use with students (see copyright page for details).

PART I
Introduction and Overview

We wrote this book to present a comprehensive system for designing, implementing, and evaluating functional assessment-based interventions (FABIs) based on a body of research developed since the early 2000s (e.g., Umbreit et al., 2004). In this book, we illustrate how to conduct a FABI as a Tier 3 intervention for students with intensive intervention needs within integrated tiered systems of support, particularly a comprehensive, integrated, three-tiered (Ci3T) model of prevention. We also feature illustrations of how FABIs can be used beyond Ci3T systems, for instance, in schools and preschool centers not yet implementing integrated tiered systems of support, in residential facilities, and in home settings.

In this first part we feature two chapters. In Chapter 1, An Introduction to Functional Assessment-Based Interventions, we provide a general introduction to using FABIs within and beyond integrated tiered systems of support. Specifically, we describe the rationale for FABIs; describe the Umbreit and colleagues (2007) manualized approach to FABIs, which has been widely studied in applied settings; and explain how FABIs are situated in integrated tiered systems of support such as Ci3T.

Next, in Chapter 2, Primer on Behavior Analysis, we begin by identifying and describing basic behavior principles needed to conduct a FABI. Then, we discuss the importance of a deeper knowledge of behavioral principles and supervised experiences. We close by defining treatment integrity and explaining its importance to the FABI process.

In Parts II–VI, we progress through the manualized process for designing, implementing, and evaluating FABIs. We include examples, resources, and illustrations throughout our discussion of each step. These steps are:

STEP #	FUNCTIONAL ASSESSMENT-BASED INTERVENTION STEPS
1	Identifying Students Who May Need a Functional Assessment-Based Intervention
2	Conducting the Functional Assessment
3	Collecting Baseline Data
4	Designing the Functional Assessment-Based Intervention
5	Testing the Intervention

Finally, in Part VII, Getting Started in Your Own Context, we provide guidance for those implementing FABIs. Specifically, we offer suggestions for educators, researchers, technical assistance providers, and university professors as they move forward with the FABI process.

CHAPTER 1

An Introduction to Functional Assessment-Based Interventions

LEARNING OBJECTIVES

- Describe the rationale for functional assessment-based interventions (FABIs).
- Describe the Umbreit et al. (2007) manualized approach to FABIs.
- Explain how FABIs are situated in integrated tiered systems of support.

From preschool through high school, students come to school with a range of skills sets—academically, behaviorally, and socially (Lane, Buckman, et al., 2020). Although some students easily negotiate relationships with adults and peers as well as self-regulate their thoughts, feelings, and behaviors, others struggle (Chafouleas et al., 2010; Walker et al., 2004). The magnitude of students struggling with internalizing (e.g., shy, anxious, and withdrawn) and externalizing (e.g., noncompliant, disruptive, and aggressive) behavior patterns is larger than many educators realize. At any time, estimates suggest that 12% of school-age youth struggle with moderate-to-severe emotional and/or behavioral disorders (EBD), and as many as 20% have mild EBD (Forness et al., 2012).

A lack of developmentally appropriate social skills and behavioral challenges are evident in early education settings as well. Preschool teachers report that disruptive behavior has become one of their biggest challenges (Friedman-Krauss et al., 2014). Six to seven percent of young children are identified with aggressive and disruptive behavior that—if not addressed—can continue to affect their experience into elementary and high school (Shaw, 2013). Preschool children are over three times more likely to be expelled than their K–12 counterparts (Gilliam, 2005).

In years past, many people assumed that students with these interfering challenging behaviors would receive support through special education services according to the Individuals with Disabilities Education Improvement Act (IDEIA; 2004) under the category of emotional disturbance (ED). However, less than 1% of students receive services for ED. Thus, most students with more broadly defined EBD will be supported by the general education community. Given that many teacher preparation programs provide as little as one class on classroom management, it is not surprising that many teachers report the need for additional support to meet the multiple needs of students who exhibit challenging behavior (Lane, 2017).

Fortunately, there have been a number of advances in the field of education to address this demand. For example, there have been decades of inquiry on the use of applied behavior analysis (ABA) principles to empower educators to design, implement, and evaluate functional assessment-based intervention to support students with intensive intervention needs (see Common et al., 2020; Lane, Bruhn, et al., 2009). This ABA inquiry is not only rigorous, but also respectful in the sense that the Behavior Analyst Certification Board (BACB; 2022) features the *Ethics Code for Behavior Analysts* to guide the professional activities of behavior analysts for whom the BACB has responsibility.

In addition, there has been an important shift away from reactive approaches to managing challenging behaviors toward a *systems approach* to preventing and responding effectively to learning and behavior challenges (Lane & Walker, 2015). Such systems originated in the field of public health. They were introduced to the educational community by Hill Walker and colleagues (Walker et al., 1996) and paved the way for a range of tiered systems, such as response to intervention (RTI; Fuchs & Fuchs, 2017; Fuchs et al., 2012) and positive behavioral interventions and supports (PBIS; Horner & Sugai, 2015), as well as integrated systems, such as multi-tiered systems of support (MTSS; Freeman et al., 2015); interconnected systems framework (ISF; Barrett et al., 2013); and comprehensive, integrated, three-tiered (Ci3T; Lane, Oakes, et al., 2014) models of prevention.

In this chapter, we introduce how to use functional assessment-based interventions (FABIs) to support students with intensive intervention needs (Umbreit et al., 2007). We introduce one specific, manualized approach developed by Umbreit and colleagues. This approach uses practical tools to empower general and special education teachers to be both effective and efficient in supporting intensive interventions. Next, we explain how FABIs are situated within integrated tiered systems of support. In this chapter, and throughout the book, we use the Ci3T (Lane, Kalberg, & Menzies, 2009) model of prevention to demonstrate how FABIs are incorporated into a cascade of supports (McIntosh & Goodman, 2016). This same logic can be applied to other tiered systems. We note that this manualized FABI process has been and can be used to design, implement, and evaluate FABIs in school-based systems where integrated tiered systems of support are not yet established. We also discuss the importance of cultural considerations when examining the context at each level of prevention (Tiers 1, 2, and 3), emphasizing FABIs specifically. Finally, we provide an overview of how this book is organized.

Functional Assessment-Based Interventions Defined

FABIs are individualized sets of procedures for decreasing challenging behaviors and increasing the development of socially appropriate, productive replacement behaviors. By individualized, we mean that the assessment and intervention procedures are tailored to fit the needs of a particular individual. In schools and other natural settings, most behavior management is a response to the occurrence of a particular behavior. For example, it is not alright to swear at the teacher or hit peers. Traditionally, school systems have used reactive approaches featuring punishment-based responses to respond to challenging behavior (Walker et al., 2014). Rather than establishing and teaching expectations as in current tiered system approaches, schools have often focused on punitive consequences that become increasingly more severe if the student continues to engage in the offense.

In contrast, a FABI aims to understand and use the reasons *why* the offensive or undesirable behavior is occurring to promote more appropriate and successful behavior by addressing those controlling conditions. A FABI begins by identifying *why* the challenging behavior is occurring. The key to understanding "why" is to identify the antecedent conditions under which the behavior occurs and the consequence(s) that reinforce the behavior. This is done through a systematic process known as functional behavioral assessment (FBA), which is more fully described throughout this book. When we can identify the behavior's *function* (i.e., the consequence that is *reinforcing* the challenging behavior), we will know why the challenging behavior is occurring.

Once we know the behavior's likely function, we can begin to systematically build an intervention that is tied to the results of the FBA and is also accomplished through a systematic process that is described throughout this book. Many professionals, even in schools, have been taught behavior management methods that are better suited for laboratories and clinics than for classrooms and other natural settings. In contrast, the FABI process has been widely studied and implemented in authentic educational environments, with demonstrated success from preschool through high school in a range of natural settings (cf. Common et al., 2017; Turton et al., 2011; Wood et al., 2015).

Early researchers who adopted a functional approach (e.g., Carr, 1977; Carr & Durand, 1985) worked with individuals with severe developmental disabilities. These individuals, who had often endured many years of institutionalization, generally had few if any effective communication skills. Central to the approach was the idea that challenging behaviors were an attempt to communicate that provided clues as to "why" a particular challenging behavior had occurred. For instance, aggressive behaviors (hitting, screaming, kicking) may be the only way a person knows to reliably gain the attention of others. In other situations, the same aggressive behavior could provide the individual with their most effective way to escape from having to engage in unwanted activities or to avoid unpleasant settings. Once the purpose—or function—of the aggressive behavior was understood, researchers were then able to teach these individuals new, socially acceptable ways to gain attention and/or avoid unpleasant activities. This approach came to be known as functional communication training (cf. Carr et al., 1994; Durand, 1990).

Before long, other researchers extended the approach to segregated special education classes for children with severe developmental disabilities (Dunlap et al., 1991; Repp et al., 1988) and those with EBD (Kern, Childs, et al., 1994). Soon after, the approach was applied to help students succeed in general education classrooms (Umbreit, 1995). The common element throughout this evolution was the basic idea of *function*, that is, the recognition that challenging behaviors occurred regularly because they were effective, providing an individual with their best chance of accessing and/or avoiding certain consequences and outcomes. Armed with this knowledge, support staff could approach behavior management in a new way. Instead of responding to the behavior itself, the focus shifted to identifying *why* the behavior occurred and to teaching new effective, socially appropriate replacement skills, thus making the challenging behavior both ineffective and unnecessary.

Behavior assessment and intervention often proceed in a linear, predictable sequence. Material in this book is presented in the same sequence in which tasks are conducted in the natural setting. Across chapters, readers will learn effective methods for defining target (i.e., problem) behaviors, identifying their function, designing effective FABI procedures, and then implementing and monitoring those interventions. We provide examples that span various ages, disabilities, and environments.

Key tools that we present include:

- The *Function Matrix*, a unique tool for organizing assessment data and identifying the function of a target behavior.
- The *Function-Based Intervention Decision Model*, which guides the identification of intervention components. These procedures will enable users to identify strategies and design interventions that are appropriate for the environment in which the behavior occurs.
- A straightforward process for selecting a valid measurement system for the behaviors and settings in which you are working. Valid measurement methods are vital to ensure effective outcomes.
- Key instruments and methods for assessing social validity and treatment integrity. To last, effective interventions must be acceptable to those responsible for their implementation (i.e., socially valid) and implemented faithfully (i.e., with treatment integrity). Instruments, tools, and methods appropriate for schools and other natural settings are discussed.

Ethical considerations in applied settings are integrated throughout the book. Relevant BACB ethics codes are identified and described as they apply within each chapter. See Box 1.1 for ethical considerations related to cultural responsiveness, nondiscrimination, awareness of personal biases, and provision of effective treatment. Rather than repeating the ethical code, each box describes the manner in which the code applies to the material within the specified chapter. In addition, we describe equitable practices that are incorporated within the FABI process (e.g., inclusion of family members on the FABI team) and provide suggestions for actions to further equity when completing individualized interventions.

FABIs in Tiered Systems

Many schools and other service systems have developed effective Tier 1 (universal) support for all students. This support typically includes establishing schoolwide expectations and procedures for positive reinforcement and data collection. In the Ci3T system, Tier 1 efforts address a student's academic, behavioral, and social and emotional well-being domains in one

> **BOX 1.1. Ethical Considerations in Chapter 1: BACB Ethics Code for Behavior Analysts**
>
> **1.07 Cultural Responsiveness and Diversity; 1.08 Nondiscrimination; 1.10 Awareness of Personal Biases and Challenges**
>
> Chapter 1 provides a broad overview of cultural and linguistic responsiveness and how it relates to intensive, individualized interventions. Importantly, the chapter highlights not only cultural, but also linguistic competence. Although the chapter provides a broader conceptualization of cultural responsiveness and more specific ideas linked to behavioral intervention, it notes only the BCBA's requirements as detailed in the BACB *Ethics Code for Behavior Analysts* (2022). These requirements include acquiring the knowledge and skills related to cultural competence and diversity, providing services that are equitable and inclusive, and evaluating personal biases and the ability to provide services. Later chapters more fully describe ways to apply this knowledge of cultural and linguistic diversity and offer suggestions for evaluating biases.
>
> **2.01 Providing Effective Treatment**
>
> Chapter 1 presents an introduction to using a specific approach to FABIs. The introduction references relevant research demonstrating that the FABI process is successful in a range of natural settings, with the weight of evidence focused on school settings. As presented in this chapter and throughout the book, the FABI is consistent with behavioral principles, is based on scientific evidence, and is focused on reinforcement. In subsequent chapters, we continue to present examples and evidence that this process produces desired outcomes and provides procedures that protect all clients and stakeholders.

integrated system. Whereas in traditional MTSS models these domains are often designed over the course of successive years, in Ci3T there is a manualized building process in which an integrated system featuring all three domains is designed over the course of one academic year (Lane, Oakes, Cantwell, et al., 2019). More specifically, during a yearlong Ci3T professional learning series, Ci3T Leadership Teams from each school develop a Ci3T implementation manual by creating the following series of blueprints (available on *www.ci3t.org/building*):

- Ci3T Blueprint A Primary (Tier 1) Plan
- Ci3T Blueprint B Reactive Plan
- Ci3T Blueprint C Expectation Matrix
- Ci3T Blueprint D Assessment Schedule
- Ci3T Blueprint E Secondary (Tier 2) Intervention Grid
- Ci3T Blueprint F Tertiary (Tier 3) Intervention Grid

As part of Tier 1 practices, roles and responsibilities are clearly articulated in academic, behavioral, and social and emotional well-being (using a validated Tier 1 curriculum) learning domains (see Lane, Menzies, et al., 2020; *www.ci3t.org*). Yet even with high levels of fidelity, there will be students who need more than Tier 1 has to offer. Tier 2 supports for these at-risk students are targeted to meet their needs. Typical targeted supports address academic tutoring, social skill development, and management systems. Ci3T includes Secondary (Tier

2) intervention grids that feature validated supports for social skill training, academic support (e.g., small-group reading instruction for targeted skills), and a check-in/check-out intervention. Students exposed to multiple risk factors and students who do not respond to Tier 2 strategies, practices, and programs are provided with individualized (Tier 3) intervention. This support can include one-to-one reading instruction and individualized deescalation plans, but most often involves FABIs—the evidence-based practice featured in this book.

Clearly building one integrated system is a formidable charge. Given the importance of multiple voices in building a Ci3T model of prevention based on current scientific knowledge as well as on a community's values and culture, Ci3T Leadership Teams include a range of stakeholders. Specifically, the teams include the principal, two general education teachers, a special education teacher, another school professional (e.g., counselor, school psychologist, behavior specialist, or other instructor), a district Ci3T coach, a family member, and the family member's child (attending sessions held after school). We contend that cultural considerations are key at each level of prevention.

Considering the Cultural Context

In 1975, the Children's Defense Fund (1975) released a report showing that issues of race contribute to disproportionate school disciplinary actions such as suspension and expulsions. More recent studies have concluded with similar findings (e.g., U.S. Department of Education & Office for Civil Rights, 2012; U.S. Government Accountability Office, 2018; Wallace et al., 2008; Whitford, 2017). It has been suggested that the same issues that lead to disproportionate disciplinary actions can also impact the evidence-based individual interventions developed for culturally and linguistically diverse (CLD) students (Bal & Perzigian, 2013).

Integrating aspects of cultural and linguistic responsiveness into tiered systems and individualized interventions has been recommended to create better outcomes for CLD students. A culturally responsive approach includes broad considerations, such as enhancing staff cultural knowledge and self-awareness; validating other cultures; appreciating and honoring different communication styles; connecting to students' prior knowledge and cultural experiences; and considering cultural relevance, validity, and equity in assessing the behavior of CLD students (Banks & Obiakor, 2015; Will & Najarro, 2022). Researchers have also noted that in addition to considering the stresses that students from immigrant families and diverse U.S. cultures experience, service providers should recognize their strengths (Bal & Perzigian, 2013; Moll et al., 1992). To better understand those stressors and strengths, it has been recommended that teachers and other service providers expand the reach of culturally responsive practices by systematically including culturally relevant input from student families and the local community (Bal et al., 2018).

We believe that attending to contextual variables through culturally and linguistically responsive practices will help you develop more effective behavioral interventions at each Tier 1 through Tier 3 level of support. Because we consider FABI as a specific Tier 3 support, sensitivity to issues of culture will help you better understand specific antecedent conditions that will impact your analysis of the observed behavioral relationships. Including diverse stakeholder perspectives in FABI interviews will improve the value of the information you collect.

A culturally responsive approach can also ensure you select elements of a FABI that are consistent with individual characteristics and cultural identities. For instance, the cultural identity of the student or teacher may impact your selection of a replacement behavior, antecedent adjustments, reinforcement procedures, and extinction procedures.

We recommend a broad and thorough understanding of equity and cultural responsiveness (cf. Mathur & Rodriguez, 2022). If you are a board-certified behavior analyst (BCBA), the BACB code of ethics requires this broader knowledge as well as an evaluation of your own biases and of your ability to provide services to individuals from diverse backgrounds. A full review of the literature on cultural and linguistic competence as it applies to behavior analysts is beyond the scope of this book. What this book will do is draw your attention throughout to opportunities to improve outcomes for CLD students by attending to variables of cultural context.

An Overview of This Book

In this book, we provide a detailed description of how to identify students who might benefit from Tier 3 support within an integrated tiered system, determine the function of the undesirable behavior, identify the most appropriate intervention method, and design and test a comprehensive intervention that includes antecedent, reinforcement, and extinction (A-R-E) components. We provide guidance on how to use effective, efficient processes to quickly detect and support students who have intensive intervention needs.

The system is comprehensive, is integrated with the other tiers of support, and is bolstered by peer-reviewed research conducted in schools and other natural settings, including preschools (e.g., Wood et al., 2011), elementary schools (e.g., Nahgahgwon et al., 2010), middle schools (e.g., Gann et al., 2014), high schools (e.g., Whitford et al., 2013), alternative high schools (e.g., Turton et al., 2011), college programs (Lansey et al., 2021), and community-based work programs with adults and seniors (e.g., Underwood et al., 2009). It has been conducted with students with autism (e.g., Reeves et al., 2013), deafness (Gann et al., 2015), emotional and behavioral disorders (Turton et al., 2007), and no identified disabilities (e.g., Liaupsin et al., 2006). See the Appendix (pp. 293–294) for a listing of the peer-reviewed studies that have tested this manualized process.

In short, this book provides the methodology for delivering effective Tier 3 supports. It is simultaneously (1) a textbook for university-level courses; (2) a training manual for BCBAs with limited school experience; and (3) a blueprint for schools, districts, and state departments attempting to create or enhance their respective tiered system of support.

Based on our collective 100-plus years as former teachers and university professors, we recognize that complex systems require careful coordination. We illustrate a five-step process that is fully integrated into a tiered system such as Ci3T. This guidance aids school personnel in getting started with the FABI process in their own integrated tiered systems, as well as individuals searching for professional learning activities to further the capacity of others to scale this process to district- and statewide levels (e.g., see Common et al., 2022).

We organize this book into seven parts, with each part including between two and nine chapters. We briefly describe the purpose and content of each part on pages 10–13.

Part I. Introduction and Overview

Part I includes two chapters. In this first chapter, we provided a general introduction to the design, implementation, and evaluation of FABIs within integrated tiered systems of support such as the Ci3T model of prevention. We provided a list of FABI studies conducted to date that you might find useful as you design, implement, and evaluate FABIs within or separate from integrated tiered systems. We also gave an overview of how the book is organized, which is centered around a five-step process.

Chapter 2, *Primer on Behavior Analysis*, includes a user-friendly overview of applied behavior analytic principles as they relate to predicting and shaping behavior. Specifically, this chapter offers information about the antecedent–behavior–consequence (A-B-C) model and five basic principles that are central to completing a FABI: behavior, antecedents, reinforcement, extinction, and punishment. We provide a basic understanding of these principles for everyone involved with the FABI. We encourage readers to explore other resources and seek additional training and supervised experience applying the principles to hone their skills. This foundational content guides readers to value the communicative intent of behavior and the respectful ways to shape behavior.

Part II. Step 1: Identifying Students Who May Need a Functional Assessment-Based Intervention

Following this introductory chapter and the primer on behavior analysis, Part II of this book features two chapters that explore Step 1: Identifying students who may need a functional assessment-based intervention.

In Chapter 3, *Working in Tiered Systems of Support: A Focus on Tier 3 Considerations*, we provide a more detailed overview of how the FABI process fits within and beyond tiered systems of support. We include sample tertiary (Tier 3) intervention grids for use in preschool, elementary, middle, and high schools implementing Ci3T models of prevention. Then we describe the five-step process for designing, implementing, and evaluating a FABI.

In Chapter 4, *Identifying Students Who May Benefit from a Functional Assessment-Based Intervention*, we explain the first step: how to identify students who might need intensive tertiary support. We discuss the circumstances in which screening data may be used to connect students to this support, as well as other circumstances in which a FABI is required by law.

Part III. Step 2: Conducting the Functional Assessment

After explaining how to determine which students may benefit from—or in fact are required to have—a FABI, the next task is to conduct the FBA to determine the reasons *why* the target behavior is occurring. Part III has four chapters that guide you through this process.

In Chapter 5, *Getting Started: Understanding the Context*, we introduce the importance of examining the context. We feature the importance of informal observations, learning about the tiered system in place (if one exists) and classroom and noninstructional settings, considering culture and community, as well as examining the integrity with which Tier 1 efforts have been implemented. We also discuss how to review students' cumulative files to learn more about students' history, including past behavior challenges and successes.

In Chapter 6, *Functional Assessment Interviews: Identifying the Problem and Establishing the Target Behaviors*, we begin by explaining how to operationally define target and replacement behaviors. Next we provide recommendations for conducting FBA interviews, followed by a closer look at the details of various informant interviews for teachers, family members (e.g., parents), and students.

In Chapter 7, *Functional Assessment: Direct Observation*, we provide a more detailed explanation of the purpose and methods of the A-B-C model. This includes step-by-step guidance on how to collect A-B-C data to determine the antecedents that set the stage for the target behavior to occur, as well as the consequences that maintain the likelihood that the target behavior will occur in the future.

In Chapter 8, *Determining the Function of the Behavior: The Function Matrix*, we introduce the Function Matrix, a simple, novel, and effective tool that is used to summarize data visually and identify the function of the behavior. We describe the purpose, layout, and use of the Function Matrix. We also explain how to write a statement of the function and provide illustrations. Then, we explain how to use these findings to select the replacement behavior.

Part IV. Step 3: Collecting Baseline Data

After explaining how to conduct the FBA and determine the reason(s) why the target behavior is occurring, the next task is to learn how to best measure the behaviors of interest (i.e., the target/challenging behavior, the replacement behavior, or both, if necessary) and collect baseline data *before* beginning intervention efforts. Part IV includes two chapters to achieve this goal.

In Chapter 9, *Identifying the Dimension of Interest and Selecting an Appropriate Measurement System*, we begin by explaining why we measure behavior. We introduce the dimensions of behavior and various measurement systems. Then we provide a practical process by which we can select the measurement system best suited for measuring the dimension of interest. We also describe and illustrate the data collection procedures needed to measure the behavior (e.g., materials needed, such as paper forms and timers, data collection sheets, and observation schedules).

In Chapter 10, *Getting Started: Collecting Baseline Data*, we explain the practicalities of data collection, including how to become reliable in the collection process before collecting baseline data. In the implementation checklist, we address topics such as when and how often to observe, why and how to collect interobserver agreement data, the factors that impact measurement, and common measurement errors.

Part V. Step 4: Designing the Functional Assessment-Based Intervention

After learning how to identify the behavioral dimension of interest, select an appropriate measurement system, and begin collecting baseline data, the next task is to design the FABI. As you might expect, this step includes multiple components. To introduce these components in a manageable manner, Part V includes nine chapters that incrementally walk readers through this process.

In Chapter 11, *Designing and Testing the Intervention*, we explain how to answer two key questions that guide the intervention focus. Chapters 12–15 provide additional directions for each intervention method. Specifically, Chapter 12 explains and illustrates *Intervention*

Method 1: Teach the Replacement Behavior. Chapter 13 explains and illustrates *Intervention Method 2: Adjust the Environment*. Chapter 14 explains and illustrates *Intervention Method 3: Shift the Contingencies*. Chapter 15 explains and describes the special situation when it is necessary to combine Methods 1 and 2. In each chapter, we provide illustrations from PreK–12 research, as well as lessons learned over the last 20 years. We also explain a range of practical A-R-E components (a̲ntecedent adjustments, r̲einforcement procedures, and e̲xtinction procedures).

Next, Chapters 16, 17, and 18 address three concepts and the associated activities needed to draw valid inferences regarding intervention outcomes. Specifically, Chapter 16 addresses *treatment integrity*; Chapter 17, *social validity*; and Chapter 18, *generalization and maintenance*. For each concept, we explain what it is, why it is important, and how to collect and use these data to inform implementation efforts.

In Chapter 19, *Designing Your Intervention*, we provide explicit directions for designing interventions. We explain how to draft A-R-E components, linking each intervention tactic to the hypothesized function of the challenging behavior. We provide guidance for introducing the intervention to the teacher and students, including checks for understanding before beginning implementation of the FABI.

Part VI. Step 5: Testing the Intervention

After designing an intervention based on the maintaining function(s), the next task is to implement the intervention and conduct a "test" to determine if the introduction of the intervention yields systematic changes in the student's behavior. As you might expect, this step includes multiple components. Part VI includes two chapters that introduce the process of determining the extent to which there is a functional relationship between the introduction of the intervention, when implemented with integrity, and changes in student performance.

In Chapter 20, *Determining Intervention Outcomes*, we introduce three key questions to address when testing the intervention: (1) Is the intervention being implemented as planned (i.e., treatment integrity)?; (2) How is it working (i.e., functional relation)?; and (3) What do stakeholders think (i.e., social validity)? We also discuss monitoring the factors that enhance an intervention's success.

In Chapter 21, *Wrapping It Up: Ending with a Defensible Functional Assessment-Based Intervention*, we provide guidance for preparing a practical report of intervention outcomes. We discuss finalizing the behavior intervention plan, having the proper documentation, and transitioning the plan and documents across time and settings.

Part VII. Getting Started in Your Own Context

This final part provides considerations for getting started with the FABI process in various systems. Here we offer two final chapters.

In Chapter 22, *Implementation Considerations*, we discuss ways to move forward with the FABI process, either in a tiered system or as individuals working on their own. We include considerations for implementation by school teams, considerations when working within a coaching model, and general tips for collaboration, with a special emphasis on the influence of culture and community.

In Chapter 23, *A Step-by-Step Training Model: One Approach to Building Capacity*, we summarize the lessons learned from professional learning projects and studies, in which the manualized FABI process has been tested at school sites in districts and in technical assistance projects. Specifically, we describe how various schools, districts, states, and technical assistance teams have taught school-site teams this systematic approach to designing, implementing, and evaluating FABIs.

Summary

This chapter served as an introduction to using FABIs to support students with intensive intervention needs (Umbreit et al., 2007). We introduced one specific, manualized approach developed by Umbreit and colleagues that features practical tools to empower general and special education teachers to be both effective and efficient. We explained how FABIs are situated within integrated tiered systems of support, such as Ci3T models of prevention (Lane, Kalberg, & Menzies, 2009), and provided an overview of how this book is organized.

Chapter 2 provides a user-friendly overview of applied behavior analytic principles relevant to all behavioral intervention, including information about the A-B-C model and a basic understanding of the behavior, antecedents, reinforcement, extinction, and punishment principles involved in completing a FABI. In addition, we define treatment integrity and explain its importance to the FABI process. This foundational content is intended to guide the reader to value the communicative intent of behavior and respectful ways to shape behavior.

CHAPTER 2

Primer on Behavior Analysis

LEARNING OBJECTIVES

- Identify and describe the basic behavioral principles needed to conduct a FABI.
- Understand the importance of a deeper knowledge of behavioral principles and supervised experiences.
- Define treatment integrity and understand its importance to the FABI.

Before we begin, it is important to understand that there is an expectation that a practitioner conducting the FABI process is competent not only in the process but also has a knowledge and understanding of and expertise in applying some key behavioral principles underlying that process. Providing services that fall within the limits of your competence is a standard of professional and ethical codes of conduct (cf. BACB, 2022; National Association of School Psychologists, 2020; National Association of Social Workers, 2021). The need for this competence holds true even if the FABI is completed by a team. The team should include at least one person who has this deeper knowledge and expertise. See Box 2.1 for ethical considerations related to competent service delivery.

Ideally, the person or team members conducting the FABI will also have the knowledge and experience to implement these behavioral principles with fidelity. Implementation fidelity of the intervention, also referred to as treatment integrity, is a key requirement of the FABI process. Treatment integrity is the extent to which an intervention is accurately implemented as written (Lane et al., 2004). For example, if I am trying to lose weight and my behavior plan calls for me to record every bite I eat, a treatment integrity measure would tell me whether I counted all or only some of what I ate. Accurate implementation of an intervention component is necessary to draw valid conclusions regarding intervention outcomes. If we do not have information on the degree to which the intervention was implemented as planned, then we cannot be certain if the intervention—or some other change in the environment in which the intervention took place—was responsible for the change. When well-designed interventions are implemented with integrity, they are more likely to result in a positive outcome (Buckman et al., 2021). More information about treatment integrity can be found in Chapter 16.

This chapter provides an overview of the five basic principles that are central to completing a FABI. It provides a beginning understanding of these principles for everyone involved with the FABI. We encourage readers to supplement this information with additional training and supervised experience in applying the principles. Many textbooks (cf. Alberto & Troutman, 2016; Cooper et al., 2020; Martin & Pear, 2019; Mayer et al., 2018) and courses include a more thorough description and discussion of behavior and the implementation of behavioral principles in applied settings. Key principles reviewed in this chapter include:

- Behavior
- Antecedents
- Reinforcement
- Extinction
- Punishment

BOX 2.1. Ethical Considerations in Chapter 2: BACB Ethics Code for Behavior Analysts

1.05 Practicing within Scope of Competence

As described in Chapter 2, there are ethical standards related to being competent in the work you perform. Applying the BACB ethics code, it means that the person developing and completing the FABI knows and understands the underlying behavioral principles and process of behavior-change interventions. Even if there is a team of people working on the FABI, at least one member must be knowledgeable about behavior change. The chapter briefly describes five key principles with which all members of a FABI team should be familiar.

1.06 Maintaining Competence

This knowledge of underlying behavioral principles and, specifically for the material in this book, in developing individualized interventions that are effective must be maintained through professional development in the field of behavior analysis, such as attending conferences and completing behavior analytic courses, presenting at conferences and teaching courses, and publishing.

2.15 Minimizing Risk of Behavior-Change Interventions

As noted in this chapter, punishment procedures are not recommended or considered for behavioral interventions. Rather, the FABI focuses on reinforcement and extinction.

Behavior

Behavior seems so ordinary and easy to understand. In fact, it is a key concept of behavior analysis, and a review of its definition is warranted. Behaviors are actions or events that are observable, result in a measurable change (i.e., can be counted), and are repeatable. Behaviors are everything a person does. In this definition there are things a behavior is not. It is not the condition in which people find themselves. For example, being hungry or dieting is not a behavior. But eating is a behavior. Behavior is also not an outcome. For example, losing weight is not a behavior. Rather, it is the outcome of several specific behaviors (eating different food, exercising, and the like).

Behavior also communicates information, although it is sometimes difficult to understand. For example, a smile may communicate "thank you," or "job well done," or simply "hello." As discussed in Chapter 1, research suggests that challenging behavior has a communicative purpose. The person who hits may be trying to communicate that they are hungry. The child who throws a tantrum may do so to get a toy. It is the purpose of the FABI to identify what the child's behavior is communicating—what the purpose of the behavior is.

There are two broad types of behavior, *operant behavior* and *respondent behavior*. Respondent behavior is the response part of a reflex. It is stimulated by something in the environment. For example, a puff of air (stimulus) may cause an eye blink. What occurs after the eye blink (i.e., its consequences) has no effect on its future occurrence. In contrast, an *operant* behavior is behavior maintained by its consequences. For example, a father picks up a crying baby and the baby stops crying. Picking up the baby is the behavior. The consequence is that the baby stops crying, so the father is more likely to pick up the crying baby in the future to "get" the consequence of ending the crying. And the baby may be more likely to cry in the future to "get" picked up. In the FBA process, only operant behavior is addressed.

In operant behavior, a basic contingency describes the temporal or functional relation between a behavior and a stimulus (i.e., the consequence) that immediately follows it. For example, a student raises their hand (behavior) and the teacher calls on the student (consequence). This statement describes a temporal relationship until it is established that the teacher calling on the student increases the likelihood that the behavior will recur. In other words, once you have established that the consequence either increases or decreases the likelihood that the behavior will occur, the contingency identifies a functional relation.

Understanding the basic contingency of behavior and consequence is vital, but operant behavior is understood to occur within a *three-term contingency* that not only describes the relationship between the behavior and the consequences, but also includes the antecedent (see Figure 2.1). It is often referred to as the A-B-C model of behavior analysis. This means that the functional behavioral assessment identifies not only the functional relation between the behavior and the consequence, but also identifies the functional relation between certain antecedent events and the behavior. In the previous example, when the student raises their hand (behavior), it is in response to an antecedent such as the teacher asking a question. Identifying that antecedent is part of understanding the purpose of the behavior and developing an intervention that is effective. The three-term contingency is completed when the A-B are followed by a consequence (C), such as the teacher calling on the student, and that consequence either increases (i.e., reinforces) or decreases (i.e., punishes) the frequency of the student raising

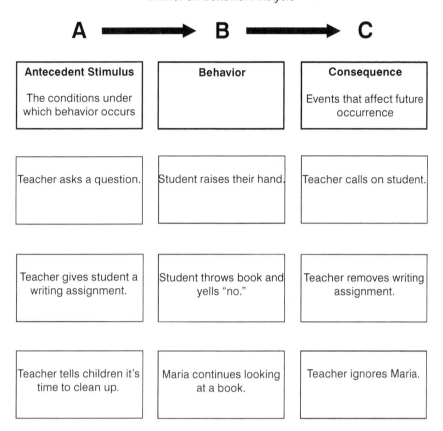

FIGURE 2.1. The antecedent–behavior–consequence (A-B-C) model: Three-term contingency examples. From Umbreit, J., Ferro, J. B., Liaupsin, C. J., & Lane, K. L. (2007). *Functional behavioral assessment and function-based intervention: An effective, practical approach.* Pearson. Reprinted by permission.

their hand in the future. You have now identified the relevant A-B-C and the function of the behavior.

Antecedents

An antecedent is a stimulus or event that occurs prior to a behavior of interest. When a behavioral response has been consistently reinforced in the presence of a stimulus, you could say that the stimulus triggers or sets the stage for the behavior. For example, the doorbell rings (antecedent stimulus) and your dog starts barking (behavior). The antecedent triggers the behavior, which is reinforced when you pet your dog and say, "Good boy."

However, the antecedent includes more than simply a specific stimulus or event that immediately precedes the behavior. The antecedent includes the conditions under which a behavior occurs (e.g., Bijou & Baer, 1961; Skinner, 1938). This condition may include other variables in the environment. For example, the behavior of braking for a yellow light or accelerating through it may be influenced by other factors, such as a camera monitoring the intersection, or a police car in the next lane, or being late for an important meeting. Each of these variables may alter your behavior such that you might accelerate through the yellow light when you are late for a meeting but brake for the yellow light when the police are nearby. In the example of your dog barking, consider what might happen if you have just provided your dog with a bone. The bone may interfere with the trigger of the doorbell so that he does not bark.

A setting event, an event that has occurred in the past (minutes, hours, or even days), may also alter the typical relationship between an antecedent and a behavior (Kantor, 1959). In our yellow light example, how might a driver react to a yellow light if they passed an accident earlier in the day? What would the effect be if their parents had died in a car accident? Either of these conditions might result in the driver slowing and stopping when they see a yellow light rather than accelerating. Setting events that may contribute to challenging behavior include a wide variety of stimuli and disruptive events (e.g., a parent moving out of the house, food insecurity, domestic violence, homelessness, community violence; Erdy & Zakszeski, 2021). Consider a student whose environment included or includes someone who argues loudly (verbal aggression) and hits (physical aggression) another adult or child. If the student exhibits challenging behavior in the presence of yelling, such as might happen during a school assembly, game, or even a classwide activity, the behavioral assessment will benefit if you know that yelling has been connected to an aversive event in the past and may trigger avoidance behaviors, such as running or aggression, in the present.

Reinforcement

Reinforcement occurs when a stimulus (1) follows a behavior and (2) strengthens or increases the probability that the behavior will occur again in the future. Reinforcement is the procedure used to strengthen or increase a behavior (Miller, 2006). A reinforcer is the stimulus (i.e., the object or action) that follows and increases a specific behavior. For example, praise, a stimulus that follows cleaning up toys, is a reinforcer only if it strengthens or increases the behavior of cleaning up toys. A thorough understanding of reinforcement and reinforcers is crucial to the success of an individualized intervention.

There are two types of reinforcement: *positive reinforcement* and *negative reinforcement*. Do not be confused by the use of the term *negative* to describe something that increases behavior. Negative does not mean bad; it means something is being removed. Although positive reinforcement increases the future occurrence of a behavior by adding something, negative reinforcement increases it by taking something away or decreasing its intensity. A simple example of positive reinforcement is a child who is given lots of attention, spoken to, and patted on the back for saying thank you. The attention and pat on the back are *added* after the child says thank you. They are positive reinforcements if the child says thank you more frequently under similar conditions in the future. An example of negative reinforcement might be the removal of a school assignment when a child screams and throws a book. Removal of the assignment is negative reinforcement if screaming and throwing the assignment occurs more often under similar conditions in the future.

The examples of positive and negative reinforcement highlight that reinforcement can increase the frequency and intensity of behaviors that may be considered appropriate (i.e., being polite) as well as those that are considered inappropriate (i.e., skipping an assignment).

It does not matter that the person removing the assignment did not *intend* to reinforce the behavior. What matters is that there is an increase in the future frequency of the behavior.

Reinforcer Effectiveness

There are conditions that make the operation of reinforcement more effective, which is what you want when you are trying to change behavior. These conditions are immediacy, individualization, motivation, and magnitude (Cooper et al., 2020). Immediacy means that the reinforcer occurs as soon after the behavior as possible. Delaying the reinforcement is especially problematic if the delay is long, but even 30 seconds may be too long a delay. The reason immediacy is vital is that other behaviors may occur during the delay between the behavior of interest and the reinforcer. The behavior that occurs closest to the reinforcer is the one that is reinforced.

Individualization refers to the idea that people are affected differently (i.e., are differentially reinforced) by objects or actions. For example, Jacko likes stories, such that giving him time to read may be identified as a reinforcer for him. However, Melanie likes working with her hands, such that building or carving may be identified as a reinforcer; in contrast, the opportunity to read means nothing to her. Verbal praise is often an efficient and effective reinforcer for most people. For example, when John's teacher says, "Good book review, John," he smiles and spends more time on assignments. The praise was reinforcing because it increased the future probability of John working on assignments. However, Ari's family has taught him that he should not be publicly recognized for doing well. Praise is not only *not* a reinforcer in this example but may decrease Ari's behavior or change it in unexpected and unwanted ways.

Cultural differences should always be considered, as they may play a role in individualizing reinforcement. That public recognition did not reinforce Ari is a good example of a difference in family values that may change what seems to be reinforcing into a neutral or aversive stimulus. Knowing this fact ahead of time would lead you to select a different reinforcer for Ari, perhaps applying private, behavior-specific praise as an alternative. In another example, some families believe that extrinsic reinforcement is not appropriate. Rather, their child should be intrinsically reinforced for an activity (e.g., reading for the love of reading or the love of learning). Similarly, families may feel that the use of food as a reinforcer is inappropriate. As you develop your reinforcement system, learn the family's expectations, find common ground, and build a trusting relationship with them. This might involve helping the family understand the scientific view of reinforcement, but may also include changing the language you use. For example, ask family members how they acknowledge their child's accomplishments to identify likely reinforcers. You could also diversify your reinforcement system so that it includes examples that may be more acceptable to the family (e.g., accessing a high-frequency or preferred activity after engaging in a low-frequency or nonpreferred activity, as provided in the Premack principle (Premack, 1959). Ensuring that family members are part of the FABI team allows the development of a reinforcement system that addresses the function of the behavior *and* is responsive to the family's values and culture.

Once you have identified a reinforcer, its value can lose or increase its effectiveness due to changes in motivation or, more specifically, changes in motivating operations (MOs; Michael, 1982, 1993). For example, food may be identified as a reinforcer for Malik. But what if Malik has just had all the chips he can eat? Hunger is an MO that establishes the value of food by increasing its effectiveness as a reinforcer. However, if Malik is satiated, food may temporarily cease to reinforce his behavior. Satiation would be considered an abolishing operation (AO) in these circumstances.

Magnitude means that the reinforcer has to be strong enough to change the behavior. For example, if Keri works all morning mowing the lawn in the hot sun for Mr. James, a dollar may not be enough to increase the probability that he will mow the lawn in the future. Magnitude also plays a role when you are trying to decrease an unwanted behavior and replace it with a new behavior. The reinforcer for the new, expected behavior must be stronger than what is reinforcing the behavior you are trying to decrease or eliminate (Horner & Day, 1991).

Types or Classification of Reinforcers

There are many types or classifications of stimuli that may be reinforcers (see Figure 2.2). Social reinforcers include verbal interactions (e.g., praise, short conversation); proximity (e.g., standing or sitting near a person); physical contact, such as a pat on the back, a hug, or a tickle; events such as a party; and attention (e.g., a smile, a wave across the room, eye contact and orienting to a person who is talking, or a phone call). Social reinforcers are some of the most effective and powerful types.

Tangible reinforcers are physical objects, such as toys, books, cosmetics, trinkets, or rocks. Any physical object, regardless of its intrinsic worth, may be a tangible reinforcer.

Activity reinforcers are everyday events or actions, such as exercise, playing a game, watching TV, hiking, and riding a bicycle. They may also be special events, such as a trip, a party, or privileges, such as cooking with a parent. Consumables, such as water or food, and sensory stimulation, such as vibration, lights, or music, may also be reinforcers.

Finally, exchangeables are items that can be used to obtain other items that are reinforcers. These include, for example, money, tokens, tickets, points, and poker chips. The exchangeables in tiered systems are often universal tickets that include the student's name, the adult's name, the location where the student was given the ticket, the date, and a list of schoolwide expectations (e.g., be respectful, be responsible, and be safe). In Ci3T modules (which you read about in Chapter 1), the school-site leadership develops a reinforcement menu or identifies schoolwide reinforcers that can be used by all. Many Ci3T Leadership Teams build function-based reinforcement menus that align with the Function Matrix that you will learn more about in Chapter 8. See Figure 2.2, Panel B, for an illustration (see *www.ci3t.org* for other illustrations).

Extinction

To many, the word *extinction* conjures images of dinosaurs or endangered species. As you might have guessed, when talking about behavior, extinction means something quite different. Extinction is a process in which previously reinforced behavior becomes weaker because it is no longer reinforced.

Let us examine each part of this definition to make sure the concept is clear.

Panel A

Social	Tangible	Activity	Consumable	Sensory	Exchangable
•Praise •Attention •Pat on the back	•Toys •Books •Cosmetics •Games	•Riding •Exercising •Watching TV •Trip	•Food •Drink	•Vibration •Light •Music	•Money •Tokens •Tickets •Points

Panel B

		In-Person/Hybrid Reinforcer Menu			
		School Name			
		Access/Get/Receive	Avoid/Pass/Skip		
Attention					
		[Item/ Activity] [No.]	[Item/ Activity] [No.]		
		[Item/ Activity] [No.]	[Item/ Activity] [No.]		
		[Item/ Activity] [No.]	[Item/ Activity] [No.]		
Activity/ Task					
		[Item/ Activity] [No.]	[Item/ Activity] [No.]		
		[Item/ Activity] [No.]	[Item/ Activity] [No.]		
		[Item/ Activity] [No.]	[Item/ Activity] [No.]		
Sensory					
		[Item/ Activity] [No.]	[Item/ Activity] [No.]		
		[Item/ Activity] [No.]	[Item/ Activity] [No.]		
		[Item/ Activity] [No.]	[Item/ Activity] [No.]		

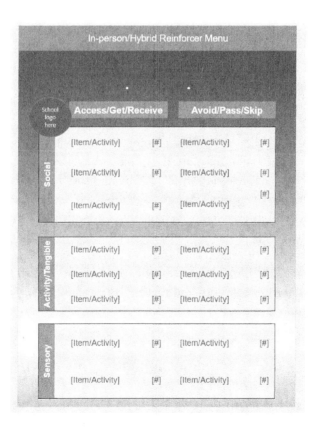

FIGURE 2.2. Panel A: Examples of types of reinforcers. Panel B: Function-based reinforcement menu. Panel B from *www.ci3t.org*. Reprinted by permission.

1. The behavior in question must have a history of reinforcement. Withholding reinforcement should make a difference only if the behavior has consistently and predictably been reinforced in the past.
2. Reinforcement must no longer follow the behavior. Sometimes extinction happens naturally, and sometimes it is programmed deliberately. Regardless, when the behavior occurs, it must no longer result in delivery of the reinforcer.
3. The behavior must become weaker (i.e., less likely to occur). If the strength of the behavior increases, or remains the same, then extinction has *not* occurred.

Extinction requires that all three conditions must be met. Consider the following example. Ms. West assigned homework every night and told the students it had to be turned in on time to get full credit. Twelve-year-old Logan almost always did his homework and always turned it in. However, he almost never turned it in on time. Logan realized that his teacher would give him full credit for his homework no matter when he turned it in. Consequently, Logan turned in his homework, but paid little or no attention to the deadlines. One day, Ms. West realized she had unintentionally reinforced Logan's behavior of turning his work in late. She told Logan that, from then on, his homework would not receive credit unless it was completed *and* turned in *on time*. Logan submitted his next homework assignment 3 days late and, to his surprise, received no credit. From then on, he made sure he turned in all homework on time.

In this example, we have a behavior (submitting completed homework after the deadline). We also have a history of reinforcement (Logan had received full credit for late assignments). Then the reinforcer (full credit) was withheld when the behavior occurred (i.e., late submissions no longer got credit). Finally, the strength of the behavior decreased, in this case, quite quickly and dramatically. The behavior of submitting assignments late virtually disappeared (you might even say it became "extinct" or "was extinguished"). However, extinction should never be used in isolation. When extinction is implemented without antecedent adjustments and shifts in rates of reinforcement for more desirable behavior, challenges can arise. Specifically, extinction can lead to aggression (Miller, 2006), and the behavior can return seemingly out of nowhere (spontaneous recovery). When used by itself, extinction is also very difficult to implement with integrity in classrooms because it can be difficult to control all sources of reinforcement. For example, peers may continue to pay attention by laughing at or commenting on the challenging behavior even if the adults in the classroom do not.

There is a simple way to think about the concept of extinction: Behavior that previously resulted in reinforcement no longer does. Janney and colleagues (2013) have demonstrated that extinction plays an essential role in FABIs.

Punishment

Punishment plays no role in FABI—we do not support the use of positive (introducing) or negative (removing) punishment. It is important that you know why, so we begin by defining it. Punishment is a stimulus or event that (1) follows a behavior and (2) decreases the probability that the behavior will be repeated. For example, if Anna looks out the window rather than working on an assignment (behavior) and the teacher makes her finish the assignment during recess (event that follows the behavior), the loss of recess is a punishment if Anna does *not* look out the window during future assignments.

A stimulus or event is only punishment if it follows a behavior (occurring contingent on the behavior) *and* decreases the behavior. If the stimulus or event does not decrease the behavior, it is not punishment. This *technical* definition of punishment can be distinguished from our everyday idea of punishment as something undesirable or aversive. In everyday life, we identify punishment as a penalty that we think will automatically decrease behavior because it is aversive or unpleasant to us. For example, if a child argues with a parent (behavior), the parent may spank the child (penalty). The parent considers the spanking to be punishment because it is an aversive event. However, if the child continues to argue with the parent (and they often do), the spanking was not punishment. It was aversive, but not punishment.

This is true of all types of behavior. If someone steals a car, they may receive ever-increasing penalties, such as fines, probation, and incarceration. However, if the person continues to steal cars when they have an opportunity, none of those penalties meet the technical definition of punishment. Conversely, events that you might consider to be pleasant or instructive can be punishing in the technical sense; that is, they can decrease behavior. For example, praise (or another instance of positive attention) is generally considered to be a reinforcer. However, under certain conditions, such as excessive public attention from an adult that the student identifies as embarrassing, a student can react as though the attention was aversive. They may stop performing the behavior for which they were praised. If this occurs, the consequence (praise) was supposed to be a reinforcer but was actually a punisher because it followed the behavior and *weakened* it. This is why it is very important to see how students respond to determine whether shifts are needed in how to reinforce the students' behaviors.

Punishment may occur naturally in the environment as a natural consequence of a behavior. For example, if you put your hand on a hot iron, you burn it. In the future, you refrain from touching an iron that you know to be hot. There are two ways that punishment can be used to decrease behavior. These two forms are called Type I and Type II punishment, also known as *positive* punishment and *negative* punishment, respectively.

In *Type I punishment*, a stimulus or event is presented after a behavior (the student gets something) and it results in the behavior decreasing. For example, if a student threatens another (behavior) and the teacher reprimands the student by telling them not to use threats (event that follows the behavior), the reprimand is a Type I or positive punisher if the student does not threaten anyone in the future. The punishment is Type I because the student received a reprimand and their behavior decreased.

In *Type II punishment*, a stimulus or event that is removed following a behavior results in the behavior decreasing. Examples include losing privileges for bad grades, being removed from a preferred environment or preferred social interaction (i.e., time-out), more severe time-out that includes isolation from others or losing your driver's license for drunk driving (response cost). Punishment is the process in which a behavior *decreases* because of the presentation of an aversive consequence or the loss of a reinforcer.

One reason people use punishment is that it can be very effective in the short term. If it works and works quickly (i.e., the punished behavior stops), the punisher is negatively reinforced for using punishment and will use it again. Unfortunately, punishment also creates many problems because it generates several negative side effects (cf. Sidman, 1989). Punishment can produce aggressive behavior and also can suppress desirable behavior. Punishment may only temporarily suppress the behavior and can also generate escape or avoidance behavior. Furthermore, the stimuli that are associated with punishment can become conditioned punishers, and children may imitate adults and deliver aversive stimuli to other children or adults.

Punishment can also have side effects for the person administering the aversive stimuli. When an aversive stimulus does not decrease the behavior or decreases it only temporarily, the person administering the punishment may resort to progressively heavier doses, thereby creating a vicious circle with a high probability of one or more of the side effects just detailed. Too often teachers and parents continue to deliver an aversive consequence simply because they believe it to be aversive and assume it will ultimately decrease the behavior. They believe that if it does not work, it is because the penalty was not aversive enough and it will work if they increase the intensity.

In addition to these side effects, punishment fails to establish new, more desirable behavior. It does not teach the student what to do—it does not build new skills. In FABI, we replace the problem behavior with one that teaches the student new skills and a new way to act in the environment that will result in positive reinforcement. To ensure that the problem behavior is eliminated for the long term, the emphasis should be on establishing new behavior that will be positively reinforced, rather than on merely eliminating old behavior.

Cultural differences may also be a factor in discussions of punishment. Some team members may have ideas of intervention for the FABI that include punishment strategies. For example, a family who sends a child to their room (time-out) or takes away the privilege of watching television as a consequence for a problem behavior may want teachers to use similar strategies at school. Teachers who send a student to the office or into the hall may want those consequences to be available as part of the FABI. It is important that all members of the FABI team, including the family member and teacher, understand and agree with the intervention components. So it is important to take the time to work with the team on developing them. Ask all the team members how they feel about the intervention through discussions about social validity—that is, whether they thought the goals and outcomes of the intervention were acceptable (see the discussion of social validity in Chapter 17). Help them understand the side effects of punishment that we want to avoid. As team members more fully understand the FABI process and implement successful interventions, they will begin to trust interventions focused on building new behaviors.

Summary

In this chapter, we identified and described five basic behavioral principles essential for understanding the function of the behavior and for completing a FABI: behavior, antecedents, reinforcement, extinction, and punishment. We also illustrated the three-term contingency that describes the functional relationship between the antecedent, behavior, and consequence. A variety of examples were used to clarify the descriptions of these principles, including a discussion of the role family values and beliefs may play in individualizing reinforcement. As you continue reading, remember that the principles of applied behavior analysis function across family, local, regional, and ethnic groups. There are observable relationships between antecedents, behaviors, and consequences. However, cultural values can influence how antecedents and consequences function in a behavioral chain and the repertoire of behaviors that a person has to choose from in order to communicate intent. We continue to highlight those examples in which cultural values may play a role.

An important note is that this chapter should be considered a supplement to a more thorough study of and experience with behavioral principles in general and with functional behavioral assessment in particular. It is important for at least one member of the FABI team to have wider experience and knowledge of behavior analysis. As we describe the steps for completing FABI in future chapters, we provide more explicit instruction about how to use the principles described here in the FABI process.

As we move forward, take a brief moment to read the Part II Introduction. Here we introduce the five-step process for designing, implementing, and evaluating FABI. Part II. *Step 1: Identifying Students Who May Need a Functional Assessment-Based Intervention* begins with Chapter 3. Here we provide a more detailed overview of how the FABI process fits within and goes beyond tiered systems of support. Specifically, we describe tiered systems of support, including components of Ci3T models of prevention (one type of tiered system). After describing we explain how a FABI is often included as one of the intensive interventions featured in tertiary (Tier 3) intervention grids for use in preschool, elementary, and middle and high schools implementing Ci3T models of prevention. Then we describe the five-step process for designing, implementing, and evaluating FABI.

PART II
Step 1: Identifying Students Who May Need a Functional Assessment-Based Intervention

Following the introductory chapter and the primer on behavior analysis, we introduce the five-step process for designing, implementing, and evaluating functional assessment-based interventions.

STEP #	FUNCTIONAL ASSESSMENT-BASED INTERVENTION STEPS
1	Identifying Students Who May Need a Functional Assessment-Based Intervention
2	Conducting the Functional Assessment
3	Collecting Baseline Data
4	Designing the Functional Assessment-Based Intervention
5	Testing the Intervention

Part II features two chapters to guide the reader through Step 1. First, we set the stage for the context when conducting a FABI as a Tier 3 intervention for students with intensive intervention needs. Specifically, in Chapter 3, we provide a more detailed overview of how the FABI process fits within and goes beyond tiered systems of support. We include sample tertiary (Tier 3) intervention grids for use in preschool, elementary, and middle and high schools implementing Ci3T models of prevention.

Next, in Chapter 4, we explain the first step: how to identify students who might need intensive tertiary support. We discuss circumstances in which screening data may be used to connect students to this support, as well as other circumstances in which a FABI is required by law.

CHAPTER 3

Working in Tiered Systems of Support
A Focus on Tier 3 Considerations

LEARNING OBJECTIVES

- Describe tiered systems of support.
- Describe the components of a Ci3T model of prevention.
- Explain where FABI is situated in a Ci3T model of prevention.
- Describe the five-step process for designing, implementing, and evaluating FABIs.

As mentioned in Chapter 1, tiered systems of support were first developed in the public health community many years ago (Grove & Hetzel, 1968; States et al., 2017). In the mid-1990s, Hill Walker and colleagues (1996) introduced these graduated systems of support to the educational community. This approach marked an important shift in how educators thought about and responded to students exhibiting challenging behavior that often disrupted positive, productive learning environments. As educational leaders began to embrace the notion of a systems approach, there was a movement away from reactive approaches to responding to challenging systems (Lane, Buckman, et al., 2020). Now, instead of waiting for problems to occur and then punishing students with the use of names and checks on the board or "clipping students down" (see McIntosh et al., 2020), there is a far greater emphasis on establishing expectations, teaching them to all students in the same way academic content is taught, and acknowledging students when they meet expectations. In short, the field is embracing a systems-level approach that features instruction about behavior and focuses on function—the reasons *why* challenging behaviors occur. These systems include proactive approaches for preventing challenging behavior from occurring and responding with validated strategies, practices, and programs when challenges arise (Lane & Walker, 2015).

Today there are many different tiered systems, with an increased emphasis on integrated systems to meet students' multiple needs (Institute of Education Sciences [IES], 2017; see Box 3.1). Some examples of tiered systems include RTI (Fuchs & Fuchs, 2017; Fuchs et al., 2012), PBIS (Horner & Sugai, 2015), and integrated systems, such as MTSS (Freeman et al., 2015), ISF (Barrett et al., 2013), and Ci3T (Lane, Oakes, et al., 2014) models of prevention.

In this chapter, we set the stage for the context when conducting a FABI as a Tier 3 intervention within an integrated tiered system for students with intensive intervention needs. Specifically, we provide a more detailed overview of how the FABI process fits within and goes beyond tiered systems of support. We do this using the Ci3T model as our example. First, we provide an overview of Ci3T models of prevention, with an emphasis on how FABI is one of the validated Tier 3 supports for students with intensive intervention needs. Then we describe tertiary (Tier 3) intervention grids for use in elementary, middle, and high school Ci3T models of prevention.

Ci3T: An Overview

Ci3T is a tiered system—a broadening of MTSS—designed to address students' academic, behavioral, and social and emotional well-being in one integrated model (Lane, Oakes, Buckman, et al., 2019). As part of a manualized building process (see Lane, Oakes, Cantwell, et al., 2019), schools assemble a Ci3T Leadership Team that includes (1) the principal; (2) two general educators; (3) one special educator; (4) at least one other person such as a school psychologist, counselor, or behavior specialist; (5) a family member and their child (at least 8 years of age); and (6) a district Ci3T coach (if possible). This team begins by attending a six-part training series with alternating 2-hour and full-day sessions. Students attend two of the 2-hour sessions held after school.

**BOX 3.1. Request for Applications 84.324N
(Institute of Education Sciences, 2017, p. 15)**

Researchers are increasingly advocating for the thoughtful integration of these tiered support systems into a single, coherent framework that is more efficient and provides optimal support to address the academic, social, emotional, and behavioral needs of all students, including those with or at risk for disabilities (e.g., Hawken et al., 2008; McIntosh & Goodman, 2016; Stewart et al., 2007; Sugai & Horner, 2009; Utley & Obiakor, 2015). Researchers have suggested that an integrated MTSS framework may have several advantages over separate tiered support systems, including more efficient service delivery and use of resources. An integrated system also has the potential to more seamlessly address students' interrelated academic and behavior problems and ensure that academic and behavioral supports are aligned without counteracting one another (McIntosh & Goodman, 2016). An integrated MTSS model may be especially beneficial for students with or at risk for disabilities who often struggle in both the academic and behavioral realm and whose difficulties in one domain are often related to difficulties in the other (e.g., Nelson et al., 2004).

During this yearlong, multi-session professional learning series, the Ci3T Leadership Team engages in a manualized, iterative process with formal input from faculty and staff using validated tools (e.g., Schoolwide Expectations Survey for Specific Settings, Primary Intervention Rating Scale; Lane, Oakes, et al., 2010) to develop a Ci3T Implementation Manual (see *www.ci3t.org* for measures). The Ci3T Implementation Manual includes the school's mission; the purpose of the Ci3T model; roles and responsibilities for key stakeholders (e.g., students, faculty, staff, families, and administrators) in academic, behavior, and social domains; a matrix of schoolwide behavioral expectations; procedures for teaching and for reinforcing; procedures for monitoring and an assessment schedule; secondary (Tier 2) intervention grids; and tertiary (Tier 3) intervention grids. The Ci3T Implementation Manual is similar to a constitution for the school, ensuring transparency among all the integrated plans and facilitating communication among stakeholders. In short, the Ci3T Implementation Manual essentially serves as an instructional tool for detailing how the school operates—including all district initiatives, programs, and practices (Lane, Oakes, Buckman, et al., 2019).

Three Domains

The Ci3T Leadership Team collaborates to create this framework for meeting students' multiple needs—academic, behavioral, and social and emotional well-being—in an integrated fashion, with each level of prevention comprising evidence-based strategies, practices, and programs. For each domain, there are specifications for students, faculty and staff, families, and administrators, making their respective roles and responsibilities transparent.

For example, for faculty and staff, the academic domain delineates (1) the core programs to be taught (e.g., English language arts [90 minutes of uninterrupted instruction] using the Scott Foresman *Reading Street: Common Core*); (2) proactive evidence-based strategies to maximize engagement (e.g., active supervision, precorrection, and instructional choice); (3) expectations for differentiating instruction; and (4) expectations for using screening and assessments to shape instruction (e.g., connect student to Tier 2 and Tier 3 interventions).

In the behavioral domain, faculty and staff are shown how to implement PBIS with integrity (e.g., teach, practice, and acknowledge students for meeting expectations), follow an instructional approach in responding to challenging behaviors (see Table 3.1), and implement the reactive plan as intended.

In the social domain, there is guidance for faculty and staff on how to teach schoolwide social and emotional well-being skills using validated resources. For example, guidance could include teaching daily Second Step lessons (15 minutes in morning meetings), modeling skills taught, reminding students how to use these skills during instruction, and acknowledging students when they participate in instruction and use the skill at other times of the day (e.g., during class discussion, cooperative learning groups, and lunchtime and in the hallways).

Students, families, and administrators are provided with the same guidance regarding Tier 1 responsibilities for each domain and how to integrate skills across domains. Essentially, this information serves as the playbook for creative, positive, productive—and even joyful—learning environments at Tier 1.

TABLE 3.1. An Instructional Approach to Respond to Challenging Behavior

An instructional approach to support students struggling to meet expectations	What would that look like?
1. Show empathy.	1. Teacher says, "I can see you are having a hard time right now. I will be back in a moment to help you get started."
2. Maintain flow of instruction.	2. Teacher says, "Class, I would like everyone to check your first three answers with your learning partner."
3. Acknowledge other students meeting expectations.	3. Teacher says, "Terrific! CJ and Bella, thank you for getting started so quickly!" Teacher gives each student a PBIS ticket.
4. Redirect and reteach expected behavior.	4. Teacher says, "Just a reminder—use a 3-second whisper voice when checking your work with your partner. That helps us all to be able to hear their feedback."
5. Allow time and space.	5. Teacher walks back to the student who was struggling and kneels down just outside of arm's length. Teacher says, "Thank you for waiting for me. OK, let's see how I can help you with that first question."
6. Recognize and reinforce appropriate behavior when demonstrated.	6. Teacher says, "That is correct, Rigley. Thank you for giving that first one a try." Teacher hands Rigley a ticket. Teacher says, "Let's try the next one."

Note. Adapted from Lane, K. L., Oakes, W. P., Cantwell, E. D., & Royer, D. J. (2019). *Building and installing comprehensive, integrated, three-tiered (Ci3T) models of prevention: A practical guide to supporting school success: Vol. 3.* KOI Education (Interactive eBook). Reprinted by permission. For additional information, see Lane, Menzies, Oakes, and Kalberg (2020).

Three Levels of Prevention

Yet, even with Tier 1 practices in place as planned, there will be students who need more than Tier 1 has to offer. As such, Ci3T—like other tiered systems—includes Tier 2 (for some) and Tier 3 (for a few) interventions. In a Ci3T model, Leadership Teams build two additional blueprints: secondary (Tier 2) intervention grids and tertiary (Tier 3) intervention grids.

The secondary (Tier 2) intervention grid features evidence-based practices for students at moderate risk, such as Tier 2 reading and math groups, check-in/check-out, and self-monitoring interventions. These moderate-intensity strategies, practices, and programs are not necessarily intended for small groups. For those who do CrossFit exercises, think about the way the coach uses a large rubber band on the rig for athletes to use when they cannot yet complete a pull-up without assistance (see Figure 3.1) or offers the option of ring row rather than pull-ups (scaling the workout). These are low-to-moderate aids that support engagement. The same is true in Ci3T models: Tier 2 interventions are low-to-moderate strategies, practices, and programs to maximize engagement, facilitate instruction, and decrease disruption.

The tertiary (Tier 3) intervention grids feature evidence-based practices for students with more intensive intervention needs. These practices include more intensive reading interventions (e.g., 4 days a week for 30 minutes), community-based mental health supports, and a FABI (see Figure 3.2)—with the latter as the focus of this book.

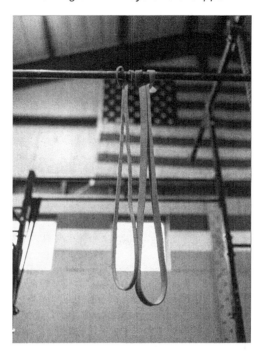

FIGURE 3.1. Providing low-to-moderate supports. Photo by Jonah Pester. Reprinted by permission.

There are no separate lists for reading, math, writing, behavioral, and social supports because the goal is to integrate these interventions. For example, a student might be engaged in a Tier 2 support for their computational skill needs, with a self-monitoring component to maximize engagement during the Tier 2 intervention time.

The grids shown in Figure 3.2 include five components:

- Support—the name of the support (e.g., the intervention), not the student.
- Description—a brief description of the supports so teachers, families, or students reading the description will know who is doing what, with whom, and under which conditions (Wolery et al., 2018).
- Schoolwide data: Entry criteria—to ensure equal access to each support, there is a listing of specific data to be reviewed to determine whether the student might benefit from this support.
- Data to monitor progress—information on how student progress will be monitored as well as information on how to know if the intervention is implemented as planned (treatment integrity) and how the stakeholders view the intervention goals, procedures, and intended outcomes (social validity) before they get started and after the intervention is under way.
- Exit criteria—specific criteria for determining whether the intervention should be concluded or faded if successful, or whether another intervention is warranted if the student's performance is not shifting even when the intervention is implemented as planned.

Panel A: Elementary School Illustration

Tertiary (Tier 3) Intervention Grid: For Elementary Schools

Support	Description	Schoolwide Data: Entry Criteria	Data to Monitor Progress	Exit Criteria
Functional assessment-based intervention	FABIs are interventions based on the function of the target behavior, as determined by the functional assessment and with the aid of the *Function Matrix*. The *Function-Based Intervention Decision Model* is used to determine the intervention focus, including Method 1: Teach the replacement behavior; Method 2: Adjust the environment; Method 3: Shift the contingencies; and a combination of Method 1 and Method 2. A package intervention is designed and implemented, including antecedent adjustments, reinforcement adjustments, and extinction procedures directly linked to the function of the target behavior.	One or more of the following: **Behavior:** ☐ SRSS-E7: High (9–21) ☐ SRSS-I5: High (4–15) ☐ SSiS-PSG Ranking of 1, 2, or 3 on the Motivation to Learn ☐ Office discipline referrals (ODRs): six or more within a grading period AND/OR **Academic:** ☐ Progress report: one or more course failures ☐ Missing assignments: five or more within a grading period ☐ AIMSweb: intensive level (math or reading)	Student behavior targeted for improvement (e.g., target or replacement behavior) using direct observation **Treatment integrity** • FABI step checklists • Treatment integrity checklist **Social validity** • IRP-15 (teacher) • CIRP (student)	The FABI will be faded once a functional relation is demonstrated using a validated single-case research design (e.g., withdrawal) and: • Behavior objective for the student is met (see Behavior Intervention Plan [BIP]).

Panel B: Middle and High School Illustration

Tertiary (Tier 3) Intervention Grid: For Middle and High Schools

Support	Description	Schoolwide Data: Entry Criteria	Data to Monitor Progress	Exit Criteria
Functional assessment-based intervention	FABIs are interventions based on the function of the target behavior, as determined by the functional assessment and with the aid of the *Function Matrix*. The *Function-Based Intervention Decision Model* is used to determine the intervention focus, including Method 1: Teach the replacement behavior; Method 2: Adjust the environment; Method 3: Shift the contingencies; and a combination of Method 1 and Method 2. A package intervention is designed and implemented, including antecedent adjustments, reinforcement adjustments, and extinction procedures directly linked to the function of the target behavior.	One or more of the following: **Behavior:** ☐ SRSS-E7: High (9–21) ☐ SRSS-I5: High (6–18) ☐ Office discipline referrals (ODRs): six or more within a grading period AND/OR **Academic:** ☐ Progress report: one or more course failures ☐ Missing assignments: five or more within a grading period ☐ AIMSweb: intensive level (math or reading) ☐ Below 2.5 GPA	Student behavior targeted for improvement (e.g., target or replacement behavior) using direct observation **Treatment integrity** • FABI step checklists • Treatment integrity checklist **Social validity** • IRP-15 (teacher) • CIRP (student)	The FABI will be faded once a functional relation is demonstrated using a validated single-case research design (e.g., withdrawal) and: • Behavior objective for the student is met (see Behavior Intervention Plan [BIP]).

FIGURE 3.2. Tertiary (Tier 3) intervention grids: functional assessment-based intervention (FABI). From *www.ci3t.org*, Tier 3 intervention grids. Reprinted by permission.

These intervention grids ensure transparency among all the available strategies, practices, and programs. The intervention grids also provide clarity for how teachers can independently (or as part of a team) review student data and connect students to Tier 2 and Tier 3 supports based on their individual needs (Oakes et al., 2014).

Data-Informed Practices

In addition to data-informed practices that connect students with a cascade of validated supports, Ci3T also features data-informed practices for adults' professional learning experiences. The Ci3T model uses treatment integrity data (i.e., "Is Ci3T happening as planned?"; Gresham, 1989) and the social validity data (e.g., "What do our faculty and staff think about the goals, procedures, and intended outcomes?"; Wolf, 1978) collected in the fall and spring each year to connect adults to various professional learning content. For example, if data suggest that students are receiving limited behavior-specific praise and if social validity data suggest that reinforcement is being confused with bribery (see Chapter 2), the principal might provide the faculty and staff with professional learning on the "hows and whys" of how behavior is learned and maintained (Cooper et al., 2020).

Meaningful Family Involvement

As you read this description of Ci3T, you may notice how Ci3T structures are constructed to create positive, productive, equitable, and safe learning environments to meet students' multiple needs. For example, family and student perspectives are integrated into the system by including them as key members of the Ci3T Leadership Teams during the data-informed, manualized building process (Lane, Oakes, Cantwell, et al., 2019).

In addition, family members engage in implementation efforts. For example, they remain part of Ci3T Leadership Teams at each school as part of regular school practices and, as members, they engage in the data-informed professional learning efforts to support implementation, reviewing treatment integrity and social validity data to examine Tier 1 efforts.

The focus on family involvement also provides an opportunity to incorporate family-based cultural issues into the intervention process. Family members and students are involved in the design, implementation, and evaluation of Tier 2 and Tier 3 interventions. For example, before moving forward with any Tier 2 or Tier 3 intervention, they complete social validity surveys to consider their priorities regarding intervention goals, procedures, and intended outcomes. Adults complete adapted versions of the Intervention Rating Profile–15 (IRP-15; Martens & Witt, 1982), and students completed adapted versions of the Children's Intervention Rating Profile (CIRP; Witt & Elliott, 1983), both of which are presented in Chapter 17. This information is reviewed and used to inform intervention design and procedures. Ensuring the family perspective is part of the systematic process of developing interventions. This procedure honors and uses the information the family and student offer to make the intervention more effective by making sure the goals and procedures are aligned with their priorities. See Box 3.2 for the ethical considerations relevant to involving clients (e.g., students) and stakeholders (e.g., families) in the intervention process.

> **BOX 3.2. Ethical Considerations in Chapter 3:
> BACB Ethics Code for Behavior Analysts**
>
> **2.03 Protecting Confidential Information**
>
> Every organization has ethical standards about confidentiality. Professionals, including the school staff, must protect the identity of those for whom they are providing services in all their communications. (In this book, a service is being provided to students and their families.) When family members and students are engaged in the school leadership team, they are also bound by confidentiality and should be provided with information during their orientation. Information about students or families that may be shared during a leadership team meeting should be coded so it does not provide identifying information. Data, such as responses to social validity questions, should be aggregated so no names are available.
>
> **2.04 Disclosing Confidential Information**
>
> Your responsibility is to ensure that confidential information about students involved in an intensive intervention and their families is only shared with designated individuals. Schools and other organizations providing services will have a policy and procedure about confidentiality and informed consent that are additions to these standards. Make sure that you know and understand this policy. If there is no policy, you must ensure that you have informed consent and that those on the FABI team and implementing the intervention also understand the need for confidentiality. Student records, including information about intensive interventions, should be kept in their confidential files that are only available to designated personnel (e.g., student's teacher, appropriate administrative staff, and professional support personnel, such as a behavior specialist or therapist).
>
> **2.05 Documentation Protection and Retention**
>
> School records will be kept confidential following school and district policy. Your responsibility is to ensure that all your documentation is also protected.
>
> **2.09 Involving Clients and Stakeholders**
>
> Family members, students, teachers, and other relevant school staff are included in both system teams and FABI teams. They contribute their cultural perspective to the development of the school's system and processes and participate in decision making in schools that implement tiered systems of support as described in this chapter. Family members are also part of the intervention team for their student, contributing both the family's perspective on a student's strengths and the goals for the intervention and participating in decisions about intervention strategies. As we continue our description of the FABI steps in later chapters, we note how clients and stakeholders are included in all parts of the process.

Creating Transparency at Tier 3: Tertiary (Tier 3) Intervention Grids

As mentioned earlier, the intervention grids are intended to ensure transparencies among the offerings at Tier 2 and Tier 3. In this book, we focus on one validated Tier 3 support, the FABI, using the manualized process described by Umbreit and colleagues (2007).

Figure 3.2 is an example of how the FABI is delineated as a Tier 3 support at the elementary (Figure 3.2, Panel A) and middle and high school levels (Figure 3.2, Panel B). School leaders can modify these grids to illustrate how the FABI process will take place in their school district. The goal is to be clear about which students may benefit from this intensive intervention.

A Closer Look at Tier 3 in Ci3T: FABIs

In the following chapters, we proceed through the five-step process of designing, implementing, and evaluating a FABI. This process can take place as a Tier 3 support within a Ci3T (see Cox et al., 2011; Germer et al., 2011) or other tiered systems or as part of the federally mandated requirement to conduct a functional behavioral assessment when designing a behavior intervention plan (BIP) as specified in the IDEIA (2004).

The five steps are as follows:

- Step 1: Identifying Students Who May Need a Functional Assessment-Based Intervention
- Step 2: Conducting the Functional Assessment
- Step 3: Collecting Baseline Data
- Step 4: Designing the Functional Assessment-Based Intervention
- Step 5: Testing the Intervention

See FABI Completion Checklists 1–5 (pp. 295–306) for a complete description of each step. These same checklists can be downloaded from *www.Ci3T.org/FABI* for your use. Throughout this book, we connect you with practical illustrations published in a range of journals from rigorous peer-reviewed articles (e.g., *Journal of Positive Behavior Interventions*) to practitioner-oriented outlets (e.g., *Preventing School Failure*). There is a list of journal articles provided in the Appendix that can be used by professors, technical assistance providers, and professional learning experts.

Summary

In this chapter, we explained how the FABI is one Tier 3 intervention that can be used as a tertiary support within an integrated tiered system for a student with intensive intervention needs. Specifically, we provided a detailed overview of how the FABI process fits within and goes beyond tiered systems of support. First, we provided an overview of Ci3T models of prevention—explaining the three levels and three domains. We explained how the FABI is one of the validated Tier 3 supports for students with intensive intervention needs. Then we described Tertiary (Tier 3) intervention grids for use in elementary, middle, and high schools.

Next, in Chapter 4, we explain the first step: how to identify students who might need intensive tertiary support. We discuss circumstances in which screening data may be used to connect students to this support as well as other circumstances in which a FABI is required by law.

CHAPTER 4

Identifying Students Who May Benefit from a Functional Assessment-Based Intervention

---

LEARNING OBJECTIVES

- Identify the circumstances in which a FABI is required.
- Determine how to use systematic screening data to detect students who might benefit from a FABI.

Many students come to school well prepared with the full set of skills needed to enjoy interactions with peers and adults and engage in instruction. However, some students start school with behavior patterns that disrupt the learning environment and impede instruction (Walker et al., 2004). In some instances, externalizing behaviors, such as aggression and extreme noncompliance, put the safety of peers and adults at risk and can even pose harm to the student demonstrating the challenging behavior (e.g., self-injurious behavior). In other instances, internalizing behaviors may also exist (e.g., extreme shyness, social withdrawal). Although internalizing behaviors are less likely to capture teachers' attention as they rarely impede instruction, these behavior challenges are no less serious (McIntosh & Goodman, 2016).

Approximately 12% of school-age youth struggle with externalizing or internalizing behavior challenges (Forness et al., 2012; Lane, Oakes, et al., 2021), but less than 1% of students qualify for special education services under the category of emotional disturbance (IDEIA, 2004). The percentage of students in need is much larger than many people realize. Over time, these behavior patterns become increasingly stable and less responsive to intervention efforts (Walker et al., 2014). As such, it is critical that general and special educators be well equipped to detect students at the first sign of concern (Gresham & Elliott, 2008b).

Fortunately, the advancement of integrated tiered systems of support can help teachers identify and support students with challenging behavior through schoolwide systematic screening efforts. All students are screened three times a year (in fall, winter, and spring). Many of these teacher-completed behavior screening tools are designed to detect internalizing and externalizing behavior patterns, which are long-standing behavioral manifestations of both major disorders of childhood (Achenbach, 1991a, 1991b). These supports might include evidence-based practices, such as check-in/check-out for K–12 students and direct instruction of problem-solving skills or self-regulation skills for preschool-age students at moderate risk (Tier 2), and FABIs for students with intensive intervention needs (Tier 3; Umbreit et al., 2007).

FABIs are effective, efficient interventions for students that are focused on understanding the "why" of behavior and then using that information to design individualized interventions that build students' skills in engaging in more adaptive behavior. This is a vast improvement from historical approaches to managing challenging behaviors that relied on harsh and exclusionary practices, such as removing students from class or school (which, for some students, is actually reinforcing!).

In this chapter, we explain the first step in developing a FABI: identifying students who might benefit from intensive intervention. We discuss circumstances in which screening data may be used to connect students to this support and other circumstances in which a FABI is required by law. See Box 4.1 for the ethical considerations when identifying students in need of intensive intervention efforts, obtaining informed consent, and gathering family and student input. We close with a brief summary and introduction to the next steps.

Identifying Students in Need of Intensive Intervention Efforts

In *Step 1: Identifying Students Who May Need a Functional Assessment-Based Intervention*, teams analyze schoolwide data collected as part of regular school practices. For example, teams

---

BOX 4.1. Ethical Considerations in Chapter 4: BACB Ethics Code for Behavior Analysts

2.09 Involving Clients and Stakeholders and 2.11 Obtaining Informed Consent

Family members are included from the beginning of the FABI process, providing consent and input into the intervention. Family members and the student are part of the FABI team. The student is also provided with the information that people will be working with them on some new skills.

2.13 Selecting, Designing, and Implementing Assessments

Ci3T serves as our example of the implementation process for intensive interventions. The process of identifying students in need of intensive intervention includes the use of data from validated systematic academic and behavior screening tools (e.g., Student Risk Screening Scale for Internalizing and Externalizing, SRSS-IE; Drummond, 1994; Lane & Menzies, 2009) and office discipline referrals (ODRs). Throughout the process, Ci3T provides checklists (e.g., Form 4.1: Referral Checklist: Functional Assessment-Based Interventions) to document the decision-making process and ensure the use of all relevant data.

may review data from academic (e.g., reading and math benchmark data) and behavior (e.g., Student Risk Screening Scale for Internalizing and Externalizing [SRSS-IE]; Drummond, 1994) screening tools, office discipline referrals (ODRs), and attendance records to determine which students may benefit from tertiary (also known as Tier 3) supports. In optimal conditions, systematic screening data are reviewed three times a year in the fall, winter, and spring, along with other data collected for all students as part of regular school practices. The intent is to support our commitment to equitable learning opportunities by ensuring equal access to a FABI as well as other evidence-based practices. More specifically, rather than relying solely on teacher or parent referrals, all students are considered for these supports in a systematic manner.

Schools implementing Ci3T models of prevention have access to the Ci3T Implementation Manuals and Tertiary (Tier 3) intervention grids of available, validated interventions. In the FABI grid (see Figure 3.2) you will find (1) the name of the FABI support, (2) a description written in a user-friendly manner, (3) schoolwide data entry criteria used to detect students, (4) data to monitor progress (e.g., on student performance, treatment integrity, and social validity), and (5) exit criteria. This information is used by teachers independently as well as by school-site teams (e.g., professional learning community teams, prereferral intervention teams) to determine which students may benefit from this support and move them through the intervention process. For example, in Figure 3.2 a FABI might be considered for an elementary-age student who scores in the high-risk range on the SRSS-I5 externalizing subscale score, a student with six or more ODRs, and/or a student with a progress report indicating one or more course failures (see Figure 4.1, Panel A). Similarly, these same objective criteria—not teacher nomination—are used to ensure elementary (Panel A), middle and high (Panel B), and preschool (Panel C) are all systematically considered for this Tier 3 support.

When detecting students with Tier 3 needs within tiered systems, you will find that some students may have required more than what Tier 1 (primary) or Tier 2 (secondary) interventions had to offer. Other students may have moved directly to Tier 3 (tertiary) supports if they have been exposed to multiple risk factors or had pronounced concerns. One key objective is to make certain all students are considered for this Tier 3 support. We do not want to risk overlooking a student in need. Moreover, we want to ensure equal access to a needed intervention, which is why we encourage the use of validated screening tools to systematically detect students three times per year (fall, winter, and spring). In addition, it is possible to examine educational records to look for behavior patterns as well as duration of difficulties. Well-kept educational records may also feature a list of interventions that were previously attempted (e.g., self-monitoring interventions, behavioral contracts) and their outcomes.

The Referral Checklist: Functional Assessment-Based Interventions (*www.ci3t.org/FABI*; see Form 4.1 at the end of this chapter) can aid the process of accurately detecting which students may benefit from a FABI. This tool can be used to document the decision-making process of how schoolwide data were used to recommend a FABI and to provide a brief description of concern. In general, a FABI may be warranted if the student's behavior impedes their learning or the learning of others or if their behavior poses a threat to themself or others. FABIs may also be warranted if validated Tier 1 and/or Tier 2 supports implemented with integrity (Buckman et al., 2021) have not yielded desired levels of student performance. In addition, FABIs may be beneficial for students exposed to multiple risk factors (e.g., high mobility, such

Panel A: Elementary Example

Tertiary (Tier 3) Intervention Grid: For Elementary Schools

Support	Description	Schoolwide Data: Entry Criteria	Data to Monitor Progress	Exit Criteria
Functional assessment-based intervention	FABIs are interventions based on the function of the target behavior, as determined by the functional assessment and as determined with the aid of the *Function Matrix*. The *Function-Based Intervention Decision Model* is used to determine the intervention focus, including Method 1: Teach the replacement behavior; Method 2: Adjust the environment; Method 3: Shift the contingencies; and a combination of Method 1 and Method 2. A package intervention is designed and implemented, including antecedent adjustments, reinforcement adjustments, and extinction procedures directly linked to the function of the target behavior.	One or more of the following: **Behavior:** ☐ SRSS-E7: High (9–21) ☐ SRSS-I5: High (4–15) ☐ SSiS-PSG Ranking of 1, 2, or 3 on the Motivation to Learn ☐ Office discipline referrals (ODRs): six or more within a grading period AND/OR **Academic:** ☐ Progress report: one or more course failures ☐ Missing assignments: five or more within a grading period ☐ AIMSweb: intensive level (math or reading)	Student behavior targeted for improvement (e.g., target or replacement behavior) using direct observation **Treatment integrity** • FABI step checklists • Treatment integrity checklist **Social validity** • IRP-15 (teacher) • CIRP (student)	The FABI will be faded once a functional relation is demonstrated using a validated single-case research design (e.g., withdrawal) and: • Behavior objective for the student is met (see Behavior Intervention Plan [BIP]).

Panel B: Middle and High School Example

Tertiary (Tier 3) Intervention Grid: For Middle and High Schools

Support	Description	Schoolwide Data: Entry Criteria	Data to Monitor Progress	Exit Criteria
Functional assessment-based intervention	FABIs are interventions based on the function of the target behavior, as determined by the functional assessment and as determined with the aid of the *Function Matrix*. The *Function-Based Intervention Decision Model* is used to determine the intervention focus, including Method 1: Teach the replacement behavior; Method 2: Adjust the environment; Method 3: Shift the contingencies; and a combination of Method 1 and Method 2. A package intervention is designed and implemented, including antecedent adjustments, reinforcement adjustments, and extinction procedures directly linked to the function of the target behavior.	One or more of the following: **Behavior:** ☐ SRSS-E7: High (9–21) ☐ SRSS-I5: High (6–18) ☐ Office discipline referrals (ODRs): six or more within a grading period AND/OR **Academic:** ☐ Progress report: one or more course failures ☐ Missing assignments: five or more within a grading period ☐ AIMSweb: intensive level (math or reading) ☐ Below 2.5 GPA	The behavior targeted for improvement (e.g., target or replacement behavior) using direct observation **Treatment integrity** • FABI step checklists • Treatment integrity checklist **Social validity** • IRP-15 (teacher) • CIRP (student)	The FABI will be faded once a functional relation is demonstrated using a validated single-case research design (e.g., withdrawal) and: • Behavior objective for the student is met (see Behavior Intervention Plan [BIP]).

FIGURE 4.1. Illustration of tertiary (Tier 3) intervention grids. Reprinted with permission from Ci3T Strategic Leadership Team. Available at *www.ci3t.org/pl*.

Panel C: Preschool or Early Childhood Example

Tertiary (Tier 3) Intervention Grid: For Preschools

Support	Description	Schoolwide Data: Entry Criteria	Data to Monitor Progress	Exit Criteria
Functional assessment-based intervention	FABIs are interventions based on the function of the target behavior, as determined by the functional assessment and as determined with the aid of the *Function Matrix*. The *Function-Based Intervention Decision Model* is used to determine the intervention focus, including Method 1: Teach the replacement behavior; Method 2: Adjust the environment; Method 3: Shift the contingencies; and a combination of Method 1 and Method 2. A package intervention is designed and implemented, including antecedent adjustments, reinforcement adjustments, and extinction procedures directly linked to the function of the target behavior.	One or more of the following: **Behavior:** ☐ SRSS-E: High ☐ SRSS-I: High ☐ Incident reports: greater than two within the month one or more for 3 months	Student behavior targeted for improvement (e.g., target or replacement behavior) using direct observation **Treatment integrity** • FABI step checklists • Treatment integrity checklist **Social validity** • IRP-15 (teacher) • CIRP (student)	The FABI will be faded once a functional relation is demonstrated using a validated single-case research design (e.g., withdrawal) and: • Behavior objective for the student is met (see Behavior Intervention Plan [BIP]).

FIGURE 4.1. *(continued)*

as more than two elementary schools, low rates of attendance) that increase the likelihood of school failure.

Finally, in some instances, FABIs are more than a good idea; they are required by law. For example, FABIs are required when a student has been placed in an alternative setting for behavior dangerous to themselves or others, placed in an alternative setting for 45 days due to drug or weapons infractions, been suspended from school for more than 10 days, or when the suspension resulted in a change in placement. In this case, a FABI is mandated by the IDEIA (2004). A 2017 Supreme Court ruling (*Endrew F. v. Douglas County Schools*) resulted in a clearer perspective on the substantive requirements of a "free and appropriate public education" and mentions behavioral intervention as an important part of a providing a student with the ability to make overall progress on IEP goals (Yell, 2019).

Step 1: Tips for Success

Box 4.2 contains a brief checklist that guides you in identifying students who will benefit from a FABI. This is a downloadable, editable form you can use with your team to walk through the three items. First, communicate with parents about their student's performance (behaviorally, academically, and socially) and get their input. Connecting with parents will also give you an opportunity to gain insight into the impact that cultural factors have in the interpretation of student needs. At this time, you may also secure their permission to conduct the FABI if your district requires parent permission for any assistance beyond Tier 1 prevention efforts. Second, after obtaining parental permission, talk with the student to explain (in developmentally appropriate terms) that people will be working with them on some new skills that will help them enjoy school and time with others (e.g., friends and teachers). Finally, complete, confirm, and turn in the Referral Checklist: Functional Assessment-Based Interventions form to document the decisions that were made.

The team conducting the FABI typically includes the teacher (or teachers) who will be implementing the FABI, one or two individuals from the school with particular expertise in applied behavior analysis and behavioral interventions (e.g., a school psychologist, a social worker, a board-certified behavior analyst), a family member (e.g., parent or guardian), and the student. The Completion Checklist for Step 1 includes some recommended readings as well as some brief tips for success. For example, make certain that Tier 1 efforts are being implemented as planned (with treatment integrity) before determining that a student needs more assistance than Tier 1 offers.

BOX 4.2. FABI Step 1: Identifying Students Who May Need a Functional Assessment-Based Intervention

Estimated Time: 1 week
Start Date: _____
End Date: _____

Check when completed	Item
☐	Communicate with parents and secure permission to conduct the functional assessment-based intervention (use your district procedures and forms for subsequent students).
☐	Talk to the student to answer questions (assent according to your district procedures).
☐	Complete, confirm, and turn in **Referral Checklist: Functional Assessment-Based Interventions** (Handout 1 [HO1] on *www.ci3t.org/fabi*).

Considerations for need:

1. ☐ Does the student's behavior impede their learning or the learning of others? Or does the student pose a threat to themselves or others (Drasgow & Yell, 2001)?
2. ☐ Has the student been nonresponsive to other intervention efforts?
3. ☐ Does the student have multiple risk factors (e.g., harsh and inconsistent parenting or high mobility) making them more susceptible to school failure and/or dangerous behavior?
4. ☐ Has the student been (1) placed in an alternative setting for behavior dangerous to themself or others, (2) placed in an alternative setting for 45 days due to drug or weapons violations, or (3) suspended from school for more than 10 days or has that suspension resulted in a change in placement (Drasgow & Yell, 2001)?

*If you answered yes to the first three questions, a FABI may be warranted. If you answered yes to the fourth question, a FABI is mandated by IDEIA, 2004).

Note. From Lane, K. L., & Oakes, W. P. (2014). *Functional assessment-based interventions (FABI): Training materials—Step-by-step checklists.* www.ci3t.org/FABI. Reprinted by permission. Copyright © 2015 by Kathleen Lynne Lane.

Summary

In this chapter, we focused on Step 1. In the subsequent chapters, we walk through the remaining four steps of this systematic process. *Step 2: Conducting the Functional Assessment*, discusses the functional assessment process that enables us to discover the reasons *why* challenging behaviors are occurring (e.g., to access or avoid attention, activities, or tangibles and/or sensory experiences). From there, teams progress to *Step 3: Collecting Baseline Data*, which focuses on behavior measurement recording and the baseline procedures used to assess the level of the target behavior *before* introducing the intervention. *Step 4: Designing the Functional Assessment-Based Intervention*, discusses the Function-Based Intervention Decision Model, which guides you through selecting an appropriate intervention method and then building specific antecedent adjustments, shifts in reinforcement contingencies, and extinction (A-R-E) components. Finally, *Step 5: Testing the Intervention*, explains how to test the effectiveness of the intervention you have designed using single case designs and measures of social validity and treatment integrity. This is very important for having a defensible plan and, even more critically, for being able to determine if the intervention is resulting in the desired change in student performance.

FORM 4.1

Referral Checklist: Functional Assessment-Based Interventions

DIRECTIONS: Please check the schoolwide data that were used to recommend this student for a functional-assessment based intervention (FABI) and include a brief description of the concern.

Academic Outcomes

☐ **State assessment scores:**

☐ **Curriculum-based measures** (e.g., DIBELS, AIMSweb):

☐ **Schoolwide formative assessments:**

☐ **Classroom assessments** *(e.g., reading inventories, chapter tests):*

☐ **Report cards** (e.g., course failures, low high school credit earnings, progress reports):

☐ **Other data used:**

Behavioral and Social Skill Outcomes

☐ **Behavior screening ratings** (e.g., ESP, SSBD, SDQ, SRSS):

☐ **Office discipline referrals:**

☐ **Attendance** (i.e., tardies/absences):

☐ **Referrals for other school services** (e.g., prereferral team, behavior specialist, special education, counseling):

☐ **Other indicator used:**

Brief Description of Concern:

From *www.ci3t.org*. Reprinted by permission.

PART III
Step 2: Conducting the Functional Assessment

STEP #	FUNCTIONAL ASSESSMENT-BASED INTERVENTION STEPS
1	Identifying Students Who May Need a Functional Assessment-Based Intervention
2	Conducting the Functional Assessment
3	Collecting Baseline Data
4	Designing the Functional Assessment-Based Intervention
5	Testing the Intervention

After identifying students who may benefit from a FABI in Step 1, we move on to *Step 2: Conducting the Functional Assessment*. Part III has four chapters that guide you through this process.

Chapter 5, Getting Started: Understanding the Context introduces the importance of examining the context. We feature the importance of informal observations, of learning about the tiered system in place (if one exists) and classroom (and other noninstructional) settings, and of considering culture and community, as well as the fidelity with which Tier 1 efforts have been implemented. We also discuss how to review students' cumulative files to learn more about past behavior challenges and successes.

Chapter 6, Functional Assessment Interviews: Identifying the Problem and Establishing the Target Behaviors begins by explaining how to operationally define target and replacement behaviors. Next, we provide recommendations for conducting functional assessment interviews, followed by a closer look at the details of various informant interviews, including those of teachers, family members (e.g., parents), and students.

Chapter 7, Functional Assessment: Direct Observation gives a more detailed explanation of the purpose and methods of the A-B-C model. This includes step-by-step guidance on how to collect A-B-C data to determine antecedents that set the stage for the target behavior to occur, as well as the consequences that maintain the likelihood the target behavior will occur in the future.

Chapter 8, Determining the Function of the Behavior: The Function Matrix introduces the Function Matrix, a simple, novel, and effective tool that is used to summarize interview and observation data visually and to identify the function of the behavior. We describe the purpose, layout, and use of the Function Matrix. We also explain how to write a statement of the function and provide some illustrations. Then we explain how to use these findings to select the replacement behavior.

CHAPTER 5

Getting Started
Understanding the Context

LEARNING OBJECTIVES

- Explain a series of tasks to determine the context in which the FABI will take place.
- Explain how to glean information about a student's history by reviewing the cumulative file.

After identifying students who may benefit from a FABI in Step 1, we move on to *Step 2: Conducting the Functional Assessment*. As discussed earlier in this book, one benefit of function-based approaches is that they feature a respectful, skill-building approach for managing challenging behavior. Rather than relying on punishment-based approaches to decrease behaviors (see Chapter 2), teachers, other educators, and families collaborate often as part of a FABI team to first understand *why* a challenging behavior occurs. When conducting the functional assessment as part of the Umbreit and colleagues (2007) method, the team recognizes the legitimacy of the target (challenging) behavior by seeking to understand what that behavior is helping students access or avoid (e.g., attention, activities and tangibles, or sensory experiences). Then the team uses this information to teach a more socially desirable behavior (replacement behavior) as part of a systematic process we are teaching in this text.

There are different ways to conduct a functional assessment to determine the reason why the target behaviors occur, including descriptive and experimental methods. In brief, we focus primarily on descriptive methods, including (1) conducting informal observations; (2) learning about Tier 1 practices; (3) reviewing educational records; (4) conducting functional assessment interviews with teachers, parents, and the student receiving the FABI; (5) completing validated rating scales to determine whether the target behavior is a "can't do" (acquisition deficit) or a "won't do" (performance deficit) problem; (6) conducting direct observations using

A-B-C recording; and (7) analyzing the multiple data sources using the Function Matrix tool (discussed in Chapter 8) to identify the function.

In Step 2, school-based teams progress through a series of tasks outlined in Box 5.1. (For a brief video overview of FABI Step 2, visit *www.ci3t.org/FABI*.) In this chapter, we explain the initial steps. Specifically, we introduce tasks to examine the students' context. We feature the importance of informal observations, learning about the tiered system in place (if one exists), the influence of the classroom and noninstructional settings, the importance of considering culture and community, as well as the fidelity with which Tier 1 efforts have been implemented. We also discuss how to review students' cumulative files to learn more about past behavior challenges and successes. Box 5.1 features the full Step 2 implementation checklist, with three shaded rows showing these initial activities. Box 5.2 presents the ethical considerations related to understanding the context and the initial steps of the FABI.

Conducting Informal Observations: Learning about the School and Classroom Setting

As a starting point, we encourage school-site FABI or Tier 3 teams to learn about the school and classroom context (Lane, Oakes, et al., 2011). For example, is the student in a school with a tiered system? If so, the team would begin by examining the implementation plans as well as the extent to which these plans were implemented as designed (i.e., examining treatment integrity). In a school implementing Ci3T, the teacher could review the Ci3T Implementation Manual to review the roles and responsibility for students, faculty and staff, families, and administrators in academic, behavior, and social domains. They could review the current procedures for teaching, reinforcing, and monitoring student performance, as well as the treatment integrity and social validity of these integrated domains. They will also have the opportunity to review the reactive plan in place for all educators to use when responding to challenging behaviors, including exactly which behaviors are considered minor and major infractions and how faculty and staff are expected to respond. In Ci3T models, the reactive plan is also instructional and consists of the following steps (Lane, Buckman, et al., 2020):

1. Show empathy.
2. Keep instruction moving forward.
3. Recognize students meeting expectations.
4. Redirect the student who is struggling and reteach expected behaviors.
5. Provide time and space for this student to get back on track.
6. Recognize the desired behaviors as soon as the student demonstrates the appropriate behavior.

Finally, the team could review the other Tier 2 and Tier 3 interventions offered as outlined in the secondary (Tier 2) intervention grids and tertiary (Tier 3) intervention grids.

After reviewing the Ci3T Implementation Manual to learn about what is offered to all (Tier 1), some (Tier 2), and a few (Tier 3) students, the team reviews the available implementation data to determine the degree to which Tier 1 efforts are in place as planned. For example,

BOX 5.1. FABI Step 2: Conducting the Functional Assessment

Check when completed	Item
☑	Complete, confirm, and turn in **data collected from Informal Observation: Classroom Map**; copy of PBIS plan; instructional schedule; classwide system for behavior management.
☑	Complete, confirm, and turn in **Universal Checklist** (Handout A [HOA] on *www.ci3t.org/fabi*).
☑	**Step 2.1 Records Review** Complete **School Archival Record Search (SARS) Forms** (Handouts 2 [HO2] and 3 [HO3]).
☐	**Step 2.2 Interviews** Complete, confirm, and turn in **Teacher Interview**, including **Operational Definition of Target Behavior** (Handout 4 [HO4] on *www.ci3t.org/fabi*).
☐	Complete and confirm **FABI Planning** for **Target Behavior** with operational definition (Handout 6 [HO6] on *www.ci3t.org/fabi*).
☐	Complete, confirm, and turn in **Parent Interview** (Handout 4 [HO4] on *www.ci3t.org/fabi*).
☐	Complete, confirm, and turn in **Student Interview** (Handout 7 [HO7] on *www.ci3t.org/fabi*).
☐	**Step 2.3 Rating Scales** Review, confirm, and turn in **Social Skills Improvement System—Rating Scale (Teacher Version)**.
☐	Review, confirm, and turn in **Social Skills Improvement System—Rating Scale (Parent Version)**.
☐ __/hours __/instances	**Step 2.4 Direct Observation (A-B-C Data Collection)** Review, confirm, and turn in **A-B-C data (data collection form)**; write in the number of hours ($N = 3$) you collected A-B-C data and the number of instances ($N = 8$ minimum) you saw the target behavior occur (check that data and time are recorded). (Handout 8 [HO8] on *www.ci3t.org/fabi*).
☐	**Step 2.5 Identify the Function** Write and confirm **FABI Planning**; for **Function Matrix**, include a **hypothesis statement** as to what is maintaining the behavior (Handout 6 [HO6] on *www.ci3t.org/fabi*).
☐	Complete, confirm, and turn in **FABI Planning** for **Replacement Behavior** with operational definitions (Handout 6 [HO6] on *www.ci3t.org/fabi*).
☐	Complete and turn in this checklist to your coach. (To clarify: Complete HO6 FABI Planning up to Function Matrix and hypothesis.)

Note. From Lane, K. L., & Oakes, W. P. (2014). *Functional assessment-based interventions (FABI): Training materials—Step-by-step checklists*. www.ci3t.org/FABI. Reprinted by permission. Copyright © 2015 by Kathleen Lynne Lane.

> **BOX 5.2. Ethical Considerations in Chapter 5:
> BACB Ethics Code for Behavior Analysts**
>
> **2.09 Involving Clients and Stakeholders**
>
> In Step 2, faculty, staff, and family members continue to provide input as part of the school and FABI teams about the school and home context to ensure that strategies fit. For example, in schools implementing Ci3T, educators, family members, and students complete social validity checklists to further provide information about intervention strategies for secondary (Tier 2) and tertiary (Tier 3) intervention, including FABIs.
>
> **2.14 Selecting, Designing, and Implementing Behavior-Change Interventions**
>
> As we progress through the steps of the FABI process, we note that each step addresses specific parts of the behavior-change intervention and therefore specific parts of code 2.14. Step 2 is designed to provide an understanding of the context in which an intensive intervention is developed. It includes the following:
>
> - Systems, structures, and interventions in the school and classroom (e.g., Tiers 1, 2, and 3 of the Ci3T system).
> - A measure of whether these systems are implemented as intended so they are most effective (i.e., treatment integrity).
> - Faculty, staff, family, and student social validity data, which provide an additional source of information for discerning whether the goals and intervention procedures of the school plan are considered acceptable within the family's cultural context.
> - Student history, including previous interventions.

in a school implementing Ci3T, to what extent are procedures for teaching, reinforcing, and monitoring in place? The school-site FABI team could review Ci3T Treatment Integrity data for each aspect of this integrated tiered system. This review could include Tiered Fidelity Inventory (TFI) data to determine the degree to which Tier 2 and Tier 3 interventions are being implemented, in addition to the Tier 1 efforts (Buckman et al., 2021).

Having this information is important for learning more about the practicalities of the context. Are schoolwide expectations taught, practiced, and reinforced? Is a schoolwide universal reinforcer (e.g., ticket) used? If so, this *same* reinforcer (e.g., Best Buck Ticket) will need to be used to help program for generalization of the new skills taught and learned as part of the FABI. Are teachers using low-intensity strategies, such as behavior-specific praise, precorrection, active supervision, instructional choices, and increased opportunities to respond? These strategies are often included in antecedent components of the FABI, and it is important to determine how these strategies can be used at Tier 1 and as elements of Tier 2 and Tier 3 supports (Lane, Menzies, et al., 2015). If these strategies are not taught as part of a district's professional learning plans, they will need to be emphasized when teaching the faculty and staff how to implement the FABI procedures. Are validated resources used to provide social and emotional well-being instruction at Tier 1? If resources such as Second Step (Committee for Children, 2002) or Positive Action (2008) are used at Tier 1, this content and language system should be aligned with the Tier 3 interventions being constructed.

FABI teams can also review social validity data to glean information about faculty, staff, and family views regarding the goals, procedures, and outcomes. This information can also be useful when designing a FABI. For example, if a common theme during initial implementation is that reinforcement is being confused with bribery, the team can anticipate the need to provide additional training on and rationale for the reinforcement procedures when designing A-R-E components.

Responses to open-ended social validity questions can begin to provide information that reflects the culture of the school, families, and community. Analyzing family responses to the questionnaire may identify differences in values. For example, do families have questions or suggestions about expectations and rules? Are families concerned about the types of reinforcement used? Follow up by identifying how potential differences in values were resolved. If the school is not implementing a tiered system, check parent input surveys, for example, and review the information gathered from parents when expectations were developed.

After reviewing Tier 1 implementation and social validity data for the school as a whole and unpackaging it by grade or department levels, the team could also look at implementation in the specific teacher's class. In addition, the team could review information in the Ci3T Tier 2 and Tier 3 Tracker, in which they keep a record of all of the interventions that have been attempted with each student, as well as the treatment integrity, social validity, and students' individual progress when receiving these interventions.

Collectively, this information provides the FABI team with a complete picture of what is happening in the school and classroom at Tier 1, as well as what has been attempted in the past to support the student who was identified for a FABI. During this time, it is often helpful to obtain or draw a map of the classroom to later inform the use of antecedent components, the instructional schedule, and the details of how the schoolwide reinforcement system operates. This information will be useful later in the process as you consider the physical classroom environments, traffic flow in the classroom, and transitions through a student's day (Lane, Menzies, et al., 2011). If a schoolwide system is not yet in place, obtain information about the classroom management system as well as any reinforcement system (e.g., token economy). Similarly, if treatment integrity data are not collected (using the Ci3T Treatment Integrity Teacher Self-Report and Direct Observation tools available on the Ci3T website), consider using another tool to glean data about what is taking place either schoolwide or in the students' classrooms. Form 5.1 (at the end of this chapter) presents the Universal Checklist constructed for use in one school system.

Learning about the Student's History: Reviewing Cumulative Files

In addition to learning about the school and classroom context, we also encourage school-site FABI or Tier 3 teams to learn about the student's history by reviewing their cumulative file. To do this review in a systematic fashion, you could use the School Archival Record Search (SARS; Walker et al., 1991). The SARS was initially developed as part of the first edition of the Systematic Screening for Behavior Disorders (SSBD; Walker & Severson, 1992). The SARS user's guide and technical manual provides instruction on how to quantify school record data on 11 archival variables: (1) transiency, (2) attendance, (3) achievement test information, (4) graduation/retention, (5) disciplinary contacts, (6) within-school referrals, (7) certification for special education, (8) nonregular classroom placement, (9) Chapter 1 services, (10) out-of-school referrals, and (11) negative narrative comments. The SARS has an excellent reliability coefficient of .96, which is helpful in being certain that the FABI or Tier 3 team has accurate information when exploring a student's previous successes and challenges.

During this step, you may also have an opportunity to review other information about the student's family that includes their goals for their child and opinions about education in general and about their child's education, in particular. During the interview phase, you will have an opportunity to ask family members more directly to identify their goals and express their feelings about the intervention. In an integrated, tiered system such as Ci3T, family members are a part of the intervention team so that they continue to have the opportunity for input that reflects their values and perspective.

Summary

In this chapter, we explained how to begin Step 2. We introduced the importance of examining the context, of conducting informal observations, of learning about the tiered system in place (if one exists) and classroom (and other noninstructional) settings, of considering culture and community, and of examining the integrity with which Tier 1 efforts have been implemented. We also discussed how to review a student's cumulative files to learn more about their history, including past behavior challenges and successes.

Next, in Chapter 6, we explain how to operationally define target and replacement behaviors and provide recommendations for conducting functional assessment interviews, followed by a closer look at the details of various informant interviews for teachers, parents, and students.

FORM 5.1

Universal Checklist

Teacher:
School/District:
Date:
Rationale for Use: The purpose of this document is to support teachers and administrators in developing an enriched and engaging classroom learning environment that meets the needs of all students.

		In Place	Needs Assistance	Comments
	ENVIRONMENTAL SUPPORTS			
	Rules, Routines, Schedules (Visual Supports)			
1	Classroom rules are posted, connected to schoolwide expectations, and number five or fewer.			
2	Rules are measurable and observable, are positively stated, and include student voice.			
3	There is evidence that rules have been taught and practiced.			
4	Evidence of routines/procedures for each part of the day in the classroom are available and when relevant connected to schoolwide expectations and routines.			
5	Adult and student routines exist and include student voice.			
6	There is evidence that routines have been taught and practiced.			
7	There is an effective attention signal, both verbal and visual, used in the classroom.			
8	Class schedule is posted and referred to often.			
9	Schedule includes all student activities, and the order of highly-to-lesser preferred activities is considered.			
10	Individual student schedules are accessible when needed, promote independence, and provide for clear transitions.			
	Physical Environment			
11	Classroom has established and defined instructional areas that provide clear, visual boundaries and communicate expectations for achievement.			
12	The classroom environment is culturally relevant, enriched with materials that are engaging, motivating, and meet the needs of all students.			
13	There are opportunities for movement within the room.			
14	Accommodations are provided to meet individual student needs.			
	Teacher–Student Interactions			
15	Positive to negative/corrective teacher-to-student interaction ratio is at least 4:1.			
16	Students are reinforced for appropriate behavior following classroom rules both individually and classwide (using behavior-specific praise and incentives).			

(continued)

From Special School District of St. Louis County (2014). *Universal Checklist* (unpublished document). Author (Lisa Powers). Reprinted by permission.

Universal Checklist *(page 2 of 2)*

		In Place	Needs Assistance	Comments
17	There is evidence that the teacher, paraprofessionals, and other adults use a consistent continuum of consequences for inappropriate behavior.			
18	Appropriate behaviors are taught to replace inappropriate behaviors.			
19	Teacher actively supervises students (scan, interact, move).			
20	Appropriate strategies to prevent or deescalate behaviors and address crisis situations are utilized to promote the care, welfare, safety, and security of all.			
Instructional Strategies				
21	There is evidence of daily, weekly, and yearly lesson planning in academics, social skills, functional skills, and vocational skills, and materials are available for instruction.			
22	Evidence-based strategies are used to increase student engagement and opportunities to respond.			
23	Student choice is embedded into instruction.			
24	Instruction is skillfully differentiated for variety of learners.			
25	Evidence of Universal Design for Learning—visual, auditory, and kinesthetic learning styles are used to plan for strengths-based instruction.			
26	There is evidence that a variety of instructional formats are used, including small-group, individual, large-group, student-initiated, and teacher-directed.			
27	Downtime is minimized or used to improve age-appropriate leisure and social skills.			
28	The pace of instruction is appropriate to promote active student engagement.			
29	There is evidence that technology is used to promote student engagement and that digital citizenship has been taught.			
30	Assistive technology and augmentative communication are utilized based on individual student needs.			
SYSTEMS SUPPORTS				
Communication System				
31	There is an effective communication system for students, staff, and families.			
32	There is evidence of regularly scheduled team meetings with the use of agendas and minutes.			
33	If there are paraprofessionals in the classroom, they receive specific and direct instruction regarding their responsibilities to the students.			
Data/Learning Outcomes				
34	There is evidence of both formative and summative assessments to guide curriculum planning.			
35	Behavior and academic data are collected weekly for both individual students and the entire class in order to guide planning and decision making.			
36	There is evidence of classroom learning systems/continuous improvement in implementation.			
37	Treatment integrity and social validity data are regularly used to assess staff effectiveness and implementation of instruction.			

CHAPTER 6

Functional Assessment Interviews
Identifying the Problem and Establishing the Target Behaviors

---

LEARNING OBJECTIVES

- Identify and operationally define target behaviors.
- Understand the contribution of interviews and informant rating scales to the FABI.
- Understand the content and format for conducting interviews with teachers, families, students, and other relevant informants.

As we continue with *Step 2: Conducting the Functional Assessment*, we note it is crucial to get as much information as possible to begin to understand all the variables influencing a challenging behavior. As you read in Chapter 5, we begin by learning about the context in which the behavior occurs. These initial activities include conducting informal observations to learn about the school and classroom setting as well as reviewing the student's cumulative file to learn more about their educational and intervention history. After these tasks are completed, we now conduct a series of interviews with the teacher, family members, and the student. Interviews are meant to identify and gather information about the behavior of concern as well as to give teachers, students, and families the opportunity to talk about their priorities and goals with reference to the behavior and the outcomes of an intervention—meeting both ethical standards and expectations about equity (see Box 6.1).

Interviews are an indirect measure of behavior. That means that they are based on recollection rather than on direct observation and interaction with the behavior. However, interviews provide vital information that can be verified as you complete the direct observation and should always be a part of the functional assessment process. In this chapter, you will learn to use a formal interview procedure to gather information about the target behavior and the circumstances and events that are present before and after the behavior occurs. This information

> **BOX 6.1. Ethical Considerations in Chapter 6: BACB Ethics Code for Behavior Analysts**
>
> **2.09 Involving Clients and Stakeholders**
>
> In Step 2, teachers, family members, and students provide input through the interview, and adults also complete the SSiS-RS (Gresham & Elliott, 2008a) as part of the FABI team. As information is gathered about goals, it is another opportunity to ensure that the family's cultural values and perspectives are considered in the discussion of the behavior and development of goals.
>
> **2.12 Considering Medical Needs**
>
> We recommend that the teacher and parent interviews used in the FABI process include questions about any acute (e.g., earache) or chronic (e.g., asthma) medical conditions. This information is addressed if needed (e.g., referrals made) and considered when designing the intervention.
>
> **2.13 Selecting, Designing, and Implementing Assessments**
>
> Although the interview is an indirect method of assessment, it can provide valuable information about the behavior, the antecedent variables occurring immediately before the behavior, other antecedents that may affect the behavior although they are not temporally close (i.e., setting events), and the consequences. This information will be verified with observations for the purposes of intervention development. Valid, reliable tools such as the SSiS-RS (Gresham & Elliott, 2008a) may also be used as part of the assessment process.

is gathered by completing an interview with significant school staff, usually the classroom teacher but also other staff as necessary, parents or other family members (if possible), and the student. Additional useful information is compiled from rating scales. For example, we have found it useful for teachers and parents to complete the Social Skills Improvement System—Rating Scale (SSiS-RS; Gresham & Elliott, 2008a) to learn more about the student's strengths and areas of concerns in terms of social skills, as well as behavior patterns and academic performance. This particular tool provides the team information about important social skills, while also learning about differences between the "can't do" (acquisition deficits) and "won't do" (performance deficits) problems that were mentioned in Chapter 5.

Box 6.2 features the full Step 2 implementation checklist, with four shaded rows detailing the interview process, including selecting the priority target behavior, operationally defining the target behavior, and completing the interviews for the FABI, and two shaded rows for completing the SSiS-RS (Gresham & Elliott, 2008a). Often the SSiS-RS surveys are handed to the teacher and parents at the end of their interview, so that they can complete the rating while the content of the interview is still fresh and a FABI team member (e.g., a BCBA specialist or school psychologist) is available to explain the surveys and answer any questions they might have.

In this chapter, we begin by explaining how to operationally define target and replacement behaviors. Then we provide recommendations for conducting functional assessment interviews, followed by a closer look at the details of various informant interviews for teachers, parents, and students.

BOX 6.2. FABI Step 2: Conducting the Functional Assessment

Check when completed	Item
☑	Complete, confirm, and turn in **data collected from Informal Observation: Classroom Map**; copy of PBIS plan; instructional schedule; classwide system for behavior management.
☑	Complete, confirm, and turn in **Universal Checklist** (Handout A [HOA] on *www.ci3t.org/fabi*).
☑	**Step 2.1 Records Review** Complete **School Archival Record Search (SARS) Forms** (Handouts 2 [HO2] and 3 [HO3]).
☑	**Step 2.2 Interviews** Complete, confirm, and turn in **Teacher Interview**, including **Operational Definition of Target Behavior** (Handout 4 [HO4] on *www.ci3t.org/fabi*).
☑	Complete and confirm **FABI Planning** for **Target Behavior** with operational definition (Handout 6 [HO6] on *www.ci3t.org/fabi*).
☑	Complete, confirm, and turn in **Parent Interview** (Handout 4 [HO4] on *www.ci3t.org/fabi*).
☑	Complete, confirm, and turn in **Student Interview** (Handout 7 [HO7] on *www.ci3t.org/fabi*).
☑	**Step 2.3 Rating Scales** Review, confirm, and turn in **Social Skills Improvement System—Rating Scale (Teacher Version).**
☑	Review, confirm, and turn in **Social Skills Improvement System—Rating Scale (Parent Version).**
☐ __/hours __/instances	**Step 2.4 Direct Observation (A-B-C Data Collection)** Review, confirm, and turn in **A-B-C data (data collection form);** write in the number of hours (*N* = 3) you collected A-B-C data and the number of instances (*N* = 8 minimum) you saw the target behavior occur (Check that data and time are recorded). (Handout 8 [HO8] on *www.ci3t.org/fabi*).
☐	**Step 2.5 Identify the Function** Write and confirm **FABI Planning**; for **Function Matrix,** include a **hypothesis statement** as to what is maintaining the behavior (Handout 6 [HO6] on *www.ci3t.org/fabi*).
☐	Complete, confirm, and turn in **FABI Planning** for **Replacement Behavior** with operational definitions (Handout 6 [HO6] on *www.ci3t.org/fabi*).
☐	Complete and turn in this checklist to your coach. (To clarify: Complete HO6 FABI Planning up to Function Matrix and hypothesis.)

Note. From Lane, K. L., & Oakes, W. P. (2014). *Functional assessment-based interventions (FABI): Training materials—Step-by-step checklists*. www.ci3t.org/FABI. Reprinted by permission. Copyright © 2015 by Kathleen Lynne Lane.

Defining and Prioritizing Problem Behaviors

A primary purpose of the interview is to select and define the behavior or behaviors that have been identified as challenging. In Chapter 2, behavior was defined as actions or events that are observable, result in a measurable change (i.e., can be counted), and are repeatable. However, a student may be referred for behavioral intervention services with one or more challenging behaviors that are not operationally defined. Or, in a school implementing Ci3T, a student may be determined to have Tier 3 needs that are due to their externalizing behaviors (e.g., high risk on the Student Risk Screening Scale for Internalizing and Externalizing [SRSS-IE]; Drummond, 1994; Lane & Menzies, 2009) and ODRs earned, thus resulting in a FABI. The interview provides the opportunity to ask questions about each behavior and carefully describe it in measurable and observable terms. For example, a student may have aggressive behavior. Aggression is a general descriptor of specific behaviors that may include hitting with a closed fist, pushing, hitting with an open fist, kicking, and spitting. You get the idea. Aggression can include different specific observable, measurable, and repeatable behaviors. In Form 6.1 (at the end of this chapter), we provide a target behavior template to help guide you in writing operational definitions. In brief, the operational definition includes (1) the label, (2) the definition, (3) examples, and (4) non-examples. It is your task to identify what those specific behaviors are for the student for whom the intervention is intended (Lane, 2013). An example of a behavioral definition for aggression might be the following:

> The target behavior is *aggression* (label), which refers to any behavior that involves putting one or both hands on another student or adult and exerting force that results in that person being displaced from their current position (pushing) and/or swinging their foot with force so that it connects with any part of another person's body (kicking) [examples in parentheses]. It does not refer to throwing objects, verbal threats (e.g., "I am going to smack you") or tantrums (e.g., screaming and flailing hands and feet) [non-examples].

This definition identifies observable behavior. You can see if the student has put their hand on another person and you can see that other person moving. You can see the foot move and connect with another person's body. The behavior is repeatable. The student can push or kick and then do it again. The behavior is also measurable. In this instance, pushing and kicking can be measured using frequency or a count of how often the behavior occurs. See Chapter 9 for additional information on how to measure behavior using frequency and other dimensions of behavior.

In this example, we used the descriptive label of *aggression*. A descriptor can be helpful when there is more than one behavior that produces the same effect. In our example, the student hit, pushed, and kicked. Although the behaviors have different topographies (i.e., what the behavior looks like) they both have the same effect on the environment, i.e., they serve the same function.

In other cases in which the student exhibits one discrete behavior, the label is the same as the behavior; thus no descriptor is needed. For example, the student's behavior is *jumping* out of their desk and falling on the floor, or the behavior is *spitting* at other children, or the behavior is *hitting the desk* with an object and making a loud noise. The definitions for discrete behaviors also include non-examples. For example: The target behavior is *hitting the desk* (label), which refers to making contact with the desk with any object (e.g., book, bag) or body part (e.g., hand) with sufficient force to make a loud noise. It does not include making contact with the desk without making a loud noise (e.g., placing a book on the desk, tapping a pencil, putting papers on the desk, laying hands on the desk).

A benefit of a behavioral definition that is observable, measurable, and repeatable is that it makes it likely that two or more people observing the behavior can agree about when it occurs and when it does not occur. It is a way to support collecting information about the frequency, duration, or other measurement of behavior (see Chapter 9) in a reliable fashion. For example, if you say that the student throws a tantrum without defining it further, one observer may identify a tantrum as the student falling out of their desk and crying. A second observer might identify a tantrum as the student tearing papers and throwing them on the floor. In fact, the student does all of those things as part of their tantrum but may not do all of them during every tantrum. Each observer will record something different and will respond differently to the student, sometimes implementing the behavioral intervention accurately and sometimes not. The consistency and accuracy with which the intervention is implemented depends on everyone responding to the target behavior as the intervention is written. If the behavior is not precisely defined, the people implementing the intervention will respond in different ways or not at all, rendering the intervention useless and ineffectual. For this reason we encourage the definition to include what the behavior "is" and "is not"—to ensure that people collecting information about the behavior are on the same page.

As you are defining the behavior, pay attention to possible errors. One error that is sometimes made is to identify the absence rather than the presence of a behavior. For example, the teacher might say that Charles does not follow directions. Ask yourself: In this description, what action is Charles performing? Does this description of Charles's behavior include movement? Is it measurable? The answer is that not doing something is not behavior. It is not action or movement, and it is your responsibility during the interview to ask questions that help you identify what Charles *does* when he is given a direction. Does he walk away? Does he begin reading a magazine? Does he talk to students in his vicinity? Identify what he is *doing*.

Another similar error is to identify and define covert (aka private) behaviors. For example, thinking or daydreaming are covert behaviors. The student may be thinking, but you cannot see it unless the thinking is verbalized. Verbal behavior is behavior that can be observed, measured, and repeated. Thinking is not. Daydreaming cannot be verified unless the student tells you that is what they are doing, and even then, the behavior is verbal behavior rather than covert behavior. In most cases, when the teacher identifies a covert behavior as a challenge, they are responding to specific visible behaviors, such as drawing pictures or doodling on a book or worksheet or mumbling.

A third error is to use a general descriptor to describe specific behaviors that do not have the same effect on the environment, in other words, behaviors that are not part of the same *response class*. For example, you might identify aggression as hitting with an open palm, kicking desks, and drawing on assignments. As noted earlier in this chapter, behaviors in the same response class may look different but have the same function. The three behaviors identified as aggression in this example are the same response class if they serve the function of avoiding tasks. It is important to clarify both through the interviews and, ultimately, through direct observation whether the behaviors you identified have the same function. If they do not, then you will need to revise the target behavior definition.

Remember that the format for developing an operational definition illustrated in Form 6.1 requires you to identify all the parts of an operational definition: the label or descriptor, the actions that are involved in the behavior, and specific examples and non-examples of the behavior. This format provides an efficient way to avoid the common errors discussed in developing an operational definition.

As a general approach for identifying the highest-priority behavior that the intervention will address, we recommend starting with a socially significant behavior—a behavior that if changed could most substantially improve the student's experience in school or more broadly in the community. You might think of this approach as dealing with the biggest problems first. Previously you learned to identify socially significant behaviors as those that are unsafe, that interfere substantially with academic engagement and learning, and that inhibit social interaction with peers. For example, you may find that the list of behaviors that the teacher identifies includes throwing materials (e.g., book or pen), yelling, and refusing to complete a task. If these behaviors occur at different times under different conditions (i.e., different stimulus or event), they may not serve the same function. Pushing a peer seems to be the most socially significant behavior and would be the first behavior to address with an intervention. If the behaviors occur at the same time or within a few seconds of each other, they may be labeled a tantrum or disruption and addressed with one behavioral definition. For example, the behavior is labeled a tantrum, which includes unsafe behavior (e.g., throwing materials), talking to and interrupting other students engaged in classroom tasks, looking at or doing activities other than working on an assigned task, saying they will not complete the task, which may be accompanied by yelling.

An important caveat is that you may be able to identify a less severe behavior that occurs prior to a significant problem behavior but is part of a behavioral chain that culminates with the more significant behavior. For example, the teacher prioritized Kim's target behavior as elopement; typically, Kim runs out of the classroom to another room in the building and off the playground to the parking area. This is certainly a significant behavior as it could result in injury. However, during the interview and subsequent observation you note that before Kim elopes, he appears to be agitated (i.e., he begins mumbling to himself; he rocks from one foot to the other, if he is standing; and rubs his hands together, if he is sitting). Prioritizing Kim's agitation as the target is a means of preventing elopement and may provide more focused information about the function of both agitation and elopement. Keep in mind that when a less serious behavior that occurs earlier in a chain of behaviors is selected for intervention, there should also be a procedure that tells the teacher what to do if the more serious behavior occurs.

In many cases, problematic behaviors in the classroom do not present a serious threat of harm or injury. If such behaviors exist, they should be addressed first, as noted. Instead, often the biggest problem behaviors are those that most *disrupt* an environment. Let us explore the example of Reggie, an 11-year-old with autism. Reggie's problem behavior is screaming in a high-pitched voice beginning within a minute after entering his general education classroom and continuing until he is removed. This was a regular pattern for Reggie, not an isolated behavior. It is safe to say that, in most classrooms, the presence of a student who is screaming in a high-pitched voice would be considered disruptive to the environment. Regardless of the particular circumstances you face, starting with the biggest problem first is usually the most productive approach.

In this section of the chapter, we reviewed the description of behavioral definitions, provided some examples, identified some common errors in defining target behaviors, and suggested a criterion for selecting the highest priority behavior. The selection and definition of the target behavior is a primary purpose of the interview. During the interview, you will ask the responding informants to list and describe the behaviors of concern. It is your task to delve deeper and identify the specific examples of what the student does when the challenging behavior occurs.

Recommendations for the FABI Interview

There are a number of good, reputable, and available FABI interviews to use for both adults (i.e., school staff and parents) and students. For example, for adults you might use the Preliminary Functional Assessment Survey (PFAS; Dunlap et al., 1993; available on *www.ci3t.org/fabi*); Bambara et al., 2005; and the Functional Assessment Checklist: Teachers and Staff (FACTS; McIntosh et al., 2008; O'Neill et al., 2015). For students, you might use the Student-Assisted Functional Assessment Interview (SAFAI; Kern, Dunlap, et al., 1994). When you complete a FABI in a preschool setting, you will need to ask questions that help you acquire information that is similar to that acquired in an elementary or high school setting but that addresses developmentally relevant problem behaviors and captures information about routines and daily activities that are developmentally appropriate (e.g., center time, free play). The National Center for Pyramid Model Innovations (2022) provides a teacher functional assessment interview form for those working in early childhood settings.

Whatever functional assessment interview form you use, you must be sure that it provides all of the information you will need to develop an effective behavioral intervention. The interview provides the beginning identification of the A-B-Cs for the FABI, helps focus your observation on the behavior and variables you have identified, and begins to give you some ideas for a functional alternative or replacement for the target behavior.

In our collective work, we have often used the PFAS (Dunlap et al., 1993; see Appendix 6.1) and the SAFAI (Kern, Dunlap, et al., 1994; see Appendix 6.2). The PFAS is used when interviewing teachers and other school staff about their observations and impressions of the target behavior. The questions on this form can also be used to interview family members after completing the teacher interview. The SAFAI is used to ask questions of the student identified as needing intensive individualized support.

In optimal conditions, interviews are conducted with the significant adults who are familiar with the student's behavior and the person for whom the FABI will be completed. In an educational setting, interviews of significant adults start with the teacher and may also include a teacher's assistant, an aide working directly with the student, and school- or program-based professionals, such as speech and language therapists. The PFAS for interviewing school personnel includes student and respondent demographic information and the date and time during which the interview occurred. For example, student information includes name, age, sex, and gender identity. Respondent information includes the respondent's name and the subject in which the behavior occurs or the subject that the respondent teaches if the student changes classes and multiple teachers are interviewed. The form should also include a way to track the amount of time spent on the interview (e.g., a start and end time) and your name as the interviewer.

Every effort should be made to also interview a family member. Families can provide insight into the student's behavior at home and any circumstances or activities that may affect the behavior in the educational setting. This information could include differences in cultural expectations and values that may affect not only the student or child's behavior, but also how the family will view the strategies chosen as part of the behavioral intervention. For example, the family interview might be their first alert to the possible influence of fatigue or hunger or changes in family circumstances (e.g., homelessness) on the student's behavior. Often in our work using this instrument with parents, we listen to their thoughts on challenging behaviors, and share the target behavior and operational definition developed with the teacher. Then, we focus the balance of the questions on that specific target behavior to get the parents' perspectives.

Unfortunately, there are no FBA interview forms specifically identified for use with families, especially interviews that directly consider the family's cultural perspective. However, we may modify the questions in the PFAS when interviewing family members. For example, rather than asking about behavior in the classroom, you might want to know whether the same behavior occurs in the home environment and, if so, under what conditions. You might want to know if the behavior is defined differently in the home or whether this behavior is a priority for the family. You will note that some questions are best answered by the student, using the student-assisted interview, or a family member because they concern events or activities that occur before the student arrives at school (e.g., hunger, sleepiness, medications).

We recommend scheduling the interview at a time that is convenient for the respondents, whether they be school staff or family members. Be considerate of the time. Remember that teachers have many responsibilities that limit their time and may make it difficult to get all the information you need during one interview. Similarly, family members often have limited time and may require appointments outside of regular school hours. When you schedule an appointment, ensure that the respondent understands the purpose of the FBA and how valuable their information is. Be efficient when collecting the information. Have all the material ready (i.e., forms and writing implements) and know which questions you might need to probe more deeply (e.g., behavior definition). Be prepared and listen with intention. This should be a collaboration between you and the other adults working with the student. It can be tempting to interview school staff in a group, but we don't recommend it. Furthermore, the interviews need to be conducted in a private location and not a more public place (e.g., coffee shop, teachers' lounge) to ensure privacy and confidentiality. If an interview is conducted using remote technology, be certain both the interviewer and interviewee (also referred to as a respondent) are in private spaces (e.g., a room with a door).

The interview should address four categories of questions: (1) questions about the behavior; (2) questions about the behavior's consequences; (3) questions about the antecedents, or what occurs immediately before the behavior, including the context or environment in which the behavior occurs; and (4) questions about setting events that occur ahead of but not immediately before the behavior. The interviews we use include questions in each of these categories. If you use another interview form, make sure it includes the questions you need to thoroughly probe the four categories listed here.

Begin with questions about the behavior: the identification and description of the behavior or behaviors of concern and the order of importance in which the respondent would place them. Discussion with the respondent during this part of the interview is an opportunity for you to do the following:

- Probe the respondent's description of each target behavior so that you can generate a preliminary behavioral definition as described earlier in this chapter.
- Identify behaviors that occur together and might be in the same response class.
- Identify when and how often the behaviors occur so that you have an idea of when to focus your observation.

Questions about when the behavior occurs should be accompanied by questions about whether there are activities or times when the behavior never occurs. Observations during these instances may illuminate differences in the antecedents or consequences that can pinpoint effective intervention strategies.

Some interview questions address consequences. They identify the circumstances or events that occur after the behavior, the consequences, and the respondent's ideas about why the behavior occurs and what they think is the motivation for the behavior. This set of questions should always include a thorough discussion of all the past and current procedures that have been used to address the behavior and how effective they have been.

Other interview questions tackle the context in which the behavior occurs and the circumstances or events that occur immediately before the behavior (antecedents). These might include questions about the tasks the student must complete, the people in the vicinity or with whom the student interacts when the behavior occurs, and any other observable event that consistently occurs before the behavior (e.g., teacher instruction). Task difficulty is a prevalent antecedent for challenging behavior (Umbreit et al., 2004) so it is important to ask questions about any skill deficits ("can't do" problems) the student might have. For example, can the student read the words required to complete their math or social studies assignment? In an early childhood classroom, does the child have the skills to problem-solve and manage their emotions?

Finally, there should be questions identifying other circumstances or events that change the relationship between the antecedent, behavior, and consequence, which are called setting events (Kantor, 1959) or motivating operations (Laraway et al., 2003). For example, hunger may change the way a person behaves in the presence of a nonpreferred task that is different than the way they behave when they are satiated. Values taught at home about cooperation and group effort may change the way a student responds to individual public praise. Previous experience with violence may change the way a student responds to events that mimic those that were part of the violent experience (e.g., a noise or similar tone of voice). Questions about possible medical issues are appropriate here. Does the student have any allergies? Is the student on medication? Does the student have any discomfort, such as an earache or stomachache? Does the student have chronic conditions, such as asthma, allergies, or diabetes? Can the student hear what the teacher says or read the writing on the board?

Family participation in the early childhood FABI is particularly important because staff are encouraged to more fully engage with families so that families participate not only in program activities, but also in decisions about the program and their child's education. Early childhood programs such as Head Start and those implementing the Pyramid Model identify parent engagement as a very high priority and emphasize the need to include them in all activities, including those addressing a child's challenging behavior.

The student interview by Kern, Dunlap, and colleagues (1994) also asks questions about the antecedents, behavior, and consequences. Specifically, it includes a few open-ended questions at the beginning of the interview asking the student to speculate on why they have problems in some settings and not others. These are followed by questions about why they do or do not like each of their school subjects. The final section assesses the student's perception of antecedents (e.g., task ease or difficulty) and consequences (e.g., Do you get the tickets you deserve?). Even young students can contribute information that informs intervention development, so it is important to make an effort to include them in the interview process. Students' responses to interview questions can provide insight into the behavior across settings, which is especially valuable in middle and high school because of the multiple settings in which students learn and interact.

As mentioned at the beginning of the chapter, if scheduling permits, reserve time at the end of teacher and family interviews for respondents to complete the SSiS-RS. This allows the team to glean the full scope of descriptive information from the adults before moving toward the next step: direct observation and ABC data collection.

Summary

In this chapter, we began by explaining how to operationally define target and replacement behaviors. Then we provided guidance for conducting functional assessment interviews, followed by a closer look at the details of various informant interviews for teachers, families, and students.

As we discussed, the FABI interview is conducted after obtaining initial information about the school and classroom context as well as from student records. Interviews are conducted with the teacher, other school staff working with the student, a family member, and the student. Interviews include questions about the behavior, its consequences, its antecedents, and possible setting events. A key part of the interview is operationally identifying target behaviors and prioritizing which behavior will be addressed for the intervention. Behaviors for intervention are often prioritized according to the risk they pose for the student and others in the classroom (i.e., they result in injury or are unsafe in some manner). Other high-priority behaviors are those that are socially significant, often including behaviors that interfere substantially with academic engagement and learning and those that inhibit social interaction with peers. This chapter also provided recommendations for completing interviews in a thorough and efficient manner.

Interviews are followed by direct observation, as discussed in the next chapter. More specifically, in Chapter 7, we explain in more detail the purpose and methods of the A-B-C model. This includes step-by-step guidance on how to collect A-B-C data to determine antecedents that set the stage for the target behavior to occur, as well as the consequences that maintain the likelihood the target behavior will occur in the future.

FORM 6.1

Target Behavior Template

Target Behavior

Label:

Refers to any behavior that involves (definition):

Examples:

Non-examples:

Complete Operational Definition of Target Behavior:

Replacement Behavior

Label:

Refers to any behavior that involves (definition):

Examples:

Non-examples:

Complete Operational Definition of Replacement Behavior:

Adapted from Lane, K. L., & Oakes, W. P. (2014). *Functional assessment-based interventions (FABI): Training materials—Step-by-step checklists*. www.ci3t.org/FABI. Copyright © 2015 by Kathleen Lynne Lane. Reprinted by permission in *Functional Assessment-Based Intervention: Effective Individualized Support for Students* by John Umbreit, Jolenea B. Ferro, Kathleen Lynne Lane, and Carl J. Liaupsin (The Guilford Press, 2024). Permission to photocopy this material, or to download and print additional copies (*www.guilford.com/umbreit-forms*), is granted to purchasers of this book for personal use or use with students; see copyright page for details.

APPENDIX 6.1. Preliminary Functional Assessment Survey (PFAS)

TIME STARTED: _____

Instructions to Positive Behavior Support Staff: The following interview should be conducted with the student's teacher. Prior to the interview, ask the teacher whether the classroom aide should participate. If yes, indicate both respondents' names. In addition, in instances where divergent information is provided, note the sources attributed to specific information.

Student: _____ Subject #: _____

Age: _____ Sex: M _____ F _____

Interviewer: _____ Date: _____

Respondent(s): _____

1. List and describe behavior(s) of concern.
   a.
   b.
   c.
   d.

2. Prioritize these behaviors. (Which is the most important?)
   a.
   b.
   c.
   d.

3. What procedures have you followed when the behaviors first occurred?
   a.
   b.
   c.
   d.

4. What do you think causes (or motivates) the behavior?
   a.
   b.
   c.
   d.

5. When do these behaviors occur?
   a.
   b.
   c.
   d.

6. How often do these behaviors occur?
   a.
   b.
   c.
   d.

(continued)

Note. From Dunlap, G., Kern, L., dePerczel, M., Clarke, S., Wilson, D., Childs, K. E., White, R., & Falk, G. D. (1993). *Preliminary Functional Assessment Survey* (unpublished document). Division of Applied Research and Educational Services, University of South Florida, Tampa. Reprinted by permission.

Preliminary Functional Assessment Survey (PFAS) *(page 2 of 3)*

7. How long has this behavior been occurring?
   a.
   b.
   c.
   d.

8. Are there any circumstances under which the behavior does not occur?
   a.
   b.
   c.
   d.

9. Are there any circumstances under which the behavior always occurs?
   a.
   b.
   c.
   d.

10. Does the behavior occur more often during certain times of the day?
    a.
    b.
    c.
    d.

11. Does the behavior occur in response to the number of people in the immediate environment?
    a.
    b.
    c.
    d.

12. Does the behavior occur only with certain people?
    a.
    b.
    c.
    d.

13. Does the behavior occur only during certain subjects?
    a.
    b.
    c.
    d.

14. Could the behavior be related to any skills deficit?
    a.
    b.
    c.
    d.

(continued)

Preliminary Functional Assessment Survey (PFAS) *(page 3 of 3)*

15. What are the identified reinforcers for this student?
    a.
    b.
    c.
    d.

16. Is the student taking any medication that might affect their behavior?
    a.
    b.
    c.
    d.

17. Could the student's behavior be signaling some deprivation condition (e.g. thirst, hunger, lack of rest)?
    a.
    b.
    c.
    d.

18. Could the behavior be the result of any form of discomfort (e.g., headaches, stomachaches, blurred vision, ear infection)?
    a.
    b.
    c.
    d.

19. Could the behavior be caused by allergies (e.g., food, materials in certain environments)?
    a.
    b.
    c.
    d.

20. Do any other behaviors occur along with this behavior?
    a.
    b.
    c.
    d.

21. Are there any observable events that signal the behavior of concern is about to occur?
    a.
    b.
    c.
    d.

22. What are the consequences when the behavior(s) occur?
    a.
    b.
    c.
    d.

TIME COMPLETED: _____

TOTAL TIME: _____

APPENDIX 6.2. Student-Assisted Functional Assessment Interview (SAFAI)

Student: _____

Date: _____

Administration Time: _____

Target Behavior: _____

1. When do you think you have the fewest problems with _____ (target behavior) in school?

    Why do you not have problems during this/these time(s)?

2. When do you think you have the most problems with _____ (target behavior) in school?

    Why do you have problems during this/these time(s)?

3. What causes you to have problems with _____ (target behavior)?

4. What changes could be made so you would have fewer problems with _____ (target behavior)?

5. What kinds of rewards would you like to earn for good behavior or good schoolwork?

Rate how much you like the following subjects:

	Don't like at all		Fair		Like very much
Reading	1	2	3	4	5
Math	1	2	3	4	5
Spelling	1	2	3	4	5
Handwriting	1	2	3	4	5
Science	1	2	3	4	5
Social Studies	1	2	3	4	5
English	1	2	3	4	5
Music	1	2	3	4	5
P.E.	1	2	3	4	5
Art	1	2	3	4	5

What do you like about _____?

What do you like about _____?

What do you like about _____?

What do you like about _____?

What do you like about _____?

(continued)

Note. From Kern, L., Dunlap, G., Clarke, S., & Childs, K. E. (1994). Student-assisted functional assessment interview. *Diagnostic, 19,* 20–39. Reprinted by permission from Sage Publications.

Student-Assisted Functional Assessment Interview (SAFAI) *(page 2 of 2)*

What do you like about _____?
What don't you like about _____?
Is there any type of _____ you have ever done that you've liked?
What could be done to improve _____?

What do you like about _____?
What do you like about _____?
What do you like about _____?
What do you like about _____?
What do you like about _____?
What do you like about _____?
What don't you like about _____?
Is there any type of _____ you have ever done that you've liked?
What could be done to improve _____?

What do you like about _____?
What do you like about _____?
What do you like about _____?
What do you like about _____?
What do you like about _____?
What do you like about _____?
What don't you like about _____?
Is there any type of _____ you have ever done that you've liked?
What could be done to improve _____?

1. In general, is your work too hard for you?   always   sometimes   never
2. In general, is your work too easy for you?   always   sometimes   never
3. When you ask for help appropriately, do you get it?   always   sometimes   never
4. Do you think work periods for each subject are too long?   always   sometimes   never
5. Do you think work periods for each subject are too short?   always   sometimes   never
6. When you do seatwork, do you do better when someone works with you?   always   sometimes   never
7. Do you think people notice when you do a good job?   always   sometimes   never
8. Do you think you get the points or rewards you deserve when you do good work?   always   sometimes   never
9. Do you think you would do better in school if you received more rewards?   always   sometimes   never
10. In general, do you find your work interesting?   always   sometimes   never
11. Are there things in the classroom that distract you?   always   sometimes   never
12. Is your work challenging enough for you?   always   sometimes   never

CHAPTER 7

Functional Assessment
Direct Observation

LEARNING OBJECTIVES

- Explain why A-B-C data are collected.
- Identify appropriate times to collect A-B-C data.
- Identify or construct an A-B-C data collection form.
- Identify the necessary amount of A-B-C data that should be collected.

At this point in Step 2 you have used the tools described in Chapter 4 (available schoolwide data, rating scales, and checklists) and determined that a student needs Tier 3 support. You have also conducted informal observations and reviewed educational records, as described in Chapter 5, to understand the context in which challenging behaviors are drawing concern. Finally, as described in Chapter 6, you have conducted structured interviews with all the adults working with the student's behavior (e.g., teachers, classroom support staff, and parents) and, if appropriate, with the student. You have also collected information on the student's strengths and areas of concern using validated rating scales (e.g., SSiS-RS; Gresham & Elliott, 2008a). As part of the interview process, you have identified and operationally defined the target challenging behavior. Now it is important to directly observe the student engaging in the target behavior in the classroom, school, or other environments in which it is causing concern.

Box 7.1 shows the full Step 2 implementation checklist, with one shaded row detailing the direct observation process for collecting A-B-C data (described next). In this chapter we explain how to conduct direct observations and how to collect direct observational data in natural contexts, such as the classroom or other school environments. Although the emphasis is on conducting direct observations in school settings, the methods described here apply to conducting observations in any natural context, including those outside of the school (e.g.,

BOX 7.1. FABI Step 2: Conducting the Functional Assessment

Check when completed	Item
☑	Complete, confirm, and turn in **data collected from Informal Observation: Classroom Map; copy of PBIS plan; instructional schedule; classwide system for behavior management.**
☑	Complete, confirm, and turn in **Universal Checklist** (Handout A [HOA] on *www.ci3t.org/fabi*).
☑	**Step 2.1 Records Review** Complete **School Archival Record Search (SARS) Forms** (Handouts 2 [HO2] and 3 [HO3]).
☑	**Step 2.2 Interviews** Complete, confirm, and turn in **Teacher Interview**, including **Operational Definition of Target Behavior** (Handout 4 [HO4] on *www.ci3t.org/fabi*).
☑	Complete and confirm **FABI Planning** for **Target Behavior** with operational definition (Handout 6 [HO6] on *www.ci3t.org/fabi*).
☑	Complete, confirm, and turn in **Parent Interview** (Handout 4 [HO4] on *www.ci3t.org/fabi*).
☑	Complete, confirm, and turn in **Student Interview** (Handout 7 [HO7] on *www.ci3t.org/fabi*).
☑	**Step 2.3 Rating Scales** Review, confirm, and turn in **Social Skills Improvement System—Rating Scale (Teacher Version)**.
☑	Review, confirm, and turn in **Social Skills Improvement System—Rating Scale (Parent Version)**.
☑ _3_/hours _17_/instances	**Step 2.4 Direct Observation (A-B-C Data Collection)** Review, confirm, and turn in **A-B-C data (data collection form)**; write in the number of hours (*N* = 3) you collected A-B-C data and the number of instances (*N* = 8 minimum) you saw the target behavior occur (check that data and time are recorded). (Handout 8 [HO8] on *www.ci3t.org/fabi*)
☐	**Step 2.5 Identify the Function** Write and confirm **FABI Planning**, for **Function Matrix**, include a **hypothesis statement** as to what is maintaining the behavior (Handout 6 [HO6] on *www.ci3t.org/fabi*).
☐	Complete, confirm, and turn in **FABI Planning** for **Replacement Behavior** with operational definitions (Handout 6 [HO6] on *www.ci3t.org/fabi*).
☐	Complete and turn in this checklist to your coach. (To clarify: Complete HO6 FABI Planning up to Function Matrix and hypothesis.)

Note. From Lane, K. L., & Oakes, W. P. (2014). *Functional assessment-based interventions (FABI): Training materials—Step-by-step checklists.* www.ci3t.org/FABI. Reprinted by permission. Copyright © 2015 by Kathleen Lynne Lane.

the home or other community settings). As part of this manualized approach, we recommend you devote approximately 3 hours to direct observations using the specific antecedent (A)–behavior (B)–consequence (C) data collection form provided, keeping track of the number of times you saw the target behavior occur. The goal is to see at least eight instances, although more may be needed to be able to analyze the data collected. We also will explain what to do if the target behavior occurs less frequently. A-B-C data recording is part of selecting and designing behavior-change interventions. See Box 7.2 for ethical considerations for this step in that process. Next, we describe the A-B-C model and then explain how to collect A-B-C data.

The Antecedent–Behavior–Consequence Model

The A-B-C model, described in Chapter 1, is the basic model used in the field of behavior analysis. It has formed the basis for all behavior analytic and *applied* behavior analytic work for more than 90 years. The model can be traced to the early work of B. F. Skinner, starting as early as 1930 (summarized by Skinner in his first major book, *The Behavior of Organisms: An Experimental Analysis*, published in 1938).

Here is how it works in the context of conducting a functional behavioral assessment (FBA). When behaviorists analyze behavior, they do so in a deliberate and particular way. Specifically, they examine a behavior in relation to two things: the context in which it occurs (referred to as the *antecedent*) and the events that follow it and affect its future occurrence (referred to as the *consequence*). Put simply, behaviorists attempt to identify (1) the conditions that exist when a behavior occurs and (2) the consequences of the behavior that influence whether it will occur again. As you learned in Chapter 2, consequences that cause the behavior to occur again in a particular situation are called *reinforcers*. Consequences that cause a behavior *not* to occur again, or to occur less often, are called *punishers*. Whenever behaviorists analyze a particular behavior, they do so by applying the A-B-C model. In every case, the goal is to identify the conditions in which the behavior occurs and the consequences that influence the likelihood that the behavior will occur again.

In conducting an FBA, structured interviews (as described in Chapter 6) are completed before collecting A-B-C data as the interview is the context in which the target behavior will

---

**BOX 7.2. Ethical Considerations in Chapter 7:
BACB Ethics Code for Behavior Analysts**

2.14 Selecting, Designing, and Implementing Behavior-Change Interventions

Part of the assessment process for a FABI is to complete a direct observation to identify the antecedents and consequences associated with a target behavior. The method described in this chapter is called A-B-C recording. The chapter further explains how to collect data using this method, how to identify when to observe, and how to determine how long to observe. Completing A-B-C observations in the setting in which the behavior occurs helps identify a wide range of variables that can affect the behavior in that specific context and may help implementation design and maintenance under naturalistic conditions. Observations continue until the analysis of the data shows a consistent pattern of antecedents, behaviors, and consequences.

be identified and operationally defined. Although interviews often provide useful information for assessment and intervention, it is still necessary to follow them with direct observations of problematic behaviors as they occur naturally. Data generated by direct observation have the potential to confirm the information provided by respondents during interviews. These data also have the potential to shed additional light on the situation. In some cases, A-B-C data also reveal important antecedents and consequences that the interview respondents have not previously recognized.

When collecting A-B-C data, the goal is to identify the specific circumstances in which a challenging behavior occurs and the specific consequences that follow the behavior that make it more likely to occur again in the future. In other words, the goal is to identify and describe the A-B-Cs for the target (challenging) behavior. At a later point (see Chapter 8), you will need to identify the *functional* properties of these events (i.e., the specific *effect* they have on the behavior). It is important to recognize that two identical events can have very different effects on behavior. Consider the example of a teacher reprimanding a student. If the reprimand makes the student *less* likely to misbehave in the future, then it is a mild form of punishment. However, consider the possibility that the student misbehaves because it is a very effective way to gain the teacher's attention, regardless of whether it is positive attention or a reprimand. If the reprimand makes it *more* likely the student will misbehave again, then it actually functions not as punishment, but as positive reinforcement. Now that we have explained what we mean by the A-B-C model and how these behaviors help us to understand the reasons why the target behavior is occurring, let us shift to learning how to collect these data.

How to Collect A-B-C Data

As we mentioned, the purpose of direct observational (A-B-C) data collection is to gather information useful for identifying the *function* of a problematic behavior (discussed in detail in Chapter 8). The method we recommend for collecting A-B-C data, as part of an FBA, uses the same principles that Bijou and colleagues identified when they provided the first description of the approach in 1968. However, the method differs in one important respect. In the original method, observers recorded all interactions that occurred during an observation without particular emphasis on any specific target or problematic behavior. In their work, Bijou and colleagues (1968) compiled a narrative, continuous recording of all behavior that occurred during the session. After the observation, these researchers applied the A-B-C model to the narrative transcript that had been produced. For example, these researchers were able to examine any behavior that occurred during the session by identifying the antecedent conditions that immediately preceded it and the consequences that immediately followed.

An understanding of this process reveals an important point about A-B-C data analysis, namely, that any particular behavior or event has both antecedents and consequences. Furthermore, an action that follows a particular behavior (i.e., is its consequence) is also the antecedent for the next behavior that occurs—building a behavioral chain (much like a necklace in which the links are connected). Antecedents and consequences become defined as such because of their relationship to a particular behavior.

Although Bijou and colleagues' (1968) methodology involved recording a comprehensive, continuing account of various behaviors as they occurred during an observation, it is not always necessary to have such a complete accounting. When conducting an FBA, our primary concern is the occurrence of a particular target or problematic behavior. Therefore, the method we recommend uses the same methods and principles that Bijou et al. first described, except the data are collected *only* with regard to the *specified target behavior*. Thus, during an observation period, occurrences of a target behavior and its relevant antecedents and consequences are recorded. The observer does *not* record the occurrence of any other behaviors nor their antecedents or consequences.

When to Observe

Conducting an FBA can take some time. However, you certainly do not want to do anything that would make the process take any longer than necessary. Prior attention to selecting productive periods for observation should save time and improve efficiency. Fortunately, the information obtained during the structured interviews can give you a head start on knowing when to observe.

In line with this approach, you want to observe when the target behavior is most likely to occur. Responses to some of the interview questions can be most helpful in this regard. For example, your interview questions may ask if there is any circumstance under which the behavior *always* occurs. Another question might ask if there is any circumstance under which the behavior does *not* occur. Close attention to the answers to these questions will help you identify the best time to observe in the classroom. Once you have identified a likely time, check with teachers or other faculty and staff to see if they agree that an observation at that time is likely to be productive.

When selecting observation times, the other important considerations are to identify (1) how long the observation period should be and (2) how many times you need to observe. Frequently, the naturally occurring length of a classroom activity will determine the length of the observation. For example, if the target behavior occurs most frequently during math lessons, and the lessons normally last for 30 minutes, then an observation length of 30 minutes would make sense. However, consider that the math lesson typically involves 10 minutes of instruction by the teacher followed by 20 minutes of independent work by the students. Based on responses during the structured interviews, you might determine that the target behavior is most likely to occur during the independent work portion of the lesson, and very unlikely to occur during the 10 minutes of teacher instruction. In this case, your observation would start once the independent portion of the lesson began (i.e., it would cover the last 20 minutes of the lesson). The same approach would be used in any observation. A high school student who is always late transferring classes would be observed from the time the bell ending class sounds until the student's arrival at their next class. A preschooler who routinely disrupts circle time would be observed during that activity, possibly during the events leading up to it, and possibly shortly after it.

Sometimes, but infrequently, a single observation session will give you all of the information you need. More likely additional sessions will be needed. It is not possible to know beforehand exactly how many times you will need to observe. Information presented in a later section ("How Much to Observe") will help you in making this decision once you have begun to collect A-B-C data. Many people prefer to observe on at least two or three occasions (we recommend at least three separate sessions) to make sure the behavior and circumstances they are recording are typical. In Box 7.1 in the shaded row, you will see we also recommend observing for approximately 3 hours and collecting information on at least eight instances of the target behavior. This is a good practice, especially if you have any concerns about the representativeness of your A-B-C data. It is also helpful to ask the teaching staff and student if what you observed was typical or unusual.

Sometimes you might want to conduct observations in multiple settings, activities, and times of day to get a broad perspective of the likely reinforcers for the target behavior. Generally speaking, this is not a good idea. The antecedents and consequences that operate in one context may be different from those in a different context. To identify relevant intervention components for the biggest problem at its worst time, you need data relevant to that setting, time, and activity. Other contexts (e.g., other subject areas, locations, or times of day) can be explored later. Your initial concern for the FABI is to address the biggest problem at the time and place in which it creates the biggest concern. To do that, all relevant assessment data need to address that time and place.

How to Observe

Before collecting A-B-C data, you will need to determine where to position yourself. If the observation is to take place in the classroom, you will need to determine where you should sit. If the observation is to take place in another school environment, such as the gym or playground, you will need to decide where you should stand or sit. In selecting a position for observation, you will need to make sure that you can (1) see and hear clearly so that you can record accurately and (2) have as little influence as possible on the naturally occurring behavior that you intend to observe. A discussion of this matter with the teaching staff *before* the observation should help you identify an acceptable place from which to observe.

Your presence may alter the behavior that occurs when you observe. This phenomenon is referred to as *reactivity*. It is a problem because your goal should be to observe naturally occurring interactions and your presence is changing that dynamic. You will be unlikely to get the data you need. To counter this, try to minimize the impact of your presence. Put simply, be as unobtrusive as possible. If the observation is to take place in a particular classroom, and you have often been in that classroom, the students may pay little attention to you. However, if the observation is to take place in a classroom in which the students do not know you or in which you have rarely been present, your presence is likely to draw their attention. One approach to handling this situation is to have the teacher introduce you to the whole class and provide a vague explanation as to why you are there (e.g., "Mrs. Cantwell is here because she wants to see how we do math in our class"). Even with a vague explanation, some students are still likely to attend to your presence for a short while. For this reason, you may want to enter the classroom 10 to 15 minutes prior to the start of your data collection. This time period will give the students a chance to forget about your presence, especially if you avoid directly looking at or interacting with any of them.

If you have previously conducted a structured interview with the student you are observing, it is possible that the student will know exactly why you are there. In these cases, your presence for a period of time prior to starting data collection will be particularly important. It is a good idea to always ask the classroom staff after the observation whether the behavior you observed was typical. One technique to avoid this problem is to complete the student interview in a more private place (e.g., in a conference room or other space), but still with another adult having you and the student in their line of sight.

Once the time for data collection begins, you will need some way to organize your observations. Form 7.1 (at the end of this chapter) presents a good example of an A-B-C data form that includes all of the information you should need to get meaningful A-B-C data. For record-keeping purposes, it is important to identify who was observed, the specific target behavior that was observed, and who conducted the observation. The form itself has six columns: *Observation number (session #), Context, Antecedent, Behavior, Consequence*, and *Function*.

Each time the behavior of interest (i.e., the target behavior) occurs, you would record in all of the columns except the *Function* column (more on this feature in Chapter 8). First, the *number* column identifies the number of the observation and the number of occurrences of the target behavior. The notation 1.1 refers to first observation session (e.g., day 1) and the first occurrence, and 1.2 refers to the second occurrence of the target behavior during that same session, whereas 2.2 indicates the second observation session and the second occurrence of the target behavior during that second observation session. You then record the activity/setting in the *Context* column (e.g., morning circle time). You would also write the conditions that preceded the target behavior in the *Antecedent* column, the student's specific action in the *Behavior* column, and the specific event that followed the occurrence of the target behavior in the *Consequence* column. (For an example of a completed A-B-C Data Collection Form, see Figure 7.1.) To save time and space, you might consider abbreviating your notations (e.g., "T accepts, then reminds" where T stands for Teacher). As noted, the *Function* column will be filled in later (see Chapter 8).

When recording data, make sure that you record actual behavior, not interpretations of the behavior (Zirpoli, 2016). For example, if Susie screams, it would be correct to record "Susie screams" in the *Behavior* column. It would not be correct to record "Susie is scared." Similarly, in the *Consequence* column, it would be appropriate to record "Teacher answers question" rather than "Teacher gets annoyed" or "Teacher reinforces student." Finally, it is important to realize that A-B-C data collection requires the observer's full attention (Cooper et al., 2020). This type of data collection cannot be conducted while carrying out other activities in the classroom.

How Much to Observe

The specific purpose of A-B-C data collection and analysis is to enable the identification of the specific antecedent conditions under which a particular behavior occurs and the specific consequences that follow the behavior and affect its future occurrence. Therefore, your goal in collecting A-B-C data is to identify a *consistent pattern* of antecedents, behavior, and consequences. How much data are needed to accomplish this goal? How many occurrences of the target behavior must be observed before your task is completed? It is not possible to

A-B-C Data Collection Form

#	Context	Antecedent	Behavior	Consequence	Function
1.1	Morning circle time	T asks question to class.	Rolling around on rug.	No response from T or P. Ben continues to roll.	
1.2	Morning circle time	P talking to each other.	Turns around and watches P.	No response from T or P, continues to watch P.	
2.1	Spanish—Rug time	Students are participating.	He hits rug, fights with hands.	No attention from T, but other students get PBIS tickets.	
2.2	Spanish—Rug time	T praises other students.	Rolling on floor with hands on head.	T ignores Ben and he continues.	
2.3	Spanish—Activity	T tells students to get a partner.	Walks away screaming.	T approaches and asks Ben to be her partner.	
3.1	Morning circle time	T is talking to class.	Blurts out of turn.	T tells Ben to sit up.	
3.2	Group activity circle time	T prompts, "Everyone sit up please."	He rolls on stomach, facing away from group.	No response from T.	
3.3	Morning circle time	T talks about book they are about to read.	He rolls on floor.	T ignores him, and he continues to roll.	
3.4	Morning circle time	T asks to come to the rug.	Says he is writing on the lines.	T praises Ben for writing on the lines.	

T = teacher; P = peers

FIGURE 7.1. Completed A-B-C Data Collection Form. From Lane, K. L., & Oakes, W. P. (2014). *Functional assessment-based interventions (FABI): ABC Data Collection Form Practice.* www.ci3t.org. Adapted by permission.

identify a specific number of occurrences that must be observed. The overriding guideline that determines how much data you need can be found in the goal of the activity: You need to collect enough data so that you can identify a consistent pattern of antecedents, behavior, and consequences.

Generally, we recommend 3 hours of observation. However, in some instances, particularly when dealing with high rates of behavior, less time may be sufficient. Similarly, in some cases, 8–10 occurrences of the target behavior will be sufficient. In other cases, 15–20 or more occurrences may be needed. In all cases, you must collect enough data so that you can identify a consistent pattern of the A-B-Cs for the target behavior. Less data would be insufficient; more data would be unnecessary. Keeping a clear eye on the activity's purpose—the identification of a consistent pattern of antecedents, behavior, and consequences—should make it possible to readily determine when you have completed the task.

As part of Step 2, conducting direct observations in which A-B-C data are recorded enables one to observe a target behavior as it occurs naturally and to identify the antecedent conditions that trigger or set the occasion for the behavior and the consequences that reinforce it (see Box 7.3). In the FBA process, direct observations are conducted after first defining the target behavior during the interviews with informants, including teachers and family members. A-B-C data from direct observations have the potential to confirm information obtained during the structured interviews. These data also have the potential to shed new light on important variables about which the respondents may not be aware.

BOX 7.3. Key Steps and Activities in Direct Observation

The following list summarizes the steps and activities involved in collecting A-B-C data as part of the FBA process.

Before the data collection session occurs:
1. Identify the biggest problem and address it first. However, if it is a severe behavior (e.g., physical aggression), identify and focus on a precursor behavior (e.g., verbal aggression).
2. Identify an appropriate time and location in which to collect data.
3. Determine the length of each observation period.
4. Identify an appropriate place to position yourself in the classroom (or other environment).
5. Identify when you should enter the classroom and when you should begin collecting A-B-C data.
6. Identify an appropriate form on which to record A-B-C data.
7. Complete the necessary identifying information at the top of the observation form (data recording sheet).

During data collection:
1. Minimize and, if possible, completely avoid interactions with anyone in the classroom.
2. For each occurrence of the target behavior, record the relevant antecedents and consequences. Make sure to record descriptions of actual behavior, not interpretations of behavior.
3. Continue collecting A-B-C data until you can identify a consistent pattern of antecedents, behavior, and consequences.

The goal of your A-B-C data collection will be to identify a consistent pattern of antecedents, behavior, and consequences. It is not possible to determine ahead of time how many occurrences of the target behavior will be needed to identify this consistent pattern. Therefore, the overriding guideline for determining when sufficient data have been collected is that you need to continue with the activity until a consistent pattern of A-B-Cs for the target behavior has been identified.

Summary

So far in the FABI process, you have learned about the importance of considering the context of the behavior (Chapter 5), identifying the problem through interviews (Chapter 6), and then collecting direct observational (A-B-C) data (Chapter 7).

In Chapter 8, we introduce a simple, novel, and effective tool that is used to summarize interview and observation data visually to identify the function of the target behavior. We describe the purpose, layout, and use of the Function Matrix. We also explain how to write a statement of the function and provide illustrations. Then we explain how to use these findings to select the replacement behavior.

FORM 7.1

A-B-C Data Collection Form

Observer: _____   Date: _____   Setting: _____

Student Name: _____   Start Time: _____   Comments: _____

Target Behavior: _____   End Time: _____

Observation Number Session #:	Context	Antecedent	Behavior	Consequence	Function
1.					
2.					
3.					
4.					
5.					
6.					
7.					
8.					

(continued)

From Lane, K. L., & Oakes, W. P. (2014). *Functional assessment-based interventions (FABI): ABC Data Collection Form. www.ci3t.org.* Reprinted by permission in *Functional Assessment-Based Intervention: Effective Individualized Support for Students* by John Umbreit, Jolenea B. Ferro, Kathleen Lynne Lane, and Carl J. Liaupsin (The Guilford Press, 2024). Permission to photocopy this material, or to download and print additional copies (*www.guilford.com/umbreit-forms*), is granted to purchasers of this book for personal use or use with students; see copyright page for details.

A-B-C Data Collection Form (page 2 of 2)

Observation Number Session #:	Context	Antecedent	Behavior	Consequence	Function
9.					
10.					
11.					
12.					
13.					
14.					
15.					
16.					
17.					
18.					
19.					
20.					

CHAPTER 8

Determining the Function of the Behavior
The Function Matrix

LEARNING OBJECTIVES

- Describe the characteristics and value of the Function Matrix.
- Plot interview and observation data in the Function Matrix.
- Write a statement of function.
- Select a replacement behavior.

In Chapter 1, we noted that one of the key features of a FABI is that it involves creating an intervention that is based on a consideration of *why* challenging behavior is occurring; the *why* is referred to as the *function* of the behavior. Intervention plans that account for the function (the why) of the behavior allow us to consider the communicative intent of the challenging behavior, reduce the use of the challenging behavior, and increase new behaviors (replacement behaviors) that promote social and academic independence and well-being.

We learned how to identify students who may benefit from a FABI (Step 1) in Chapters 3 and 4. Step 2 involves conducting an assessment of function that identifies the why, or function, of the behavior. This includes understanding the context of the behavior (Chapter 5), identifying the problem through interviews (Chapter 6), and collecting direct observational (A-B-C) data (Chapter 7). This chapter covers the last activities of Step 2 (see Box 8.1) as we progress in developing a FABI: determining the function of the behavior, creating a statement of function, and selecting a socially valid replacement behavior (e.g., one that the stakeholders view to be important; see Box 8.2 for the ethical considerations relevant for including stakeholders and selecting the replacement behavior).

BOX 8.1. FABI Step 2: Conducting the Functional Assessment

Check when completed	Item
☑	Complete, confirm, and turn in **data collected from Informal Observation: Classroom Map**; copy of PBIS plan; instructional schedule; classwide system for behavior management.
☑	Complete, confirm, and turn in **Universal Checklist** (Handout A [HOA] on *www.ci3t.org/fabi*).
☑	**Step 2.1 Records Review** Complete **School Archival Record Search (SARS) Forms** (Handouts 2 [HO2] and 3 [HO3]).
☑	**Step 2.2 Interviews** Complete, confirm, and turn in **Teacher Interview**, including **Operational Definition of Target Behavior** (Handout 4 [HO4] on *www.ci3t.org/fabi*).
☑	Complete and confirm **FABI Planning** for **Target Behavior** with operational definition (Handout 6 [HO6] on *www.ci3t.org/fabi*).
☑	Complete, confirm, and turn in **Parent Interview** (Handout 4 [HO4] on *www.ci3t.org/fabi*).
☑	Complete, confirm, and turn in **Student Interview** (Handout 7 [HO7] on *www.ci3t.org/fabi*).
☑	**Step 2.3 Rating Scales** Review, confirm, and turn in **Social Skills Improvement System—Rating Scale (Teacher Version)**.
☑	Review, confirm, and turn in **Social Skills Improvement System—Rating Scale (Parent Version)**.
☑ _3_/hours _17_/instances	**Step 2.4 Direct Observation (A-B-C Data Collection)** Review, confirm, and turn in **A-B-C data (data collection form)**; write in the number of hours (*N* = 3) you collected A-B-C data and the number of instances (*N* = 8 minimum) you saw the target behavior occur (check that data and time are recorded). (Handout 8 [HO8] on *www.ci3t.org/fabi*)
☐	**Step 2.5 Identify the Function** Write and confirm **FABI Planning**, for **Function Matrix**, include a **hypothesis statement** as to what is maintaining the behavior (Handout 6 [HO6] on *www.ci3t.org/fabi*).
☐	Complete, confirm, and turn in **FABI Planning** for **Replacement Behavior** with operational definitions (Handout 6 [HO6] on *www.ci3t.org/fabi*).
☐	Complete and turn in this checklist to your coach. (To clarify: Complete HO6 FABI Planning up to Function Matrix and hypothesis.)

Note. From Lane, K. L., & Oakes, W. P. (2014). *Functional assessment-based interventions (FABI): Training materials—Step-by-step checklists.* www.ci3t.org/FABI. Reprinted by permission. Copyright © 2015 by Kathleen Lynne Lane.

> **BOX 8.2. Ethical Considerations in Chapter 8: BACB Ethics Code for Behavior Analysts**
>
> **2.09 Involving Clients and Stakeholders**
>
> As members of the FABI team, staff and family members continue to participate in the behavior-change intervention. It is important for them to understand the hypothesized function of the target behavior and the method by which it was identified. Their knowledge and understanding of the function will give them the information they need to be involved in the development of the intervention. As described in this chapter, the client, family members, and staff will be able to provide a contextual and cultural perspective for identifying a replacement behavior that not only addresses the function of the behavior but is also relevant and valid for the environment in which the intervention will be implemented.
>
> **2.14 Selecting, Designing, and Implementing Behavior-Change Interventions**
>
> This chapter addresses the last activities for Step 2 of the FABI process for designing a behavior-change intervention. It describes a method for analyzing the observation data, the information collected during the interview, and rating scales to:
>
> - Determine the function of the behavior.
> - Create a statement of function.
> - Select a replacement behavior.
>
> This chapter introduces the Function Matrix, a tool that provides a means for organizing and analyzing interview and observational data so that a function can be hypothesized. There is a clear description of how to use the Function Matrix and how to write a statement of function based on the analysis of assessment data. The chapter ends with a description of how to select the replacement behavior.

The Function Matrix

Two Functions of Behavior

As explained in Chapter 2, behavior is maintained by reinforcement. The principles of behavior analysis describe two ways that behavior is reinforced; positive reinforcement and negative reinforcement. Put simply, when individuals engage in behavior to access something, we say that the behavior is maintained by positive reinforcement. When they engage in behavior to avoid or escape something, we say that the behavior is maintained by negative reinforcement. For instance, if Adrian yells in class, does that behavior result in access to something, like individual teacher assistance (positive reinforcement), or does it allow Adrian to avoid something, like an independent math activity (negative reinforcement)? It is also often the case that a behavior is maintained by both positive and negative reinforcement; Adrian's yelling might allow him to access teacher assistance and avoid the math activity at the same time!

Three Categories of Behavior

Discerning the "something" that a person is trying to access or avoid is the second part of understanding the intent of a target behavior. In other words, what is the social, tangible, or sensory reinforcer that an individual is seeking by engaging in the target behavior? In our research and teaching, we have had a great deal of success by using the categories of (1) attention, (2) tangibles or activities, and (3) sensory.

The category of attention includes instances in which a target behavior results in access to social interaction with others (e.g., teacher assistance, peer laughter, time with a counselor) or avoidance of social interaction (e.g., teacher requests, embarrassing praise, peer bullying). The category of tangibles or activities covers situations that often go together, though not always. A person might try to access or avoid an activity that does not involve a tangible (e.g., going for a walk). They also might try to access or avoid a tangible that does not involve an activity (e.g., having a favorite colorful eraser on their desk). However, in most cases we see that tangibles are tied to activities (e.g., having a phone to text, having a ball to shoot baskets).

The sensory category can help ensure that we consider some important communicative intents (e.g., avoiding a loud lunchroom, accessing enjoyable music using headphones), but it can be a bit tricky because it requires that we find evidence for internal states. For instance, a student who does not have the skills to make requests may seek to avoid a loud room by engaging in behavior (e.g., yelling, hitting) that leads to leaving the assigned area (e.g., going to the principal's office or a quiet corner). Another example would be a nonverbal child who is pulling roughly on their ear to attenuate, or reduce the impact of, a painful ear infection. As we discuss later, interview data collected are also critical in considering whether behaviors fall into this category.

Combining Functions and Categories of Reinforcers

If you consider the two functions of behavior (positive and negative reinforcement) and the three categories of reinforcers (attention, tangibles/activities, and sensory), you will note that there are six possible combinations to describe how behavior is maintained.

1. Positive reinforcement: attention
2. Positive reinforcement: tangible/activity
3. Positive reinforcement: sensory
4. Negative reinforcement: attention
5. Negative reinforcement: tangible/activity
6. Negative reinforcement: sensory

Table 8.1 provides examples of the combinations of functions and reinforcers, which can be visualized in multiple ways (see Panels A and B).

Purpose of the Function Matrix Tool

To simplify the process of determining function, we have organized the six possible combinations of functions and reinforcers into a tool called the *Function Matrix* (Figure 8.1). Organizing the possible combinations of functions and reinforcers in the Function Matrix has a few benefits. First, it provides a visual structure that makes it easier to remember all six of the possible combinations of reinforcement. Considering behavior through the Function Matrix also

TABLE 8.1. Examples of the Six Combinations of Functions and Reinforcers

Panel A

- Positive reinforcement: attention
  - Emerson yells in class to get individualized teacher support.
- Positive reinforcement: tang/activity
  - Tatum hits peers to gain alone time on the computer.
- Positive reinforcement: sensory
  - River rocks back and forth because it feels interesting.
- Negative reinforcement: attention
  - Dakota threatens peers to avoid sitting near them.
- Negative reinforcement: tang/activity
  - Riley digs in his backpack to avoid starting independent math activities.
- Negative reinforcement: sensory
  - Kendall leaves the lunchroom without permission to avoid loud noises.

Panel B

	Positive reinforcement	Negative reinforcement
Attention	Emerson yells in class to get individualized teacher support.	Dakota threatens peers to avoid sitting near them.
Tang/activity	Tatum hits peers to gain alone time on the computer.	Riley digs in his backpack to avoid starting independent math activities.
Sensory	River rocks back and forth because it feels interesting.	Kendall leaves the lunchroom without permission to avoid loud noises.

Note. From Umbreit, J., Ferro, J. B., Liaupsin, C. J., & Lane, K. L. (2007). *Functional behavioral assessment and function-based intervention: An effective, practical approach.* Pearson. Reprinted by permission.

	Positive Reinforcement	**Negative Reinforcement**
Attention		
Tangible/Activity		
Sensory		

FIGURE 8.1. The Function Matrix. From Umbreit, J., Ferro, J. B., Liaupsin, C. J., & Lane, K. L. (2007). *Functional behavioral assessment and function-based intervention: An effective, practical approach.* Pearson. Reprinted by permission.

helps us to plan for the possibility that a behavior may be maintained by multiple functions. In our experience, it is common for challenging behaviors to be maintained by multiple functions (e.g., Gann et al., 2014; Turton et al., 2007, 2011; Whitford et al., 2013). For example, a student's disruptive verbal outbursts may be maintained by escaping the task (negative reinforcement: activity) and the laughter of classmates (positive reinforcement: attention). A FABI would have to address both functions of the disruptive behavior to be fully effective (see Table 8.1, Panel B). Table 8.2 uses some of the same examples from Table 8.1 to show some instances in which a behavior might be maintained by multiple functions.

Finally, through the Function Matrix tool we can consider the interview and observation data collected earlier in the FABI process. The next section describes this procedure.

Using the Function Matrix

The *Function Matrix* helps a FABI team analyze interview, observation, and rating scale data. The process of using this tool begins by reading through the data you collected through interviews (Chapter 6), direct A-B-C observations (Chapter 7), and SSiS-RS summaries. The goal is to review each behavioral chain in your A-B-C Data Collection Form to determine which of the six combinations of functions and reinforcers each behavioral chain represents (e.g., positive or negative reinforcement in the form of attention, tangibles/activity, or sensory experiences). We start with the A-B-C data because they often provide the clearest examples of potential behavioral function.

Next you can review the interview data as well as information from rating scales for additional examples and context. As a reminder, when these data were collected, the process started with the interviews to properly identify and define the target behavior to observe and to determine when to observe so that you would be sure to see examples of the target behavior in action. The final task in our process of determining function is to enter data from these multiple sources into the six cells constituting the Function Matrix.

A note of caution is relevant at this point. After completing your interviews and observations, you may be tempted to skip a detailed examination of your data. The combination of function and reinforcer may seem obvious to you while you are collecting the data. We

---

TABLE 8.2. Examples of Multiple Functions

- Positive reinforcement: attention
- Negative reinforcement: attention
  - Emerson yells in class to get individualized teacher support.
  - Emerson yells in class to avoid working with peers.
- Positive reinforcement: tang/activity
- Negative reinforcement: attention
  - Tatum hits peers to gain alone time on the computer.
  - Tatum hits peers so they will not pick on him.
- Positive reinforcement: sensory
- Negative reinforcement: sensory
  - River pulls at own hair to gain interaction from the paraprofessional.
  - River pulls at own hair to avoid pain from inner ear infection.

Note. From Umbreit, J., Ferro, J. B., Liaupsin, C. J., & Lane, K. L. (2007). *Functional behavioral assessment and function-based intervention: An effective, practical approach.* Pearson. Reprinted by permission.

recommend against taking this shortcut. A careful examination of the data will ensure that you do not miss situations in which a behavior is maintained by multiple functions or additional contexts in which the connection to the behavior is not as obvious.

Returning to the A-B-C Observations

In Chapter 7, you learned how to record individual instances of the target behavior in a chart with columns for context, antecedent, target behavior, and consequence. The form we recommended using had one additional column that we did not complete: the Function column. At this point, it is time to return to your A-B-C Data Collection Form and complete the Function column. For each line of data in your form, record which of the six combinations of function and reinforcer each instance of the target behavior appears to represent.

Figure 8.2 shows the sample data that were collected in Chapter 7 and how we would record the combination of function and reinforcer for each instance in the Function column. In this example, Ben is the focus of an observation that takes place during a group activity (circle time) in an early childhood classroom. Note that in the first four recorded A-B-C chains there are various antecedent conditions, the behavior consists of Ben rolling around on the floor and hitting the rug, and in the consequence column it is noted that the teacher and peers do not appear to provide any attention to Ben's behavior. In this case, we have selected negative reinforcement: activity because Ben is escaping involvement in circle time. In the next two behavior chains, we have selected positive reinforcement: attention because, after Ben's disruptive behavior, the teacher approaches Ben and engages with him. In the last behavior chain, we have selected multiple functions (positive reinforcement: attention *and* negative reinforcement: activity) because Ben is engaging in writing at his desk instead of coming to the carpet and the teacher engages with him but does not require him to come to the group.

Returning to the Interview Data

Once you have completed the Function column in your A-B-C Data Collection Form, it is time to return to the interview data. Start by paying particular attention to the interview questions that deal directly with the circumstances that occur after the target behavior (the consequences). Also look at questions respondents were asked directly about what they considered to be the motivation for the behavior. Make a note on your interview form or on a separate sheet of paper (that you can keep with your interview forms) about the combination of function and reinforcer that these responses appear to represent.

Plotting Your Data in the Function Matrix

The final step in using the Function Matrix to determine the function of the target behavior is to enter the data you have analyzed. To plot your A-B-C observation data, write the numerical notation for each line of your observation in the Function Matrix box that matches the Function column for that behavioral instance. For example, if line 1.1 showed a function/reinforcer combination of "positive reinforcement: activity," write *1.1* into the box on the Function Matrix that corresponds to *positive reinforcement: activity*. The resulting Function Matrix will provide

A-B-C Data Collection Form

#	Context	Antecedent	Behavior	Consequence	Function
1.1	Morning circle time	T asks question to class.	Rolling around on rug.	No response from T or P. Ben continues to roll.	Negative reinforcement: Activity
1.2	Morning circle time	P talking to each other.	Turns around and watches P.	No response from T or P, continues to watch P.	Negative reinforcement: Activity
2.1	Spanish—Rug time	Students are participating.	He hits rug, fights with hands.	No attention from T, but other students get PBIS tickets.	Negative reinforcement: Activity
2.2	Spanish—Rug time	T praises other students.	Rolling on floor with hands on head.	T ignores Ben and he continues.	Negative reinforcement: Activity
2.3	Spanish—Activity	T tells students to get a partner.	Walks away screaming.	T approaches and asks Ben to be her partner.	Positive reinforcement: Attention
3.1	Morning circle time	T is talking to class.	Blurts out of turn.	T tells Ben to sit up.	Positive reinforcement: Attention
3.2	Group activity circle time	T prompts, "Everyone sit up please."	He rolls on stomach, facing away from group.	No response from T.	Negative reinforcement: Activity
3.3	Morning circle time	T talks about book they are about to read.	He rolls on floor.	T ignores him, and he continues to roll.	Negative reinforcement: Activity
3.4	Morning circle time	T asks to come to the rug.	Says he is writing on the lines.	T praises Ben for writing on the lines.	Positive reinforcement: Attention / Negative reinforcement: Activity

T = teacher; P = peers

FIGURE 8.2. Completed A-B-C Data Collection Form. Adapted from Lane, K. L., & Oakes, W. P. (2014). *Functional assessment-based interventions (FABI): ABC Data Collection Form Practice. www.ci3t.org.* Reprinted by permission.

a detailed map allowing you to visually assess the strength of each function and allow anyone to see the interview and observational evidence leading to the determination of function(s).

Figure 8.3 shows an example of a completed Function Matrix. In this case, you can clearly see that the data demonstrate two functions are responsible for maintaining the target behavior: positive reinforcement: attention *and* negative reinforcement: tangible/activity.

Writing a Statement of Function

The next step in the FABI process is to create a statement of the function(s) of the behavior. This simple statement will contain much of the information and insights we need to create an effective FABI. The statement of function has four parts: context, student, target behavior, and maintaining function (see Table 8.3).

Context

The statement of function starts with a description of the conditions and context under which the target behavior occurs. Review the incidents you included on the Function Matrix. What environmental elements are consistent across these incidents? Be sure to consider factors like

	Positive Reinforcement	**Negative Reinforcement**
Attention	A-B-C Data: 23 incidents during independent work: 1.1, 1.2, 1.3, 1.6, 1.8, 1.11, 1.12, 1.15, 2.2, 2.3, 2.5, 2.7, 2.10, 2.11, 2.12, 3.2, 3.3, 3.4, 3.6, 3.7, 3.8, 3.10, 3.11 Teacher Interview: Peers commonly laugh at outbursts.	
Tangible/ Activity		A-B-C Data: 30 incidents during independent work: 1.1, 1.2, 1.3, 1.4, 1.5, 1.6, 1.8, 1.11, 1.12, 1.15, 2.1, 2.2, 2.3, 2.5, 2.7, 2.8, 2.9, 2.10, 2.11, 2.12, 3.1, 3.2, 3.3, 3.4, 3.6, 3.7, 3.8, 3.10, 3.11, 3.12 Teacher Interview: Outbursts often result in student not completing the activity. Student Interview: Says that the work assigned independently is too much.
Sensory		

FIGURE 8.3. Sample completed Function Matrix. From Umbreit, J., Ferro, J. B., Liaupsin, C. J., & Lane, K. L. (2007). *Functional behavioral assessment and function-based intervention: An effective, practical approach.* Pearson. Reprinted by permission.

TABLE 8.3. Examples of Function Statements

Context	Student	Target behavior	Function
During group lessons,	Alex	engages in off-task activities (drawing, coloring)	to access preferred activities (positive reinforcement: activity).
At the lunch table,	Blair	hits or slaps peers	to avoid the noise of the lunchroom (negative reinforcement: sensory).
When in long lines,	Carmen	is verbally abusive to peers	to access teacher interaction (positive reinforcement attention) and avoid standing in line (negative reinforcement: activity).

Note. From Umbreit, J., Ferro, J. B., Liaupsin, C. J., & Lane, K. L. (2007). *Functional behavioral assessment and function-based intervention: An effective, practical approach.* Pearson. Reprinted by permission.

time of day, physical location, social interactions, task demands, and so forth. Having a clear understanding of the context in which the target behavior is likely to occur will help the FABI team consider any adjustments to the environment that might be necessary to limit the target behavior and promote a more appropriate alternative behavior. It also underscores that the intervention to be designed should be implemented under the conditions when and where it is needed most.

Student

Including the name of the student in the statement of function may seem like a formality. However, including the student's name ensures that the focus of the FABI supports remain on them. Incorporating this element also ensures that the statement of function clearly communicates the focus of the intervention to other professionals and family members who may be part of a team creating or implementing the FABI.

Target Behavior

The target behavior is another essential element of a useful statement of function. We described the development of an observable, measurable definition of the target behavior in Chapter 6. In the statement of function, we include the target behavior to clarify that the statement is a summary related directly to a specific behavior. Clearly stating the target behavior in the statement of function also helps avoid having the FABI drift into dealing with other behaviors that have not been part of the focus of the data collected so far.

Hypothesized Function

This part of the statement of function summarizes what we discovered from the interviews, direct observations, and use of the Function Matrix about how the target behavior is maintained or reinforced. Depending on the results of your analysis using the Function Matrix, your statement of function may name only one function, or it may include two or more if your analysis identified the importance of multiple functions. As we noted earlier, we have found it to be very common for a single target behavior to be maintained by multiple functions. For examples of multiple functions, look back at Table 8.2.

Examples of Completed Function Matrices

In Chapters 12–15, we provide additional examples of how to use the Function Matrix tool to analyze data collected from interviews, direct observations, and rating scales as part of Step 2. In these chapters, we also illustrate how the information collected throughout Step 1 and Step 2 is organized in the Functional Assessment and Behavior Intervention Plan: Planning Form, which we discuss in detail in Chapter 11 (see Form 11.1; Handout 6 on *www.ci3t.org/FABI*). This planning form is a living document that supports the team's efforts in the design, implementation, and evaluation of FABIs. The information in the form will be transferred to the FABI Behavior Intervention Plan (BIP) and/or district standard forms after completing *Step 5: Testing the Intervention* (Handout 6.1 on *www.ci3t.org/FABI*). Chapter 21 features an example of a completed BIP (see Form 21.1).

Selecting the Replacement Behavior

After the hypothesized function statement has been drafted, the next step in the process of creating an effective FABI is to select the replacement behavior. There are four criteria you should consider when selecting an appropriate replacement behavior. The replacement behavior should:

- Be measurable, observable, and repeatable.
- Describe what the student can do or learn to do.
- Have support in the natural environment.
- Logically fit with the statement of function.

More specifically, we require the replacement and target behaviors to be operationally defined by providing the following four components: (1) label (which is important for facilitating communication about the behavior of interest); (2) definition of the behavior (one simple sentence); (3) examples (specific to this particular student); and (4) non-examples (specific to this specific student).

Table 8.4 provides examples of common errors in selecting replacement behaviors. When writing out the replacement behavior statement, include the same components as the target behavior: a label, the behavior, examples, and non-examples. For instance, On task (label): Alex will be on task during group activities (behavior). Examples include looking at materials, on-topic conversations with peers, and answering questions. Non-examples include interacting with nontask materials, off-topic conversations with peers, and leaving the group activity area.

TABLE 8.4. Examples of Replacement Behaviors

Student	Function statement	Replacement behavior	
Alex	During group activities, Alex engages in off-task behavior (drawing, coloring) to access preferred activities (positive reinforcement: activity).	*Wrong* Alex will not draw during group activities. *Better* On task: Alex will be on task during group activities.	*Error* The "absence" of behavior
Blair	At the lunch table, Blair hits or slaps peers to avoid the noise of the lunchroom (negative reinforcement: sensory).	*Wrong* Blair will enjoy crowded lunchroom time with peers. *Better* Personal space: Blair will keep hands and feet to self at the table in the lunchroom.	*Error* Not easily measurable; not something the student "can do"
Carmen	When in long lines, Carmen is verbally abusive to peers to access teacher interaction (positive reinforcement: attention) and avoid standing in line (negative reinforcement: activity).	*Wrong* Carmen will be respectful in lines. *Better* Communicate needs: Carmen will raise a hand to talk to an adult or ask for a break from a line.	*Error* Not easily measurable

Note. From Umbreit, J., Ferro, J. B., Liaupsin, C. J., & Lane, K. L. (2007). *Functional behavioral assessment and function-based intervention: An effective, practical approach.* Pearson. Reprinted by permission.

Measurable, Observable, and Repeatable

A replacement behavior should identify what you want the student to do. Just as we state the target behavior in clear terms to measure and monitor it, the same is true for the replacement behavior. Not only does this assist us in measuring and monitoring the replacement behavior, it also helps us recognize the behavior so we can reinforce it when we see it. A common mistake in defining the replacement behavior is to state it in terms of what we don't want, such as "not yelling" or "not scratching staff." Not doing something is *not* a behavior. It is merely the absence of behavior. Instead, replacement behaviors should identify what you want the person to do; they should describe observable, measurable, repeatable actions, like "interrupt with a raised hand" or "request a break from activities."

Can Do or Learn to Do

The replacement behavior should be some action that the student already has in their behavioral repertoire or that we agree they can learn to do. What we have learned about the family and school context, student interests, and social–emotional behavior could provide more of the information we need to identify the most effective replacement behavior that meets the needs of the student as well as the classroom. For example, you may identify a replacement behavior for a student to participate in an academic task. Academic engagement can be defined in a number of ways but often includes behaviors such as looking at the teacher, responding to questions, taking notes about the lecture, and raising a hand to ask for help. Non-examples may include looking away from instructional materials for more than 30 seconds or engaging in tasks and conversation that are not related to an assignment.

Increasing opportunities to respond (OTRs) is a valuable strategy for improving student engagement (e.g., Common et al., 2020). However, if the student is a dual or multilanguage learner, you may want to identify different ways to present the material and/or varying response modalities that would engage the student's strengths while also increasing opportunities to respond. For example, a dual language learner may have difficulty processing the language used during group instruction quickly enough to provide a quick, individual response. Instead, a strategy such as choral responding is mediated by the teacher and provides multiple correct models through the responses of other students. The student may be more successful if responding is peer mediated or limited to a small group. Participation might consist of hands-on activities and practice rather than oral responding. It may include allowing the student to respond using practical examples from their own and their family's historical knowledge. The point is, it is important to consider academic engagement, or any replacement behavior, in a way that meets the needs of both the classroom context and the student, as well as the behavioral function.

This is also a time to consider any overarching goals the family might have for the student. For example, family members may want the student to make friends. Consider how that goal might be addressed if the function of the challenging behavior is to get attention from the teacher. The intervention strategies would include an appropriate way to request attention from the teacher, and the teacher would provide attention as the consequence. However, an additional strategy might be to assign a peer buddy that the student could ask for help under certain conditions (e.g., when the teacher is busy or in a workgroup). The replacement behavior might then be to ask for help from the teacher or a peer. Reviewing all the information you have gathered from the teacher, family members, and the student during Step 2 of the FABI process will provide what you and the team need to identify the most suitable replacement behavior.

We should also consider whether the student has the physical, sensory, and cognitive abilities to engage in or develop the behavior. We may find that the student can perform a suitable replacement behavior if they are provided with instruction or with environmental modifications or accommodations. For instance, if the replacement behavior involves the student requesting a change in activities, a nonverbal student with limited cognitive abilities may need to learn a new sign or be provided with a technology solution. In any case, we should plan for those supports in our FABI. We demonstrate how to incorporate those elements into a FABI in Chapter 11.

Supported by the Natural Environment

As we know from the principles of behavior analysis, behaviors maintain or increase through reinforcement. We actively plan for the reinforcement of the replacement behavior in our FABI. However, we can expect the process to be simpler and more successful if we choose a replacement behavior for which there are already appropriate reinforcers available in the natural environment or that already exist in the setting.

Unfortunately, some environments are not rich in appropriate reinforcers. That is why our FABI plan considers whether adjustments in the environment are needed to ensure the availability of natural reinforcers. In our FABI, we may initially have to add contrived reinforcers, or reinforcers that are not natural to the situation or environment. However, we plan to pair contrived reinforcers with naturally occurring reinforcers so that, over time, the replacement behavior can be maintained as naturally as possible. We review adjustments to the environment in Chapter 11 and in Chapters 12–15, which detail the various intervention methods described in Chapter 11.

Logical Fit for the Function

As we mentioned in the opening chapter of this book, FABI procedures are based on earlier efforts to consider the communicative intent of challenging behavior. In most cases, we select a replacement behavior that serves the same function and communicative intent as the target behavior. For instance, we may find that a student scratches a staff member to get a break from tasks (negative reinforcement: activity). In this case, signing for a break would be a replacement behavior that serves the same function and communicative intent.

In other cases, the best replacement behavior is one that allows the student to avoid the need to engage in the problem behavior. In the previous example, we might see that the student could easily complete the task if they were taught how to do it. Of course, it might also be necessary to promote success by altering the difficulty of the task (Umbreit et al., 2004). We explain how our process for developing a FABI incorporates adjustments to the environment in Chapter 11.

Summary

This chapter focused on the last activities in Step 2 of the process of creating a FABI: using the collected data (interviews and observations) to determine the function of the behavior, to write a function statement, and to select a replacement behavior. We started with a review of the functions of behavior and reinforcers. Next we presented a simple yet efficient tool—the Function Matrix—designed to assist FABI teams in organizing and interpreting data collected from multiple sources (e.g., direct observations, interviews, and rating scales) with the goal of identifying the hypothesized function of a behavior. When completed, the Function Matrix should provide a clear picture of the individual or multiple functions of the target behavior.

After determining the function of the target behavior, we create a *function statement* that provides a clear way to communicate the single or multiple functions of the behavior to other professionals. It also serves as a synopsis of the important elements of the problem that we can return to as we craft the intervention plan. Once we have the function statement, we can select a replacement behavior. The replacement behavior should be measurable, observable, and repeatable; describe what the student can do or learn to do; be supported in the natural environment; and fit logically with the statement of function.

As we mentioned previously, we provide additional examples of how to use the Function Matrix to analyze collected data as part of Step 2 in Chapters 12–15. These chapters also feature examples of how the information gleaned throughout Step 1 and Step 2 is organized in the Functional Assessment and Behavior Intervention Plan: Planning Form (Form 11.1; also Handout 6 on *www.ci3t.org/FABI*). This living document supports FABI team efforts in designing, implementing, and evaluating functional assessment-based interventions.

With Step 2 complete, we turn our focus to Part IV: *Step 3: Collecting Baseline Data*. Moreover, after explaining how to conduct the functional behavior assessment and determine the reason(s) why the target behavior is occurring, the next task is to learn how to best measure the behaviors of interest (i.e., the target/challenging behavior, the replacement behavior, or both, if necessary) and collect baseline data *before* beginning intervention efforts. Part IV includes two chapters to achieve this goal. In Chapter 9, we begin by explaining why we measure behavior. We introduce the dimensions of behavior and various measurement systems. Then we provide a practical process by which we can select the measurement system best suited to measure the dimension of interest. We also describe and illustrate the data collection procedures needed to measure the behavior (e.g., materials needed, data collection sheets, and observation schedules).

In Chapter 10, we explain the practicalities of data collection, including how to become reliable in data collection before colleting baseline data. More specifically, we explain the importance of baseline data, when to measure both target and replacement behaviors, what procedures to use to collect baseline data, common errors and factors impacting measurement, and when and how to measure reliability.

PART IV
Step 3: Collecting Baseline Data

STEP #	FUNCTIONAL ASSESSMENT-BASED INTERVENTION STEPS
1	Identifying Students Who May Need a Functional Assessment-Based Intervention
2	Conducting the Functional Assessment
3	Collecting Baseline Data
4	Designing the Functional Assessment-Based Intervention
5	Testing the Intervention

After conducting the functional assessment in Step 2, we move on to *Step 3: Collecting Baseline Data.* This task involves learning how to best measure the behaviors of interest (i.e., the target/challenging behavior, the replacement behavior, or both, if necessary) and to collect baseline data *before* beginning intervention efforts. Part IV includes two chapters to achieve this goal.

In Chapter 9, Identifying the Dimension of Interest and Selecting an Appropriate Measurement System, we begin by explaining why we measure behavior. We introduce the dimensions of behavior and various measurement systems. Then we provide a practical process by which we can select the measurement system best suited to measure the dimension of interest. We also describe and illustrate the data collection procedures needed to measure the behavior (e.g., various materials, data collection sheets, and observation schedules).

In Chapter 10, Getting Started: Collecting Baseline Data, we examine the practicalities of data collection, including how to become reliable in data collection before colleting baseline data. In the implementation checklist (see Boxes 9.1 and 10.1), we address several topics, such as when and how often to observe, why and how to collect interobserver agreement data, and how to identify the factors that impact measurement and common measurement errors.

CHAPTER 9

Identifying the Dimension of Interest and Selecting an Appropriate Measurement System

LEARNING OBJECTIVES

- Explain why we measure behavior.
- Identify the dimensions of behavior.
- Identify and understand measurement systems.
- Identify an appropriate measurement system.

At this point the FABI team has completed the first two steps in the process. As you will recall, Step 1 involved determining which students might benefit from a FABI. Step 2 included a series of tasks that are conducted to complete a functional assessment. Now that the target and replacement behaviors are operationally defined and a hypothesis statement has been written indicating why the target behavior is occurring, we move to *Step 3: Collecting Baseline Data* (see Box 9.1).

Box 9.1 features a detailed listing of tasks to be completed in this step. For example, after the FABI team has completed and confirmed the function of the target behavior using the Function Matrix, the team will address a series of questions: What is the behavioral dimension you are focusing on? What measurement system is most appropriate to measure the behavior? What are the specific procedures your FABI team will use to measure the behavior (e.g., various materials, data collection sheets, observation schedules)? How will the team become reliable in data collection?

It is important to identify an appropriate measurement system so you can test whether the FABI you develop is effective and monitor its effectiveness when it is implemented (to be addressed in Chapters 20–23). In this chapter, we begin by explaining why we measure

> **BOX 9.1. FABI Step 3: Collecting Baseline Data**

Check when completed	Item
☑	Complete and confirm through **Determining the Function of the Behavior: Using the Function Matrix** on **Planning Sheet** (Handout 6 [HO6] on *www.ci3t.org/fabi*).
☑	What is the behavioral dimension you are focusing on (in **Planning Sheet**)? (Handout 6 [HO6] on *www.ci3t.org/fabi*). Explain here:
☑	What measurement system did you select to measure behavior (in **Planning Sheet**)? (Handout 6 [HO6] on *www.ci3t.org/fabi*). Explain here:
☑	Describe the data collection procedures you will use to measure the behavior: materials needed, data collection sheet, scheduled observation times. Explain here:
☐	How did your team become reliable in data collection? Explain here:
☐ ___ sessions	How many reliability data observations were completed?
☐ ___ %	What was the percent of agreement between observers (interobserver agreement [IOA]) on the data collection training (reliability training)?
☐ ___ data points	How many baseline data points did you collect?
☐ ___ points with IOA	How many baseline data points included IOA (at least 25% of observations)?
☐ ___ %	What was your IOA for baseline?
☐	Graph your baseline data.
☐	Complete and turn in this checklist to your coach.

Note. From Lane, K. L., & Oakes, W. P. (2014). *Functional assessment-based interventions (FABI): Training materials—Step-by-step checklists.* www.ci3t.org/FABI. Reprinted by permission. Copyright © 2015 by Kathleen Lynne Lane.

behavior. We introduce the dimensions of behavior and various measurement systems. Then we provide a practical process by which we can select the measurement system best suited to measure the dimension of interest. We also describe and illustrate data collection procedures needed to measure the behavior (e.g., paper forms and timers, data collection sheets, and observation schedules; see shaded rows in Box 9.1).

All reputable textbooks about applied behavior analysis cover the basics of behavioral measurement. Some good examples include books by Zirpoli (2016), Alberto and Troutman (2016), Martin and Pear (2019), Miller (2006), Mayer and colleagues (2018), and Cooper and colleagues (2020). These texts provide solid overviews of the types and methods of behavioral measurement as they might be used in any positive behavioral support program in the school, home, workplace, or community. Our goal is to cover this topic specifically as it pertains to conducting FBAs and testing and monitoring a FABI. Although our focus is on using these methods appropriately in school settings, the same methods and considerations apply equally

> **BOX 9.2. Ethical Considerations in Chapter 9:
> BACB Ethics Code for Behavior Analysts**
>
> **2.17 Collecting and Using Data**
>
> Chapter 9 describes the first step in the process of collecting and using data to make decisions about behavior-change interventions. It describes why and how we measure behavior and what we measure (i.e., dimensions of behavior) and closes with suggestions for how to choose which behavioral measure is appropriate in specific circumstances.

to FABIs conducted in other settings (e.g., homes, clinics, and communities). In short, this chapter begins the discussion of collecting and using data to make decisions about a behavior-change intervention. See Box 9.2 to review ethical considerations around data collection.

Why Measure Behavior?

To many people on the school staff, the idea of collecting data is about as welcome as the idea of volunteering for root canal surgery. They cope with many demands in a typical school day. Furthermore, they may question the value of spending considerable time generating data that may or may not be used. Prior to the introduction of tiered systems, some teachers were frustrated when asked to collect data given that they had exhausted their knowledge of what to try by the time they reached out for support from experts (e.g., school psychologists). In short, teachers were in urgent need of intervention support. The process of collecting data seemed too long, and the connections to interventions were not clear. Given a demanding workload, not to mention the ever-increasing amount of time and effort staff must devote to other types of assessment, record keeping, and grading, their reluctance is not surprising.

Applied behavior analysts may not have helped the situation when, during the 1960s and 1970s, they developed and promoted many elegant data collection systems that benefited research but held little practical value for practitioners. This period has been referred to by some (e.g., Wetzel & Hoschouer, 1984) as the "documentation mania" phase of our field. The term is apt because the methods used often produced mounds of data, much of which was not useful. Wetzel and Hoschouer recommended that practitioners try to collect the *least* amount of data that tells them what they need to know. This is a good guideline because data collection is undertaken for a specific purpose—to find out something in particular about a person's behavior.

So why do we bother collecting data at all? The answer is simple: Data provide the only objective way to know whether a FABI is effective. Because we have no better way to evaluate our efforts to improve behavior, it is helpful to understand how to identify appropriate methods for measuring behavior and how to use them efficiently.

It may be helpful to rethink what data collection really means. Bijou and colleagues (e.g., Bijou, 1970; Lund et al., 1983) suggested long ago that data collection is nothing more than *record keeping*. People who run businesses keep "data" of all sorts (e.g., inventories of stock, sales receipts, salaries paid, taxes). Banks keep a record of every customer's deposits, transfers, and expenditures. Schools keep records of every course a student takes, every grade that is given, and every diploma that is awarded. In fact, schools also keep track of every day that a student attends and every class session that the student attends or misses. Although people rarely think of this information as data, it is.

School personnel who attempt to improve behavior also keep data, but these data pertain to what students do. In essence, the data collected about a FABI's effectiveness are nothing more than a form of record keeping about the impact of the FABI. If a student's behavior is so problematic that it warrants a Tier 3 intervention, then the effectiveness of the FABI must be evaluated. Without objective evaluation measures (via data on the student's behavior), there is no way to justify the time spent conducting the FBA or in implementing the resulting intervention.

Data collection is not a luxury; it is a necessity. That said, it is important that you know how to collect meaningful behavioral measures and how to collect them efficiently. We now take up that task by addressing the different dimensions of behavior that can be measured.

Dimensions of Behavior

Behavior has several different dimensions. It is important to understand these dimensions before you attempt to select an appropriate method of behavioral measurement. Just as objects are not one-dimensional, neither is behavior. For example, a car could be "measured" with regard to its physical properties (e.g., height, length, width, or weight). It could also be measured with regard to its performance (e.g., maximum speed, time going from 0 to 60 mph, and fuel efficiency in average miles per gallon). Similarly, it can be "measured" with regard to its value (e.g., initial cost, age, or resale value).

In this respect, behavior is no different because it is also multidimensional. In fact, most experts agree that behavior has at least six dimensions. These dimensions are frequency/rate, duration, latency, topography, locus, and force.

- *Frequency* refers to how often a behavior occurs. *Rate* refers to how often a behavior happens within a certain time frame. For example, does a student hit other people once per day, once per hour, or once per minute?
- *Duration*, the second possible dimension of behavior, pertains to how long the behavior lasts. For example, is the student off task for 5 minutes per hour, or 55 minutes per hour?
- *Latency*, the third possible dimension of behavior, refers to the length of time between when a behavior is requested and when it actually starts. For example, if a parent tells a child it is time to get ready for bed, how long does it take until the child actually starts to get ready for bed? Immediately, after 5 minutes, or a full 15 minutes after the fifth reminder?
- *Topography*, the fourth possible dimension of behavior, refers to the shape or form of the behavior (i.e., what it looks like). For example, does a student hold a pencil with an immature grip or a mature one? Does a student type using the two-finger hunt-and-peck method or use all 10 fingers while looking away from the keyboard? Does a person

text fluently using their thumbs, or slowly using only one index finger tapping one letter at a time?
- *Locus*, the fifth possible dimension of behavior, addresses where the behavior occurs. For example, does the student eat in the cafeteria, on the playground, in the hallway, or in the classroom?
- *Force*, the final dimension of behavior, addresses the strength or intensity of the behavior. For example, does the student scream or speak softly? More specifically, does the child speak loudly enough to be heard from 5 feet away, from 20 feet away, or from across the playground?

Any behavior can be measured with respect to all six dimensions. For example, 7-year-old Evan often uses a profane gesture (can you guess which finger?). Assume we know certain facts about his use of this gesture. For example, we know that Evan uses the gesture, on average, three times per hour and that each occurrence lasts for less than 5 seconds. The gesture occurs immediately after someone else makes a disparaging comment to him, and within 5 minutes after his teacher tells him to read or do math. Furthermore, he uses the same gesture repeatedly (i.e., it always has the same shape), uses it in all school environments (classroom, hallways, playground, cafeteria), and is always dramatic in presenting it (waves and shakes his arms at the same time). With this information, we can describe several relevant dimensions of Evan's gestures: their rate (three times per hour); their duration (5 seconds or less); their latency (immediately in response to comments or within 5 minutes of receiving an academic assignment); their topography (both arms raised with middle fingers extended); their locus (all school environments); and their force (arms and fingers waving rapidly).

Fortunately, we rarely, if ever, need to address all six possible dimensions of behavior. In fact, only one or two dimensions are addressed in most cases. At this point, your task is to determine which dimensions of the target behavior are most relevant. Are you most concerned about how often the behavior occurs? If so, you will concentrate on the behavior's frequency or rate. Perhaps you are not particularly concerned with the behavior's rate, but rather with how long it lasts or how long it takes before it starts. If so, you would focus on the behavior's duration or latency. Perhaps the behavior is acceptable in some environments (e.g., the playground) but not in others (e.g., the classroom). If so, you would be concerned with the behavior's locus. Similar questions apply to the other two dimensions of behavior. As you move through this decision-making process, the FABI team's discussion and decisions would be written on the FABI Planning Sheet (illustrations to follow in Chapter 13).

Measuring Behavior

Several different methods can be used to measure behavior. Miller (2006) suggested classifying these methods as either *event-based* or *time-based* by considering the behavior's uniformity. *Uniform* behaviors are those in which every performance takes about the same length of time as every other. Uniform behaviors are often brief. For example, each swear word a student utters will last roughly the same length of time. Each hit of another student also lasts approximately the same length as all other hits. Whenever each performance of a behavior lasts about the same length of time, we can describe it as *uniform*. In contrast, many behaviors are *nonuniform* in length. A student may be "off task" for 30 seconds on one occasion and for 10 minutes on the next occasion. Other behaviors such as crying, reading, and talking are similar in that each occurrence can last a very different length of time. Behaviors that can vary in length are *nonuniform*.

This basic classification helps in identifying an appropriate measurement system. In most cases, uniform behaviors are likely to be best measured by *event-based* methods, whereas nonuniform behaviors are likely to be best measured by *time-based* methods.

Event-Based Methods

This section presents four event-based methods for measuring behavior—permanent products, frequency of behavior, rate of behavior, and the intensity/magnitude of behavior.

Permanent Products

The first event-based method, permanent product recording, actually does not measure behavior directly. Rather, it measures the *products* of behavior that last long after the behavior's occurrence. Many examples can be found in school settings. For example, when students take a spelling or math test, they often write answers on a sheet of paper. These written answers are products of the student's actual behavior (solving the problem and writing). When students write graffiti on bathroom walls or carve their initials into a school desk, the products of their behavior (the graffiti and the initials) can be observed and recorded long after the occurrence of the behavior that produced them. Anytime a behavior generates products that last, the permanent product recording method can be used.

The procedure for measuring these products is fairly simple. For example, with the spelling or math test, the teacher would record, at a later time, the number or percentage of words spelled correctly or math problems calculated correctly.

Frequency

The measurement of the frequency of behavior (i.e., how often it occurs) is perhaps the most basic unit of measurement in the field of applied behavior analysis. Frequency recording (see Figure 9.1) is appropriate for measuring uniform behaviors that have a clear beginning if the observation periods are equal in length (e.g., always 10 minutes long; Zirpoli, 2016). If observation periods vary in length (e.g., if some last 10 minutes and others last 15 or 20 minutes), you will need to convert the frequencies into rate data.

Rate

Rate recording is identical to frequency recording except that the data come from observation sessions that vary in length. Specifically, rate identifies the number of times a behavior occurs within a specified time frame. Nonbehavioral rate measures (e.g., miles per hour) are common in our society. Behavioral measures of rate are essentially the same.

Student: Jimmy	Observer: Mrs. Robbins
Setting: Math Class	Date: 2-1-23
Behavior: Profanity	
Start: 10:05	Stop: 10:25

~~卌~~ ~~卌~~ ||

Total = 12

Student: Jimmy	Observer: Mrs. Robbins
Setting: Math Class	Date: 2-2-23
Behavior: Profanity	
Start: 10:05	Stop: 10:25

~~卌~~ ~~卌~~ ||||

Total = 14

Student: Jimmy	Observer: Mrs. Robbins
Setting: Math Class	Date: 2-3-23
Behavior: Profanity	
Start: 10:05	Stop: 10:25

~~卌~~ ~~卌~~ |

Total = 11

FIGURE 9.1. Example of frequency recording. From Umbreit, J., Ferro, J. B., Liaupsin, C. J., & Lane, K. L. (2007). *Functional behavioral assessment and function-based intervention: An effective, practical approach.* Pearson. Reprinted by permission.

To calculate rate, simply divide the number of occurrences of the behavior (i.e., its frequency) by the number of minutes the student was observed. The result is usually expressed as number-per-minute or number-per-hour. Rate data often produce somewhat "funny" numbers, such as a rate of 0.2 swear words per minute. This is somewhat akin to the report that the average American couple has 1.96 children. Of course, no one has 1.96 children, and no one emits 0.2 responses per minute. Nevertheless, the method enables us to compare the relative strength of behavior when observation sessions vary in length. For convenience and communication, you may find it helpful to convert fractional numbers to whole numbers. For instance, we can convert rate-per-minute to a rate-per-hour or rate-per-day. A rate of 0.2 responses per minute, when multiplied by 60 minutes, results in a rate of 12 times per hour. If the school day is 6 hours long, multiplying the hourly rate (12) by 6 (i.e., the number of hours in the school day) produces a daily rate of 72. Many school staffers find these converted rates to be easier to manage.

Intensity/Magnitude

The measurement of the intensity or magnitude of a behavior addresses its force. These measures usually require a judgment by the observer, which makes them less attractive than other options. Measures of intensity or magnitude are usually estimates based on a predetermined qualitative scale in which an observer rates a behavior's force as "very strong, strong, weak, or very weak" or as "very loud, loud, quiet, or very quiet." Ratings like these are subjective, which is problematic, but they may be improved by using more objective criteria (loud enough to be heard from 5 feet, 10 feet, or 20 feet away, etc.). Fortunately, the intensity or magnitude of a behavior is usually not a school staff's primary concern. Frequency and rate measures are typically much more useful when the need to measure uniform behaviors arises.

Generally speaking, event-based measures are fairly demanding on the observer, often requiring the individual to watch carefully throughout an entire observation session. However, they provide very useful information when assessing a behavior's strength. Time-based methods can be equally demanding, but may be less so, are fairly easy to do, and can provide a useful estimate of a behavior's strength.

Time-Based Methods

This section covers five time-based methods that can be used to measure behavior, specifically, methods involving duration, latency, partial-interval and whole-interval recordings, and time sampling.

Duration

The recording of a behavior's duration (i.e., how long it lasts) is fairly straightforward. To do this, simply keep track of how long each occurrence of the behavior lasts by using any clock that has a seconds hand, including a stopwatch, a wristwatch, or a clock on the classroom wall. You may simply record the duration of each occurrence of the behavior (called *response duration*) or may restart and stop the timer every time the behavior occurs, which results in a *total duration* for the session. If a student has a tantrum, you may be interested in the duration of each instance (response duration), or you may be more interested in the total amount of time spent across tantrums (total duration).

Latency

The measurement of latency is identical to the measurement of duration except the observer is not measuring how long the behavior lasts. Rather, the observer measures the length of time that elapses between when an instruction is given and when the behavior starts. For instance, many parents know that their children do not always go to bed immediately when told to. A measure of latency would tell us how much time elapses between hearing "time for bed" and actually starting to go to bed.

Partial-Interval and Whole-Interval Recordings

The interval recording methods are used quite often in research and in practice because they are flexible and provide useful data. Their common feature is that an observation period is divided into blocks of time (called intervals) and observations are recorded separately for each interval. Typically, the blocks of time are equal intervals. For example, a 15-minute observation period may be divided into a total of 30 intervals, each of which is 30 seconds long. The observer then makes recordings based on what occurs during each interval. The recordings are usually fairly simple, such as a "+" or "−" for each interval to indicate occurrence or nonoccurrence of the behavior. The observer does not record the frequency of the behavior during the interval, but rather its presence or absence.

The observer may choose to use either the partial-interval or whole-interval recording method. With the *partial-interval* method, the observer records whether the behavior occurred *at all* during the interval. If the behavior occurs even once, the observer would record a "+" for that interval (see Figure 9.2). It does not matter whether the behavior occurs once or 10 times during the interval because the observer scores only its presence ("+") or its absence ("−"). This process continues interval by interval throughout the entire recording session. When the session is finished, the observer calculates the *percentage of intervals* in which the behavior occurred. In Figure 9.2, the observer determined that that behavior occurred during 45% of the intervals. This percentage was determined by dividing the number of intervals in which the behavior occurred (9) by the total number of intervals (20), then multiplying the result by 100%. This percentage provides a useful estimate of the overall strength of the behavior.

If the *whole-interval* method is used, the procedures are identical with one exception: A "+" is scored only if the behavior lasts *throughout the entire interval*. The whole-interval method is most appropriate when observing behaviors that are nonuniform, such as on-task behavior. Conversely, the partial-interval method is most appropriate when observing brief, uniform behaviors that have distinct beginnings and endings. Common examples include profanity, hitting, or making noises. Both interval methods place considerable demands on the observer because they typically require constant attention throughout the observation period. Nevertheless, many school staffers find the interval methods attractive because they are easy to perform and usually result in a useful estimate of a behavior's strength. By comparing the data from one observation session to another over time, the staff can easily determine whether an intervention is effective.

When reporting interval data, it is important to remember that the data represent a percentage of observed intervals, not a percentage of total time. For instance, if we consider the data in Figure 9.2, it should not be reported as "Jimmy engaged in profanity 45% of the time." Instead, it should be reported as "Jimmy engaged in profanity in 45% of observed intervals."

It is important to understand that the interval recording methods provide an estimate of the level of a behavior. Partial-interval recording systems tend to overestimate the level of behavior. In contrast, whole-interval recording systems tend to underestimate the occurrence of behavior (Cooper et al., 2020). In addition, there have been broader concerns and criticisms about the use of interval methods in the fields of applied behavior analysis and single-case design (Ledford & Gast, 2018; Ledford et al., 2015), particularly regarding whole-interval recording. We encourage the FABI team to be conservative when selecting a recording system. If your goal is to increase a behavior (e.g., academic engagement), it would be most conservative to use a whole-interval system because a response is credited only if it lasts throughout the entire interval. In contrast, if your goal is to decrease a behavior (e.g., disruption), it would be most conservative to use a partial-interval recording system because even one brief occurrence during an interval is counted.

Student: **Jimmy** Observer: **Ms. Smith**
Setting: **Math Class** Date: **2-1-23**
Behavior: **Profanity**
Start: **10:05** Stop: **10:15**

10 minutes: 30-second intervals

1	2	3	4	5	6	7	8	9	10	11	12	13	14	15	16	17	18	19	20
+	+	+	−	−	−	−	−	−	+	−	+	−	−	+	+	−	+	−	+

+ = occurrence
− = nonoccurrence

Summary:

Profanity occurred during 9/20 = 45% of the intervals.

FIGURE 9.2. Partial-interval recording. From Umbreit, J., Ferro, J. B., Liaupsin, C. J., & Lane, K. L. (2007). *Functional behavioral assessment and function-based intervention: An effective, practical approach.* Pearson. Reprinted by permission.

Time Sampling

The final time-based method, time sampling, is also very popular because of its simplicity and usefulness. Time sampling (sometimes called *momentary* time sampling) is identical to the interval methods with one important exception: A behavior is scored as occurring ("+") or not occurring ("−") based solely only on whether it is happening at the end of the interval. Therefore, the observer only needs to observe directly at the end of the interval. The method of recording and calculating the percentage of intervals in which the behavior occurred is the same as with the interval methods.

How to Collect Data: Methods and Considerations

The topics in this section include how to choose the appropriate measurement method, how to identify the information that needs to be included on data collection forms, and when and how often to observe.

Picking an Appropriate Measurement Method

There is no simple formula or set of questions that would identify exactly the "right" measurement method for every occasion. Therefore, the FABI team will need to use their collective knowledge of the different measurement methods and of the student and situation to identify an appropriate measurement method. Sometimes, more than one method may be appropriate. The ultimate choice among appropriate methods will rest on the ease of data collection, the demands made on the observer, and personal preferences for one method over another.

Fortunately, common sense and reason can help you identify which methods are potentially appropriate and which are clearly inappropriate for a given situation. Earlier we stated that your first task is to identify the dimension of the student's target behavior that concerns you the most. Assume a student's target behavior is "off task" and the replacement behavior is "on task." In this instance, your greatest concern is most likely how long each type of behavior lasts (i.e., its duration). Knowing this, you can eliminate the event-based methods. You can also eliminate the partial-interval recording method because it is most appropriate for measuring brief, uniform behaviors. You are left with three options: duration recording, whole-interval recording, and time sampling. Each of these methods would give you useful information about the strength of the student's on- and off-task behaviors. Now, consider which of these methods is the easiest to implement, makes the fewest demands on your time, and provides the most useful information. In this situation, many people would select time sampling because it is easy to do and makes relatively few demands on their time. However, others might choose the whole-interval method, especially if their goal is for the student to be on task all or nearly all of the time. Although the whole-interval method makes greater demands on the observer's time, as we mentioned earlier, it provides the most conservative possible estimate of on-task behavior because credit is given for being on task only if the behavior occurs throughout the entire interval.

With a different student, the target behavior might be profanity. Once again, begin by identifying the dimension of behavior that is of greatest concern. Most of the staff would focus on how often the behavior occurs. Each use of profanity is brief, and the behavior is uniform, so you can automatically eliminate most of the time-based methods as being inappropriate. Once again, you are left with three options: frequency, rate, or partial-interval recording, each of which could provide useful information. Some of the staff may count frequencies because they want precise data and are able to observe each day at the same time and for the same length of time. Others may choose the rate method because they are not always able to observe at the same time or for the same length of time. Still others may select the partial-interval method because it provides a useful estimate of the behavior's strength and is easier to implement.

Given that there is often not a single "right" method for every situation, how do you proceed? Identify which methods are potentially appropriate for measuring the dimension of behavior you are most concerned about (see Figure 9.3).

- Make sure the method chosen provides useful information.
- Weigh the relative demands of each potentially appropriate method.
- Select the one that is easiest to do given your knowledge of the student, their behavior, and the setting and situation in which data must be collected.

If you are not the person collecting data, be sure you have consulted with the data collector to identify what they think is easiest and fits most appropriately in the classroom. For example, if the teacher is collecting the data, make sure you have the teacher's input. This may require some negotiation so that you ensure the best method is selected while still meeting the needs of the teacher and classroom environment.

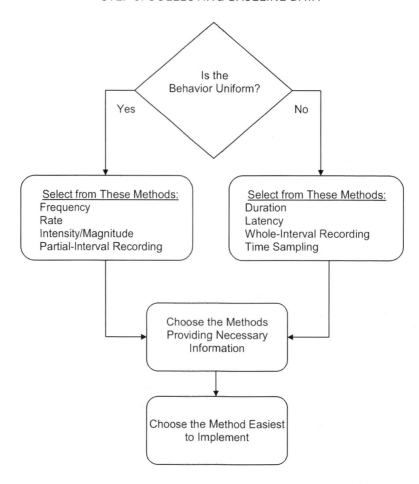

FIGURE 9.3. Process for selecting a measurement method. From Umbreit, J., Ferro, J. B., Liaupsin, C. J., & Lane, K. L. (2007). *Functional behavioral assessment and function-based intervention: An effective, practical approach.* Pearson. Reprinted by permission.

This process of decision making, combined with your judgment and experience, should enable you to identify at least one measurement method that is appropriate for your needs.

Identifying Information

Remember, data collection is a form of record keeping. Make sure your data collection form contains certain identifying information. Zirpoli (2016) has recommended that every data collection form should include the following: the student's name, the target behavior (and replacement behavior if both are being recorded), the environment or situation in which the student is being observed, the observer's name, and the date of the observation. We suggest also noting the time at which the observation begins and ends. Figures 9.1 and 9.2 are good examples of data collection forms that include this information. Store receipts include similar information (date, time of day, item purchased, cost, etc.). Data collection should be no different. Proper record keeping requires that you include the identifying information listed here. Without it, you may have potentially good data that are unusable. If you cannot identify whose data (name) it is or where it fits with other data that were collected (date), you cannot use the information.

When and How Often to Observe

There are no hard-and-fast rules to determine exactly how long each observation session should last. The decision is a judgment you will make on the basis of your knowledge of the student, the student's behavior, and the setting or situation in which the target behavior occurs. Natural circumstances combined with information from the FBA often will help you identify an appropriate observation length. For example, assume an FBA indicates that a student uses profanity during independent seatwork assignments in reading and math, that these academic areas are addressed every day, that 40 minutes per day is devoted to both reading and math, and that the independent seatwork portion of each day's lesson, which is typically when the target behavior occurs, occupies the last 20 minutes of each session. Armed with this information, you could reasonably set your observation length as the 20 minutes of independent seatwork in each academic area.

With a different student, the target behavior might be aggressive behavior (pushing, grabbing, and hitting other children). From the FBA, you determine that the behaviors are most likely to occur during midmorning recess times and after lunch. Knowing this, you could reasonably observe during these recess periods. If the morning recess lasted 15 minutes and the after-lunch recess lasted for 20 minutes, these periods would naturally define the observation length.

The same approach applies whether you are using event-based or time-based methods. For example, assume an FBA reveals that a student's target behavior involves lengthy transition times getting from one class to another, and that transitions are most problematic with certain classes and not much of a problem with others. Given this information, you could reasonably collect data during the problematic transition times. The length of the observation would be determined by how long it takes the student to get to the next class. With a different student, the primary concern might be with on- and off-task behavior. Use the natural length of the activity (e.g., 20 minutes) to identify the observation length.

When using an interval method, you will need to determine an appropriate *interval length*. Simply changing the length of the intervals can produce drastically different results. For example, assume a behavior occurs, on the average, once every minute. With a 15-second interval, we would expect the behavior to occur once every four intervals, indicating that the behavior occurred during no more than 25% of the intervals. However, if the interval length was 1 minute or longer, it might occur during as many as 100% of the intervals. These different interval lengths would produce very different results and conclusions, even though the strength of the behavior *never changed*. Thus, finding an appropriate interval length is important.

When collecting interval data, you will need enough intervals to see changes in behavior as they occur. Usually, 20–30 intervals per observation will be sufficient. A smaller number of intervals can be problematic. For example, assume a behavior occurs, on the average, once every minute, and that data are recorded for total of 10 minutes. In this case, each data point counts for 10% of the total result. This creates a risk that your data can be misleading. With 20–30 data points per session, you are likely to avoid this risk.

Summary

This chapter explained why we measure behavior, described the dimensions of behavior, reviewed the measurement systems available, and presented a systematic process for identifying an appropriate measurement system. In Chapter 10, we explain the practicalities of data collection, including how to become reliable in data collection before colleting baseline data. In the implementation checklist, we provide more information about when and how often to observe, why and how to collect interobserver agreement (IOA) data, the factors that impact measurement, and common measurement errors.

CHAPTER 10

Getting Started
Collecting Baseline Data

LEARNING OBJECTIVES

- Develop baseline procedures.
- Collect baseline data.
- Understand reliability and how to calculate interobserver agreement.
- Identify common factors affecting measurement and how to address them.

This chapter completes Step 3. In Chapter 9, you learned the reasons we measure behavior, the dimensions of behavior, and how to select a measurement system that is best suited to the target and replacement behaviors you have identified in your FABI. That information provides the foundation for beginning data collection. In this chapter, we explain the practicalities of data collection, including how to become reliable in data collection before colleting baseline data. More specifically, we explain the importance of baseline data, when to measure both target and replacement behaviors, what procedures to use to collect baseline data, common errors and factors impacting measurement, and when and how to measure reliability. In the implementation checklist, we detail the specific tasks the FABI team will complete, including when and how often to observe, why and how to collect interobserver agreement (IOA) data, and how to identify the factors that impact measurement and common measurement errors.

Baseline Data

You have already begun collecting data during observations within the functional assessment process. You observed students and collected A-B-C data to identify the behavioral function and pinpoint the environmental stimuli that occur before the behavior and reliably trigger the behavior. In this step, you will measure the student's present level of responding by collecting baseline data.

Baseline data serve two purposes. First, these data provide more information about the target and replacement behaviors. They verify that the target behavior continues to pose a significant problem that needs to be addressed with an individualized intervention and provide more information about when and how often the replacement behavior occurs. The second purpose was identified in Chapter 9. Baseline data serve as a "control" condition against which you can assess whether the intervention impacts the behaviors of interest and the strength of that impact. In other words, baseline data allow you to compare the student's behavior before and after intervention so that you can reliably assess intervention effectiveness.

A question that must be considered at this point is which behaviors are to be measured in collecting baseline data. You have already identified a target and replacement behavior, but you must decide whether to measure both or only one of those behaviors. Often the choice is to measure both. For example, if a student pushed other people and that behavior was to be replaced with the student asking other people to play, you would measure both the target behavior of pushing and the replacement behavior of asking to play. The intervention is deemed effective if the target behavior of pushing decreases and the replacement behavior of asking to play increases, which can be done independently of each other.

Measuring the replacement behavior is as important an indication of the effectiveness of the intervention as is measuring the target behavior, if not more so. In fact, we emphasize in our classes that you *always* measure the replacement behavior. The replacement behavior has the important purpose and benefit of building and strengthening the skills the student needs to obtain reinforcement in an appropriate and desirable manner. Furthermore, it often feels much better for families to see the more desirable replacement behavior graphed (and progressing!) than to see the less desirable target behavior.

In some cases, the target and replacement behaviors are *dichotomous*, meaning that they cannot occur together in the same moment. An example of nondichotomous target and replacement behaviors would be calling out and raising a hand; a student could do both at the same time. On the other hand, a classic example of dichotomous behaviors is being on task and off task. If a student is engaged in learning (i.e., on task), they cannot at the same time be disengaged (i.e., off task). Remembering our recommendation to always measure the replacement behavior, in this circumstance you would only collect data for on-task behavior, knowing that the student was off task for any time remaining in the observation. For example, if you are using an interval measurement system, any interval that is not marked with a plus denoting that the student is on task is an interval in which off-task behavior occurred.

Remember, if the target and replacement behaviors are not dichotomous, you must identify an appropriate measurement system, as discussed in Chapter 9, and then measure both behaviors when collecting data. In some cases, doing so will mean using two different measurement systems. For example, if profanity (operationally defined, of course) has been identified as the target behavior, you would determine that this behavior is uniform and could measure it using a frequency count. However, the replacement behavior might be identified as on-task or student engagement, which would be nonuniform and would be measured using a time-based system such as whole-interval or momentary time sampling. A final point to remember is that what you measure in collecting baseline data will continue to be the measurement system throughout the intervention. More specifically, the baseline data collected, the first introduction of the intervention, the withdrawal of the intervention, and the reintroduction of the intervention (e.g., A-B-A-B design, where A is the baseline and B is the intervention) all reflect data collected using the same measurement system in each phase.

Baseline Data Collection Procedures

Once you have identified the measurement method you will use for data collection, it is time to formalize data collection procedures. You will:

- Identify and gather needed materials, such as data collection protocols or timing forms.
- Identify a primary and secondary observer and complete reliability training.
- Schedule and complete all observations.
- Schedule reliability data observations.
- Calculate IOA.
- Graph baseline data.

Materials

The materials used for data collection vary, depending on the measurement method and the level of technology employed. For example, you might use a paper form to make a tally mark each time a behavior occurs (frequency) and count all the marks at the end of your observation for the total number of occurrences, or you could use a device that you click each time the behavior occurs so that at the end you have a record of the total number of occurrences. A timer may be useful when recording duration, or you can simply use a clock to note the time a behavior begins and ends. Several data collection apps developed in recent years can also be useful for data collection.

In thinking about materials, remember that the target and replacement behaviors may require different measurement systems and, therefore, different materials. For example, if the target behavior is tantrums, you will collect both frequency and duration data, and would need a tool to accurately measure the length of the tantrum and a recording form or tool to measure frequency. If the replacement behavior is reading, you could also measure reading duration, but you might use a different time-based measure, such as time sampling. Examples of downloadable data collection forms for frequency and momentary time sampling are available at *www.ci3t.org/FABI*.

The point is to be sure that you have thought about what the data collector will need, have gathered all the materials before beginning data collection, and have labeled all the materials with identifying information as discussed in Chapter 9.

Data Collectors and Reliability

Identify at least two people to collect data during baseline observations. One person will serve as the primary data collector and at least one other person will serve as the secondary collector. The primary data collector collects data during all observations. These data are then recorded and graphed for baseline purposes. The secondary data collector collects data during reliability observations, and these data are used solely to calculate the IOA (addressed later in this chapter). Sometimes you may want to train more than one secondary data collector to ensure that reliability checks can always be completed.

Each data collector is trained prior to collecting any data so that they consistently and accurately recognize the target and replacement behaviors as described in their operational definitions. Training also includes the measurement system used and procedures (e.g., how and when to collect the data, forms to use, identifying information needed). Training may include modeling as well as descriptions of the definitions and procedures.

Primary and secondary data collectors are trained until they are reliable, meaning until they accurately recognize the behavior and use the correct procedures. They then practice to a specified criterion of agreement with each other. For example, prior to collecting baseline data, data collectors may conduct 10- to 15-minute observations of the behavior of interest via video or in the classroom at a time other than when the intervention is to be implemented. Both sets of data are compared until they achieve the specified criterion. There is no set

---

BOX 10.1. FABI Step 3: Collecting Baseline Data

Check when completed	Item
☑	Complete and confirm through **Determining the Function of the Behavior: Using the Function Matrix** on **Planning Sheet** (Handout 6 [HO6] on *www.ci3t.org/fabi*).
☑	What is the behavioral dimension you are focusing on? (in **Planning Sheet**) (Handout 6 [HO6] on *www.ci3t.org/fabi*). Explain here:
☑	What measurement system did you select to measure behavior? (in **Planning Sheet**) (Handout 6 [HO6] on *www.ci3t.org/fabi*). Explain here:
☑	Describe the data collection procedures you will use to measure the behavior: materials needed, data collection sheet, scheduled observation times. Explain here:
☑	How did your team become reliable in data collection? Explain here:
☑ ___ sessions	How many reliability data observations were completed?
☑ ___ %	What was the percentage of agreement between observers (interobserver agreement [IOA]) on the data collection training (reliability training)?
☑ ___ data points	How many baseline data points did you collect?
☑ ___ points with IOA	How many baseline data points included IOA (at least 25% of observations)?
☑ ___ %	What was your IOA for baseline?
☑	Graph your baseline data.
☑	Complete and turn this checklist into your coach.

Note. From Lane, K. L., & Oakes, W. P. (2014). *Functional assessment-based interventions (FABI): Training materials—Step-by-step checklists.* www.ci3t.org/FABI. Reprinted by permission. Copyright © 2015 by Kathleen Lynne Lane.

number of practice observations. Observations continue until the data collectors achieve the specified point of agreement. These data are not the baseline data, but are considered part of the training process to ensure that the data collectors are accurate and reliable. We recommend at least 90% agreement for three consecutive observations. At this point the FABI team could detail the results of the reliability training (e.g., we conducted five training sessions, with reliabilities of 80%, 85%, 90%, 95%, and 95%, and we concluded reliability training after the last three sessions, which were 90% or above). Later in this chapter we describe how to calculate agreement between observers across various data recording methods.

Scheduling Observations

Once data collectors have been trained and are reliable, it is time to schedule baseline data collection. Scheduling includes not only when to observe, but also how often to observe and the length of time the observation will last.

The time and setting for data collection are determined by identifying when the target behavior is most likely to occur, much the same way that you determined when to collect A-B-C data for the FBA direct observation. Use the information gathered in the interview and direct observation to more precisely pinpoint when the target behavior is most likely to occur and is most problematic. You will develop your intervention around the antecedents and consequences that occur during this time. This is the period during which it will be most productive to schedule a baseline observation.

To ensure that data can be compared from day to day, it is important to observe the behavior as closely as possible at the same time and in the same setting. The reason is that different people, activities, or instruction will invariably be present at different times and settings. Any of these differences can change the behavior and the effectiveness of your intervention. For example, Tom sits near Bernard during reading but not during math. If Tom's presence is an antecedent that triggers Bernard's target behavior, you will only have an accurate measure of the target behavior if you observe Bernard during reading. Or you may find that Bernard exhibits different physical states at different times of the day. The FABI interview (Chapter 6) includes questions about establishing operations, for example, whether the student is hungry or sleepy or has an allergy. If these conditions or states are reliable establishing operations for the target behavior, it's important to observe them at the same time of day so that the data are consistent. For example, the student may be hungry before lunch but not after. The variability that may occur when behaviors are observed at different times and settings can mask changes that are due to the intervention.

We recommend that baseline observations occur on consecutive days, when possible. This will provide the most accurate information about the current state of the behavior. However, if circumstances make it necessary to collect baseline data on nonconsecutive days, keep the days you do collect data as close together as possible and try for a minimum of 3 days in the same week.

There is no explicit guideline for the number of observations that need to occur during baseline data collection. We recommend that the primary data collector plan to collect baseline data for approximately five observations. However, if the behavioral data fall within a small range of values after a minimum of three observations, you may have complete baseline data. This also assumes that the data are collected at the same time in the same environment.

For example, after 3 days of baseline data collection during reading, Jamie was observed to be on task for 0%, 10%, and 0% of observed intervals. There is no upward or downward trend in these data and the range of values is small, so baseline data may be considered complete for Jamie. In another example, after three days of observation Mark had one tantrum on Day 1, six tantrums on Day 2, and no tantrums on Day 3. In this example, there is a large range of values, so that you would want to continue for at least the five suggested observations. In most cases, you will likely need the five observations to ensure stability of baseline data.

If, after five observations, baseline data continue to be variable, it is possible that the data accurately depict the current behavior. However, there are also some common mistakes you can check for in the following list:

1. Review your operational definitions for the target and replacement behaviors. See the description in Chapter 6 on defining behavior. Include the data collectors and the teacher, if the teacher is not one of the data collectors, in this review. Tighten your definitions, if needed (e.g., revisit the label, definition, examples, and non-examples).
2. Make sure that data collectors are reliable. If not, you may need to do some additional training.
3. Ensure that you have selected an appropriate measure (Chapter 9). Reassess whether the behavior is uniform or nonuniform. For example, tantrums are nonuniform and require a time-based measure but also need a measure of frequency. Frequency alone is an insufficient measure unless the tantrum lasts exactly the same number of minutes each time.
4. Identify any variability in the environment during the baseline process that might account for variability in the data. For example, the student may have been absent for a few days between observations, or a class was shortened one day because of an assembly. When these variables are resolved, additional baseline data should result in stability.
5. Check that the behavior is observed at the same time each day, that the observation is long enough, and that it occurs at the optimal time for detecting the behavior.

If the issue is not the operational definition or the method of collecting data, it may be that the student's behavior commonly varies widely from day to day. In this situation, more baseline observations will not result in stability. Review your functional assessment data and talk to the teacher to ascertain if there are any identifiable differences in antecedents and the delivery of consequences that account for this variability. If you cannot identify any differences and have addressed any mistakes as identified previously, proceed with designing and testing the intervention as described in Chapter 11 even though the baseline is not stable. In most cases, you will find that the test is successful (i.e., the target behavior becomes more stable while also decreasing as the replacement behavior increases). In other words, the intervention is working.

As mentioned in Chapter 9, you should use the knowledge gained during the assessment process combined with your knowledge of the student and setting to determine the optimal length of the observation. An observation must be long enough to provide a good example of how often the behavior occurs. In some cases, the observation will be scheduled for the length of the activity in which the behavior occurs. For example, Desmond's target behavior has been identified as tantrums and his replacement behavior as being "on task." If the target behavior occurs during reading, which is scheduled for 20 minutes every day, you would schedule baseline observations for 20 minutes, for 5 consecutive days, during the entire reading activity. In other cases, you will collect enough baseline data in a 10- to 15-minute observation of part of an activity. For example, the FABI shows that Anna's behavior is verbal aggression and refusal to follow instructions. It occurs at the beginning of gym class, and she sits quietly on the sidelines during the remainder of the class. Gym occurs only 3 days a week. You would schedule your baseline observation for the first 20 minutes of gym class, so you can observe the beginning of the class and some of the time that Anna sits on the sidelines. Data would be collected for 3 days of one week and 2 days, if needed, in the second week.

The same basic approach can be used to determine the length of the observation whether you are using an event-based or a time-based method for collecting data. In our examples, "on task" is measured using a time-based method and tantrums can be measured using both an event-based method (e.g., a frequency count of the number of tantrums) and a time-based method (e.g., the duration of each tantrum).

If you are using interval-recording or time-sampling methods, the length of the interval must also be identified and there must be a sufficient number of intervals to allow you to see changes in the behavior, as described in the previous chapter. Intervals could be short or could be extended to as much as 5 minutes in length. To capture sufficient data when using a whole- or partial-interval method, many authorities recommend shorter intervals ranging from 6 to 30 seconds. For example, Iwata and colleagues (1982) used 15-second intervals to conduct functional analyses, whereas Northup and colleagues (1991) used 6-second intervals. In making your decision, consider that shorter intervals (e.g., less than 15 seconds) may be very difficult to manage in a classroom because of the focus required. In contrast, intervals that are too long may underestimate the occurrence of the behavior. For example, if incidents last 1 minute or less and occur infrequently during the observation, collecting data using the whole-interval method, in which the behavior must last throughout the interval to be recorded, with a 1-minute interval could miss many instances of the behavior. Another way to select an appropriate interval length for whole- or partial-interval data collection is to consider the average interresponse time. *Interresponse time* is the duration of time between the end of one target behavior and the initiation of the next target behavior (Cooper et al., 2020). For instance, if you determine that the average interresponse time for a discrete behavior (like spitting) is 10 seconds, then a data collection interval of 10 seconds will make it more likely that target behaviors will occur in separate intervals, thus helping to avoid over- or underreporting of the target behavior.

We recommend that data be recorded for a minimum of 20 intervals using a 15-, 20-, or 30-second interval length. If your baseline observation lasts 10 minutes and you are using a 30-second interval, you would record 20 data points per observation.

Interobserver Agreement

Beginning with baseline data collection, we recommend scheduling reliability observations once every 4 days for each phase of data collection. If you are scheduled to collect baseline data for 5 days, schedule 2 days for reliability observations. Schedule the first observation on the first or second day of collecting baseline data so that you are sure that at least one reliability observation can be completed if you collect only 3 days of baseline data. Scheduling your reliability checks early in the process also helps ensure that your initial baseline data are accurate. We encourage using the same timing during each subsequent phase of testing, as described in later chapters.

IOA, the extent to which there is agreement between the data collected by the primary and secondary data collectors, is calculated for every reliability observation. Knowing that our data are reliable allows us and others to trust that our data represent the true state of the behavior and that changes are accurately measured. IOA also allows us to recognize and correct measurement errors (discussed in a later section). Remember that the data collected by the primary data collector are the data to be reported for the purposes of baseline observations even when the secondary observer is also collecting reliability data. Sometimes graduate students, when they first collect data, have wanted to combine the data of the two observers and calculate an average, but that would not be correct. The secondary observer's data are used solely for calculating IOA.

Calculating IOA

The method for calculating IOA depends on the recording method you are using to collect data (Kazdin, 1982). However, all IOA calculations are generally reported as a percentage of agreement between the two observers.

Permanent Product

IOA is calculated by dividing the number of agreements by the total number of items scored and then multiplying the result by 100%. For example, each observer might score a 20-item spelling test. The primary data collector scores 19 items as being correct and the secondary observer scores 20 items as correct. The IOA calculation is the number of agreements (19) divided by the total number of items (20), resulting in .95 multiplied by 100% for an IOA of 95%.

Frequency and Rate

IOA is calculated by dividing the lower-reported frequency by the higher-reported frequency and multiplying that number by 100%. Consider an example in which the primary data collector reported that there were 8 tantrums and the secondary data collector reported 12 tantrums. To calculate IOA, you would divide 8 by 12, yielding a result of .67, and then multiply that by 100% for a 67% IOA. This would be considered an inadequate IOA, as noted earlier in this chapter, and would require efforts to improve it (e.g., additional training).

Intensity/Magnitude

IOA for intensity/magnitude is a little more complicated to calculate. Each data collector's rating of the behavior is compared individually and identified as an agreement (i.e., the rating is the same) or as a disagreement (i.e., the rating is different). For example, if the first rating for the primary data collector is a magnitude 10 and the first rating for the secondary data collector is a magnitude 10, you would mark this as an agreement. If, however, the first rating for the primary data collector is a 9 and the first rating for the secondary data collector is a 10, you would mark it as a disagreement. This process continues for each rating. IOA is calculated by dividing the number of agreements by the total number of ratings and multiplying the result by 100%. If there are 20 ratings and 18 agreements, you would divide 18 by 20. The result of .90 would then be multiplied by 100% for a 90% IOA.

Duration and Latency

IOA for these measures is calculated by dividing the shorter duration by the longer duration and multiplying the result by 100%. For example, the primary data collector may report that the time between a teacher instruction and when Alex began work (latency) was 5 minutes, but the secondary data collector reported that it was 4 minutes. To calculate IOA, you would divide 4 by 5, yielding a result of .80, and then multiply by 100% for an 80% IOA.

Whole- and Partial-Interval and Time-Sampling Methods

IOA for interval data is calculated in the same manner for all three measures. To calculate IOA, compare each observer's data interval by interval and identify whether the data agree

---

Observer: *Primary (Rivas)/Secondary (Jones)* Date: *10/10*
Start Time: *10:15 AM* End Time: *10:35 AM*
Setting: *Math Class* Activity: *Trigonometry Lesson*
No. Adults: *2* No. Students: *29* Behavior: *On-Task*

20 minutes: 1-minute interval/time sampling

Ms. Rivas

1	2	3	4	5	6	7	8	9	10	11	12	13	14	15	16	17	18	19	20
+	+	+	+	−	+	−	−	+	+	+	+	−	+	+	+	−	+	−	+

Mr. Jones

+	+	+	+	+	+	−	−	+	+	+	−	−	+	+	+	+	+	−	+

Agreement

Y	Y	Y	Y	N	Y	Y	Y	Y	Y	Y	Y	N	Y	Y	Y	Y	N	Y	Y

On-Task % = *14/20 = 0.7 × 100% = 70%*

Agreement = *17/20 = 0.85 × 100% = 85%*

FIGURE 10.1. Example of assessment of IOA. From Umbreit, J., Ferro, J. B., Liaupsin, C. J., & Lane, K. L. (2007). *Functional behavioral assessment and function-based intervention: An effective, practical approach.* Pearson. Reprinted by permission.

or disagree (Cooper et al., 2020). Figure 10.1 on the previous page provides an example of a reliability observation using the time-sampling method consisting of 20 intervals of 1 minute each. Data for both the primary and secondary data collectors are presented with a third set of boxes noting agreement or disagreement for each interval. Each observer has marked a plus (+) if the behavior occurred at the end of the interval or a minus (–) if the behavior did not occur. Individual intervals are identified with a Y, signifying that the data collectors had made the same mark in that interval (agreement), or an N, signifying that the data collectors had a different mark in the interval (disagreement). In this example, three disagreements occur, one each in intervals 5, 12, and 17. To calculate IOA, divide the number of agreements (17) by the total number of intervals (20). The result of .85, multiplied by 100% yields an IOA of 85%. The example in Figure 10.1 also identifies the calculation of the percentage of intervals that the student was on task, using the data from Ms. Rivas, who was the primary data collector.

Factors Affecting Data Reliability

Measurement Error

Measurement error occurs when data consistently over- or underreport the true value of the occurrence of the behavior. Reliability observations provide a way to address measurement error by checking the accuracy of the primary data collector against the accuracy of a secondary data collector. Factors affecting measurement include *observer drift* and *reactivity*.

Observer drift usually refers to a change in the observer's definition of the behavior being measured from the operational definition applied during training (Cooper et al., 2020). The change may be gradual and unintentional. Observer drift may occur if a person collects data infrequently, such as a reliability data collector who only does some of the reliability observations. Observer drift may also occur over time if the data collector does not review the operational definition of the behavior. For example, a data collector who is observing behavior such as aggression that includes hitting might begin to also report touching, a behavior that was not part of the original definition, with the result that the occurrence of the behavior is overestimated. Conversely, a data collector might fail to record a tantrum if they have omitted some behaviors that were in the original definition, with the result that the occurrence of the behavior is underestimated. If observer drift is identified through reliability observations, it can be addressed through additional training in the definition of the behavior. It can be lessened in the future by ensuring that the data collectors review the behavior definition before each observation.

Reactivity refers to a person behaving differently because they are being observed; they react to the presence of the observer. Reactivity can cause either an increase or decrease in the behavior and is especially likely if the observer is obvious and/or the student knows they are being observed. Reactivity can occur even if you regularly work in the school, program, or classroom and students expect to see you. Reactivity can even occur if you are the teacher collecting data. The good news is that the effects of reactivity on the behavior are often temporary (Cooper et al., 2020) and can be minimized or prevented with a few simple practices (Cooper et al., 2020; Kerr & Nelson, 2010) as follows:

- Be as unobtrusive as possible in entering or leaving the classroom and as you collect data. Each classroom environment will suggest ways to be unobtrusive. Suggestions for those who are not part of the classroom staff include:
  - Choose an observation area that allows you to fade into the background, such as a corner.
  - Sit down. Sitting is likely to be less obtrusive than standing.
  - Spend some time in the classroom before beginning to collect data. Enter the room prior to each observation so students will become used to seeing you. This is helpful especially in early childhood classrooms in which the children tend to want to greet all those entering the room.
- Observe until the reactivity subsides.
- Plan what students should be told about what you are doing to minimize reactivity. Students may know you are observing but not who or why.
- Do not participate in classroom activities or interact with the students if you are not part of the classroom staff. Interactions will distract from data collection and may also increase a student's sensitivity to your presence.
- Whether you are or are not part of classroom staff, use a data collection tool that is as unobtrusive as possible. A counter worn on the wrist or other electronic device that cues an interval and records behavior can be an important tool to address reactivity.

Reactivity can also affect the observer (i.e., *observer* reactivity). In this case, the observer's behavior changes due to an awareness that someone is evaluating the data they are collecting. Reviewing operational definitions and retraining the data collector are often sufficient to address observer reactivity.

If any of these errors occur, document what happened and how you addressed the error so you can be sure of what those data represent. Your goal is to collect accurate data so that you can evaluate the effectiveness of your intervention. When these measurement errors occur, your data will not represent a real and long-term change in the student's behavior. You must be vigilant in identifying them and address them each time they appear.

**BOX 10.2. Ethical Considerations in Chapter 10:
BACB Ethics Code for Behavior Analysts**

2.17 Collecting and Using Data

Chapter 10 describes recommended practices for baseline data collection procedures for behavior-change interventions. In this chapter, you have learned the practicalities of data collection, including how to become reliable before you begin. You also have learned that baseline data are important for documenting the student's level of responding before implementation of an intervention so you can document how effective the intervention is in changing that behavior. This chapter introduces the idea of a secondary data collector for some observations to assess the reliability of the data collected. Training all data collectors to accurately observe and reliably report the student's behavior is key to ensuring that any changes are, in fact, a result of the intervention. IOA measures the extent of agreement between two observers measuring the same behavior, and is calculated for every reliability observation, including baseline observations.

Summary

In this chapter, we have described recommended practices for baseline data collection procedures, including reliability observations, calculating IOA for each dimension of behavior, and the factors that can affect measurement. Recommended baseline practices include:

- Identify at least two data collectors, one primary and one secondary.
- Develop adequate behavioral definitions.
- Train data collectors to be reliable in their data collection.
- Observe at the same time of day and in the same setting.
- Observe on consecutive days, if possible.
- Plan approximately five baseline observations. A minimum of three observations is acceptable if the data are stable.
- Use information accumulated during the FABI process to determine the observation length.
- If the behavior requires using a time-based method, consider the behavior and how often it occurs when identifying the length of the interval.
- Schedule one reliability observation for every four observations.
- Calculate IOA as a percentage of agreement based on the measurement method used.
- Plan data collection to minimize measurement error that may be caused by reactivity and observer drift.
- Address measurement errors immediately.

We encourage you to keep this content in mind as you navigate the decisions before beginning the baseline data collection process (see Box 10.1 on page 120). In addition, consider the ethical considerations noted in Box 10.2 on page 127 regarding collecting baseline data and IOA.

This chapter completes Step 3. The next step, *Step 4: Designing the Functional Assessment-Based Intervention*, explains how to design the FABI and includes multiple components, as you might expect. To introduce these components in a manageable manner, Part V includes nine chapters that incrementally walk readers through this process. The next chapter, Chapter 11, explains how to use the Function-Based Intervention Decision Model to ask and answer two key questions that guide the intervention focus.

PART V
Step 4: Designing the Functional Assessment-Based Intervention

STEP #	FUNCTIONAL ASSESSMENT-BASED INTERVENTION STEPS
1	Identifying Students Who May Need a Functional Assessment-Based Intervention
2	Conducting the Functional Assessment
3	Collecting Baseline Data
4	Designing the Functional Assessment-Based Intervention
5	Testing the Intervention

After learning how to identify the behavioral dimension of interest, selecting an appropriate measurement system, and collecting baseline data in Step 3, the next task is to design the FABI in *Step 4: Designing the Functional Assessment-Based Intervention*. To introduce the multiple components of Step 4 in a manageable manner, Part V includes nine chapters that incrementally walk readers through this process.

In Chapter 11, Designing and Testing the Intervention, we explain how to answer two key questions that guide intervention focus. Chapters 12–15 provide additional direction on each intervention method. Specifically, Chapter 12 explains and illustrates Intervention Method 1: Teach the Replacement Behavior. Chapter 13 explains and illustrates Intervention Method 2: Adjust the Environment. Chapter 14 explains and illustrates Intervention Method 3: Shift the Contingencies. Chapter 15 explains and describes the special situation when it is necessary to combine Methods 1 and 2. In each chapter, we provide illustrations from PreK–12 research, as well as lessons learned over the last 20 years. We also explain a range of practical A-R-E components.

Next, Chapters 16, 17, and 18 address three concepts and the associated activities needed to draw valid inferences regarding intervention outcomes. Specifically, Chapter 16 introduces treatment integrity, Chapter 17 introduces social validity, and Chapter 18 introduces generalization and maintenance. For each concept, we explain what it is, why it is important, and how to collect and use these data to inform implementation efforts.

In Chapter 19, Designing Your Intervention, we provide explicit directions for designing interventions. We explain how to draft A-R-E components and link each intervention tactic to the hypothesized function of the challenging behavior. We provide guidance for introducing the intervention to the teacher and students, including checks for understanding before beginning implementation of the FABI.

CHAPTER 11

Designing and Testing the Intervention

LEARNING OBJECTIVES

Designing the Intervention

- Use the Function-Based Intervention Decision Model to select an intervention method.
- Develop A-R-E intervention components.
- Draft components related to valid inference making: treatment integrity, social validity, and generalization and maintenance.
- Develop a plan for preparing the teacher, the student, and sometimes family members to learn to implement intervention procedures.
- Collect any additional baseline data, if needed.

Testing the Intervention

- Select a design that allows the FABI team to determine if there is a functional relation between the introduction of the intervention and the student's behavior.
- Implement the intervention.
- Collect treatment integrity data.
- Continue to collect data on student performance; include IOA during 25% of sessions in each phase.
- Collect maintenance and generalization data.
- Assess social validity before the intervention is put in place and after the "test" is complete.

As you might recall, the FABI team has already completed three steps prior to designing the intervention.

- Step 1: Identifying Students Who May Need a Functional Assessment-Based Intervention
- Step 2: Conducting the Functional Assessment
- Step 3: Collecting Baseline Data

To briefly review, Chapter 4 discussed the first step in developing a FABI: Identifying students who might benefit from intensive intervention. We discussed the circumstances in which screening data may be used to connect students to this support and other circumstances in which a FABI is required by law.

Part III featured four chapters to guide you through Step 2. Chapter 5 explained the importance of informal observations; learning about the tiered system in place (if one exists) and classroom and noninstructional settings; the importance of considering culture and community; and the fidelity with which Tier 1 efforts have been implemented. We also discussed how to review students' cumulative files to learn more about past behavior challenges and successes. Chapter 6 explained how to operationally define target and replacement behaviors. We provided recommendations for conducting functional assessment interviews, followed by a closer look at the details of various informant interviews (teacher, parents, and student). Chapter 7 explained in more detail the purpose and methods of the A-B-C model. We included step-by-step guidance on how to collect A-B-C data to determine antecedents that set the stage for the target behavior to occur, as well as the consequences that maintain the likelihood the target behavior will occur in the future. Chapter 8 introduced the Function Matrix, a tool that is used to summarize data visually and identify the function of the behavior. We described its purpose, layout, and use, and also explained how to write a statement of the function and provide illustrations. Then, we explained how to use these findings to select the replacement behavior.

Part IV featured two chapters to guide you through Step 3. After explaining how to conduct the FBA and determine the reason(s) for the target behavior, these chapters explored how to best measure the behaviors of interest (i.e., the target/challenging behavior, the replacement behavior, or both, if necessary) and collect baseline data before beginning intervention efforts. Chapter 9 discussed why we measure behavior. We introduced the dimensions of behavior and various measurement systems and provided a practical process for selecting the measurement system best suited to measure the dimension of interest. We also described and illustrated the data collection procedures that measure the behavior (e.g., various materials, data collection sheets, and observation schedules). In Chapter 10, we explained the practicalities of data collection, including how to train to become reliable in data collection before colleting baseline data. We addressed topics, such as when and how often to observe, why and how to collect IOA data, and how to identify the factors that impact measurement and common measurement errors. In these chapters, we have identified the ways in which the FABI process includes culturally responsive and equitable methods (e.g., including family members and students in the FABI team, using interviews and measures of social validity). We have also provided suggestions for additional ways to include family and student voice and ways to consider culture, values, and perspectives in the assessment and development of the FABI (e.g., replacement behavior selection).

Information from each of these steps is summarized in the Functional Assessment and Behavior Intervention Plan: Planning Form (Form 11.1 at the end of this chapter) that supports FABI team efforts in the design, implementation, and evaluation of functional assessment-based interventions.

Now we are ready for the final two steps in this process: designing and testing the intervention.

- Step 4: Designing the Functional Assessment-Based Intervention
- Step 5: Testing the Intervention

These steps focus on the practicalities of designing an intervention based on the maintaining function(s) (Step 4) and then putting the intervention in place and conducting a test to determine if the introduction of the intervention yields systematic changes in the student's behavior (Step 5).

Purpose

In this chapter, we provide an overview of Steps 4 (Box 11.1) and 5 (Box 11.2). First, we walk through Step 4. We explain how answers to two key questions guide teams' intervention efforts by showing them how to select the appropriate intervention method. Then we explain how specific A-R-E intervention components are developed. As noted previously, A-R-E stands for antecedent adjustments, reinforcement adjustments, and extinction procedures that are needed regardless of which intervention methods you use. Next we introduce three additional components to consider when designing the intervention so that you will be able to draw accurate conclusions about intervention outcomes: treatment integrity (Is the intervention happening as planned?); social validity (What do stakeholders think about the goals, procedures, and intended outcomes?); and generalization and maintenance (Does the replacement behavior(s) occur in new settings, with new people, and over time?). In the final section of Step 4, we provide guidance on when additional baseline data may need to be collected during the intervention design step.

Next, we walk through Step 5. Here we provide an overview of the how the testing should be conducted so that the FABI team can be confident that the changes in the student's behavior(s) are due to the intervention and not something else happening in the environment. For example, we explain the importance of picking a design (e.g., withdrawal or multiple-baseline design; Ledford & Gast, 2018) that allows you to determine if a functional relation exists: namely, are changes in the student's behavior only present when the intervention is in place? Let us now turn to the "big picture" of designing and testing a FABI, knowing that we will fill in all the details as we go along.

Designing the Intervention: An Overview

During Step 4, the team works through the building process. First, they select an intervention method using the Function-Based Intervention Decision Model (see Figure 11.1 on page 138). Next the team develops the intervention by drafting A-R-E components. During the planning process, the team links each possible intervention tactic to the hypothesized function on the planning sheet to make certain all maintaining functions are addressed. Then the team develops the additional components needed to draw accurate conclusions regarding intervention outcomes. Finally, it may be necessary to collect additional baseline data before the intervention is introduced.

BOX 11.1. FABI Step 4: Designing the Intervention

Check when completed	Item
☐	**Step 4.1 Select an Intervention Method.** Select intervention method and confirm with teacher—**FABI Planning** (Handout 6 [HO6] on *www.ci3t.org/fabi*).
☐	**Step 4.2 Develop Intervention Components** Draft A-R-E components (**A**ntecedent adjustments, **R**einforcement adjustments, and **E**xtinction components). Link each intervention tactic to the hypothesized function on the planning sheet (*depending on the method* you select according to the Function-Based Intervention Decision Model).
☐	**Step 4.3 Components Related to Valid Inference Making** Draft a treatment integrity form, including quality rubric: **Treatment Integrity Checklist** (Handout 11 [HO11] on *www.ci3t.org/fabi*).
☐	Select and review social validity forms: **Adapted-IRP-15 and Adapted-CIRP**.
☐	Prepare a plan for introducing the intervention to the teacher—include a check for understanding. Describe how it was done here:
☐	Prepare a plan for introducing the intervention to the students—include a check for understanding. Describe how it was done here:
☐	Revise and finalize A-R-E intervention components using feedback from the teacher and draft final treatment integrity form (Handout 11 [HO11] on *www.ci3t.org/fabi*).
☐	Prepare intervention materials.
☐	Collect additional baseline data after any school breaks (three points) with at least one IOA.
☐	Complete and turn in this checklist to your coach.

Note. From Lane, K. L., & Oakes, W. P. (2014). *Functional assessment-based interventions (FABI): Training materials—Step-by-Step checklists.* www.ci3t.org/FABI. Reprinted by permission. Copyright © 2015 by Kathleen Lynne Lane.

Using the Function-Based Intervention Decision Model to Select an Intervention Method

Now that you are clear about the target and replacement behaviors, the next step is to figure out which intervention method is the best fit for this student. To simplify this important task, ask two key questions:

1. Can the student perform the replacement behavior?
2. Do antecedent conditions represent effective practices for this student?

BOX 11.2. FABI Step 5: Testing the Intervention

Check when completed	Item
☐	Implement intervention.
☐	Collect treatment integrity data daily (teacher perspective) with IOA for 25% of sessions (outside team observer).
☐	Collect a minimum of five data points (behavior measurement—same behavior and measurement system as baseline)—with 25% IOA [report as number of sessions, % of sessions, and actual IOA %].
☐ ___ data points	How many intervention data points did you collect?
☐ ___ points with IOA	How many intervention data points included IOA?
☐ ___ %	What was your IOA for intervention?
☐	Graph your intervention data *(coaches' review for support for deciding when to withdraw the intervention)*.
☐	Withdrawal of the intervention with at least three data points (1 IOA) ***Note phase-change decisions for each phase are guided by student performance on variables measured.**
☐	Complete the treatment integrity form (daily by interventionist [teacher]; 25% of sessions for IOA).
☐	Graph withdrawal data *(coaches' review for support for deciding when to reintroduce the intervention)*.
☐	Reintroduce the intervention. ***Note phase-change decisions for each phase are guided by student performance on variables measured.**
☐	Collect treatment integrity data daily (teacher perspective) with IOA for 25% of sessions (outside team observer).
☐	Collect a minimum of three data points (behavior measurement—same behavior and measurement system throughout all phases)—with 25% IOA [report as number of sessions, % of sessions, and actual IOA %].
☐	Plan for follow-up data collection to assess maintenance. **FABI Planning** and **Behavior Intervention Plan (BIP)** (Handouts 6.0 [HO6.0] and 6.1 [HO6.1] on *www.ci3t.org/fabi*).
☐	Work with your coaches to complete the behavior intervention plan and graphed data to share with the teacher and parents.
☐	Conduct a final check of ethical considerations from the **Ethics Checklist** (Handout 14 [HO14] on *www.ci3t.org/fabi*).
☐	After reviewing the final graph, assess POST social validity: **Adapted-IRP-15** and **Adapted-CIRP**.
☐	Complete and turn in this checklist to your coach.

Note. From Lane, K. L., & Oakes, W. P. (2014). *Functional assessment-based interventions (FABI): Training materials—Step-by-step checklists. www.ci3t.org/FABI*. Reprinted by permission. Copyright © 2015 by Kathleen Lynne Lane.

Question 1: Can the Student Perform the Replacement Behavior?

The first question focuses on determining if the desired replacement behavior is in the student's repertoire. More specifically, it is important to determine if the student's behavior is a "can't do" or "won't do" problem. The "can't do" means that the student has not yet learned how to do the replacement behavior or cannot do it fluently enough to be reinforced naturally. Therefore, no amount of contingent reinforcement is going to make it happen. For example, if you set a new year's goal for yourself to "do double unders" with your jump rope (where the rope passes under your feet two times each time you jump), you cannot just "will" those actions to happen or expect praise from your coach to "make" them happen. If you have not learned the skill yet, or you are not fluent enough to use that behavior, it is a "can't do" problem. This means the skill (behavior) needs to be taught.

On the other hand, a "won't do" problem means that the student is capable of performing the desired behavior, but acts differently because of the prevailing contingencies (i.e., it is more effective to behave otherwise; Horner & Day, 1991). Performance "won't do" problems are common and usually develop because the antecedent conditions are inadvertently structured to set the occasion for the target behavior to occur, rather than the replacement behavior. For example, Sammie may have learned that misbehaving gets him much more attention than "being good" and following the rules.

Question 2: Do Antecedent Conditions Represent Effective Practices for This Student?

The second question focuses on carefully considering the environment in order to learn more about the context in which the FABI will take place. In schools implementing Ci3T or other integrated tiered systems, it is important to understand how the planned experiences affect students academically, behaviorally, and socially. As we discussed in an earlier chapter, educators implementing Ci3T have a Ci3T Implementation Manual that features the roles and responsibilities of all stakeholders: students, faculty and staff, families, and administrators. Information is collected about the extent to which these Tier 1 features are implemented as planned (treatment integrity) and what the stakeholders think about the goals, procedures, and outcomes (social validity). Treatment integrity data are collected using validated tools and are obtained from multiple perspectives (e.g., educators and outside observers; Ci3T Treatment Integrity tools; Tiered Fidelity Inventory; Algozzine et al., 2014; Lane, 2009a, 2009b), just as adults' views are measured using the Primary Intervention Rating Scale (PIRS; Lane, Kalberg, Bruhn, et al., 2009) to reliably assess social validity.

The FABI team can determine what is happening at Tier 1 by reviewing these data as summarized for the school as a whole. They can also review individual teachers' data to assess implementation efforts in specific classrooms. For example, if a FABI team reviewed an individual teacher's treatment integrity data, the team may notice one or more of the following:

- Behavior-specific praise is rarely used.
- Schoolwide expectations are not revisited before activities (precorrection).

- Limited use of low-intensity supports that increase engagement (e.g., instructional choice, increased opportunities to respond, or active supervision).
- Routines need to be refined (e.g., beginning with starter activities, ending a lesson with a closing activity, and providing guidance on how to ask for help).
- Challenges with the physical layout of the classroom (e.g., traffic flow).
- Location of instructional materials (e.g., materials placed by the classroom door, causing a backup when students are trying to enter the classroom).
- Challenges with how instructions are provided (e.g., limited or no checks for understanding).
- Challenges with how reinforcement takes places (e.g., tickets passed out without providing behavior-specific feedback).

Similarly, the FABI team could review the social validity data for the school as a whole and for an individual teacher to determine if there are areas in need of refinement. For example, there could be some confusion about the differences between bribery and reinforcement. There could be a lack of understanding about "consequences," which are simply those events that follow any behavior and that influence the future probability of the behavior occurring. These are but a few of the considerations FABI team members could explore as they review treatment integrity data collected at Tier 1.

Function-Based Intervention Decision Model to "Figure" It Out

In Figure 11.1, we illustrate how answers to these questions lead to one of the following methods. Method 1, *Teach the Replacement Behavior*, is used when the student does not have the replacement behavior in their skill set yet, meaning the student has an acquisition deficit or a "can't do" problem (Question 1: Answer = no). As we discussed in Chapter 5, no amount of incentive will make it happen—the individual has not yet acquired the skill or developed sufficient fluency to use that skill in natural settings. However, the classroom environment does represent effective practices for this particular student (Question 2: Answer = yes; see Chapter 12).

Method 2, *Adjust the Environment*, is used when the student is able to fluently perform the replacement behavior, meaning the challenge is more of a performance deficit or a "won't do" problem (Question 1: Answer = yes), but the classroom environment could be enhanced for this student to maximize learning opportunities and harmony in the classroom (Question 2: Answer = no). This adjustment can often be accomplished via small—but important—shifts in routines, procedures, physical arrangements, or other adjustments that set the stage for the replacement behavior to occur (see Chapter 13).

Method 3, *Shift the Contingencies*, is used with students when they can perform the replacement behavior (Question 1: Answer = yes) *and* the classroom environment features effective practices for this student (Question 2: Answer = yes). If the student can perform the replacement behavior and the environment is setting the occasion for the replacement behavior, then the challenge is likely related to reinforcement. More specifically, behaviors other than the desired behaviors are being reinforced. In this method, a shift in reinforcement is

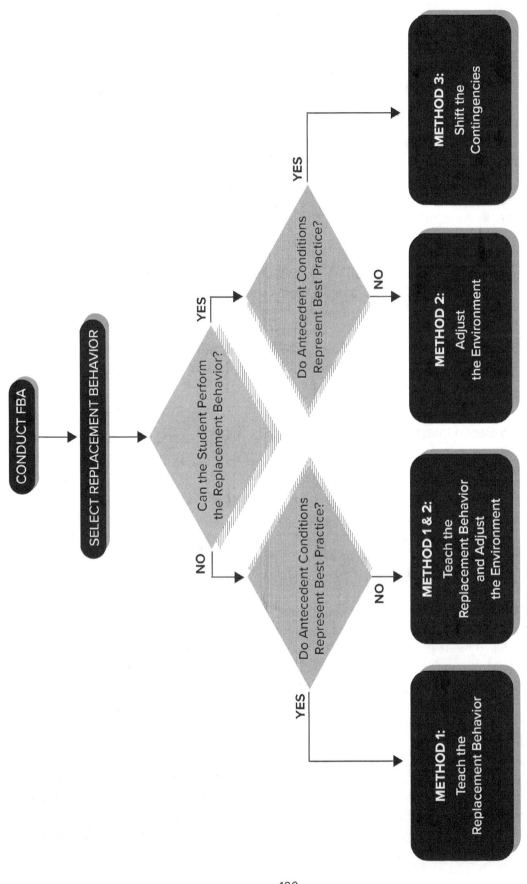

FIGURE 11.1. The Function-Based Intervention Decision Model. Adapted from Umbreit, J., Ferro, J. B., Liaupsin, C. J., & Lane, K. L. (2007). *Functional behavioral assessment and function-based intervention: An effective, practical approach*. Pearson. Reprinted by permission.

needed to ensure that the student receives positive feedback when meeting expectations (e.g., when the replacement behavior occurs) and far less, if any, reinforcement when challenging behavior occurs (see Chapter 14).

Finally, a fourth option is the combination of Methods 1 and 2: *Teach the Replacement Behavior* and *Adjust the Environment*. This combination is needed when the student cannot perform the replacement behavior yet (Question 1: Answer = no) and the environment could be adjusted to better meet the student's individualized needs (Question 2: Answer = no; see Chapter 15). In the next four chapters we provide additional detail for each intervention method, including demonstrations of how to use a planning document we developed to guide you through the whole functional assessment process (see Form 11.1 at the end of this chapter). For now, know that after the method is selected, the FABI team collaborates to draft A-R-E components, with each element linked to the function(s) of the target behavior.

Developing A-R-E Components: Linking to the Function of the Target Behavior

Each of the previous methods includes A-R-E components. When an intervention method is selected, the FABI team will develop A-R-E components with the specific emphasis aligned to the specific method selected. In this section, we provide additional details on the A-R-Es to set the stage for your own learning. Before you read this section, it might be useful to review Form 11.1 (the Functional Assessment and Behavior Intervention Plan: Planning Form at the end of this chapter; also available on *ci3t.org/FABI*), which can be used to organize your FABI team's conversations, decisions, and data.

A: Antecedent Adjustments

Antecedent adjustments refer to shifts that take place in a given context (e.g., classrooms, hallways, centers) before challenges occur. These adjustments to routines, procedures, and environment are developed to prompt the occurrence of the new replacement behavior. For example, a teacher might provide instructional choices during an entry activity, placing three problems on the whiteboard and inviting students to complete two of the three). Or a teacher might refer to the expectation matrix posted in the front of the room and by the door to the hallways and remind students of three ways they are going to show responsibility as they transition from the classroom to the hallways on their way to a pep rally before the Friday night football game. The goal here is to make adjustments that will make it more likely the student will engage in the replacement behavior instead of the targeted challenging behavior.

R: Reinforcement Shifts

Reinforcement shifts refer to changes in reinforcement types, rates, or schedules to ensure that students receive higher rates of reinforcement when they engage in the replacement behavior (e.g., engagement) than when they engage in the target behavior you would like eliminated or reduced (e.g., off-task or disruptive behavior). Reinforcement shifts should also include more opportunity to connect with reinforcement occurring naturally in the environment to ensure the behavior is sustainable. In short, the new behaviors need to "work better" for students, resulting in higher rates of reinforcement. In schools and classrooms that have a Ci3T model or other integrated tiered system, this shift might include the faculty and staff being on the lookout for opportunities to acknowledge the students when they engage in the replacement behavior, such as receiving a ticket paired with sincere behavior-specific praise. The goal here is to make certain the new behavior is more effective for the student in getting or avoiding attention, activities, tangibles, or sensory experiences according to their individual maintaining functions.

E: Extinction of Target Behavior

Extinction refers to withholding reinforcement for a target behavior (e.g., off-task or disruption) that had been previously reinforced (oftentimes unintentionally). Extinction plays a key role in a FABI (Janney et al., 2013). For example, if a student who engaged in disruptive behaviors was often sent to the office when such behaviors occurred and the frequency of these behaviors increased in the future, then being removed from class was likely a reinforcer for that student. In this case, extinction using planned ignoring and keeping the student in class when such behaviors occurred might be implemented. In extreme cases, it might even be necessary to remove the other students from the classroom for safety reasons. If we accidentally acknowledge or reinforce the student's behavior occasionally, it could actually strengthen the behavior. So we must be careful with extinction procedures to ensure that they are feasible (a point we discuss more fully in Chapter 19). The goal in this case is to withhold reinforcing the target behavior to reduce the future probability of it occurring.

Including Components Needed to Draw Valid Inferences

The FABI team will collaborate to design specific A-R-E intervention tactics to be considered, selected, and implemented with integrity (treatment integrity), assess the reliability of how student performance is measured (interobserver agreement, discussed in Chapter 10), and ensure that the intervention agents (e.g., teachers, families, students) agree that the intervention goals are socially significant, the intervention procedures are socially acceptable, and the intended outcomes are socially important (Wolf, 1978). These elements are just as important in intervention design as is planning an intervention that will produce meaningful, lasting change (Baer et al., 1968, 1987). As such, we have future chapters dedicated to each of these elements: Chapter 16 addresses treatment integrity, Chapter 17 covers social validity, and Chapter 18 discusses generalization and maintenance. Yet, because of their important role in intervention design, we provide a brief introduction to these important elements here.

In brief, the FABI team will make plans for assessing treatment, including developing treatment integrity forms to collect information on the extent to which each A-R-E component is implemented as intended. They will also assess social validity before the intervention plans are finalized using validated tools (e.g., Intervention Rating Profile–15 for adults [Martens & Witt, 1982]; Children's Intervention Rating Profile for children [CIRP; Witt & Elliott, 1983]) or draft their own tools to get formal input from stakeholders (e.g., teacher, family members, and student) before the intervention is agreed upon to ensure it is a good fit for all. This can make a difference, because people may be more likely to implement an intervention as planned if they view the goals, procedures, and intended outcomes favorably (Lane, Kalberg, Bruhn, et al., 2009). Finally, the FABI team will make plans to assess generalization and maintenance from the start to ensure the newly acquired behaviors occur in other locations, with other people, and over time.

Once all these details are drafted, the intervention procedures are reviewed and clarified with everyone implementing the intervention (e.g., the teacher who is on the FABI team; other intervention agents)—and decisions are made as to which A-R-E components are retained. For example, the initial planning may include four antecedent adjustments to set the stage for engagement: (1) a starter activity featuring instructional choices to allow students to be independently engaged when the teacher is taking attendance and welcoming students to the classroom, (2) a schoolwide expectation matrix posted at the front of the classroom and by the classroom door, (3) a teacher-led song to review schoolwide expectations, and (4) a self-monitoring checklist designed for the student and placed on their desk. After revisiting these drafted components with the teacher, they might decide they are not comfortable with the third choice because they think middle school students would make fun of the teacher for singing the song, finding it "babyish." As such, the FABI team may elect to move forward with the other three antecedent adjustments (1, 2, and 4). After the procedures are finalized, a check for understanding is conducted to make certain each person is familiar with how each component may take place. This might include modeling, role play, or using a series of questions and answers.

Next this plan is shared with the student, family members, and other intervention agents, as necessary. This practice provides the opportunity to explain procedures to stakeholders and to ask them to complete a preintervention social validity form. Their input is used to make initial revisions and gives them an opportunity to reflect on the whole intervention. It also enables them to provide more private feedback that may be difficult to share publicly. After A-R-E intervention components are finalized with feedback from everyone, the team completes the treatment integrity form (examples are included in Chapter 16) and prepares any needed intervention material. Then all intervention agents complete a check for understanding by answering a few questions or role-playing specific A-R-E components (a point discussed more fully in Chapter 19).

Collect Additional Baseline Data If Needed

Depending on how long this process takes, it may be necessary to collect additional baseline data. For example, if the planning process takes a week (or more), you will continue collecting baseline data throughout this time period until the intervention is ready to be put in place. As you learned in Chapter 10, ideally you will collect IOA data on 25% of the data points collected in each phase, including the baseline.

Testing the Intervention: An Overview

At the end of Step 4, the FABI team will have a fully designed intervention linked to the function of the target behavior. Then it is time to "test" the intervention using a design that allows the FABI team to determine whether there is a functional relation between the introduction of the intervention and the student's behavior. We go into more detail on this process in Chapter 20, but be forewarned that it will not be enough to simply introduce the intervention, continue to collect student performance data, compare the data from the two phases, and think that your work is completed. We encourage you to read over the explicit items in the completion checklist for *Step 5: Testing the Intervention* (see Box 11.2 on page 135) so that you are aware of additional items, such as (1) collecting treatment integrity data during each introduction of the intervention; (2) continuing to collect student performance data using the same measurement system used in the baseline process, including collecting IOA during 25% of the sessions in each phase; (3) collecting maintenance and generalization data as planned; and (4) assessing social validity before the intervention is considered ready and after the "test" is complete. Ethical considerations regarding these topics are presented in Box 11.3.

Part VI goes into greater detail about the multiple components of Step 5. In Chapter 20, we introduce three key questions to address when testing the intervention: (1) Is the intervention being implemented as planned (i.e., treatment integrity)?; (2) How is it working (i.e., functional relation)?; and (3) What do stakeholders think (i.e., social validity)? We also discuss monitoring factors that enhance an intervention's success. Then, in Chapter 21, we provide guidance for preparing a practical report of intervention outcomes. We discuss finalizing the behavior intervention plan, having the proper documentation, and transitioning the plan and documents for future use.

BOX 11.3. Ethical Considerations in Chapter 11: BACB Ethics Code for Behavior Analysts

1.07 Cultural Responsiveness and Diversity

The inclusion of family members and teachers as part of the intervention team provides the opportunity to individualize strategies that best fit the intervention within the context of the classroom, the family's values, the diversity of their experience, and student interest.

2.01 Providing Effective Treatment

The use of the Function-Based Intervention Decision Model to select and design intervention strategies has been proven to be an efficient and effective way to select strategies for an effective behavior-change intervention. See the table of peer-reviewed studies using the Function-Based Intervention Decision Model in the Appendix following Chapter 23.

2.08 Communicating about Services

Although this ethical code refers to communicating with stakeholders about services in the larger sense of their scope (what will be done) and how long they will last, it was included here because of the beginning statement about using understandable language, dispensing with jargon, and ensuring that the intervention is understood. Chapter 11 describes explaining the intervention strategies to teachers, family members, and the student so they understand and have an opportunity for input before implementation. This is also the time at which a social validity assessment is completed by family members and teachers.

> **2.09 Involving Clients and Stakeholders**
>
> Once the intervention is designed (i.e., A-R-E procedures are identified), teachers, family members, and students have a preintervention opportunity to comment on intervention procedures, goals, and expected outcomes. They are also part of the FABI intervention team and have input throughout the development, design, and implementation of the intervention. The chapter describes considerations that might be made if a strategy is not a good fit and notes that procedures could still be revised at this stage.
>
> **2.13 Selecting, Designing, and Implementing Assessments**
>
> The answers to Function-Based Intervention Decision Model questions and therefore the selection of an intervention method are grounded in assessment and observation data that include student skill assessment, observations, the procedural integrity of implementing the tiered system of support, and the assessment of the quality of instruction.
>
> **2.14 Selecting, Designing, and Implementing Behavior-Change Intervention**
>
> The primary focus of Chapter 11 is to overview a method for selecting and designing an intervention using the Function-Based Intervention Decision Model, to describe what is included in the A-R-E components of the intervention, and to provide a method for testing the intervention. The chapter includes all the components of a behavior-change intervention as identified in Code 2.14.
>
> The Function-Based Intervention Decision Model asks two questions that are key to identifying one of four intervention methods that best fits the student's ability to perform the replacement behavior (Question 1) and the status of effective practices in the classroom—the antecedent conditions (Question 2). The answers to these decision-model questions and therefore the selection of an intervention method are grounded in data as required in Code 2.13.
>
> Chapter 11 goes on to describe the development of the intervention to include antecedent, reinforcement, and extinction components for each method and concludes with an overview of procedures for testing the intervention. Each method and all intervention components are more fully described with illustrations in Chapters 12–15.
>
> The chapter also provides a handy tool for the selection and design of the intervention in the Functional Assessment and Behavior Intervention Plan: Planning Form. The form includes space for all intervention components, including treatment integrity, social validity, and generalization and maintenance, all of which are important but sometimes neglected in the intervention process. These intervention components are more fully addressed in Chapters 16–18.

For now, just know that there is a formal plan for testing the FABI—one that is rigorous, feasible, and meets the standards for a defensible plan (see Chapter 21).

Summary

In this chapter, we introduced Step 4. After briefly reviewing Steps 1 through 3, we explained how to (1) use the Function-Based Intervention Decision Model to select the relevant intervention method(s); (2) develop proposed A-R-E components, linking each tactic to the hypothesized function on the planning sheet; (3) draft components needed to draw valid inferences about intervention outcomes; (4) create a plan to prepare the teacher, student, and sometimes family members to learn how to implement the intervention procedures; and (5) collect any addition baseline data, if needed. We also briefly introduced *Step 5, Testing the Intervention*, so that you have a general overview of what is coming next. We also discuss finalizing the behavior intervention plan, proper documentation, and transitioning the plan and documents across time and settings.

In Chapters 12–15, we illustrate how the interventions were designed—and tested (Step 5)—for each method. We also explain a range of practical A-R-E components that are part of each method.

FORM 11.1

Functional Assessment and Behavior Intervention Plan: Planning Form

Directions: Functional Assessment and Behavior Intervention Plan: Planning Form is a living document to support team efforts in the design, implementation, and evaluation of functional assessment-based interventions. This information will be transferred to the Behavior Intervention Plan (BIP) and/or school district standard forms after completing *Step 5: Testing the Intervention*.

Student Name:	**Student ID:**
School:	**Date of Birth:**
Current Grade Level:	**Special Education:** ☐ Yes ☐ No
Gender:	**Disability Eligibility:**
Parent(s):	**Parent(s) Contact Number:**
Date of Assessment:	**Classroom Teacher:**

Persons Conducting the Assessment:

Role: ☐ Classroom Teacher   ☐ SPED Teacher   ☐ Teacher (Other)   ☐ Teacher (Other)
☐ School Psychologist   ☐ Counselor   ☐ Behavior Specialist   ☐ Intern
☐ University Student   ☐ BCBA/ABA   ☐ Other:

Identifying the Problem: Defining Target and Replacement Behaviors

Target Behavior (observable, measurable, repeatable):

Drafting:

Label:	
Definition:	
Examples:	
Non-examples:	

Operational Definition (include label, definition, examples, and non-examples):

Dimension of Behavior (e.g., frequency, rate, duration, latency):

(continued)

From Lane, K. L., Menzies, H., Bruhn, A., & Crnobori, M. (2011). *Managing challenging behaviors in schools: Research-based strategies that work.* Guilford Press. Reprinted by permission in *Functional Assessment-Based Intervention: Effective Individualized Support for Students* by John Umbreit, Jolenea B. Ferro, Kathleen Lynne Lane, and Carl J. Liaupsin (The Guilford Press, 2024). Permission to photocopy this material, or to download and print additional copies (*www.guilford.com/umbreit-forms*), is granted to purchasers of this book for personal use or use with students; see copyright page for details.

Functional Assessment and Behavior Intervention Plan: Planning Form *(page 2 of 10)*

Replacement Behavior (observable, measurable, repeatable):

Drafting:

Label:	
Definition:	
Examples:	
Non-examples:	

Operational Definition (include label, definition, examples, and non-examples):

Dimension of Behavior (e.g., frequency, rate, duration, latency):

Rationale for Replacement Behavior (e.g., Why do you want to teach this behavior or increase the likelihood of this behavior occurring?):

Functional Behavioral Assessment: Interviews and Direct Observations

Interviews Completed: ☐ YES ☐ NO

Interviewees: ☐ Teacher ☐ Parent ☐ Student

Rating Scales:

Hours of Total Direct Observation (A-B-C):

Setting(s) of Observations:

1) 2) 3)

(continued)

Functional Assessment and Behavior Intervention Plan: Planning Form *(page 3 of 10)*

Determining the Function of the Behavior: Using the Function Matrix

	Positive Reinforcement (Access Something)	Negative Reinforcement (Avoid Something)
Attention		
Tangible/ Activity		
Sensory		

Source: Umbreit, Ferro, Liaupsin, and Lane (2007).

Rating Scales Summary Statement:

Outcome of Function Matrix: Hypothesized Function:

Determining the Behavior Objective

What behavior are you progress-monitoring with direct observation? *(select minimum of one)*

☐ Target Behavior ☐ Replacement Behavior

Rationale for behavior to progress monitor *(e.g., replacement behavior focuses on the desired behavior—focusing on the positive)*:

Check the measurement system used for your data collection: *(select minimum of one)*

☐ Frequency ☐ Whole-Interval Recording
☐ Rate ☐ Partial-Interval Recording
☐ Duration ☐ Momentary Time Sampling
☐ Latency ☐ Other (discuss with coach):
☐ Interresponse Time

(continued)

Functional Assessment and Behavior Intervention Plan: Planning Form *(page 4 of 10)*

Baseline (e.g., number of observations, level, trend, stability to describe present levels of student performance and to inform the development of behavior objective)

Baseline Descriptive Statistics describing level and trend for baseline:

Mean (*SD*):

Slope (*SE YX*):

Baseline Statement:

Behavioral Objective:

Function-Based Intervention Decision Model

CONDUCT FBA
↓
SELECT REPLACEMENT BEHAVIOR
↓
Can the Student Perform the Replacement Behavior?
- NO → Do Antecedent Conditions Represent Best Practice?
  - YES → **METHOD 1:** Teach the Replacement Behavior
  - NO → **METHOD 1 & 2:** Teach the Replacement Behavior and Adjust the Environment
- YES → Do Antecedent Conditions Represent Best Practice?
  - NO → **METHOD 2:** Adjust the Environment
  - YES → **METHOD 3:** Shift the Contingencies

(continued)

Functional Assessment and Behavior Intervention Plan: Planning Form *(page 5 of 10)*

Determining the Intervention Method

Method Selected *(select and complete one)*:

☐ Method 1: Teach the Replacement Behavior

☐ Method 2: Adjust the Environment

☐ Method 3: Shift the Contingencies

☐ Methods 1 and 2: Teach the Replacement Behavior and Adjust the Environment

Note. After you have selected the appropriate method, draft an intervention for the selected intervention on page 6, 7, 8, **OR** 9. ***Do not draft ALL interventions.***

Method	Description
Method 1: Teach the Replacement Behavior	• Adjust antecedent conditions so new behaviors are learned and aversive conditions avoided. • Provide appropriate reinforcement for the replacement behavior. • Withhold the consequence that previously reinforced the target behavior.
Method 2: Adjust the Environment	• Adjust antecedent variables so the conditions that set the occasion for the target behavior are eliminated and new conditions are established in which the replacement behavior is more likely to occur. • Provide appropriate positive reinforcement for replacement behavior. • Withhold the consequence that previously reinforced the target behavior.
Method 3: Shift the Contingencies	• Provide the consequence that previously reinforced the target behavior, but only for the replacement behavior. • Withhold the consequence when the target behavior occurs (extinction). • Adjust the antecedent conditions to make it more likely that the replacement behavior will occur.
Methods 1 and 2: Teach the Replacement Behavior and Adjust the Environment	• Adjust antecedent variables so (1) new behaviors are learned and aversive conditions avoided and (2) the conditions that set the occasion for the target behavior are eliminated and new conditions are established in which the replacement behavior is more likely to occur. • Provide appropriate positive reinforcement for replacement behavior. • Withhold the consequence that previously reinforced the target behavior.

(continued)

Functional Assessment and Behavior Intervention Plan: Planning Form *(page 6 of 10)*

Method 1: Teach the Replacement Behavior

Adjust Antecedents	Adjust antecedent conditions so new behaviors are learned and aversive conditions avoided.	
Reinforcement Rates	Provide appropriate reinforcement for the replacement behavior.	
Extinguish Target Behavior	Withhold the consequence that previously reinforced the target behavior.	

(continued)

Functional Assessment and Behavior Intervention Plan: Planning Form *(page 7 of 10)*

Method 2: Adjust the Environment

Adjust Antecedents	Adjust antecedent variables so the conditions that set the occasion for the target behavior are eliminated and new conditions are established in which the replacement behavior is more likely to occur.	
Reinforcement Rates	Provide appropriate positive reinforcement for replacement behavior.	
Extinguish Target Behavior	Withhold the consequence that previously reinforced the target behavior.	

(continued)

Functional Assessment and Behavior Intervention Plan: Planning Form *(page 8 of 10)*

Method 3: Shift the Contingencies

Adjust Antecedents	Adjust the antecedent conditions to make it more likely that the replacement behavior will occur.	
Reinforcement Rates	Provide the consequence that previously reinforced the target behavior, but only for the replacement behavior.	
Extinguish Target Behavior	Withhold the consequence when the target behavior occurs (extinction).	

(continued)

Functional Assessment and Behavior Intervention Plan: Planning Form

Methods 1 and 2: Teach the Replacement Behavior and Adjust the Environment

Adjust Antecedents	Adjust antecedent variables so (1) new behaviors are learned and aversive conditions avoided and (2) the conditions that set the occasion for the target behavior are eliminated and new conditions are established in which the replacement behavior is more likely to occur.	
Reinforcement Rates	Provide appropriate positive reinforcement for replacement behavior.	
Extinguish Target Behavior	Withhold the consequence that previously reinforced the target behavior.	

(continued)

Functional Assessment and Behavior Intervention Plan: Planning Form

Data to be collected:

Student Outcome (What behavior(s) is (are) being measured? What measurement system? When/Where?)
Target Behavior:

Replacement Behavior:

Treatment Integrity (e.g., checklist)
Treatment Integrity:

Social Validity (e.g., IRP-15, CIRP)
Social Validity:

Supporting Success (e.g., evaluating the intervention)
Fading and Generalization:

Program Review Date:

Personnel and Roles:

Emergency Procedures:

CHAPTER 12

Intervention Method 1
Teach the Replacement Behavior

LEARNING OBJECTIVES

- Describe how to determine whether the failure to perform the replacement behavior is an acquisition, fluency, or performance problem.
- Describe issues associated with different types of replacement behaviors (i.e., issues with communication, social, and academic skills).
- Describe how the A-R-E components are applied within Intervention Method 1.
- Describe how the elements for Method 1 apply in a case study.

In Chapter 11, we learned how to use the Function-Based Intervention Decision Model to select one of four intervention options: Method 1: Teach the Replacement Behavior, Method 2: Adjust the Environment, Method 3: Shift the Contingencies, or a combination of Methods 1 and 2: Teach the Replacement Behavior and Adjust the Environment. This chapter focuses on how to develop a Method 1 intervention. We start by taking a more detailed look at the differences between acquisition, fluency, and performance problems. Then we consider some issues with communication, social, academic, and self-management skills that are specific to different types of replacement behaviors. Next, we look at how to create A-R-E components that are appropriate for a Method 1 intervention. We end this chapter with a step-by-step example of how a Method 1 intervention was developed for a young child with a behavior disorder (see Form 12.1 at the end of this chapter). As in previous chapters, ethical considerations are also included (see Box 12.1).

> **BOX 12.1. Ethical Considerations in Chapter 12: BACB Ethics Code for Behavior Analysts**
>
> **2.08 Communicating about Services and 2.09 Involving Clients and Stakeholders**
>
> The FABI process for communicating with stakeholders and involving them in the intervention selection and design process is detailed in the Functional Assessment and Behavior Intervention Plan: Planning Form. The chapter provides some examples, including an illustration of a full FABI using a published study. As part of the FABI team, the student, teacher, and family members provide information about preferences and goals as well as about the student's behavior. Although a family member was not interviewed in the illustration, a family interview is always the goal. Social validity is measured before an intervention proceeds, and teachers, the student, and family members should have multiple opportunities for input during intervention development. Involving family members and the student in the development of the intervention provides multiple opportunities to identify important cultural and linguistic perspectives that might affect intervention development and implementation.
>
> **2.13 Selecting, Designing, and Implementing the Assessment**
>
> This chapter describes collecting and using data to determine whether the replacement behavior needs to be taught. Assessments include observations of the student during instruction, evaluating academic competence, and using validated rating scales that measure both academic and social behavior.
>
> **2.14 Selecting, Designing, and Implementing Behavior-Change Intervention**
>
> Chapter 12 begins the first of four chapters that describe the process of selecting each intervention option described in the Function-Based Intervention Decision model. Chapters 12–15 provide a more detailed description of each method and the core of selecting, designing, and implementing a behavior-change intervention using this model.
>
> Chapter 12 is a step-by-step description and the illustration of a study in which Intervention Method 1 was used. It takes a closer look at issues specific to different types of replacement behaviors—all in the interest of designing an effective intervention. The A-R-E component selection for Method 1 is explicitly described with examples. Proper selection of the replacement behavior is always important, but Method 1 emphasizes this aspect of intervention development. An emphasis is placed on identifying behaviors that can recruit reinforcement in the natural environment with the purpose of sustaining outcomes under naturalistic conditions.
>
> The Functional Assessment and Behavior Intervention Plan: Planning Form is an example of the intervention using Method 1. The form provides a complete example of each step of the FABI process in detail, beginning with selection of the student and progressing through data collection.
>
> This illustration of Method 1 is based on assessment results and scientific evidence. It relies on the data gathered during the FBA and identifies the additional data needed for an evaluation of student performance. Positive reinforcement and extinction procedures are specified and are based on the results of the FBA. The description includes ideas for how to identify and address the diverse needs of the family, the student, and the classroom environment.
>
> **2.15 Minimizing Risk of Behavior-Change Interventions**
>
> No punishment procedures are suggested for use in interventions designed using the Function-Based Intervention Decision Model. Care is taken to ensure that all intervention strategies are supported

in the natural environment and are acceptable to the teacher and family. Extinction procedures are designed to minimize side effects by identifying an appropriate replacement behavior that, in most cases, serves the same function as the challenging behavior and ensuring that reinforcement for the replacement behavior occurs at a rate higher than or comparable to that previously reported for the target behavior.

2.16 Describing Behavior-Change Interventions Before Implementation

The FABI process described in this book includes describing and fully developing intervention procedures and strategies as part of the team process so that team members understand and approve the final intervention. Strategies are also described and all members of the implementation team (e.g., teachers) are thoroughly trained in implementing the intervention.

Can the Student Perform the Replacement Behavior?

In Chapter 8, you learned to select a replacement behavior that is observable, measurable, and repeatable; that describes what a student can do or learn to do; that can be supported by the natural environment; and that logically fits the statement of function. In this chapter, we begin to probe the replacement behavior more deeply. We are specifically concerned with the answer to the first key question in the Function-Based Intervention Decision Model: "Can the student perform the replacement behavior?" You will use Method 1: Teach the Replacement Behavior when the answer to this question is *no* and the answer to the second question "Do antecedent conditions represent effective practices for this student?" is *yes*. Best practice identifies antecedent conditions that set the stage for the student to perform the replacement behavior once it is learned. To answer Question 1, we need to understand the difference between acquisition, fluency, and performance issues. These differences were discussed in Chapter 11, but they bear repeating here because a clear understanding of these terms and the underlying issues will help you develop a plan that supports a student in using a replacement behavior.

Acquisition Problems

Sometimes the answer to the question is simple. If the behavior has seldom or never been observed in the environment, the likelihood is pretty good that the student cannot perform the behavior. We would consider this an acquisition problem; the student has never acquired the skill. If you select the replacement behavior early on, you can ask others on the team about this during interviews and you can look for it during your own observations. If you choose the replacement behavior later in the process (i.e., after FABI interviews and observations), you can review what has been completed, ask the teacher about it, do a short observation, and/or review records. Clearly, if a student does not know how to perform the replacement behavior, then our intervention can be designed to help them acquire that skill. For example, if you want a student to use the sign for "more" to make a request at lunch and it is something completely new to them that requires you to teach that hand sign, you will want to add instructional strategies, such as modeling, direct instruction, and practice to the intervention.

Fluency Problems

In some cases, it may be that a student has been seen to use the replacement behavior, but not in a way that is adequate for it to fulfill its function in a situation. This can be referred to as a fluency problem. For instance, a student may raise a hand and wait to be called on, but does not get their hand up high enough for the teacher to see it. Or a student may be able to struggle through reading a grade-level sentence but do it so slowly that they do not understand the meaning. Or they may greet peers on the playground but do so using awkward language that is not appropriate for their age. In each case, the student cannot perform the behavior in a way or with the fluency required for the behavior to function in the environment as needed. In these cases, our intervention components should include instructional strategies that help the student perform the replacement behavior quickly and easily.

Performance Problems

In some cases, a student can perform the replacement behavior fluently, but chooses to use other behaviors. To return to an example, a child may be able to "raise a hand and wait to be called on," but they instead choose to call out because they find that behavior to be more effective (they get called on immediately!). These are considered performance issues. Rather than teaching the behavior, our intervention should focus on shifting the contingencies to make the replacement behavior effective and the problem behavior ineffective. You will learn to deal with those situations in Chapter 14.

Assessing Acquisition, Fluency, and Performance

One way we can distinguish between performance, fluency, and skill deficits is to use validated tools, such as the *Social Skills Improvement System—Rating Scale* (SSiS-RS; Gresham & Elliott, 2008a). The SSiS-RS assesses a range of social skills (i.e., communication, cooperation, assertion, responsibility, empathy, engagement, and self-control), behavior problems (externalizing and internalizing), and academic competence (e.g., in reading and math and motivation to learn). This information, coupled with the A-B-C data used to determine function, can help provide a clear picture of the nature of the student's capabilities.

Issues Related to Types of Behaviors/Skills

The literature on challenging behavior and the FBA process demonstrates that challenging behavior may often be centered around a deficit in social skills (Maag, 2005, 2006), an academic skill (Liaupsin et al., 2006), or communication skills (Heath et al., 2015). Because Method 1 strongly focuses on teaching the student a replacement behavior, this section reviews the behaviors related to communication, social, academic, and self-management skills around which a deficit often occurs and some issues related to each one.

Communication Skills

As discussed in Chapter 2, behavior has a meaning and a communicative intent. Sometimes students engage in problem behavior when they do not have the skills to express their wants and needs in other ways. For example, students with speech or language deficits may not be able to easily speak or sign. They may have trouble making themselves understood. Communication problems can occur for students who speak a language that is different from the general population in their school, classroom, or community. They can also occur for students who live in families, communities, or cultures where they have not needed or learned school-related communication behaviors. In such cases, you may identify a replacement behavior that provides the student with a more appropriate means to communicate their wants and needs. For example, a student may be taught to raise their hand, say a word, or make a sign to obtain help when they need it. A student may be taught to use an electronic communication system or board to obtain materials or to ask for a break. There is a rich research history of using function-based interventions that teach communication skills to help students with developmental disabilities and emotional and behavioral disorders, as well as students at risk and those without any identified disability (cf. Reichle & Wacker, 2017).

The most important point to remember is that we should not assume that a student has learned or can fluently use a specific communication skill. Be sure to ask questions in the initial interviews or follow-up interviews to help you answer the question of whether the student can perform the communication skill as a replacement behavior.

Social Skills

Social skills are often chosen as replacement behaviors when an individual's existing social behavior is not appropriate for the environment (e.g., a young child who takes a peer's toys, a youth who gets frustrated with work instead of asking for help, an adult who does not respect the personal space of others). In schools implementing Ci3T models of prevention, social skills are taught at Tier 1 as part of regular school practices (Lane, Oakes, et al., 2014). This teaching at Tier 1 essentially levels the playing field for all students, building a foundational set of skills that are common for everyone. Within these and other integrated tiered systems, some students may require additional support to fully master these and other social skills, such as those provided in Tier 2 and Tier 3 interventions.

When addressing social skills within a Tier 3 support, such as a FABI, you will likely want to focus on a small number of specific social behaviors. Social skills rating scales can be useful in selecting specific acquisition deficits to remedy as part of a Method 1 intervention. It is also important to consider carefully the particular situations in which the student will use the skill and provide more frequent opportunities for practice.

This holds true for early childhood classrooms as well. Social skills instruction is a necessary part of early childhood learning. It can range from problem-solving skills, such as different ways to calm down, to friendship skills, such as sharing, taking turns, and how to get a friend's attention. However, the replacement behavior identified in a behavioral intervention must be specific to the behavior that is being replaced and address the same function as the target behavior. For example, if Davi screams and hits other children when they enter his play space, you might identify a replacement behavior of using the Turtle Technique to calm him down (social skill) and asking a peer to please leave him alone (communication skill).

The interviews and observations conducted by the FABI team will likely provide enough information for you to answer the question of whether the student can perform the replacement social skill. There are also social skills assessments that can help you make the determination. As described earlier, the SSiS-RS (Gresham & Elliot, 2008a) is appropriate for individuals ages 3–18. It uses ratings from multiple informants (i.e., teacher, parent, child) to provide information that can identify specific social skill acquisition ("can't do") and performance ("won't do") deficits as well as social skills strengths. It also assesses behaviors that might interfere with the expression of social skills and gathers teacher impressions of a student's academic competence.

Academic Skills

The literature on challenging behavior and academic achievement of K–12 students shows that problem behaviors can be related to academic achievement deficits in areas such as reading (Preciado et al., 2009; Thomas et al., 2008) and math (Liaupsin et al., 2006). School settings can create situations in which students engage in problem behavior because they lack a required academic skill. In many cases of challenging behavior during an academic task, the replacement behavior will be identified as *on-task* behavior or *task engagement*. Additional engagement with the task (e.g., listening to the teacher, reading aloud, working on math problems) should result in the student learning the academic skill. However, if the instruction does not result in the student learning the academic skill, it may be necessary to teach the academic skill so that the student actually can be on task.

As with social skills, there are standardized assessments (e.g., reading and math diagnostic tools) that can help you identify whether a student can perform a specific academic skill with the fluency necessary to be successful. However, the complex nature of some academic skills may require that you conduct interviews and observations to determine the exact nature of the issue. For instance, if the replacement behavior is for the student to be on task during math activities, you would want to evaluate the math activity and identify which step was a problem for the student. If the student was working on becoming more proficient in adding two-digit numbers with regrouping, one strategy would be to sit with the student and observe them attempting to solve a few problems. Also keep in mind that fluency of a component skill can be the underlying problem in the case of complex academic skills. For example, lack of fluency (automaticity) in multiplying single digit numbers makes it impossible to learn how to do division and other, more complex math procedures.

Self-Management Skills

Teaching self-management skills can be very useful when an intervention plan is focused on developing a replacement behavior. This can include teaching a student to count and record their own use of the replacement behavior (self-recording); having them systematically judge their own performance (self-evaluation); and/or having them determine whether they earned reinforcement and provide it to themselves (self-reinforcement). These self-management techniques can be adapted for use with even very young children with strategies such as using charts with pictures. Self-management strategies can also be popular with teachers who find that the method reduces the burden of intervention implementation. Because this can be the case, it is important to understand that the literature on self-management strategies shows that a significant amount of adult assistance is often required for proper implementation in an intervention plan (Briesch & Chafouleas, 2009).

The A-R-E Components for Method 1

In Chapter 11, we described that the basic components of each intervention method involved adjusting the A-R-E components, that is, the antecedent conditions, reinforcing the replacement behavior, and extinguishing the target behavior. Although all the intervention methods include A-R-E components, when using Method 1, these components should be crafted with a broad focus that facilitates learning and developing fluency in performing the replacement behavior.

Adjusting the Antecedent Conditions

You choose the Method 1 intervention when the student cannot fluently perform the replacement behavior. Thus, the primary focus of the antecedent adjustments is to provide explicit instruction in the replacement behavior. However, you must also adjust any antecedent conditions that prevent the student from performing the replacement behavior. For instance, to help a student "follow directions," you might help the teacher in breaking down lengthy instructions into smaller segments that the student can learn more easily, in addition to teaching the student simple steps for following instructions.

Reinforcing the Replacement Behavior

As described in Chapter 2, behaviors are more likely to continue when they are reinforced. You want to be sure that the replacement behavior results in the student accessing the reinforcer that makes the behavior "functional." As discussed in Chapter 11, this starts with selecting the appropriate replacement behavior. You should be sure to select a replacement behavior that really does "recruit" natural reinforcement in the environment.

In some cases, you should plan your intervention to include short-term reinforcement, particularly if the natural reinforcer is likely to be delayed. Short-term reinforcement is also useful in a Method 1 intervention because you may be teaching the student a behavior that is brand new to them and for which they have no experience with its long-term benefits. For example, if the replacement behavior is "raise a hand and wait to be called on," a student may have difficulty waiting as long as it takes for the teacher to respond with assistance. A short-term (interim) reinforcer could be for the teacher to acknowledge the student's appropriate use of the replacement behavior while they wait (e.g., provide an immediate thumbs-up, a verbal thank-you, and a request to wait). In schools implementing Ci3T, the teacher or other adult can give the student a ticket, paired with behavior-specific praise. As mentioned in earlier chapters, these tickets are the universal reinforcers used by all adults to acknowledge students for meeting expectations. In Ci3T schools, it is important to retain the use of this one universal reinforcer to avoid introducing confusion with a second acknowledgment system.

Extinguishing the Target Behavior

The purpose of the extinction procedure in a Method 1 intervention is to make sure that the target behavior no longer works—that it no longer provides the student an effective or efficient way to achieve the intended function. Part of this goal is met by the previous two intervention components; you have already directly taught the replacement behavior and made sure that its use would result in reinforcement. For the extinction component to work, you need to be sure that the function (reinforcer) is no longer available when the student performs the target behavior. For example, if the student is sent out of the room for yelling and pushing papers off their desk, and you have identified the function of the behavior as negative reinforcement, that is, avoiding a task, you must find some way that the task continues to be presented to the student. One way might involve keeping the student in the classroom, or you may send the unfinished task (e.g., worksheet, book) home to be completed there by the student. The point is that extinction means that the student can no longer avoid the task by performing the target behavior.

Calli and Her Teachers

More than two dozen scholarly, peer-reviewed articles have been published on the efficacy of our approach to developing effective FABIs. In the section that follows, we provide an illustration adapted from Reeves and colleagues (2017). The purpose of the study was to demonstrate that students with skill acquisition deficits show better outcomes when the intervention includes direct instruction in the replacement behavior. This particular example describes a Method 1 intervention developed for Calli, a 12-year-old sixth grader who was diagnosed with autism spectrum disorder (ASD) and speech/language impairment.

Step 1: Identifying Students Who May Need a FABI

Calli was selected because she had specific characteristics. She (1) was between the ages of 4 and 13, (2) was diagnosed with some form of ASD, (3) had an individualized education plan (IEP), (4) displayed chronic challenging behavior, (5) was in a classroom with high levels of effective teaching practices, and (6) demonstrated an inability to perform necessary replacement behaviors independently.

Calli spent most of her day in a self-contained classroom, though she received science and language arts instruction in resource class settings. Her teacher reported that Calli could read at grade level and received additional special education support in math, writing, speech, and counseling. The resource classroom for language arts, where the intervention was needed, consisted of one teacher, 17 students, and an educational assistant who provided Calli with academic and behavioral support. The arrangement of the classroom consisted of a basic set of student desks arranged into five rows. The class routine would also be familiar to many teachers or school professionals: entry activities, daily assignment review, independent writing, group reading, and class discussions.

Calli clearly met researchers' criteria for age, diagnosis, and identification for special education services. In terms of chronic challenging behavior, the special education teacher reported that Calli's behavioral issues (rude comments, complaining, screaming, banging her head on the desk, falling to the floor, hitting her head with her fist) were accelerating in frequency and intensity.

The researchers wanted to ensure that Calli's problem was not likely to be caused by ineffective classroom teaching practices. To this end, the researcher conducted a classroom environmental assessment using a checklist of quality classroom teaching practices (Ferro et al., 2008). They independently observed the classroom for 30 minutes, noting whether each of the 33 items on an environmental checklist was fully in place in the classroom. Then they compared the results of their observations to ensure they agreed on what they had seen. In Calli's case, the observers were in 100% agreement that indicators of a high-quality classroom environment were in place.

The last qualifying criterion for inclusion in the study was that the student demonstrated an inability to perform a suitable replacement behavior fluently and independently. The researchers explored this criterion as they entered the next step in the FABI process.

Step 2: Conducting the Functional Assessment

The researchers began the functional assessment process by conducting interviews and engaging in direct classroom observations. They interviewed Calli's teacher and the classroom assistant using the PFAS (Dunlap et al., 1993). The teacher was most concerned about Calli's rude comments, acting out, and off-task behavior in response to work demands. The assistant was concerned about essentially the same issues, although they noted that the behavior problems appeared to be escalating across the last month.

Direct observations took place when and where the behavior was reported (during interviews) to happen most often. The observations involved collecting ABC data during five sessions over 3.5 hours. When the researchers reviewed the interview and observational data through the Function Matrix (see Figure 12.1), it confirmed what they had been told during the interviews. The resulting statement of function was that Calli engaged in rude and off-task behavior when she was given an assignment. The target behaviors allowed her to access attention from the teacher and peers while also escaping assignments.

Step 3: Collecting Baseline Data

The researchers planned their baseline data collection carefully. They selected a 30-second whole-interval recording method because the target and replacement behaviors (off-task and on-task) are nonuniform behaviors. They kept the observation sessions brief; just 12 minutes each. This choice was likely made for two reasons; maintaining whole-interval recording requires constant attention from an observer, and they determined from previous interviews and observations that they could get a reasonable sample of behavior (24 intervals) in a short amount of time. Calli's on-task behavior averaged 14% of intervals (range = 6–31%) during the initial baseline.

	Positive Reinforcement (Access Something)	**Negative Reinforcement** (Avoid Something)
Attention	A-B-C Data: 1.3, 1.5, 1.9, 2.3, 2.5, 3.2, 3.4, 4.3, 5.2, 5.5 Teacher Interview: Calli is sometimes offered a break after making rude comments or complaining. Assistant Interview: Gives Calli a break or an office referral.	
Tangible/ Activity		A-B-C Data: 1.1, 1.4, 1.7, 2.2, 2.4, 3.1, 3.3, 4.1, 5.1, 5.4 Teacher Interview: Calli uses rude comments when asked to do work. Assistant Interview: Says Calli is rude when asked to complete nonpreferred activities.
Sensory		

FIGURE 12.1. Function Matrix for Calli.

Step 4: Designing the FABI

The next step in the process was to work through the Function-Based Intervention Decision Model. As explained previously, this involved asking the two key questions: (1) Can the student perform the replacement behavior? and (2) Do antecedent conditions represent effective practices for this student? As described earlier, the researchers confirmed the high quality of the classroom environment as a condition of including Calli in the study. Therefore, the answer to Question 2 was yes, the classroom environment reflected effective practices for this student and in fact other students as well. To answer Question 1, the researchers used a novel method to determine whether Calli could perform the replacement on-task behavior. It involved creating a task analysis of exactly what "on-task" behavior by Calli would look like in the classroom: engaging in assignments, raising a hand to ask a question, saying "No thank you" when called on, and saying "excuse me" to gain attention. Furthermore, each of these behaviors was separated into component steps. For instance, "engaging in assignments" meant that Calli could get materials, start the task within 30 seconds, maintain focus, sit quietly, and put materials away at the end of the assignment. This process made it possible to determine the specific skills that would be needed to address acquisition or fluency deficits or skills that might be sufficiently in place. This careful analysis found that Calli had acquisition deficits in "hand raising" and "getting attention," with performance deficits in "maintaining focus" and "saying no thanks." In summary, this was going to be a Method 1 intervention.

In this study, the purpose was to show just how important including instruction in the replacement behavior is for students who cannot perform it fluently. To prove this point, the researchers created two interventions. The first intervention for Calli was designed to include all three A-R-E components but did not include any instruction about the replacement behavior. The antecedent was adjusted by reminding Calli of the behavioral expectations at the beginning of each class session. When the replacement on-task behavior occurred, the teacher provided verbal praise as reinforcement. There was also a point system in place. Calli received a point for every 5 minutes she was on task; if she earned 80% of the points available during a session, she got to leave class 10 minutes early for free play. In other words, Calli was provided with "escape" from tasks by completing them instead of avoiding them. The teacher and assistant did not respond to any instances of the target off-task behavior.

The second intervention for Calli (see Figure 12.2) was identical to the first intervention but included additional antecedent elements to teach Calli the replacement behaviors that were necessary for her to be on task. In a set of four lessons that included examples, non-examples, and practice, Calli was taught how to raise her hand more effectively. Calli was provided with instruction in making appropriate versus inappropriate comments. Finally, a sign with reminders of how to get attention appropriately was created, was reviewed with Calli, and was placed where she could see it.

Step 5: Testing the Intervention

In most situations, you can test your intervention using a simple A-B-A-B withdrawal design, where the A condition is baseline and the B condition involves implementation of your FABI. In this case, the researchers wanted to demonstrate the importance of teaching the replacement behavior, so they used an A-B-A-C-A-(B or C) research design to test whether no intervention (the A condition), intervention without teaching the replacement behavior (the B condition), or intervention with teaching the replacement behavior (the C condition) worked best for Calli. Data were collected daily, and the data recording sessions lasted 12 minutes. A 30-second whole-interval recording system was used to collect data on Calli's on-task behavior. Each 12-minute session was divided into 30-second intervals. If Calli was on task across the entire interval, a plus was recorded. If she was off task during any part of an interval, a minus was recorded. To summarize the data for each session, the observer divided the total

Required Components	Resulting Intervention Elements
A = Adjust the antecedent conditions so new behaviors are learned and aversive conditions avoided. (Method 1).	• Remind Calli of the behavioral expectations at the start of class. • Teach Calli replacement behaviors necessary to be on task. • Provide a list of acceptable ways to get attention. • Create a sign with reminders and post it where Calli can see it.
R = Provide appropriate reinforcement for replacement behavior.	• Provide attention/praise when Calli is on task. • Implement a point system to earn free time.
E = Withhold the consequence that previously reinforced the target behavior.	• Briefly redirect (minimal attention) to continue working. • Maintain task and keep in class.

FIGURE 12.2. Function-based intervention for Calli.

number of plus marks by the total number of opportunities (24) and multiplied the number by 100%. The result would be the percentage of observed intervals Calli was completely on task.

A second observer collected data simultaneously during 38% of Calli's sessions to check on IOA. The IOA checks showed an average agreement between observers of 93% (range = 87–97%). Treatment integrity (TI), or whether the intervention was delivered as planned, was assessed during 33% of Calli's sessions by having an observer review a checklist of the intervention procedures and mark whether each component took place. To summarize TI at the end of a session, the observer would simply divide the number of check marks by the number of components in the procedure and multiply by 100%. This calculation yielded the percentage of procedural components properly implemented. There was also a second observer to ensure that TI was being measured accurately. The second observer completed the same TI checklist and summarized the data by dividing agreements on each procedural component by the total number of procedural components. Across implementation, this second check on TI showed 100% agreement.

Social validity was assessed using the Treatment Acceptability Rating Form—Revised (TARF-R; Reimers & Wacker, 1988). The instrument includes 17 items that measure several components of acceptability, including reasonableness, effectiveness, side effects, disruptiveness/time, cost, and willingness. Each item is assessed using a 7-point, Likert-type scale, with higher scores representing greater acceptability. The teacher completed the TARF-R prior to the first intervention, with a score of 115/117, and again prior to the second intervention, with a perfect score of 117/117.

Figure 12.3 presents the comparative results of the two interventions. During the initial no intervention (A) condition, Calli's on-task behavior averaged just 14% (range = 6–31%). Her on-task behavior increased to 29% of observed intervals (range = 0–56%) when the first

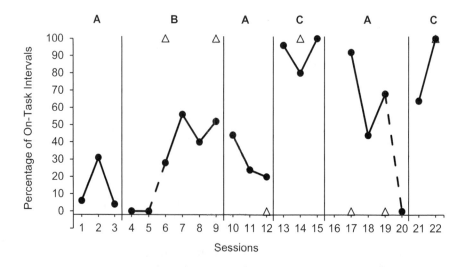

FIGURE 12.3. Levels of on-task behavior in Calli's intervention testing (closed circles are on-task percentage of intervals observed; open triangles are session treatment integrity). From Reeves, L. M., Umbreit, J., Ferro, J. B., & Liaupsin, C. J. (2017). The role of the replacement behavior in function-based intervention. *Education and Training in Autism and Developmental Disabilities, 52,* 305–316. Reprinted by permission.

intervention (B) was implemented and remained at 29% (range = 20–44%) when the no-intervention (A) condition was put back in place. When the second intervention with teaching of the replacement behavior (C) was implemented, Calli's on-task behavior jumped to an average of 92% (range = 80–100%). A return to no intervention (A) resulted in lower average on-task behavior (51%; range = 0–92%). The second implementation of the intervention with replacement behavior instruction (C) demonstrated an increase in on-task behavior to 82% (range = 64–100%).

Summary

In this chapter, we focused on the development of an intervention using Method 1: Teach the Replacement Behavior. This method is used when it is determined that the student cannot perform the replacement behavior and that the antecedent conditions (i.e., environment) represent best practices for this student. We reviewed the difference between acquisition, fluency, and performance issues to ensure that we have properly considered whether the student can perform the replacement behavior. Acquisition issues occur when the student has not acquired the replacement behavior. Fluency issues exist when a student has been seen to use the replacement behavior, but not in a way that is adequate for it to fulfill its function in a situation. Performance issues exist when a student can fluently perform the replacement behavior, but chooses another behavior that is perceived to be more effective.

In Chapter 13, we focus on the method needed when designing an intervention for students who are able to perform the replacement behavior fluently, but who need environmental adjustments that set the stage for the replacement behavior to occur.

FORM 12.1

Functional Assessment and Behavior Intervention Plan: Planning Form for Calli

Directions: Functional Assessment and Behavior Intervention Plan: Planning Form is a living document to support team efforts in the design, implementation, and evaluation of functional assessment-based interventions. This information will be transferred to the Behavior Intervention Plan (BIP) and/or school district standard forms after completing *Step 5: Testing the Intervention*.

Student Name: Calli
School: Middle School
Current Grade Level: 6
Gender: Female
Parent(s): Harriet and Marcus
Date of Assessment: 10/12/2022

Student ID: 022208
Date of Birth: 5/20/2010
Special Education: ☐ Yes ☑ No
Disability Eligibility: ASD and Speech Lang. Impaired
Parent(s) Contact Number: 555-296-4432
Classroom Teacher: Ms. Thomas

Persons Conducting the Assessment:

Role: ☐ Classroom Teacher ☑ SPED Teacher ☐ Teacher (Other) ☐ Teacher (Other)
☐ School Psychologist ☐ Counselor ☐ Behavior Specialist ☐ Intern
☑ University Student ☐ BCBA/ABA ☑ Other: University Consultants

Identifying the Problem: Defining Target and Replacement Behaviors

Target Behavior (observable, measurable, repeatable):

Drafting:

Label:	Off-task behavior
Definition:	Off-task behavior refers to engaging in activities other than the assigned task.
Examples:	rude comments; speaking rudely to teachers or peers (e.g., saying "I hate you"); complaining; raising her voice; screaming; whining; crying; banging on the desk; falling to the floor; hitting her head.
Non-examples:	Working quietly; completing assignments; raising a hand to ask a question; being polite to gain attention (e.g., saying "no thank you" or "excuse me").

Operational Definition (include label, definition, examples, and non-examples): Off-task behavior refers to engaging in activities other than the assigned task. Examples include rude comments to teachers and peers, raising her voice, whining or crying, banging on desk or own head, and falling to the floor. Non-examples include working quietly, completing assignments, raising a hand to gain attention, using polite language.

Dimension of Behavior (e.g., frequency, rate, duration, latency):
Frequency (average frequency across intervals using a whole-interval measurement)

(continued)

Form adapted from Lane, K. L., Menzies, H., Bruhn, A., & Crnobori, M. (2011). *Managing challenging behaviors in schools: Research-based strategies that work.* Guilford Press. Reprinted by permission. Graph from Germer, K. A., Kaplan, L. M., Giroux, L. N., Markham, E. H., Ferris, G. J., Oakes, W. P., & Lane, K. L. (2011). A function-based intervention to increase a second-grade student's on-task behavior in a general education classroom. *Beyond Behavior, 20,* 19–30. Reprinted by permission of Sage Publications.

Functional Assessment and Behavior Intervention Plan: Planning Form for Calli *(page 2 of 7)*

Replacement Behavior (observable, measurable, repeatable):

Drafting:

Label:	On-task behavior
Definition:	Being engaged quietly and interacting politely
Examples:	Working quietly; completing assignments; raising a hand to ask a question; being polite to gain attention (e.g., saying "no thank you" or "excuse me").
Non-examples:	rude comments; speaking rudely to teachers or peers (e.g., saying "I hate you"); complaining; raising her voice; screaming; whining; crying; banging on the desk; falling to the floor; hitting her head.

Operational Definition (include label, definition, examples, and non-examples): *On-task behavior is defined as being engaged quietly and interacting with teacher and peers politely. Examples include working quietly, completing assignments, raising a hand to gain attention, using polite language. Non-examples include rude comments to teachers and peers, raising her voice, whining or crying, banging on desk or own head, and falling to the floor.*

Dimension of Behavior (e.g., frequency, rate, duration, latency):
Duration: Average duration across intervals using a whole interval measurement)

Rationale for Replacement Behavior (e.g., Why do you want to teach this behavior or increase the likelihood of this behavior occurring?): *On-task behavior was selected as the replacement behavior because it would be likely to lead to academic and social success for Calli. In addition, on-task behavior was identified by the teacher and classroom assistant in interviews as a highly desirable behavior and a good replacement for Calli's off-task behavior. Finally, the examples of on-task behavior are natural and expected in the environment.*

Functional Behavioral Assessment: Interviews and Direct Observations

Interviews Completed: ☑ YES ☐ NO

Interviewees: ☑ Teacher ☐ Parent ☑ Student

Rating Scales: *No Standardized Rating Scales Used*

Hours of Total Direct Observation (A-B-C): *3.5 hours*

Setting(s) of Observations:

1) *Classroom* 2) 3)

(continued)

Functional Assessment and Behavior Intervention Plan: Planning Form for Calli *(page 3 of 7)*

Determining the Function of the Behavior: Using the Function Matrix

	Positive Reinforcement (Access Something)	**Negative Reinforcement (Avoid Something)**
Attention	ABC Data: 1.3, 1.5, 1.9, 2.3, 2.5, 3.2, 3.4, 4.3, 5.2, 5.5 Teacher Interview: Calli is sometimes offered a break after making rude comments or complaining. Assistant Interview: Gives Calli a break or an office referral.	
Tangible/ Activity		ABC Data: 1.1, 1.4, 1.7, 2.2, 2.4, 3.1, 3.3, 4.1, 5.1, 5.4 Teacher Interview: Calli uses rude comments when asked to do work. Assistant Interview: Says Calli is rude when asked to complete nonpreferred activities.
Sensory		

Source: Umbreit, Ferro, Liaupsin, and Lane (2007).

Rating Scales Summary Statement:
There were no rating scales administered.

Outcome of Function Matrix: Hypothesized Function:
When Calli is given an assignment, she engages in rude and off-task behavior to access attention from teacher and peers (positive reinforcement) AND escape the assigned activity (negative reinforcement).

Determining the Behavior Objective
What behavior are you progress-monitoring with direct observation? *(select minimum of one)*

☐ Target Behavior   ☑ Replacement Behavior

Rationale for behavior to progress monitor *(e.g., replacement behavior focuses on the desired behavior—focusing on the positive)***:**
Our defined replacement is incompatible with the target; they cannot occur together; they are opposites.

Check the measurement system used for your data collection: *(select minimum of one)*

☐ Frequency
☐ Rate
☐ Duration
☐ Latency
☐ Interresponse Time

☑ Whole-Interval Recording
☐ Partial-Interval Recording
☐ Momentary Time Sampling
☐ Other (discuss with coach):

(continued)

Functional Assessment and Behavior Intervention Plan: Planning Form for Calli *(page 4 of 7)*

Baseline (e.g., number of observations, level, trend, stability to describe present levels of student performance and to inform the development of behavior objective)
We have selected a 30-second whole-interval method because the replacement behavior is nonuniform; 12-minute observations, with three initial baseline sessions, but with a return to baseline in a withdrawal design (A-B-A-C-A-C).

Baseline Descriptive Statistics describing level and trend for baseline:

Mean (*SD*):

Slope (*SE YX*):

Baseline Statement:
Calli's on-task behavior during baseline averaged 14% (range 6–31%). After an initial low level of on-task behavior in the first session, it rose for one session to 31% before returning to a low level (6%).

Behavioral Objective:
Increase on-task behavior to a minimum mean of 70% for three consecutive observation sessions during intervention. In addition, we will be considering two interventions (B = without instruction in the replacement behavior; C = with instruction in the replacement behavior).

Function-Based Intervention Decision Model

```
CONDUCT FBA
     ↓
SELECT REPLACEMENT BEHAVIOR
     ↓
Can the Student Perform the Replacement Behavior?
  NO ↙                          ↘ YES
Do Antecedent Conditions          Do Antecedent Conditions
Represent Best Practice?          Represent Best Practice?
 YES ↙    ↘ NO                     NO ↙       ↘ YES
METHOD 1:  METHOD 1 & 2:         METHOD 2:    METHOD 3:
Teach the  Teach the             Adjust       Shift the
Replacement Replacement Behavior the          Contingencies
Behavior   and Adjust            Environment
           the Environment
```

(continued)

Functional Assessment and Behavior Intervention Plan: Planning Form for Calli *(page 5 of 7)*

Determining the Intervention Method

Method Selected *(select and complete one)*:

☑ Method 1: Teach the Replacement Behavior

☐ Method 2: Adjust the Environment

☐ Method 3: Shift the Contingencies

☐ Methods 1 and 2: Teach the Replacement Behavior and Adjust the Environment

Method	Description
Method 1: Teach the Replacement Behavior	• Adjust antecedent conditions so new behaviors are learned and aversive conditions avoided. • Provide appropriate reinforcement for the replacement behavior. • Withhold the consequence that previously reinforced the target behavior.
Method 2: Adjust the Environment	• Adjust antecedent variables so the conditions that set the occasion for the target behavior are eliminated and new conditions are established in which the replacement behavior is more likely to occur. • Provide appropriate positive reinforcement for replacement behavior. • Withhold the consequence that previously reinforced the target behavior.
Method 3: Shift the Contingencies	• Provide the consequence that previously reinforced the target behavior, but only for the replacement behavior. • Withhold the consequence when the target behavior occurs (extinction). • Adjust the antecedent conditions to make it more likely that the replacement behavior will occur.
Methods 1 and 2: Teach the Replacement Behavior and Adjust the Environment	• Adjust antecedent variables so (1) new behaviors are learned and aversive conditions avoided and (2) the conditions that set the occasion for the target behavior are eliminated and new conditions are established in which the replacement behavior is more likely to occur. • Provide appropriate positive reinforcement for replacement behavior. • Withhold the consequence that previously reinforced the target behavior.

(continued)

Functional Assessment and Behavior Intervention Plan: Planning Form for Calli *(page 6 of 7)*

Method 1: Teach the Replacement Behavior

Adjust Antecedents	Adjust antecedent conditions so new behaviors are learned and aversive conditions avoided.	Remind Calli of the behavioral expectations at the start of class. Teach Calli replacement behaviors necessary to be on task. Provide a list of acceptable ways to get attention. Create a sign with reminders and post where Calli can see it.
Reinforcement Rates	Provide appropriate reinforcement for the replacement behavior.	Provide attention/praise when Calli is on task. Implement a point system to earn free time.
Extinguish Target Behavior	Withhold the consequence that previously reinforced the target behavior.	Briefly redirect (minimal attention) to continue working. Maintain task and keep in class.

(continued)

Functional Assessment and Behavior Intervention Plan: Planning Form for Calli

Data to be collected:

Student Outcome (What behavior(s) is (are) being measured? What measurement system? When/Where?)

Target Behavior: *Off task—not measured as an outcome.*

Replacement Behavior: *On task—measured using 30-second whole-interval recording; reported as "percentage of observed intervals."*

Treatment Integrity (e.g., checklist)

Treatment Integrity: *Component checklist; observer records during each interval whether elements of the intervention were properly implemented as needed; level determined by dividing the number of observed intervals in which the intervention was properly implemented by the total number of intervals (and multiplying by 100%).*

Social Validity (e.g., IRP-15, CIRP)

Social Validity: *The Treatment Acceptability Rating Form-Revised (TARF-R; Reimers & Wacker, 1988) for the teacher and family member. The student was not able to respond to social validity items.*

Supporting Success (e.g., evaluating the intervention)

Fading and Generalization: *We are evaluating two interventions using a withdrawal design where we start with baseline (A), intervention w/o teaching replacement behavior (B), return to baseline (A), intervention w/teaching replacement behavior (C), return to baseline, then final implementation of the more effective intervention (B or C). Fading of some intervention elements will begin after achieving the behavioral objective in the last phase of intervention. Generalization will be considered for the lunchroom where similar behaviors sometimes occur.*

Program Review Date: *The university student will review the results at least weekly with the university mentors, teacher, and assistant.*

Personnel and Roles: *The university student will lead assessment and intervention; university mentors will provide consultation; teacher and assistant will implement intervention.*

Emergency Procedures: *The school has crisis plans in place and specific requirements for the students in the self-contained classrooms. The school procedures should be followed when there is an emergency.*

CHAPTER 13

Intervention Method 2
Adjust the Environment

LEARNING OBJECTIVES

- Describe practical, research-based antecedent adjustments used to increase engagement and limit disruption.
- Describe how to examine the environment to see if antecedent adjustments can be made to set the stage for the replacement behavior to occur.
- Describe how A-R-E components are developed with Intervention Method 2: Adjust the Environment.

As discussed in Chapter 11, Intervention Method 2 focuses on building an intervention with A-R-E components to enhance the environment to set the stage for success. The team makes antecedent adjustments designed to remove aversive events and introduces structures and supports to prompt the student to engage in the desired replacement behavior.

In this chapter, we begin by first understanding the current environment, attending to whether there are specific antecedent adjustments that could be made to enhance the environment. Specifically, we describe how to determine what is happening at Tier 1 in the current context and then consider specific antecedents that set the stage for positive, productive, safe, and enjoyable experiences. To complete the chapter, we provide an example of how antecedent adjustments to the environments were applied in one general education class in a southern state. We include ethical considerations for Method 2 in Box 13.1.

Understanding the Current Environment

Reviewing Tier 1 and Classroom Happenings

As we mentioned in Chapter 11, the Function-Based Intervention Decision Model is used to answer the second question: Do the antecedent conditions represent effective practices for this

> **BOX 13.1. Ethical Considerations in Chapter 13: BACB Ethics Code for Behavior Analysts**
>
> **2.08 Communicating about Services and 2.09 Involving Clients and Stakeholders**
>
> As we noted in Chapter 12, the FABI process includes identifying and addressing the diverse needs of the family, student, and classroom environment. A process for gathering information about student and family preferences and goals, implementation efficiency, and cost-effectiveness is described (e.g., by assessing social validity data because all stakeholders, as members of the intervention team, have multiple opportunities for input).
>
> **2.13 Selecting, Designing, and Implementing Assessment**
>
> The chapter identifies data sources that document the implementation integrity of evidence-based practices in the school, program, or classroom and provides checklists to examine the instructional environment. This information augments the FABI interview and A-B-C observation to determine the antecedent adjustments that are necessary to address an individual student's needs. This is the core of the Method 2 intervention. Assessing the environment is not just about what is happening to the student but also about the context and supports that are in place to ensure that a replacement behavior can be maintained in the environment. If you are in a school or program that implements an integrated, multi-tiered system of support (e.g., Ci3T, PBIS, or pyramid model), Tier 1 and Tier 2 data provide the necessary foundation of prevention that is needed to make sure the intervention is necessary, effective, and sustainable. The instructional environment is evaluated to ensure it is differentiated, varied, and designed to prompt student engagement. Social validity data from teachers and families address whether the process and intervention are feasible and acceptable.
>
> **2.14 Selecting, Designing, and Implementing Behavior-Change Intervention**
>
> Chapter 13 is a step-by-step description of the Method 2 intervention. It describes how to use the Function-Based Intervention Decision Model to identify antecedent adjustments that remove stimuli and the events that trigger challenging behavior and introduces supports that prompt engagement in the replacement behavior. The Functional Assessment and Behavior Intervention Plan: Planning Form is used to guide you through the FABI process of selecting, designing, and implementing an intervention using Method 2. The completed form is based on an illustration of an intervention for a second-grade student, providing a complete and detailed example of the process and A-R-E components for designing the intervention.
>
> **2.15 Minimizing Risk of Behavior-Change Interventions**
>
> As noted in all intervention illustration chapters, the use of punishment procedures is discouraged. Social validity checklists ensure that behavior-change strategies are supported and feasible in the natural environment and are acceptable to the teacher and family. Strategies minimize the side effects of extinction by using a replacement behavior based on the data gathered during the FABI. The intervention provides a high rate of reinforcement for the replacement behavior.
>
> **2.16 Describing Behavior-Change Interventions Before Implementation**
>
> Intervention procedures and strategies are developed and fully described as part of the team process so that team members understand and approve of the final intervention. Strategies are also described and thoroughly trained for those implementing the intervention (e.g., teacher).

student? The FABI team needs to review what is happening in the school as a whole as well as what is happening in the classroom settings. If the school leaders are implementing Ci3T or another tiered system of support, the first step is to review the schoolwide data regarding Tier 1 implementation to determine the extent to which Tier 1 efforts are being implemented as planned, as well as the social validity data to see what people think about the goals, procedures, and outcomes (Lane, Buckman, et al., 2020). Here, FABI teams might review various data, which include teacher self-reported information as well as direct observations, to answer the following questions:

- Are expectations clear in all school settings?
- Are adults using tickets paired with behavior-specific praise to recognize students meeting expectations?
- Are social skills lessons being taught schoolwide?
- Are these same skills prompted throughout instructional activities to afford students opportunities to practice using these skills with their peers?

The second question on antecedent conditions also addresses instruction. The FABI team will want to examine the instructional environment and ask the following questions (Lane, Menzies, et al., 2011):

- Are adults using low-intensity strategies to increase engagement and minimize disruption (e.g., behavior-specific praise, instructional choice)? (See Table 13.1 for a full listing.)
- Is instruction varied enough to include a range of techniques (e.g., cooperative learning, facilitated discussions, independent work, scaffolded instruction)?
- Is the curriculum differentiated in terms of context, process, and products? (See Table 13.2.)
- Did the teacher or other adult check for students' understanding before asking the students to get started?

For readers interested in learning more about the questions to consider regarding instructional variables, see Lane, Menzies, and colleagues (2011).

TABLE 13.1. Low-Intensity Strategies to Increase Engagement and Minimize Disruption

- Behavior-specific praise
- Precorrection
- Active supervision
- Increased opportunities to respond
- Instructional choice
- Instructional feedback
- High-probability requests

Note. See *www.ci3t.org/PL* for resources for teaching and using these strategies. From Lane, K. L., Menzies, H. M., Ennis, R. P., & Oakes, W. P. (2015). *Supporting behavior for school success: A step-by-step guide to key strategies.* Guilford Press. Reprinted by permission.

TABLE 13.2. Instructional Delivery: Consideration for Differentiation

Content	Process	Products
• Using varied materials • Using varied tools: graphic organizers, advanced organizers, note-taking structures • Concept-based teaching • Curriculum compacting • Mini-lessons	• Cooperative learning groups • Computer-assisted instruction • Learning centers	• Essays or written products • Simulations • Performances or demonstrations • Presentations

Note. From Lane, K. L., Menzies, H., Bruhn, A., & Crnobori, M. (2011). *Managing challenging behaviors in schools: Research-based strategies that work.* Guilford Press. Reprinted by permission.

In the classroom, the FABI team will use available Tier 1 data (e.g., treatment integrity and social validity) as well as direct observations to answer the following questions:

- Is there a positive climate or tone in the classroom?
- Is the physical environment of the classroom arranged to make it easy to follow directions as students move about the classroom and to enable teachers to supervise students?
- Is there a dedicated workspace for independent work and small-group and whole-class activities?
- Are the materials needed for instruction well organized and accessible?
- Is the classroom environment inviting and calming, without being overdecorated to the point of distraction?
- Are the routines and procedures needed for day-to-day happenings clear and followed consistently by students (e.g., requesting work when absent, requesting permission to use the restroom, asking for help) and by teachers (e.g., taking attendance, collecting and returning work)?

Next, the FABI team will want to learn more about previous attempts at implementing other interventions. If the team is working in a Ci3T school, they will be able to review (1) the school's Tier 2 and 3 tracking systems to see which of the strategies, practices, and programs listed in the secondary (Tier 2) and tertiary (Tier 3) intervention grids included in the Ci3T Implementation Plan have been implemented and (2) the data collected as part of these interventions. For example, the FABI team may learn that systematic screening data determined that the student might benefit from a check-in/check-out intervention and that the intervention was put in place for 4 weeks as planned, but the student rarely achieved the 80% goal.

For the next intervention, the teacher attempted another option: a self-monitoring intervention. Yet that too was not effective in increasing engagement and minimizing disruption. As such, the teacher looked through their Ci3T Implementation Manual's tertiary (Tier 3) intervention grids to select a more intensive intervention. Based on the schoolwide entry criteria, the teacher determined a FABI would be the best Tier 3 support to shift to at this time. Then the teacher reached out to the FABI team, confirmed their agreement, and got started.

As noted in this illustration, the data collected within integrated tiered systems like Ci3T can be invaluable in demonstrating that Tier 2 interventions have been ineffective and that more intensive Tier 3 interventions, like a FABI, are warranted. In the next section we discuss antecedent adjustments that hold particular importance when designing, implementing, and evaluating FABI.

Antecedent Adjustments

Reviewing Tier 1 efforts, the classroom context, and previous intervention efforts can be useful in identifying antecedent adjustments. The results of your FABI interviews and A-B-C observation data will also determine which antecedent adjustments are necessary for the student. Antecedent adjustments are shifts that can be made in the environment before challenging behaviors occur. Shifts may include adjusting instruction and task demands, as well as social and physiological adjustments. Our goal here is to identify adjustments that will set the stage for the replacement behavior to occur (see Table 13.3).

Answers to the previous questions on current classroom practices, along with the data gathered during the interviews and A-B-C observations, help direct the FABI team to consider a host of antecedent conditions that can be adjusted according to an individual student's needs. For example, if you have determined that the student's challenging behavior occurs most often when the teacher is giving instruction for an activity or when instructional activities get started, examining the instructional environment may identify specifically where an

TABLE 13.3. Examples of Antecedent Adjustments

Variables	Illustrations
Environment	• Expectations posted and visible in the setting • Room arranged to support varied instructional groupings (independent, partner, and group activities) • Room arranged for easy traffic flow • Materials well organized and accessible
Instruction and task demands	• Objectives (academic, behavioral, and social) written on the board and reviewed • Starter and closing activities provided • Understanding checked before beginning work • Reminder of what is expected (precorrection) • Instructional choices provided • Instructional feedback provided • Clear instructions given to support transitions
Social	• A learning partner or buddy provided • Small-group activities provided
Physiological	• Adequate sleep • Adequate food and drink • Adequate exercise

Note. From Lane, K. L., Menzies, H., Bruhn, A., & Crnobori, M. (2011). *Managing challenging behaviors in schools: Research-based strategies that work.* Guilford Press. Reprinted by permission.

antecedent adjustment should be made. In this example, you learn that after a teacher explains an activity, several students do not begin the task right away. Instead, they ask the teacher multiple follow-up questions, or whisper questions to their peers, indicating that the instructions are not clear. Some possible antecedent adjustments to make instructions clearer could include the following:

- The teacher holds up a red traffic-light symbol that says "STOP: It is time to listen."
- The three-step direction sequence is written on the whiteboard.
- The teacher verbally states the three instructions while gesturing to the whiteboard.
- The teacher quickly checks for understanding by asking, "Who can tell me the first thing we're going to do when we get started?" while pointing to step one on the board, and follows up with similar questions for the second and third steps.
- The teacher provides time for any additional questions.
- The teacher holds up a green traffic-light symbol that says "GO: It is time to work."
- If other students ask questions at this point (e.g., "Wait! What are we supposed to be doing?"), the teacher can say, "Please look at the board and double check with your learning partner."

Making instructions clearer may only partially eliminate the condition that set the occasion for the target behavior. In this case, additional adjustments may be needed to establish the conditions in which the target is more likely to occur. In our example, further examination of previous interventions or contexts in which the behavior seldom or never occurs indicates that the student works best with a learning partner or when there are choices embedded through parts of a lesson (e.g., starting or closing activities, independent work). Each of these strategies may enhance the antecedent conditions.

Keeping in mind the focus on antecedent adjustments, in the next section we describe the components of Method 2 and the intervention focus. Following this section, we provide an illustration adapted from Germer and colleagues (2011) at the elementary school level that models how antecedent adjustments are determined.

Method 2: Adjust the Environment

Description

As we discussed in Chapter 11, Method 2 is selected when (1) the student can perform the replacement behavior (Question 1: Answer = yes) and (2) antecedent conditions do not yet represent effective practices for this student (Question 2: Answer = no). More specifically, this method is used when the student is capable of performing the replacement behavior and the challenge is a performance ("won't do") deficit, not an acquisition or fluency ("can't do") deficit.

In Chapters 11 and 12, you learned the importance of this distinction. The answer to this first question determines whether it is necessary to explicitly teach the behavior that is not yet in the student's repertoire or to enhance the environment to address performance or fluency deficits (or both!). When the answer to the first question is that the student can perform the replacement behavior, the second question directs the focus to the environment or context to determine if there are adjustments that could be made in the classroom or other setting to enhance the learning environment for this student. In short, the intent here is to determine if adjustments in routines, procedures, or physical arrangements or the use of low-intensity supports will increase engagement by setting the stage for the replacement behavior to occur. For example, in a Ci3T classroom, enhancements might involve the following:

- Projecting a starter activity on the whiteboard—offering the student the opportunity to choose one of two journal prompts to respond to while the teacher takes attendance and greets students at the door.
- Referring to the schoolwide expectation matrix, reminding students that they will "be respectful, be responsible, and be safe" when rotating through centers during the 90 minutes of an uninterrupted English language arts instructional block.
- Checking for understanding before students transition to centers.
- Providing opportunities for the student to practice the replacement behavior.

Method 2 includes three components (see Form 13.1 at the end of this chapter for the FABI Planning sheet): antecedent adjustments, shifts in rates of reinforcement, and extinction procedures. More specifically:

1. Adjust antecedent variables so the conditions that set the occasion for the target behavior are eliminated and new conditions are established in which the replacement behavior is more likely to occur.
2. Provide appropriate positive reinforcement for the replacement behavior.
3. Withhold the consequence that previously reinforced the target behavior.

Each of the three components is important no matter which intervention method you use. However, Method 2 requires a more comprehensive look at the conditions that set the occasion for the target behavior to occur and generally encompasses many more antecedent strategies.

A-R-E components depicting specific tactics are developed by the team, which includes those implementing the intervention (i.e., the teacher, family members, or caregivers) and the student themself. Including a family member provides another opportunity to investigate how cultural considerations may suggest strategies to enhance the environment. An early childhood classroom example might include a recording of music or a family member speaking as an added calming strategy for a child. A family member may alert the team to a possible clash between an intervention strategy and a cultural value, such as respecting cooperative learning over individual achievement.

In the next section, we provide an illustration for Method 2 with a student at the elementary school level. This illustration is adapted from an article featured in a special issue of *Beyond Behavior* (Germer et al., 2011), a journal designed for practitioners learning how to design, implement, and evaluate the use of evidence-based practices such as FABIs (Common et al., 2020).

At the Elementary Level: David and Ms. Jones

Step 1: Identifying Students Who May Need a FABI

Germer and colleagues (2011) conducted a FABI with David, a 7-year-old second-grade student in a general education classroom in a school implementing Ci3T in a large urban school district. He was not receiving special education services, but the previous year his guardian had tried medication and counseling to address David's challenges with inattention and hyperactivity. They ultimately discontinued medication. He was placed in a class with a reduced class size of 10 students, an extended school day, and counseling services.

According to his teacher, Ms. Jones, David struggled with being engaged. He often left assigned instructional areas without permission to interact with his peer and used materials inappropriately. These off-task behaviors disrupted not only his learning, but the learning of others. Ms. Jones did a good job of implementing Tier 1 practices outlined in her school's Ci3T Implementation Manual. She had tried several informal strategies to support David in being more engaged (e.g., using proximity, talking with David, and having a "behavior conference" with him). Ms. Jones reviewed available Tier 2 and Tier 3 interventions in the Ci3T manual.

In reviewing the schoolwide entry criteria, she decided it would be best to move directly to a FABI. Her decision was based on the high number of ODRs David had earned in first grade and the fact that he scored in the high-risk range on the SSRS (Drummond, 1994) and on the externalizing dimension of the SSBD (Walker & Severson, 1992). These screening tools were completed for all students in the fall, winter, and spring. In addition, David was beginning to fall behind in reading according to the Dynamic Indicators of Basic Early Literacy Skills (DIBELS; Good & Kaminski, 2002), which showed he fell in the "some risk" category on oral reading fluency (score = 37) in the fall.

Ms. Jones wanted to intervene as efficiently and effectively as possible given that David was already not meeting grade-level expectations in three classes. The prereferral intervention team he was referred to had recommended an inflatable seat cushion. Yet Ms. Jones felt the FABI could be more useful, and she had been offered support from two liaisons from a local university who were learning this manualized FABI process.

David was often off task throughout the day. Morning instruction was particularly challenging for him. During the informal observations, David's peers were seated at desks facing the whiteboard where instruction took place. To minimize distractions, David's desk was facing a bookshelf on the left side of the classroom. Ms. Jones frequently stood in front of the whiteboard when leading instruction, which was outside of David's view. He could hear what she was saying, but often could not see her or get a full view of the content on the whiteboard.

As part of Tier 1 instruction, teachers used their DIBELS data to inform instruction and ensured that the PBIS plan was in place—with the expectations of "Be Respectful, Be Responsible, and Give Your Best" posted in the classroom and throughout the school. The school used the *Character Counts!* program as their social skills resource, teaching and modeling the skills throughout the day. As part of the schoolwide reinforcement procedures, teachers and staff provided PBIS tickets to students when they met academic, behavioral, and social skills expectations. These tickets were paired with behavior-specific praise so that students understood why they were receiving these reinforcers. In addition, David's teacher used a calendar to communicate with families and monitor daily behaviors. If students met expectations throughout the day, she put a sticker on the calendar, which was taken home daily and shared with their families. If expectations were not met, Ms. Jones provided a written comment for students to take home.

In reviewing Tier 1 fidelity data, it appeared that implementation was going well. Ci3T Teachers Self-Report and Ci3T Direct Observations (from both the teachers and outside observer perspectives) showed that scores in the fall ranged between 92.72% (SD =10.61; self-report) and 79.48% (SD =20.10; observation by an outside observer). In addition, the School-wide Evaluation Tool (SET; Sugai et al., 2001) data also indicated high levels of fidelity at 93.75%, well above the goal of 80%. Although Tier 1 practices were in place as planned, David appeared to need more than Tier 1 offered to support him in engaging in instruction and enjoying time with his peers.

Step 2: Conducting the Functional Assessment

When it came time to begin the functional assessment, the team began by first conducting functional assessment interviews with the teacher, Ms. Jones. One liaison interviewed her using the PFAS (Dunlap et al., 1993). Ms. Jones shared several concerns about David, but felt that his off-task behavior was the most serious one, as previously mentioned. She went on to share that David was very capable of doing well with the task assigned during independent seat time when the work was adjusted for each student's instructional level. However, he struggled to stay focused and was highly social with his peers, often falling out of his chair and making others laugh. She went on to explain that she was most concerned about David's off-task behavior because it interfered with him being engaged academically, which negatively impacted his academic performance. Ms. Jones and the liaisons (the FABI team) collaborated to operationally define David's target behavior to make sure that everyone agreed what it meant to be "off task" (see Form 13.1 at the end of this chapter for the planning sheet completed by the FABI team). They decided to focus on on-task behavior as the replacement behavior. This was a logical replacement behavior given their goal of increasing David's engagement so that he could access instruction and ultimately improve his academic performance and social standing in class.

At the end of the teacher interview, the liaison conducting the interview handed the teacher the SSiS-RS (Gresham & Elliott, 2008a). Ms. Jones completed the rating scale, while the liaisons began collecting A-B-C data and arranging the next functional assessment interviews.

The FABI team planned to connect with David's guardian. However, after multiple attempts to schedule an interview, the guardian was unable to attend and decided not to reschedule. However, David's guardian was willing to complete the parent version of the SSiS-RS, so Ms. Jones sent it home for him.

Next, both liaisons met with David to administer the Student-Assisted Functional Assessment Interview (Kern, Dunlap, et al., 1994). During the interview, David explained several times that he definitely did not "do those things," but his friends did. He said that he had some ideas as to why they did these things, such as falling out of their seats during independent work time. For example, he said that sometimes other students fell "on the floor on purpose . . . so people look at them . . . to get the teacher's attention." Later in the interview, David shared that he liked having help from his friends, classmates, and Ms. Jones. When asked about preferred reinforcers, he said he liked taking breaks and getting extra time to play with his friends.

After the interviews and both SSiS-RS forms were completed, the FABI team met to score the teacher- and guardian-completed SSiS-RS forms. They looked at the social skills strengths as well as areas of concern to determine if there were acquisition deficits (e.g., completing tasks without bothering or getting distracted by others, introducing himself to others, and remaining calm if teased) and performance deficits (e.g., cooperation in class, following directions, and respecting others' property). Ms. Jones rated David's social skills as below average, with a standard score of 73, whereas David's guardian reported average social skills with a score of 91. Both Ms. Jones and the guardian reported David as having higher-than-average behavior problems with standard scores of 130 and 149, respectively. Ms. Jones's academic rating was also below average (75; see Form 13.1 at the end of this chapter).

After the teacher interview was conducted, the liaisons began the A-B-C data collection. Observations took place in the classroom for 1 hour per day for 3 days. Each time David was off task, the liaison noted the antecedent (A) that happened before the behavior (B) and the consequences (C) that immediately followed. Later they all met to talk through and determine the function of each instance of the target behavior (i.e., was the function accessing or avoiding attention, tangibles or activities, and/or sensory experiences). At the end of the first day, the data collector numbered the instances of each target behaviors: 1.1, 1.2, 1.3, and so on. Then they numbered them at the end of the second day (2.1, 2.2, 2.3, etc.) and at the end of the third day (3.1, 3.2, 3.3, etc.). Gathering these data allowed them to look for patterns across and within days.

Key information from the interviews and SSiS-RS data were placed into the Function Matrix, along with the numbered A-B-C data (see Form 13.1 at the end of this chapter). Then, Ms. Jones and the liaisons met to review the collected data and organize it into the matrix. For example, they noticed the target behavior occurred quite often, with 97 instances resulting in David accessing attention and 84 instances in which David was able to avoid work-related tasks. In 42 instances of the target behavior, it served two functions: accessing attention and escaping an instructional task. From there, they collaborated to develop a hypothesis for the function of the target behavior. Based on their review of the information they collected, they drafted the following hypothesized function (see Form 13.1):

When given assignments or tasks to do, David engages in off-task behavior (e.g., leaving assigned area, doing things other than the assigned task, making inappropriate comments to others) to access attention from his teacher and peers and escape completing assigned tasks (positive reinforcement in the form of attention and negative reinforcement: activity).

After the team completed Step 2, they used this hypothesis to start designing the intervention components. They would need to address *both* functions of the target behavior—after they determined the main intervention method by using the Function-Based Intervention Decision Model in Step 4. However, to keep moving forward, they next started *Step 3: Collecting Baseline Data.*

Step 3: Collecting Baseline Data

In their conversation during the functional assessment interview, the FABI team (Ms. Jones and both liaisons) decided to collect and graph baseline performance of the replacement behavior, because they felt it would be more comfortable for David and his family to focus on the behavior they would like to see more of (on task), rather than the target behavior they wanted to be reduced or eliminated (off task). After reviewing the options for measuring the behavior (see Chapter 9), they selected a time-based recording procedure. Specifically, they decided to assess the duration of engagement in each session using the total-duration recording procedure because David's on-task behaviors varied in length (Cooper et al., 2020).

They decided to collect total-duration data for 20-minute sessions 2–4 days per week. There was one day (November 4) when they observed for only 10 minutes because the lesson was cut short for student vision and hearing testing. Before starting baseline data collection, the two liaisons defined the procedures and checked to make sure they were accurately measuring on-task behavior. Training involved practicing the operational definitions using the video clips provided in the SSBD recording system, then practicing in the classroom by observing David before formal data collection began. They kept practicing observing at the same time until they achieved three consecutive sessions of 90% agreement (see Chapter 10). They computed IOA by dividing the shorter duration (from one of the liaisons) by the longer duration of on-task behavior (from the other liaison, who was measuring behavior simultaneously in the exact same sessions) and then multiplying the result by 100% to compute the percentage of agreement (Gast & Hammond, 2010).

In brief, a liaison sat in a spot in the room where they could see the classroom activities, particularly making sure they could see David's instructional context clearly. When a session began, one of the liaisons doing the observation started their stopwatch as soon as David become engaged but waited 3 seconds before measuring the behavior. When David stopped being engaged, the observer waited 3 seconds and then pushed stop on the stopwatch—being careful *not* to reset the watch. This pattern was repeated through each session, resulting in a cumulative amount of on-task behavior for each observation. This amount was divided by the total time observed and multiplied by 100% to obtain percentage agreement. By waiting 3 seconds before a behavior was measured as an occurrence or nonoccurrence, they were able to accurately measure engagement. Next, the team graphed the baseline data (see Phase A1 in Figure 13.1).

Step 4: Designing the FABI

After generating the hypothesized functions at the end of Step 2 and reviewing the baseline data collection in Step 3, Ms. Jones and the liaisons met to select the appropriate intervention method and design the intervention.

First, they reviewed information gathered to this point to answer the two questions mentioned previously:

1. Can David perform the replacement behavior? (Question 1: Answer = yes.) Data indicated that David was capable of engaging in the assigned tasks during independent

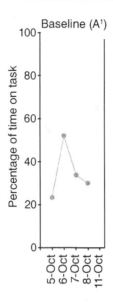

FIGURE 13.1. David's engagement. From Germer, K. A., Kaplan, L. M., Giroux, L. N., Markham, E. H., Ferris, G. J., Oakes, W. P., & Lane, K. L. (2011). A function-based intervention to increase a second-grade student's on-task behavior in a general education classroom. *Beyond Behavior, 20,* 19–30. Reprinted by permission of Sage Publications.

work time that had been crafted for him. The teacher and other adults had seen him engage in activities and finish assigned tasks. He had far more performance deficits ("won't do" problems) than acquisition deficits ("can't do" problems). Simply put, he could do the work.

2. Do antecedent conditions represent effective practices for David? (Question 2: Answer = no.) In reviewing information from the interviews and direct observations, it was clear there was room for improving routines, procedures, and practices in the classroom environment to facilitate David's success. For example, providing instructions that included checks for understanding and giving David specific tools to keep on track and communicate his needs were some of the specific adjustments discussed by the team.

More specifically, the team selected Method 2: Adjust the Environment given that David was capable of performing the replacement behavior and his challenges were more related to performance ("won't do") deficits, not acquisition or fluency ("can't do") deficits.

After selecting Method 2, the next step was to brainstorm the specific, appropriate A-R-E components linked to both maintaining functions: accessing attention and escaping tasks. The team recognized it was important for the intervention to be designed to address *both* maintaining functions, as it would be far less likely to be effective if it only addressed accessing attention or only addressed escaping tasks. An invention addressing both functions was needed.

The FABI team met to brainstorm ideas for possible A-R-E components (see Figure 13.2), each of which would be linked to a maintaining function. They decided on five antecedent adjustments (A1–A5), four shifts in reinforcement contingencies (R1–R4), and three extinction

Component	Intervention Procedures	Mon	Tue	Wed	Thu	Fri
Antecedent Adjustments						
A1	Was the student seated alongside a designated peer and facing the board?					
A2	Did the student use the stoplight system as instructed?					
A3	Was the self-monitoring form displayed on the student's desk during independent work time?					
A4	Did I review the picture schedule on the board prior to independent work time?					
A5	Did I check in with the student to ensure that they understood the assignment after general instructions were provided to the class?					
Reinforcement Contingencies						
R1	Did I provide behavior-specific praise when the student was on task?					
R2	Did I acknowledge the student when their stoplight was on red and assist them as soon as possible?					
R3	Did I check the student's work when they signaled "I'm finished!" with their stoplight and provide them with a brief break?					
R4	At the end of independent work time did I check the student's self-monitoring form and write one thing that they did well on their self-monitoring sheet?					
Extinction						
E1	Did I provide no praise or attention when the student was off task with the exception of one verbal or gestural redirect per minute?					
E2	Did I provide assistance without praise and provide the most minimal instruction possible when student's stoplight was on red?					
E3	When the student was off task, did I provide praise to other students who were on task?					
Rating Scale: 0 = Never; 1 = Sometimes; 2 = Always						

FIGURE 13.2. David's intervention procedures and Treatment Integrity Form. From Germer, K. A., Kaplan, L. M., Giroux, L. N., Markham, E. H., Ferris, G. J., Oakes, W. P., & Lane, K. L. (2011). A function-based intervention to increase a second-grade student's on-task behavior in a general education classroom. *Beyond Behavior, 20,* 19–30. Reprinted by permission of Sage Publications.

tactics (E1–E3). The team developed an intervention that set the stage for success. David was able to access attention from his peers and teachers, along with brief breaks contingent upon on-task behavior (see Form 13.1 at the end of this chapter). The reinforcement components relied on using the schoolwide reinforcer (PBIS tickets) paired with behavior-specific praise to acknowledge David for being engaged (i.e., provided attention for on-task behavior). It also provided David with a short break when he finished a task (to address the escape function). The extinction components were designed to ensure that David would *not* receive attention for being off task or *not* be allowed to escape tasks (see Janney et al., 2013).

After the intervention was designed, Ms. Jones and the two liaisons met to take a final look at the proposed intervention plan and complete a social validity measure (the Intervention Rating Profile–15 [IRP-15]; Martens & Witt, 1982) to make sure that she was comfortable with all of the components (more on this in Chapter 17). David completed the Children's Intervention Rating Profile (CIRP; Witt & Elliott, 1983) to get his views as well. Then the team walked through the implementation plans, with some brief verbal checks for understanding to make sure everyone was on the same page regarding implementation plans (e.g., completing each tactic, completing the treatment integrity form). The liaisons were in the classroom during the first day of the agreed-upon intervention to support implementation and provide feedback.

Step 5: Testing the Intervention

The FABI team used an A-B-A-B withdrawal design with a maintenance phase to see how well the intervention increased David's time on-task behavior (see Figure 13.3). On-task behavior

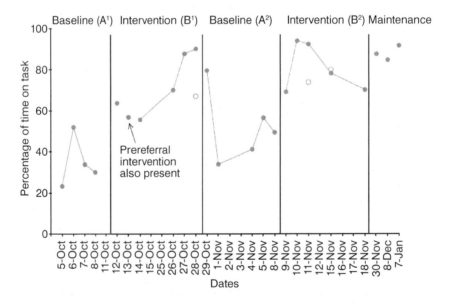

FIGURE 13.3. David's intervention outcomes (closed circles denote percentage of on-task behavior; open circles denote percentage of on-task behavior during generalization probes in the afternoon). From Germer, K. A., Kaplan, L. M., Giroux, L. N., Markham, E. H., Ferris, G. J., Oakes, W. P., & Lane, K. L. (2011). A function-based intervention to increase a second-grade student's on-task behavior in a general education classroom. *Beyond Behavior, 20,* 19–30. Reprinted by permission of Sage Publications.

data were collected as they were during the baseline phase. Ms. Jones assessed treatment integrity each day using the form shown in Figure 13.2 (see Chapter 16 for more information on treatment integrity). The liaisons also measured treatment integrity when they were in the room. Generalization data were collected in 20-minute sessions during afternoon instructional periods during both intervention phases to examine David's engagement in other classes (see Form 13.1 at the end of this chapter; see Chapter 18 for more information on generalization and maintenance).

Treatment integrity data suggested that the intervention was generally carried out as planned during both intervention phases. When the intervention was in place, David's on-task behavior was at a higher level than when the intervention was not in place. Social validity data collected postintervention suggested that the intervention was acceptable to both Ms. Jones and David.

Summary

In this chapter, we discussed the importance of understanding the current environment. We discussed how to determine what was taking place at Tier 1 for all students. We explored specific antecedent conditions that could be used, introduced, or adjusted to create positive, productive, safe, and enjoyable experiences. Then we shared an illustration about how Method 2 was used to support David, a second-grade student.

In Chapter 14, we focus on how to design, implement, and evaluate an intervention when the students are capable of performing the replacement behavior *and* antecedent conditions represent effective practices for the student.

FORM 13.1

Functional Assessment and Behavior Intervention Plan: Planning Form for David

Directions: Functional Assessment and Behavior Intervention Plan: Planning Form is a living document to support team efforts in the design, implementation, and evaluation of functional assessment-based interventions. This information will be transferred to the Behavior Intervention Plan (BIP) and/or school district standard forms after completing *Step 5: Testing the Intervention*.

Student Name: David **Student ID:** 138599

School: MLK Elementary School **Date of Birth:** 1/30/2015

Current Grade Level: **Special Education:** ☐ Yes ☑ No

Gender: male **Disability Eligibility:** NA

Parent(s): Bob and Tamekia **Parent(s) Contact Number:** 555-867-5309

Date of Assessment: 9/15/2022 **Classroom Teacher:** Ms. Jones

Persons Conducting the Assessment:

Role: ☑ Classroom Teacher ☐ SPED Teacher ☐ Teacher (Other) ☐ Teacher (Other)

☐ School Psychologist ☐ Counselor ☐ Behavior Specialist ☐ Intern

☐ University Student ☐ BCBA/ABA ☑ Other: Liaisons Kathryn & Eric

Identifying the Problem: Defining Target and Replacement Behaviors

Target Behavior (observable, measurable, repeatable):
Drafting:

Label:	Off-task behavior
Definition:	Off-task behavior referred to engaging in behaviors or making verbal comments unrelated to instructional tasks.
Examples:	Examples include leaving the assigned instructional area without permission from teachers or adult, making inappropriate comments to others not related to instruction, engaged in activities other than the assigned activities, using instructional materials in ways not related to assigned activities, taking more than 30 seconds to get started on assigned activities.
Non-examples:	Non-examples include remaining in the assigned instructional area, making comments to others appropriately related to instruction, attending to or engaged in the assigned tasks, using instructional materials as intended, and getting started on assigned activities within 30 seconds.

Operational Definition (include label, definition, examples, and non-examples): Off-task behavior referred to engaging in behaviors or making verbal comments unrelated to instructional tasks. Examples include leaving the assigned instructional area without permission from teachers or adult; making inappropriate comments to others not related to instruction, engaged in activities other than the assigned activities, using instructional materials in ways not related to assigned activities, taking more than 30 seconds to get started on assigned activities. Non-examples include remaining in the assigned instructional area, making comments to others appropriately related to instruction, attending to or engaged in the assigned tasks, using instructional materials as intended, and getting started on assigned activities within 30 seconds.

(continued)

Form adapted from Lane, K. L., Menzies, H., Bruhn, A., & Crnobori, M. (2011). *Managing challenging behaviors in schools: Research-bsed strategies that work*. Guilford Press. Reprinted by permission. Graph from Germer, K. A., Kaplan, L. M., Giroux, L. N., Markham, E. H., Ferris, G. J., Oakes, W. P., & Lane, K. L. (2011). A function-based intervention to increase a second-grade student's on-task behavior in a general education classroom. *Beyond Behavior, 20*, 19–30. Reprinted by permission of Sage Publications.

Functional Assessment and Behavior Intervention Plan: Planning Form for David *(page 2 of 8)*

Dimension of Behavior (e.g., frequency, rate, duration, latency): *duration per session*

Replacement Behavior (observable, measurable, repeatable):

Drafting:

Label:	*On-task behavior*
Definition:	*On-task behavior referred to engaging in behaviors or making verbal comments related to instructional tasks.*
Examples:	*remaining in the assigned instructional area, making comments to others appropriately related to instruction, attending to or engaged in the assigned tasks, using instructional materials as intended, and getting started on assigned activities within 30 seconds.*
Non-examples:	*leaving the assigned instructional area without permission from teachers or adult; making inappropriate comments to others not related to instruction, engaged in activities other than the assigned activities, using instructional materials in ways not related to assigned activities, taking more than 30 seconds to get started on assigned activities.*

Operational Definition (include label, definition, examples, and non-examples): *On-task behavior referred to engaging in behaviors or making verbal comments related to instructional tasks. Examples include remaining in the assigned instructional area, making comments to others appropriately related to instruction, attending to or engaged in the assigned tasks, using instructional materials as intended, and getting started on assigned activities within 30 seconds. Non-examples include leaving the assigned instructional area without permission from teachers or adult; making inappropriate comments to others not related to instruction, engaged in activities other than the assigned activities, using instructional materials in ways not related to assigned activities, taking more than 30 second to get started on assigned activities.*

Dimension of Behavior (e.g., frequency, rate, duration, latency): *Duration per session*

Rationale for Replacement Behavior (e.g., Why do you want to teach this behavior or increase the likelihood of this behavior occurring?): *We decided to focus on on-task behavior, because we wanted to make sure David was engaged constructively in the assigned tasks so that he could benefit from instruction academically and interact more easily with others in ways that protect his peers' learning opportunities and enhance his social standing by limiting off-task and disruptive behaviors.*

Functional Behavioral Assessment: Interviews and Direct Observations

Interviews Completed: ☑ YES ☐ NO

Interviewees: ☑ Teacher ☐ Parent ☑ Student

Rating Scales: *Social Skills Improvement System—Rating Scale (SSiS-RS)*

Hours of Total Direct Observation (A-B-C): *3 hours*

Setting(s) of Observations:

1) 2) 3)

(continued)

Functional Assessment and Behavior Intervention Plan: Planning Form for David *(page 3 of 8)*

Determining the Function of the Behavior: Using the Function Matrix

	Positive Reinforcement (Access Something)	**Negative Reinforcement (Avoid Something)**
Attention	Student interview: "They be falling on the floor on purpose . . . so people look at them and the teacher gets annoying [sic] . . . to get the teacher's attention." Direct observation A-B-C data: 97 incidences during morning work time: 1.1, 1.2, 1.3, 1.6, 1.8, 1.10, 1.15, 1.16, 1.17, 1.18, 1.20, 1.21, 1.22, 1.23, 1.24, 1.25, 1.26, 1.27, 1.30a, 1.31, 1.34a, 1.37, 1.38a, 1.40a, 1.41a, 1.42, 1.43, 1.46a, 1.48a, 1.50, 1.51, 1.53, 1.54a, 1.55, 1.56a, 1.58, 1.59a, 1.60, 1.61a, 1.62a, 1.63a, 1.64a, 1.66a, 1.67a, 1.68, 2.2a, 2.5a, 2.6a, 2.7, 2.9, 2.12, 2.13a, 2.14a, 2.15a, 2.16, 2.18, 2.19a, 2.20a, 2.21, 2.22, 2.23, 2.24, 2.25a, 2.27a, 2.28a, 2.29a, 2.30a, 2.32a, 2.33, 2.34, 2.35a, 2.37, 2.38a, 2.39, 2.41a, 2.42a, 2.43a, 2.44a, 3.1a, 3.3, 3.4a, 3.5a, 3.7, 3.8, 3.9, 3.10, 3.11a, 3.12, 3.15c, 3.18a, 3.19, 3.20, 3.23, 3.24a, 3.25, 3.26, 3.28	
Tangible/ Activity	Teacher interview: Motivated to finish morning math work but does not complete during assigned time; finishes by copying during review of work, likes to turn it in. Direct observation A-B-C data: three incidences during morning work time: 1.4b, 2.8, 3.6b	Teacher interview: "He never finishes an assignment." It typically happens during independent work, "when I'm not directing it . . . he takes advantage of the freedom." The second-grade-level work might be too hard, but he has average math and reading ability compared to class. There's "nothing that interests him enough." Sometimes he will start an activity OK, but often he's not interested enough to stop engaging in off-task behavior. Direct observation A-B-C data: 84 incidences during morning work time: 1.4b, 1.5, 1.7, 1.9, 1.11, 1.12, 1.13, 1.14, 1.19, 1.28, 1.29, 1.30a, 1.32, 1.33, 1.34a, 1.35, 1.36, 1.38a, 1.39, 1.40a, 1.41a, 1.44, 1.45, 1.46a, 1.47, 1.48a, 1.49, 1.52, 1.54a, 1.56a, 1.57, 1.59a, 1.61a, 1.62a, 1.63a, 1.64a, 1.65, 1.66a, 1.67a, 1.69, 2.1, 2.2a, 2.3, 2.4, 2.5a, 2.6a, 2.10, 2.11, 2.13a, 2.14a, 2.15a, 2.17, 2.19a, 2.20a, 2.25a, 2.26, 2.27a, 2.28a, 2.29a, 2.30a, 2.32a, 2.35a, 2.36, 2.38a, 2.40, 2.41a, 2.42a, 2.43a, 2.44a, 3.1a, 3.2, 3.4a, 3.5a, 3.6b, 3.11a, 3.13, 3.14, 3.16, 3.17, 3.18a, 3.21d, 3.22, 3.24a, 3.27

(continued)

Functional Assessment and Behavior Intervention Plan: Planning Form for David *(page 4 of 8)*

	Positive Reinforcement (Access Something)	**Negative Reinforcement (Avoid Something)**
Sensory	Teacher interview: "He's not an unreasonable child . . . he intends to behave, but can't. He's not physically able to sit still." Student interview: Tends to be off task "when I feel ticklish" Direct Observation A-B-C data: two incidences during morning work time: 3.15c, 3.21d	

Note.
a. Behaviors maintained by access to attention and avoidance of activities/tangibles.
b. Behaviors maintained by access to and escape from activities/tangibles.
c. Behaviors maintained by access to attention and sensory.
d. Behaviors maintained by access to sensory and escape from activities/tangibles.

Source: Umbreit, Ferro, Liaupsin, and Lane (2007).

Rating Scales Summary Statement:
Ms. Jones (teacher): below average in social skills (standard score of 73) and academic competence (75); above average for problem behaviors (130). Guardian: average social skills (91); problem behaviors were well above average (149).

Performance deficits:
- cooperation in class
- following directions
- respecting others' property

Acquisition deficits:
completing tasks without bothering to get help

Outcome of Function Matrix: Hypothesized Function:
When given assignments or tasks to do, David engages in off-task behavior (e.g., leaving assigned area, doing things other than the assigned task, making inappropriate comments to others) to access attention from his teacher and peers and escape completing assigned tasks (positive reinforcement in the form of attention and negative reinforcement: activity).

Determining the Behavior Objective

What behavior are you progress-monitoring with direct observation? *(select minimum of one)*

☑ Target Behavior   ☑ Replacement Behavior

Rationale for behavior to progress monitor *(e.g., replacement behavior focuses on the desired behavior—focusing on the positive)*:
Replacement behavior focuses the desired behavior—focusing on the positive

Check the measurement system used for your data collection: *(select minimum of one)*

☐ Frequency
☐ Rate
☑ Duration
☐ Latency
☐ Interresponse Time

☐ Whole-Interval Recording
☐ Partial-Interval Recording
☐ Momentary Time Sampling
☐ Other (discuss with coach):

(continued)

Functional Assessment and Behavior Intervention Plan: Planning Form for David

Baseline (e.g., number of observations, level, trend, stability to describe present levels of student performance and to inform the development of behavior objective)

Baseline Descriptive Statistics describing level and trend for baseline:

    Mean (*SD*):

    Slope (*SE YX*):

Baseline Statement: *During the baseline condition, David's on-task behavior was variable (range 23.24% to 52.00%, M = 34.79%). An initial low level of on-task behavior was followed by a sharp increase in on-task behavior during the second observation (David spent part of this time working 1:1 with Ms. Jones). Between the second and fourth observation probes, a downward trend was noted.*

Behavioral Objective: *Increase on-task behavior to a minimum mean of 70% for three consecutive observation sessions during the intervention phase.*

Function-Based Intervention Decision Model

CONDUCT FBA
↓
SELECT REPLACEMENT BEHAVIOR
↓
Can the Student Perform the Replacement Behavior?
- NO → **Do Antecedent Conditions Represent Best Practice?**
  - YES → **METHOD 1:** Teach the Replacement Behavior
  - NO → **METHOD 1 & 2:** Teach the Replacement Behavior and Adjust the Environment
- YES → **Do Antecedent Conditions Represent Best Practice?**
  - NO → **METHOD 2:** Adjust the Environment
  - YES → **METHOD 3:** Shift the Contingencies

(continued)

Functional Assessment and Behavior Intervention Plan: Planning Form for David *(page 6 of 8)*

Determining the Intervention Method

Method Selected *(select and complete one)*:

- ☐ Method 1: Teach the Replacement Behavior
- ☑ Method 2: Adjust the Environment
- ☐ Method 3: Shift the Contingencies
- ☐ Methods 1 and 2: Teach the Replacement Behavior and Adjust the Environment

Method	Description
Method 1: Teach the Replacement Behavior	• Adjust antecedent conditions so new behaviors are learned and aversive conditions avoided. • Provide appropriate reinforcement for the replacement behavior. • Withhold the consequence that previously reinforced the target behavior.
Method 2: Adjust the Environment	• Adjust antecedent variables so the conditions that set the occasion for the target behavior are eliminated and new conditions are established in which the replacement behavior is more likely to occur. • Provide appropriate positive reinforcement for replacement behavior. • Withhold the consequence that previously reinforced the target behavior.
Method 3: Shift the Contingencies	• Provide the consequence that previously reinforced the target behavior, but only for the replacement behavior. • Withhold the consequence when the target behavior occurs (extinction). • Adjust the antecedent conditions to make it more likely that the replacement behavior will occur.
Methods 1 and 2: Teach the Replacement Behavior and Adjust the Environment	• Adjust antecedent variables so (1) new behaviors are learned and aversive conditions avoided and (2) the conditions that set the occasion for the target behavior are eliminated and new conditions are established in which the replacement behavior is more likely to occur. • Provide appropriate positive reinforcement for replacement behavior. • Withhold the consequence that previously reinforced the target behavior.

(continued)

Functional Assessment and Behavior Intervention Plan: Planning Form for David

Method 2: Adjust the Environment

Adjust Antecedents	Adjust antecedent variables so the conditions that set the occasion for the target behavior are eliminated and new conditions are established in which the replacement behavior is more likely to occur.	A1 Student seated alongside designated peer and facing the board (access peer attention). A2 Stoplight system (access attention; brief escapes from tasks). A3 Self-monitoring form for use during independent work time (access attention, brief break from task). A4 Review picture schedule on the board prior to independent work time (access attention). A5 Individual check for understanding after general instructions were provided to class (access teacher attention).
Reinforcement Rates	Provide appropriate positive reinforcement for replacement behavior.	R1 Provide behavior-specific praise when David was on task (access attention). R2 Acknowledge David when his stoplight was on red and assist him as soon as possible (access attention, briefly escape too difficult task). R3 Check David's work when he signaled "I'm finished!" with his stoplight and provide him with a brief break (access attention; brief escapes from tasks). R4 Check David's self-monitoring form at the end of independent work time and write one thing that he did well on his self-monitoring form (access attention).
Extinguish Target Behavior	Withhold the consequence that previously reinforced the target behavior.	E1 Provide no praise or attention when David was off task with the exception of one verbal or gestural redirect per minute (remove attention for off-task behavior). E2 Provide assistance without praise and provide the most minimal instruction possible when his stoplight was on red (remove attention for off-task behavior). E3 Provide praise to other students who were on task when David was off task. (remove attention for off-task behavior).

(continued)

Functional Assessment and Behavior Intervention Plan: Planning Form for David

Data to be collected:

Student Outcome (What behavior(s) is (are) being measured? What measurement system? When/Where?)

Target Behavior: *Off task*

Replacement Behavior: *On-task—measured using total duration recording procedures; during independent work time.*

Treatment Integrity (e.g., checklist)

Treatment Integrity: *Component checklist; with each intervention component phrased as a question and assessed using a three-point Likert-type scale: 0 = never; 1 = sometimes; 2 = always*

Social Validity (e.g., IRP-15, CIRP)

Social Validity: *Adapted Version of the Intervention Rating Profile-15 (IRP-15)–Teacher; Children's Intervention Rating Profile (CIRP)*

Supporting Success (e.g., evaluating the intervention)

Fading and Generalization: *Generalization data (20-minute probes) to be collected during afternoon instructional periods during both intervention phases. Maintenance was assessed at the completion of the intervention.*

Program Review Date: *1 week after intervention was under way*

Personnel and Roles: *teacher and liaisons*

Emergency Procedures: *schoolwide crisis plan*

CHAPTER 14

Intervention Method 3
Shift the Contingencies

LEARNING OBJECTIVES

- Use the decision model to identify the need for Method 3 interventions that focus on the contingencies.
- Describe practical, research-based methods to shift the contingencies to reinforce the replacement behavior and extinguish the target behavior.
- Describe how A-R-E components are developed with Intervention Method 3.

As discussed in Chapter 11, Intervention Method 3: Shift the Contingencies, is used when the student can fluently perform the replacement behavior *and* the environment is setting the occasion for the replacement behavior. In this situation, the basic problem is that the target behavior has been very effectively reinforced; in contrast, the replacement behavior has been on extinction. A-R-E components shift the contingencies so that the reinforcement follows performance of the replacement behavior while the target behavior is put on extinction. An illustration of how this method is applied in a classroom setting completes the chapter.

Method 3: Shift the Contingencies

Description

In some cases, there is no need to explicitly teach the replacement behavior because it is already in the student's repertoire and the student can perform it fluently. See Chapter 12 for a discussion of acquisition and fluency deficits (i.e., "can't do") as compared to performance problems (i.e., "won't do"). There is also no need to make substantial adjustments to antecedents in the classroom because after a review of Tier 1 efforts, the classroom context, and the instructional environment, it is determined that antecedents are effective for supporting the replacement behavior. See Chapter 13 for examples of assessing and examining the environment. In such a situation, Method 3: Shift the Contingencies is the appropriate choice.

Research on Method 3 describes both positive and negative reinforcement functions (Janney et al., 2013; Lane, Weisenbach, et al., 2006), a variety of target and replacement behaviors (e.g., engagement, off task, and disruption), and implementation across grade levels (Nahgahgwon et al., 2010; Turton et al., 2011). For example, Turton and colleagues (2011) identified Method 3 for an eighth-grade student whose target behavior of disruption served two functions: positive reinforcement: attention and positive reinforcement: activity/tangible.

Method 3 includes the A-R-E components that were also identified in Chapters 12 and 13: antecedent adjustments, shifts in rates of reinforcement, and extinction, with a primary focus on the reinforcement contingencies. More specifically,

1. As needed, adjust the antecedent conditions so that the replacement behavior is more likely to occur.
2. Provide the consequence for the replacement behavior that previously reinforced the target behavior.
3. Withhold the consequence that previously reinforced the target behavior.

All three components are important, but Method 3's focus on reinforcement requires careful tracking of the reinforcers and contingency so it is *more* efficient, effective, and robust for the replacement behavior than it was for the target behavior (Horner & Day, 1991). Method 3 also requires an antecedent adjustment that encourages and supports the replacement behavior, such as an additional reminder about the expected behavior or a reminder to peers that they should ignore the student's target behavior.

The next section provides an illustration for Method 3 that has been adapted from an article featured in *Journal of Emotional and Behavioral Disorders* (Lane, Rogers, et al., 2007). The article included two participants: Aaron, who received a FABI using Method 2: Adjust the Environment, and Claire, who received a FABI focused on Method 3: Shift the Contingencies. In this chapter, we focus on Claire, a first-grade student.

At the Early Elementary Level: Claire

Step 1: Identifying Students Who May Need a FABI

Lane, Rogers, and colleagues (2007) conducted a FABI with Claire, a typically developing 7-year-old first-grade student in a general education classroom in a rural school district. Claire's teacher had 15 years of experience and a master's degree in educational administration. There were 21 children in Claire's class. Desks were arranged in rows or were clustered in sets of four so students could work together. There was also a carpeted area for whole-class instruction where students had assigned spots to sit.

The district implemented PBIS and was also part of Project PREVENT, a large research project that contributed to the development and refinement of Ci3T. In Project PREVENT, teachers used a combination of systematic screenings to identify students who were at risk for emotional and behavioral disorders (Lane, Weisenbach, et al., 2007). The screenings included (1) the SSBD (Walker & Severson, 1992), (2) the SRSS (Drummond, 1994), and (3) the *Teacher Rating Form* (TRF; Achenbach, 1991a, 1991b). Identified students in Project PREVENT benefited from Tier 1 universal prevention methods that were implemented schoolwide, but also received Tier 2 interventions designed to address their specific behaviors.

Claire had received Tier 2 behavioral intervention services throughout the previous school year because of high levels of internalizing behavior as measured by the SSBD and because she exceeded gender norms on the internalizing subscale of the elementary version of the SSRS (Gresham & Elliott, 1990). Although the Tier 2 intervention resulted in some decreases in internalizing behavior, Claire's behavioral team did not feel that the behavior change was substantial enough to be considered effective. In the classroom, Claire was described as extremely withdrawn and shy. She infrequently interacted with peers, participated in class discussion, or responded to teachers. Claire was selected for a tertiary intervention based on the following:

1. Teacher's observations of high levels of internalizing behavior as measured through systematic screening, and
2. Inadequate response to Tier 2 behavioral intervention.

Step 2: Conducting the Functional Assessment

Both Claire's teacher and her mother were interviewed using the PFAS (Dunlap et al., 1993). Claire was interviewed using the SAFAI (Kern, Dunlap, et al., 1994).

Claire's teacher was most concerned with Claire's nonparticipation because she felt it affected both academic and social skills. The teacher noted that Claire refrained from initiating during class; that is, she did not raise her hand to answer teacher-directed questions and did not ask questions or let the teacher know when she had a problem understanding any part of the lesson. She indicated that Claire appeared to be "afraid" to respond when other children could hear her response, such as during whole-class, teacher-directed instruction. Whole-class instruction occurred either while students sat in a row at their desks or in assigned seats on the carpet. The students were required to respond in the presence of the other children by raising their hands and waiting for the teacher to call on them.

During the parent interview, Claire's mother agreed that Claire did not want to respond verbally at home when they did academic-related tasks such as homework. Claire's interview indicated that she liked school but had the most trouble with responding during reading instruction. According to the interviewers, Claire stated that she got nervous and was afraid of giving the wrong answer. Claire's team felt that the three interviews supported the idea that Claire avoided responding when others were present such as during whole-class instruction and especially during whole-class reading instruction.

A-B-C observations were completed during whole-class instruction. One recommendation was to collect A-B-C data long enough and often enough to establish a clear pattern of A-B-Cs (e.g., 3 hours, with a minimum of eight instances of the target behavior; see Chapter 7 for addition considerations in how long to observe). In Claire's case, observations occurred over 3 days for 30 minutes per observation. The team agreed that the target behavior (B) was nonparticipation (see Form 14.1 at the end of this chapter to review the FABI team's planning sheet and behavioral definitions). This behavior can be difficult to observe because it seems like the absence of behavior. Remember that in Chapter 2 we identified behavior as an action that can be observed, measured, and repeated, and we made it clear that not doing something is *not* behavior. Therefore, it was important for the team to be very precise in their operational definition, writing it so that the examples included actions that could be observed. Claire's target behavior of nonparticipation was operationally defined as "any behavior that was nonresponsive to teacher- or peer-initiated interactions or to a lack of initiation of any social interaction. Examples included keeping her hand down when the teacher asked a question of the group or remaining quiet during whole-class choral responding. Non-examples included raising her hand and/or verbally responding to teacher-initiated questions" (Lane, Rogers, et al., 2007, p. 172).

The team also identified, operationally defined, and recorded Claire's replacement behavior during A-B-C observations (see Form 14.1 at the end of this chapter for the planning sheet, with the operational definition identified by the team). Claire's replacement behavior of participation was operationally defined as "responding to teacher- or peer-initiated interactions. Examples included raising her hand and/or verbally responding to teacher-led questions and volunteering information during an academic task. Non-examples included keeping her hand down and making no verbal utterances during an academic task" (Lane, Rogers, et al., 2007, p. 172).

Each time Claire failed to participate when an opportunity occurred, the team member doing the observations recorded the antecedent (A) that happened before the behavior (B) and the consequences (C) that immediately followed the behavior. At the end of each day of observation, the observer numbered the instances of the target behavior beginning with 1.1 for Day 1, 2.1 for Day 2, and 3.1 for Day 3. This numbering system describes patterns both across and within days.

Information from the interviews, the rating scale (SSRS), the screening scores (e.g., SSBD), and the numbered A-B-C data were placed into the Function Matrix (see Form 14.1 at the end of this chapter) for the team to review. During this process of determining the function, the team could also review all the interviews and the observation data collection forms available as needed.

The team identified antecedents (A) as teacher- or peer-initiated interactions that provided an opportunity for Claire to respond. Examples included the teacher instructing the class to respond together (choral responding), the teacher asking the class a question, a peer asking Claire a question, or the teacher asking Claire a question. They noticed that Claire often avoided responding when opportunities were presented. For example, in each observation, Claire's teacher gave her 12–15 (average 13.5) opportunities to respond by raising her hand. Of these, Claire responded by raising her hand 0–4 (average 2) times per observation. In every instance of the target behavior, Claire avoided attention from her teacher and peers. These observations led to the team drafting the following hypothesized function (see Form 14.1 at the end of this chapter): "During periods of whole-class instruction, Claire displayed nonparticipation to escape attention from teacher and peers" (Lane, Rogers, et al., 2007, p. 174). The team then moved forward with *Step 3: Collecting Baseline Data*.

Step 3: Collecting Baseline Data

Because the target and replacement behavior were mutually exclusive (meaning, if Claire was responding by raising her hand and asking questions, she could not be nonresponsive at the same time), the team decided to collect and graph baseline performance of only the replacement behavior. This allowed the team to focus on improving what Claire should be doing (i.e., participating) rather than on what she was not doing.

First, Claire's teacher was trained on the event-based method for recording data. Then Claire's teacher and the research assistant for the study collected frequency data simultaneously but independently. Their data were reviewed to ensure they were accurate and reliable, using a reliability criterion of at or above 90% for three consecutive sessions. See Chapter 10 for more information about reliability data collection during the baseline process and Chapter 16 for a more thorough description of IOA. The level of IOA was computed by taking the lower number of replacement behaviors reported and dividing it by the higher number of the replacement behaviors reported, and then multiplying the result by 100% to obtain the percentage of agreement (Gast & Hammond, 2010).

The baseline data consisted of practices currently in place in the classroom. Nine observations were conducted across 21 days for 30 minutes each session until the data were stable. Claire's teacher and the research assistant independently marked each time Claire participated, and graphed the data as shown in Figure 14.1.

Step 4: Designing the Intervention

In Step 4, Claire's behavioral team met to review the information gathered during the FABI process and answer the following two questions related to the decision model:

1. Can Claire perform the replacement behavior? (Questions 1: Answer = yes.)
   Observations indicated that Claire was able to participate in class. She could perform all the behaviors identified in the definition of participation (i.e., she could raise her hand and verbally respond to teacher- and peer-initiated interactions). Although academically Claire scored below the 25th percentile in Broad Reading on the Woodcock–Johnson III Tests of Achievement (WJ-III; Woodcock et al., 2001), the teacher was already providing the additional reading support and instruction that Claire needed. Therefore, her replacement behavior focused on participation rather than on reading. However, Claire needed additional positive reinforcement to increase participation.
2. Do antecedent conditions represent effective practices for Claire? (Question 2: Answer = yes.)

Observations and classroom assessment of social and instructional activities indicated that the antecedents represented effective practice. Claire's teacher had a system of classwide Tier 1 strategies in place, which included expectations and rules that were taught and posted, and individual and group reinforcement strategies (e.g., student groups received "paw points" for expected behavior). The class received additional "paw points" for specified levels of accumulation. She also had procedures for challenging behaviors (e.g., verbal warnings followed by

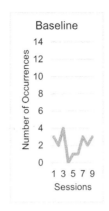

FIGURE 14.1. Claire's participation. From Lane, K. L., Rogers, L. A., Parks, R. J., Weisenbach, J. L., Mau, A. C., Merwin, M. T., & Bergman, W. A. (2007). Function-based interventions for students who are nonresponsive to primary and secondary prevention efforts: Illustrations at the elementary and middle school levels. *Journal of Emotional and Behavioral Disorders, 15*(3), 169–183. Reprinted by permission of Sage Publications.

recording the incidents). Finally, the teacher used a variety of instructional strategies, such as choral responding, small workgroups, and multiple opportunities for students to respond. Based on the responses to the two questions, the team selected Method 3: Shift the Contingencies.

The next activity for the team involved designing the intervention by identifying the A-R-E components that were specific to Claire's circumstance and addressed the maintaining function of escaping attention. As a Method 3 intervention, the team focused primarily on the reinforcement and extinction components (see Form 14.1 at the end of this chapter).

Claire's team identified only two antecedent adjustments that were relatively simple but still increased the likelihood the replacement behavior would occur. Claire and the teacher set a goal each morning that identified a specified number of times she would participate during a whole-class activity (A1). Once Claire met or exceeded the goal for 3 consecutive days the number of times Claire had to participate was increased (A2). Claire's first goal was to participate three times.

The FABI team identified five reinforcement (R) components. They considered how to allow Claire to escape attention, the consequence that previously reinforced nonparticipation. In this intervention, Claire was allowed to escape attention with a break from participation and attention once she met her daily goal (R1). The teacher counted each time Claire participated. When she met her daily goal, the teacher reported the goal completion to Claire and gave her the choice of not participating (R2). Although she was not required to participate (R3), Claire was required to remain in her seat with the rest of the students. Additionally, when Claire participated, she received positive reinforcement in the form of verbal praise and recognition (R4), as well as a daily certificate she took home to her family (R5) if she reached her goal.

Because the use of positive reinforcement seems counter to the information gleaned during the FBA, it is important to consider the rationale for its inclusion in the intervention.

The authors of this study explained their rationale for using positive reinforcement—attention in a couple of ways. First, Claire's teacher and mother identified praise as very reinforcing for Claire under nonacademic conditions. That meant there was a known history of the effectiveness of praise on Claire's behavior. Second, the authors speculated there was a difference in the way Claire perceived the nature of the attention she might receive during whole-class instruction. Specifically, prior to the intervention, Claire indicated that she avoided the kind of attention that would occur if she answered incorrectly. As attention during the intervention was focused on participation rather than on correct responses, Claire would be more open to answering. In fact, Claire responded well to the positive attention she received.

Another important consideration was that the teacher used positive reinforcement—giving extensive attention in her classroom. The plan for maintenance of the replacement behavior should always include opportunities for the student to contact consequences that occur naturally in the environment. In this case, programming positive reinforcement into Claire's intervention was designed to increase and maintain participation once the intervention was concluded. Maintenance is discussed more completely in Chapter 18.

Extinction of the target behavior was the third component of Claire's intervention. It included four strategies. Claire was no longer allowed to escape attention when she did not participate (E1). If she felt unsure of the answer, the teacher was to tell Claire that not participating was OK, and she would keep asking her questions (E2). The extinction strategy included asking Claire a direct question even if she had not raised her hand (E3) and repeating the question every few minutes until Claire responded (E4).

Once the intervention was designed, the research assistants trained Claire's teacher on data collection using event recording and the specific intervention procedures created for Claire. The training occurred during an initial 6-hour session and was followed with weekly follow-up meetings to ensure that Claire's teacher implemented the intervention correctly.

Social validity was also assessed using the IRP-15 (Martens & Witt, 1982) to assess the teacher's view of the acceptability, possible effectiveness, and usefulness of the intervention procedures. Claire was also asked to complete the CIRP (Witt & Elliott, 1983).

Step 5: Testing the FABI

The FABI team used a changing criterion design (i.e., changing the goal) with a maintenance phase to assess the effectiveness of the intervention compared to baseline (see Figure 14.2). If you recall, the antecedent strategies described that Claire and her teacher set a daily goal for the number of times she would participate and that the goal was increased once it had been met for 3 consecutive days. During the intervention phase, Claire's goal was increased from 3 to 4, then 5, and then 6 instances of participation during whole-class instruction. During intervention, participation was measured using event recording. The teacher marked each time Claire participated by raising her hand and/or answering a question.

Treatment integrity data were also collected for 30% of the sessions during each phase of the intervention using a checklist of intervention components. Claire's teacher completed a weekly self-rating, and the research assistants completed separate, independent rating of treatment integrity (see Figure 14.3 for the Treatment Integrity Checklist).

During all phases of intervention, Claire performed above baseline levels, gradually increasing her participation as the goals increased. The initial goal of three participations in a

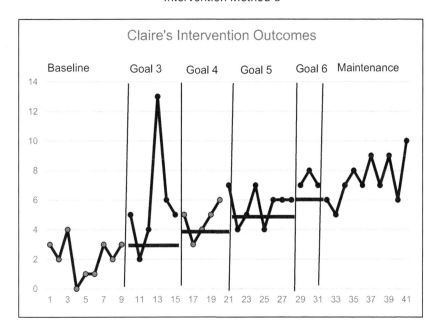

FIGURE 14.2. Claire's intervention outcomes. From Lane, K. L., Rogers, L. A., Parks, R. J., Weisenbach, J. L., Mau, A. C., Merwin, M. T., & Bergman, W. A. (2007). Function-based interventions for students who are nonresponsive to primary and secondary prevention efforts: Illustrations at the elementary and middle school levels. *Journal of Emotional and Behavioral Disorders, 15*(3), 169–183. Reprinted by permission of Sage Publications.

20-minute session was gradually increased to six participations per 20-minute session. When Claire reached six participations, the intervention was deemed successful, and the maintenance phase began. The intervention team set a goal based on average student participation in the classroom, set intermediate steps toward that goal, and planned for maintenance in their intervention development rather than continuing the intervention without an end date in mind. This point is important to remember as you develop interventions. Set a final goal based on classroom expectations (e.g., how often a student participates or responds, what percentage of intervals a student must be on task to be successful in the classroom). Identify intermediate objectives for reinforcement. For example, if the goal is for the student to be on task for 80% of intervals, but the student's baseline shows they are only on task for 30% of intervals, your initial objective might be 40% or 50% of intervals so you can be sure the student is able to access the reinforcement. Gradually increase the goal criterion until it reaches 80% (e.g., goal is 40% of intervals, then 60% of intervals, then 80% of intervals).

Withdraw the intervention when the behavior is stable at the level identified in the final goal (Common et al., 2015). Have a plan ready for maintenance and generalization and continue to monitor the behavior to ensure it remains at the goal level. During the maintenance phase, Claire's intervention was discontinued, but her participation remained at the highest level achieved during intervention. Treatment integrity data indicated the intervention was implemented as intended during all intervention phases. The intervention was rated acceptable (social validity rating) by both Claire and her teacher before the intervention began and after it was completed. Relevant ethical considerations are presented in Box 14.1.

Component	Intervention Procedure	Mon	Tue	Wed	Thu	Fri
Antecedent Adjustments						
A1	With Claire, set a goal each morning for the number of times she will participate in each whole-class activity.					
A2	If Claire has met or exceeded the goal for 3 consecutive days, increase the goal by one.					
Reinforcement Contingencies						
R1	Inform Claire that she has met her goal.					
R2	Offer Claire the choice to take a break from attention once she has met daily goal.					
R3	Claire remains in her seat during break but is not expected to participate.					
R4	Provide verbal praise and recognition upon goal completion.					
R5	Send a certificate for goal completion home to her family daily.					
Extinction						
E1	Prompt Claire to participate by asking her a direct question if she has not participated by raising her hand.					
E2	If Claire is unsure of the answer, tell her that is OK, and you will return to her in a minute.					
E3	Provide another opportunity for Claire to answer the question she was unsure of in a few minutes until Claire responds.					
E4	Ask Claire a question every few minutes if she has not participated.					
Rating Scale: 0 = never, 1 = sometimes, 2 = always						

FIGURE 14.3. Claire's intervention procedures and Treatment Integrity Checklist.

BOX 14.1. Ethical Considerations in Chapter 14: BACB Ethics Code for Behavior Analysts

2.08 Communicating About Services and 2.09: Involving Clients and Stakeholders

As we noted in Chapters 12 and 13, the FABI process includes procedures that rely on input and ongoing feedback from the family, student, and classroom staff as part of the intervention team and as respondents for functional assessment interviews. Data are collected in the form of social validity checks completed by classroom staff and family members. The teacher and family member are given an opportunity for additional feedback once the intervention plan is completed but before implementation.

2.14 Selecting, Designing, and Implementing Behavior-Change Intervention

Chapter 14 is a step-by-step description of Intervention Method 3: Shift the Contingencies. To answer the two questions related to the decision model, all assessments and data identified in Method 1: Teach the Replacement Behavior and in Method 2: Adjust the Antecedent are reviewed so you know that the environment represents effective practice, and the student can perform the replacement behavior. This intervention focuses on shifting the contingencies, so the target behavior no longer receives reinforcement, and reinforcement for the replacement behavior is at least comparable to the level at which the target behavior was previously reinforced. Antecedent adjustments are usually minor when this method is used. A-R-E components enable the development of intervention strategies that are effective and sustainable. The Functional Assessment and Behavior Intervention Plan: Planning Form again provides a useful guide through the process of selecting, designing, and implementing an intervention so that that nothing is omitted (e.g., training, intervention data collection, monitoring, social validity and reliability checks, and generalization and maintenance).

This chapter completes the description of the three methods presented in the Function-Based Intervention Decision Model.

2.15 Minimizing Risk of Behavior-Change Interventions

As noted in all intervention illustration chapters, the use of punishment procedures is discouraged when using the FABI process and the Function-Based Intervention Decision Model.

2.16 Describing Behavior-Change Interventions Before Implementation

Intervention procedures and strategies are developed and fully described as part of the team process so that team members understand and approve of the final intervention. Strategies are also described and everyone implementing the intervention is thoroughly trained.

Summary

In this chapter, we reviewed A-R-E procedures when Method 3: Shift the Contingencies is identified as the appropriate intervention method. We pointed out that the three intervention components (A-R-E) were all necessary even when environmental conditions already represented effective practice. We also described how antecedent conditions may be minimally shifted to increase the opportunity for the replacement behavior to occur. Within the illustration of how Method 3 was used to support Claire, we discussed how and why positive reinforcement might be used even when the function of the behavior is identified as negative reinforcement.

In our explanation of Method 3, we emphasized the need to include a family member and the student in the FABI process through interviews and social validity checks. In the illustration of Claire's intervention planning and implementation, we noted that both Claire and her mother were interviewed to provide valuable information that informed the intervention development. Claire was able to participate in selecting the goal she would meet for her replacement behavior. Her mother also continued to be informed about the outcome of the intervention through the daily certificate that Claire brought home.

In Chapter 15, we describe an intervention in which both Methods 1 and 2 are needed. The student is unable to perform the replacement behavior *and* the environment does not represent effective practice.

FORM 14.1

Functional Assessment and Behavior Intervention Plan: Planning Form for Claire

Directions: Functional Assessment and Behavior Intervention Plan: Planning Form is a living document to support team efforts in the design, implementation, and evaluation of functional assessment-based interventions. This information will be transferred to the Behavior Intervention Plan (BIP) and/or school district standard forms after completing *Step 5: Testing the Intervention*.

Student Name: Claire   **Student ID:** 145111
School: MLK   **Date of Birth:** 1/30/2015
Current Grade Level: 1   **Special Education:** ☐ Yes ☑ No
Gender: Female   **Disability Eligibility:** NA
Parent(s): Leslie and Ruth   **Parent(s) Contact Number:** 555-867-9914
Date of Assessment: 2/24/2022   **Classroom Teacher:** Ms. Reading
Persons Conducting the Assessment:

Role: ☑ Classroom Teacher   ☐ SPED Teacher   ☐ Teacher (Other)   ☐ Teacher (Other)
         ☐ School Psychologist ☐ Counselor   ☐ Behavior Specialist ☐ Intern
         ☐ University Student   ☐ BCBA/ABA   ☑ Other: Research Assistants

Identifying the Problem: Defining Target and Replacement Behaviors

Target Behavior (observable, measurable, repeatable):

Drafting:

Label:	Nonparticipation
Definition:	Nonparticipation behavior is any that was nonresponsive to teacher- or peer-initiated interactions, or to a lack of initiation of any social interaction.
Examples:	Keeping hands down when the teacher asked a question of the group or failing to verbalize during whole-class choral responding.
Non-examples:	Raising her hand and/or verbally responding to teacher-initiated questions.

Operational Definition (include label, definition, examples, and non-examples): Nonparticipation behavior is any that was nonresponsive to teacher- or peer-initiated interactions, or to a lack of initiation of any social interaction. Examples include keeping hands down when the teacher asked a question of the group or failing to verbalize during whole-class choral responding. Non-examples include raising her hand and/or verbally responding to teacher-initiated questions.

Dimension of Behavior (e.g., frequency, rate, duration, latency): Not measuring—only replacement behavior

(continued)

Adapted from Lane, K. L., Rogers, L. A., Parks, R. J., Weisenbach, J. L., Mau, A. C., Merwin, M. T., & Bergman, W. A. (2007). Function-based interventions for students who are nonresponsive to primary and secondary prevention efforts: Illustrations at the elementary and middle school levels. *Journal of Emotional and Behavioral Disorders, 15*(3), 169–183. Reprinted by permission. Lane, K. L., Menzies, H., Bruhn, A., & Crnobori, M. (2011). *Managing challenging behaviors in schools: Research-based strategies that work*. Guilford Press. Reprinted by permission.

Functional Assessment and Behavior Intervention Plan: Planning Form for Claire *(page 2 of 7)*

Replacement Behavior (observable, measurable, repeatable):

Drafting:

Label:	Participation
Definition:	Participation behavior is defined as responding to teacher- or peer-initiated interactions.
Examples:	Raising her hand and/or verbally responding to teacher-led questions and volunteering information during an academic task.
Non-examples:	Keeping hands down and making no verbal utterances during an academic task.

Operational Definition (include label, definition, examples, and non-examples): Participation behavior is defined as responding to teacher- or peer-initiated interactions. Examples include raising her hand and/or verbally responding to teacher-led questions and volunteering information during an academic task. Non-examples include keeping hands down and making no verbal utterances during an academic task.

Dimension of Behavior (e.g., frequency, rate, duration, latency): Frequency

Rationale for Replacement Behavior (e.g., Why do you want to teach this behavior or increase the likelihood of this behavior occurring?): We decided to focus on participation to ensure that Claire was engaged in learning activities and increased her responses so that correct responses could be reinforced, and errors could be corrected. Participation includes asking questions when she needs help, which should result in a better understanding of the instruction and, therefore, the academic task.

Functional Behavioral Assessment: Interviews and Direct Observations

Interviews Completed: ☑ YES ☐ NO

Interviewees: ☑ Teacher ☑ Parent ☑ Student

Rating Scales: SSRS; SSBD—elevated internalizing behaviors

Hours of Total Direct Observation (A-B-C): 1.5 hours (3 observations)

Setting(s) of Observations:

1) Whole-group instruction   2) Whole-group instruction   3) Whole-group instruction

(continued)

Functional Assessment and Behavior Intervention Plan: Planning Form for Claire

Determining the Function of the Behavior: Using the Function Matrix

	Positive Reinforcement (Access Something)	Negative Reinforcement (Avoid Something)
Attention		ABC data: 1.1, 1.2, 1.3, 1.4, 1.6, 1.7, 1.8, 1.9, 1.10, 1.11, 1.12, 1.14, 1.15, 2.1, 2.2, 2.3, 2.4, 2.5, 2.6, 2.7, 2.8, 2.9, 2.10, 2.11, 2.12, 3.1, 3.3, 3.4, 3.5, 3.6, 3.7, 3.8, 3.9, 3.10, 3.11, 3.12, 3.13 Teacher interview: Avoids raising her hand to answer or ask questions. Avoids asking for help. Appears to be afraid when other children can hear her response. Student interview: Gets nervous; afraid will answer incorrectly. Parent interview: Does not want to respond verbally to academic-related tasks at home. Rating Scale: SSRS: Exceeded gender norms on internalizing subscale. Screening Score: SSBD: High levels of internalizing behavior.
Tangible/ Activity		
Sensory		

Note: a. Behaviors maintained by avoidance and escape of attention. *Source:* Umbreit, Ferro, Liaupsin, and Lane (2007).

Rating Scales Summary Statement: Teacher: exceeded gender norms on internalizing subscale of the Social Skills Rating System (SSRS) and earned a broad reading score less than the 25th percentile on the Woodcock-Johnson III Test of achievement (Woodcock et al., 2001).

Outcome of Function Matrix: Hypothesized Function: During periods of whole-class instruction, Claire displayed nonparticipation to escape attention from teacher and peers.
Source: Observation and Interview

Determining the Behavior Objective

What behavior are you progress-monitoring with direct observation? *(select minimum of one)*

☑ Target Behavior   ☑ Replacement Behavior

Rationale for behavior to progress monitor *(e.g., replacement behavior focuses on the desired behavior—focusing on the positive)*: Replacement behavior focuses on the desired behavior—focuses on learning

Check the measurement system used for your data collection: *(select minimum of one)*

☑ Frequency ☐ Whole-Interval Recording
☐ Rate ☐ Partial-Interval Recording
☐ Duration ☐ Momentary Time Sampling
☐ Latency ☐ Other (discuss with coach):
☐ Interresponse Time

(continued)

Functional Assessment and Behavior Intervention Plan: Planning Form for Claire *(page 4 of 7)*

Baseline (e.g., number of observations, level, trend, stability to describe present levels of student performance and to inform the development of behavior objective) *Nine baseline observations of 30 minutes each over 21 days.*

Baseline Descriptive Statistics describing level and trend for baseline:

Mean (SD): *Averaged twice for each of the nine 30-minute observations; SD 1.47. (Ranged from a high of 4 on the third day of baseline to a low of 0 on the fourth day.)*

Slope (SE YX):

Baseline Statement: *Baseline data showed that Claire's participation varied (range 0 to 4 and a mean of 2) over the nine sessions. During the first three baseline sessions, Claire's participation averaged three times a session, dropping to zero during the fourth observation. The second three sessions averaged one participation, and the final three sessions showed a slight increase to an average of 2.6.*

Behavioral Objective: *Increase participation to three instances per session for three consecutive observation sessions during the intervention phase. Once that objective is met participation will continue to increase in increments of one until the team deems that the number of participations is sufficient for Claire to be successful in the classroom.*

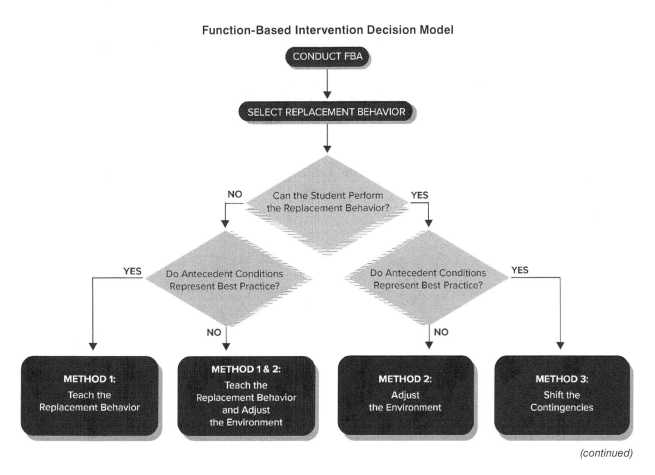

(continued)

Functional Assessment and Behavior Intervention Plan: Planning Form for Claire *(page 5 of 7)*

Determining the Intervention Method

Method Selected *(select and complete one)*:

☐ Method 1: Teach the Replacement Behavior

☐ Method 2: Adjust the Environment

☑ Method 3: Shift the Contingencies

☐ Methods 1 and 2: Teach the Replacement Behavior and Adjust the Environment

Note. After you have selected the appropriate method, draft an intervention for the selected intervention on page 6, 7, 8, **OR** 9. ***Do not draft ALL interventions.***

Method	Description
Method 1: Teach the Replacement Behavior	• Adjust antecedent conditions so new behaviors are learned and aversive conditions avoided. • Provide appropriate reinforcement for the replacement behavior. • Withhold the consequence that previously reinforced the target behavior.
Method 2: Adjust the Environment	• Adjust antecedent variables so the conditions that set the occasion for the target behavior are eliminated and new conditions are established in which the replacement behavior is more likely to occur. • Provide appropriate positive reinforcement for replacement behavior. • Withhold the consequence that previously reinforced the target behavior.
Method 3: Shift the Contingencies	• Provide the consequence that previously reinforced the target behavior, but only for the replacement behavior. • Withhold the consequence when the target behavior occurs (extinction). • Adjust the antecedent conditions to make it more likely that the replacement behavior will occur.
Methods 1 and 2: Teach the Replacement Behavior and Adjust the Environment	• Adjust antecedent variables so (1) new behaviors are learned and aversive conditions avoided and (2) the conditions that set the occasion for the target behavior are eliminated and new conditions are established in which the replacement behavior is more likely to occur. • Provide appropriate positive reinforcement for replacement behavior. • Withhold the consequence that previously reinforced the target behavior.

(continued)

Functional Assessment and Behavior Intervention Plan: Planning Form for Claire *(page 6 of 7)*

Method 3: Shift the Contingencies

Adjust Antecedents	Adjust the antecedent conditions to make it more likely that the replacement behavior will occur.	A1 With Claire, set a goal each morning for the number of times she will participate in a whole-class activity. A2 Increase the goal by one each time Claire meets or exceeds the goal.
Reinforcement Rates	Provide the consequence that previously reinforced the target behavior, but only for the replacement behavior.	R1 Inform Claire when she meets her goal. R2 Offer a choice to take a break from participation and attention once she has met her daily goal. R3 Claire remains in her seat during break but is not required to participate. R4 Provide verbal praise and recognition upon goal completion. R5 Send a certificate for goal completion home to her family daily.
Extinguish Target Behavior	Withhold the consequence that previously reinforced the target behavior.	E1 Prompt Claire to participate by asking her a direct question if she has not participated by raising her hand. E2 If Claire is unsure of the answer, tell her that is OK and you will return to her in a minute. E3 Provide another opportunity for Claire to answer the questions she was unsure of. E4 Prompt Claire every few minutes if she has not participated.

(continued)

Functional Assessment and Behavior Intervention Plan: Planning Form for Claire

Data to be collected:

Student Outcome (What behavior(s) is (are) being measured? What measurement system? When/Where?)

Target Behavior: *N.A.*

Replacement Behavior: *Participation measured using frequency during whole-group activities.*

Treatment Integrity (e.g., checklist)

Treatment Integrity: *Component checklist; with each intervention component assessed using a three-point, Likert-type scale: 0 = never; 1 = sometimes; 2 = always*

Social Validity (e.g., IRP-15, CIRP)

Social Validity: *Adapted Version of the Intervention Rating Profile–15 (IRP-15)—Teacher; Children's Intervention Rating Profile (CIRP)—Student*

Supporting Success (e.g., evaluating the intervention)

Fading and Generalization: *Data (20-minute probes) to be collected during afternoon instructional periods during all intervention phases. **Fading and maintenance probes** will be implemented when the FABI team agrees that Claire's participation is sufficient for her to be successful and that the intervention phase is complete. Gradually fade the amount of time Claire spends in break while maintaining the number of required participation events for Claire during the activity in which intervention was implemented. Begin maintenance probes once weekly. If participation remains sufficient, fade the maintenance probe to every 2 weeks. Continue to fade maintenance data collection gradually. Implement **generalization** probes daily during other instructional periods. As fading begins, continue to probe for generalization during other instructional periods once daily. If generalization occurs, gradually fade generalization probes to weekly, etc. If generalization does not occur, implement generalization strategies.*

Program Review Date: *1 week after intervention is under way and weekly until the intervention is completed.*

Personnel and Roles: *teacher and liaisons*

Emergency Procedures: *schoolwide crisis plan*

CHAPTER 15

Intervention Methods 1 and 2
Teach the Replacement Behavior and Adjust the Environment

LEARNING OBJECTIVES

- Explain why an intervention might require the application of both Method 1: Teach the Replacement Behavior and Method 2: Adjust the Environment to increase engagement and limit disruption.
- Describe how A-R-E components are developed for a combined Method 1 and Method 2 intervention.

At this point in the process, you have learned how to develop a FABI using Method 1: Teach the Replacement Behavior, Method 2: Adjust the Environment, and Method 3: Shift the Contingencies. All three intervention methods include A-R-E components. **A**ntecedent adjustments make the replacement behavior more likely to occur. **R**einforcement procedures increase the strength of the replacement behavior. **E**xtinction procedures make the target (challenging) behavior ineffective so that it no longer results in reinforcement.

Although the three intervention methods include A-R-E components, the primary differences between the different methods occur in the antecedent adjustments that are needed. If the student cannot perform the replacement behavior fluently, you will need to use Method 1. If the classroom environment is setting the occasion for the target behavior, rather than the replacement behavior, you will need to use Method 2. If the student can fluently perform the replacement behavior and the environmental conditions are arranged to occasion the replacement behavior, you will need to use Method 3, in which the replacement behavior is merely prompted.

However, looking back at the Function-Based Intervention Decision Model (see Chapter 11) leaves one more possibility that we need to address. What if the student needs to learn or strengthen their ability to perform the replacement behavior *and* also needs the antecedent conditions to be adjusted? In this case, the answer to both key questions is no. The student cannot perform the replacement behavior fluently, and the environmental conditions are setting the occasion for the target behavior, rather than for the replacement behavior. This exact situation is fairly common, especially in natural settings.

In this case, the team needs to use a combination of Methods 1 and 2. Using one method but not the other may provide some benefit, but not nearly as much as applying both. Fortunately, combining Methods 1 and 2 is straightforward and not particularly difficult. You will need two types of antecedent adjustments instead of just one—one type for learning or strengthening new behavior (Method 1) and another type for the environmental adjustments that are needed (Method 2). The reinforcement and extinction procedures remain the same for both methods, so the only difference when combining the methods is the need to address both types of antecedent adjustments.

You already know how to design a FABI using Method 1 (Chapter 12) and how to design a FABI using Method 2 (Chapter 13). This chapter focuses on how to combine and integrate these methods when both are needed as part of the same behavior intervention plan (BIP). Ethical considerations for combining Methods 1 and 2 are the same as those presented in Chapters 12 and 13. Review Boxes 12.1 and 13.1 for more information.

In the next section, we illustrate how to combine both intervention methods when the answers to both key questions is no, the participant cannot fluently perform the replacement behavior, and the environment is setting the occasion for the target behavior, not the replacement behavior. This example is adapted from Turton and colleagues (2007). A FABI was developed for Saida, an adolescent girl with EBD. She was of Black African descent and a citizen of Bermuda, an Atlantic Island territory of the United Kingdom. We do not explain how to determine the answers to questions constituting the Function-Based Intervention Decision Model because this information has been provided in earlier chapters.

Saida and Her Social Studies Teacher

Step 1: Identifying Students Who May Need a FABI

Saida was a 16-year-old girl who attended an alternative high school for students with significant, persistent behavior problems. Even though Bermuda used a noncategorical approach, Saida had received services for her behavior problems continuously since the age of 5, when she was first evaluated because of her short attention span, impulsiveness, and aggressive and "acting-out" behaviors. Early evaluations described Saida as a student who participated only when prodded, reacted negatively to teacher questions unless she was doing what she preferred, made little effort to relate to others (either her teachers or peers), and claimed that her behavior was not a problem. Before being placed in the alternative school, Saida had attended typical schools, but with increasingly less and less success. She had been attending the alternative school for 6 months when the FABI was initiated.

Saida's school did not have a three-tiered system of support (e.g., Ci3T) in place, nor any screening measures to help identify the need for a FABI. All students were served in the regular school programs, with additional support provided on an individual basis. Learning support specialists employed by the Ministry of Education responded to requests for assistance from school administrators.

Assessments were conducted when Saida transferred to the alternative school. The results indicated that she was she was at least 3 years below her age and grade levels (i.e., as a 10th grader, she was functioning at the seventh-grade level). Saida lived with her mother and, at 6 feet, was tall for a woman of any age. She had a large frame and was often teased about it. She had developed a reputation for fighting, threatening peers, and hitting or grabbing both peers and members of the staff. Saida's school day included classes in language arts, math, science, and social studies, in addition to a homeroom period every day. The FABI was conducted by the learning support specialist at the request of the school's principal and teaching staff. See Form 15.1 (at the end of the chapter) for an overview of Saida's FABI.

Step 2: Conducting the Functional Assessment

The FBA included interviews with all of Saida's teachers. Each of them was interviewed individually using the PFAS (Dunlap et al., 1993) that was described in previous chapters. They reported that she used profanity in all classes, but it was most pronounced in social studies. All of her teachers reported that Saida sometimes completed her assignments. They also reported that occurrences of physical aggression were always preceded by profanity, which then escalated to threats, and then hitting or grabbing.

The staff noted that Saida was teased a lot and did not have any real friends in the school. She swore and sometimes also made threats of physical harm when she thought people were talking about her. The teachers reported that this pattern occurred during class, immediately when she entered class, or just before transitioning to another class. The staff suspected that Saida was trying to avoid having to do her work and/or having to interact with her peers. When she had previously been sent to a break room, she often sat calmly and completed the assigned task. One teacher noted that Saida often claimed the work she was given was too easy. However, even when Saida appeared to be on task, she was often sitting quietly but not doing any of her work. In contrast, she never displayed behavioral problems when she used a computer.

Saida was interviewed using the SAFAI (Kern, Dunlap, et al., 1994), described in the previous chapters, and was quite happy to participate. She claimed she often missed school because her mother would not give her a ride. She admitted that, on some days, she did not want to be at school at all. She said that those were the days when she did not do schoolwork because the staff and her peers "annoyed" her. Saida asserted that the work she was given was too easy. However, she loved playing computer games and reading in school. Among her classes, she liked math and science the most, and language arts and social studies the least. Saida said that she did not receive enough support in those classes and that she used profanity when the staff "bugged" her. As a group, the teachers, principal, and the learning support specialist identified "profanity" as the first target behavior to address in a FABI.

The target behavior was the use of profanity in response to teacher directives. Profanity included any words considered to be profane by the teachers. Non-examples included working quietly, completing assignments, raising a hand to gain attention, using polite language, and nodding or saying yes or no to teacher directives.

The replacement behavior was responding to teacher directives appropriately by nodding or saying yes or no; working quietly; working on assignments; and raising a hand to gain attention. Non-examples included using profanity in response to teacher directives.

Direct observational (A-B-C) data (Bijou et al., 1968) were collected in her social studies classroom during three 30-minute periods of instruction and assigned activity. An observer recorded the antecedents and consequences each time profanity occurred. In total, there were 19 occurrences of profanity in response to a teacher directive. They occurred when Saida was (1) redirected to her work, (2) asked to show how she had done her work, (3) questioned about the truthfulness of something she had said, or (4) asked to come into class. The consequences included attention from the teacher in the form of reprimands and being sent out of class. If Saida was not sent out immediately, she typically continued with profanity until she was sent out. The staff suspected that Saida used profanity to be removed, so they redirected her initially but removed her when her behavior escalated.

Interviews and direct observational data were analyzed using the Function Matrix (see Form 15.1 at the end of the chapter). These data indicated that Saida used profanity to gain attention from the staff through reprimands, through attempts to calm her down once she was removed from class, and through one-to-one time with her. She also used profanity to be removed from class and to avoid doing her work in class. Therefore, the use of profanity served two functions: positive reinforcement: attention and negative reinforcement: activities.

Step 3: Collecting Baseline Data

Baseline data were collected in the social studies class on 6 consecutive school days. Each session lasted 20 minutes, and event (frequency) data were recorded. Following each teacher directive (average = 10.25 directives per session; range = 9–12), an observer recorded whether Saida responded appropriately (the replacement behavior) or with profanity (the target behavior). A second observer independently recorded the same data during two of the baseline sessions to establish IOA. Events scored identically were considered agreements. IOA was calculated by dividing the number of agreements by the total number of events recorded and multiplying by 100%. The result was that IOA averaged 94% (range = 86–100%).

Step 4: Designing the FABI

The intervention for Saida was developed using the Function-Based Intervention Decision Model (Umbreit et al., 2007; see Form 15.1 at the end of the chapter). In Saida's case, the answer to both questions was no: Saida could not fluently perform all aspects of the target behavior, and the classroom conditions were not setting the occasion for the replacement behavior to occur. Therefore, both Methods 1 and 2 were needed. The resulting intervention is presented in Form 15.1 (at the end of the chapter). Please note that there are two groups of antecedent adjustments—one for Method 1 and a group of different adjustments for Method 2. The reinforcement and extinction procedures are the same as they would be if either Method 1 *or* Method 2 was used alone.

For Saida, the Method 1 antecedent adjustment involved starting each school day with social skills instruction and practice in using her new skills. This instruction involved modeling, role play, and feedback to provide opportunities for her to improve her fluency in responding appropriately.

Several Method 2 antecedent adjustments were needed. First, the staff identified those days on which Saida rode the bus to school. She began those mornings planning her school day with the homeroom teacher. Second, she was reminded to be on time *and* to use her new skills. Third, Saida was shown how to monitor her own behavior. Fourth, teachers gave Saida more challenging work during class, more homework, and additional task-related assistance. Finally, the teacher modified the class assignments so Saida could participate in whole-class instruction.

The reinforcement and extinction procedures were addressed as well. Profanity enabled Saida to gain attention and escape from certain nonpreferred activities (a dual function). To address the attention function, any appropriate responding by Saida resulted in praise and other forms of attention (e.g., a thumbs-up, a call home). To address the escape function, Saida was given access to a preferred activity whenever she finished her work. In contrast, instances of profanity resulted in very brief redirection (to create attention extinction) and maintenance of the existing task (to create escape extinction).

Step 5: Testing the Intervention

An A-B-A-B (reversal) design was used to test the effects of the intervention in the social studies class. Event data were collected for 20 minutes each day. The response to each teacher directive was either profanity or appropriate responding. To assess reliability, a second observer independently recorded these same data during one baseline and one intervention condition to establish interobserver agreement (IOA).

Events scored identically were considered agreements. IOA data were collected once during each baseline condition and during 6 of 14 intervention sessions (four times during the first intervention condition and twice during the second intervention). IOA averaged 98% (range = 89–100%). During the intervention testing, the number of teacher directives per session averaged 9.8 (range = 6–25).

Treatment integrity and social validity data were also collected on the same days that were used to assess IOA. For treatment integrity, a 10-point checklist that addressed implementation of the components of the intervention was used. Across sessions, treatment integrity averaged 98% (range = 90–100%).

Social validity was assessed before and after the intervention by the social studies teacher and teacher assistant. Each completed the Behavior Intervention Rating Profile (BIRP; Martens & Witt, 1982). This instrument includes six questions that address whether the intervention targets an important goal, is warranted and reasonable within the classroom, and is likely to improve behavior. Each item is rated on a 6-point Likert-type scale (1 = *Strongly disagree*; 6 = *Strongly agree*). Scores range from 6 to 36, with higher scores indicating higher social validity.

Saida and one of her classmates also provided input on social validity, but did so only after the intervention. These data were collected using the CIRP (Witt & Elliott, 1983), an instrument that includes seven items that address whether the intervention was fair, helpful, acceptable, appropriate with other students, and likely to cause problems with the target student's friends. Each item is rated on a 6-point Likert-type scale (1 = *Strongly disagree*; 6 = *Strongly agree*), with some items reverse coded. Scores range from 7 to 42, with higher scores indicating higher social validity.

Figure 15.1 presents the intervention results. Appropriate responding averaged 28% (range = 16–40%) of opportunities during the initial baseline condition and rose to an average of 84% (range = 56–100%) during the first intervention condition. During the return-to-baseline

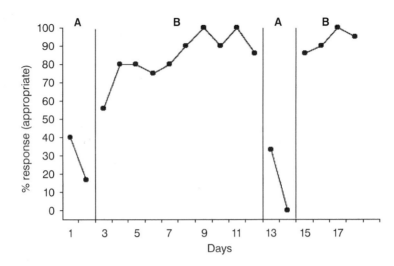

FIGURE 15.1. Results of intervention implementation in ongoing social studies classes. From Turton, A. M., Umbreit, J., Liaupsin, C. J., & Bartley, J. (2007). Function-based intervention for an adolescent with emotional and behavioral disorders in Bermuda: Moving across culture. *Behavioral Disorders, 33,* 23–32. Reprinted by permission of Sage Publications.

condition, appropriate responding fell to an average of 20% (range= 0–40%), but rose again to an average of 91% (range = 82–100%) during the second intervention condition. No baseline data points overlapped with any intervention data points.

The teacher's scores on the social validity rating were 34 (out of 36) both preintervention and postintervention. The teacher assistant's scores were 28 (preintervention) and 34 (postintervention). Saida rated the intervention 42 (out of 42). Her classmate's rating gave the intervention a score of 40.

Summary

This chapter has presented the combined use of Methods 1 and 2: Teach the Replacement Behavior and Adjust the Environment. This particular combination of intervention methods is needed when students cannot perform the replacement behavior fluently enough to be reinforced naturally *and* the environmental conditions are not setting the occasion for the replacement behavior to occur. The need for two different types of antecedent conditions makes this situation unique. Fortunately, the reinforcement and extinction procedures are the same for both methods.

Next, Chapters 16, 17, and 18 address the key concepts and associated activities needed to draw valid inferences regarding intervention outcomes. For each concept, we explain what it is, why it is important, and how to collect and use these data to design implementation efforts. Read on to learn more about the hows and whys of treatment integrity—measuring the extent to which the A-R-E intervention components are implemented as designed.

FORM 15.1

Functional Assessment and Behavior Intervention Plan: Planning Form for Saida

Directions: Functional Assessment and Behavior Intervention Plan: Planning Form is a living document to support team efforts in the design, implementation, and evaluation of functional assessment-based interventions. This information will be transferred to the Behavior Intervention Plan (BIP) and/or school district standard forms after completing *Step 5: Testing the Intervention*.

Student Name: Saida
School: Alternative School
Current Grade Level: 10
Gender: Female
Parent(s): Florence
Date of Assessment: 10/12/2006

Student ID: 123456
Date of Birth: 5/23/1990
Special Education: ☑ Yes ☐ No
Disability Eligibility: Behavior Disorders
Parent(s) Contact Number: 555-123-4567
Classroom Teacher: Ms. Jones

Persons Conducting the Assessment:

Role: ☐ Classroom Teacher ☑ SPED Teacher ☐ Teacher (Other) ☐ Teacher (Other)
☐ School Psychologist ☐ Counselor ☑ Behavior Specialist ☐ Intern
☐ University Student ☐ BCBA/ABA ☐ Other: University Consultants

Identifying the Problem: Defining Target and Replacement Behaviors

Target Behavior (observable, measurable, repeatable):

Drafting:

Label:	Profanity
Definition:	Profane responses to teacher directives
Examples:	Any words considered to be profane.
Non-examples:	Responding to teacher directives by nodding or saying yes or no.

Operational Definition (include label, definition, examples, and non-examples): The behavior was profanity in response to teacher directives. Profanity includes any words considered to be profane by teachers. Non-examples include working quietly, completing assignments, raising a hand to gain attention, using polite language, and nodding or saying yes or no to teacher directives.

Dimension of Behavior (e.g., frequency, rate, duration, latency): Frequency, as part of the calculation of percentage of opportunity

(continued)

Adapted from Turton, A. M., Umbreit, J., Liaupsin, C. J., & Bartley, J. (2007). Function-based intervention for an adolescent with emotional and behavioral disorders in Bermuda: Moving across culture. *Behavioral Disorders, 33,* 23–32. Reprinted by permission. Lane, K. L., Menzies, H., Bruhn, A., & Crnobori, M. (2011). *Managing challenging behaviors in schools: Research-based strategies that work.* Guilford Press. Reprinted by permission.

Functional Assessment and Behavior Intervention Plan: Planning Form for Saida *(page 2 of 7)*

Replacement Behavior (observable, measurable, repeatable):

Appropriate behavior, indicated by nodding or saying yes or no to teacher directives

Label:	Appropriate behavior
Definition:	Nodding or saying yes or no to teacher directives
Examples:	Saying yes or no to teacher directives; working quietly; working on assignments; raising a hand to gain attention
Non-examples:	Profanity

Operational Definition (include label, definition, examples, and non-examples): *Appropriate responding; nodding or saying yes or no to teacher directives; working quietly; working on assignments; raising a hand to gain attention Non-examples include using profanity in response to teacher directives.*

Dimension of Behavior (e.g., frequency, rate, duration, latency): *Frequency, as part of the calculation of percentage of opportunity*

Rationale for Replacement Behavior (e.g., Why do you want to teach this behavior or increase the likelihood of this behavior occurring?): *Current social behavior is interfering with school attendance and success. The FABI should teach new skills and better match her academic levels with the instruction being provided, leading to both social and academic success.*

Functional Behavioral Assessment: Interviews and Direct Observations

Interviews Completed: ☑ YES ☐ NO

Interviewees: ☑ Teacher ☐ Parent ☑ Student

Rating Scales: *No Standardized Rating Scales Used*

Hours of Total Direct Observation (A-B-C): *1.5 hours*

Setting(s) of Observations:

1) *Social Studies classroom* 2) 3)

(continued)

Functional Assessment and Behavior Intervention Plan: Planning Form for Saida *(page 3 of 7)*

Determining the Function of the Behavior: Using the Function Matrix

	Positive Reinforcement (Access Something)	**Negative Reinforcement (Avoid Something)**
Attention	ABC data: 1.1, 1.3, 1.4, 1.6, 2.1, 2.2, 2.6, 3.1, 3.2 Student Interview: Saida happy to be interviewed	
Tangible/Activity		ABC data: 1.2, 1.5, 2.3, 2.4, 2.5, 3.2, 3.3, 3.5, 3.6, 3.7
Sensory		

Source: Umbreit, Ferro, Liaupsin, and Lane (2007).

Rating Scales Summary Statement: There were no rating scales administered.

Outcome of Function Matrix: Hypothesized Function: Saida uses profanity to gain attention from the staff through reprimands, attempts to calm her down once removed from class, and 1:1 time with her. She also uses profanity to be removed from class and to avoid doing her work in class.

Determining the Behavior Objective

What behavior are you progress-monitoring with direct observation? *(select minimum of one)*

☑ Target Behavior ☑ Replacement Behavior

Rationale for behavior to progress monitor *(e.g., replacement behavior focuses on the desired behavior—focusing on the positive)*: We need to monitor both the target and the replacement behavior to calculate the percentage of opportunities that Saida appropriately responds to teacher directives.

Check the measurement system used for your data collection: *(select minimum of one)*

- ☑ Frequency
- ☐ Rate
- ☐ Duration
- ☐ Latency
- ☐ Interresponse Time
- ☐ Whole-Interval Recording
- ☐ Partial-Interval Recording
- ☐ Momentary Time Sampling
- ☐ Other (discuss with coach):

(continued)

Functional Assessment and Behavior Intervention Plan: Planning Form for Saida *(page 4 of 7)*

Baseline (e.g., number of observations, level, trend, stability to describe present levels of student performance and to inform the development of behavior objective) *Frequency data were recorded. In particular, Saida's response to each teacher directive was recorded and classified as "appropriate responding" or as "profanity." These data were then used to calculate a percentage of opportunity, that is, the percentage of responses by Saida that were appropriate rather than profane.*

Baseline Descriptive Statistics describing level and trend for baseline:

  Mean (*SD*):

  Slope (*SE YX*):

Baseline Statement: *Appropriate responding occurred in 20–30% of opportunities.*

Behavioral Objective: *Increase appropriate responding to 85% of opportunities for 10 consecutive days.*

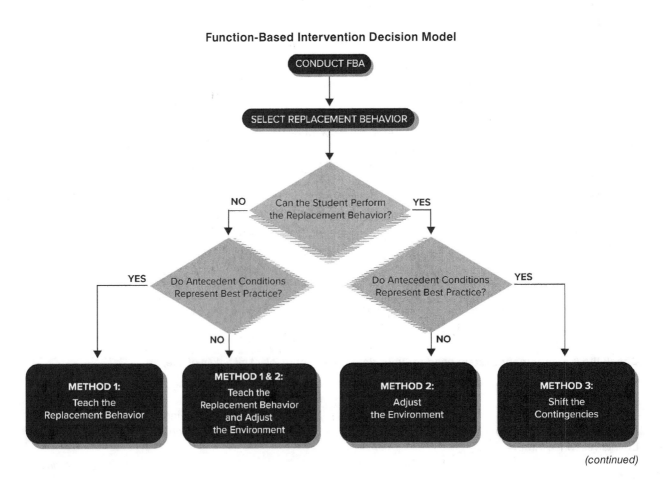

(continued)

Functional Assessment and Behavior Intervention Plan: Planning Form for Saida *(page 5 of 7)*

Determining the Intervention Method

Method Selected *(select and complete one)*:

☐ Method 1: Teach the Replacement Behavior

☐ Method 2: Adjust the Environment

☐ Method 3: Shift the Contingencies

☒ Methods 1 and 2: Teach the Replacement Behavior and Adjust the Environment

Method	Description
Method 1: Teach the Replacement Behavior	• Adjust antecedent conditions so new behaviors are learned and aversive conditions avoided. • Provide appropriate reinforcement for the replacement behavior. • Withhold the consequence that previously reinforced the target behavior.
Method 2: Adjust the Environment	• Adjust antecedent variables so the conditions that set the occasion for the target behavior are eliminated and new conditions are established in which the replacement behavior is more likely to occur. • Provide appropriate positive reinforcement for replacement behavior. • Withhold the consequence that previously reinforced the target behavior.
Method 3: Shift the Contingencies	• Provide the consequence that previously reinforced the target behavior, but only for the replacement behavior. • Withhold the consequence when the target behavior occurs (extinction). • Adjust the antecedent conditions to make it more likely that the replacement behavior will occur.
Methods 1 and 2: Teach the Replacement Behavior and Adjust the Environment	• Adjust antecedent variables so (1) new behaviors are learned and aversive conditions avoided and (2) the conditions that set the occasion for the target behavior are eliminated and new conditions are established in which the replacement behavior is more likely to occur. • Provide appropriate positive reinforcement for replacement behavior. • Withhold the consequence that previously reinforced the target behavior.

(continued)

Functional Assessment and Behavior Intervention Plan: Planning Form for Saida

Methods 1 and 2: Teach the Replacement Behavior and Adjust the Environment

Adjust Antecedents	Adjust antecedent variables so (1) new behaviors are learned and aversive conditions avoided and (2) the conditions that set the occasion for the target behavior are eliminated and new conditions are established in which the replacement behavior is more likely to occur.	Start each school day with social skills training and practice on appropriate responding that includes modeling (positive and negative examples), role playing, and feedback to develop fluency. Identify when Saida will ride the bus to school and spend homeroom time planning for the day. Remind Saida to be on time and use appropriate language. Give Saida a Behavior Monitoring Sheet (BMS) to track her own performance. Give Saida work that is more challenging and on the same topic as the rest of the class. Address Saida's work along with the work of the whole class.
Reinforcement Rates	Provide appropriate positive reinforcement for replacement behavior.	Provide attention/praise when Saida responds appropriately to directives. Praise verbally and in writing in the BMS, and call Saida's mother when she does well. Make computer time available when Saida speaks appropriately and completes work.
Extinguish Target Behavior	Withhold the consequence that previously reinforced the target behavior.	Briefly redirect (minimal attention) to continue working. Maintain task and keep in class.

(continued)

Functional Assessment and Behavior Intervention Plan: Planning Form for Saida

Data to be collected:

Student Outcome (What behavior(s) is (are) being measured? What measurement system? When/Where?)

Target Behavior: *The behavior was profanity in response to teacher directives. Profanity includes any words considered to be profane by teachers. Non-examples include working quietly, completing assignments, raising a hand to gain attention, using polite language, and nodding or saying yes or no to teacher directives.*

Replacement Behavior: *Appropriate responding saying yes or no to teacher directives; working quietly; working on assignments; raising a hand to gain attention. Non-examples include using profanity in response to teacher directives.*

Treatment Integrity (e.g., checklist)

Treatment Integrity: *Treatment integrity was assessed using a 10-point checklist that addressed implementation of the components of the intervention.*

Social Validity (e.g., IRP-15, CIRP)

Social Validity: *BIRP (Social studies teacher and classroom aide); CIRP (Saida and peer)*

Supporting Success (e.g., evaluating the intervention)

Fading and Generalization: *The intervention's effects will be evaluated through an ABAB format. Fading of some intervention elements will begin after achieving the initial behavioral objective. Generalization will be assessed in other classrooms and in different subject areas.*

Program Review Date: *Monthly by the school team. Sooner if the initial behavioral objective has been met.*

Personnel and Roles: *The behavior specialist will lead the team and provide consultation, as needed. The social studies teacher and instructional aide will implement the intervention.*

Emergency Procedures: *The school has crisis plans in place and specific requirements for the students in the self-contained classrooms. The school procedures should be followed when there is an emergency.*

CHAPTER 16

Treatment Integrity

LEARNING OBJECTIVES

◎ Define treatment integrity.

◎ Explain why it is important.

◎ Understand how to collect and use treatment integrity data to inform intervention efforts.

As you read earlier, treatment integrity is an essential—and sometimes forgotten—component of intervention efforts. At each level of prevention—Tier 1, Tier 2, and Tier 3—it is important for educators to know the extent to which strategies, practices, and programs were put in place as designed. Just as it is important to assess the reliability of the dependent variables (e.g., student engagement, oral reading fluency, initiating social interactions; see Chapter 10), it is equally important to know if the intervention components (i.e., A-R-E components in a FABI) are implemented with integrity (Lane & Beebe-Frankenberger, 2004). Without this information, it is not possible to evaluate accurately the effects of an intervention or Tier 1 efforts on student performance. In other words, we cannot determine if shifts (or lack of shifts) in student performance are due to an intervention if we do not have explicit information about the degree to which that intervention was actually implemented. In more practical terms, it is just like a person talking about their dating life in high school—maybe it happened as described, maybe it did not. We need data to know whether the actual happenings took place.

In this chapter, we introduce treatment integrity. Specifically, we explain what it is, why it is important, and how to collect and use these data to inform implementation efforts. Ethical considerations related to collecting and using treatment integrity data are included in Box 16.1.

> **BOX 16.1. Ethical Considerations in Chapter 16: BACB Ethics Code for Behavior Analysts**
>
> **2.17 Collecting and Using Data**
>
> Chapter 16 identifies treatment integrity as an important data tool to ensure that the intervention is being implemented correctly. When an intervention has been implemented correctly, we can attribute the behavior change (i.e., effectiveness), or lack thereof, to the intervention strategies. Knowing what works for the student within the context of a specific classroom is information that can be used to design generalization strategies, implement prevention procedures in other environments, and/or develop individualized interventions if needed in the future. Without treatment integrity data, it is difficult—if not impossible—to draw conclusions about whether the intervention strategies have resulted in the changes in student behavior.
>
> If treatment integrity is low, indicating that the intervention has not been implemented correctly, coaching and/or retraining those implementing the intervention is one strategy for improving effectiveness.

Treatment Integrity Defined

We defined treatment integrity as the extent to which intervention components or tactics are implemented as designed (Gresham, 1989; Peterson et al., 1982; Yeaton & Sechrest, 1981). When conducting a FABI—or any other intervention—it also important to carefully plan for and implement baseline as well as intervention conditions. This includes developing plans for measuring the extent to which all procedures in each condition are put into practice as planned, also referred to as procedural reliability (Billingsley et al., 1980), treatment integrity (Gresham, 1989), or implementation fidelity or integrity (Ledford & Gast, 2018). We also want to make sure that the person(s) who conducted the intervention is well prepared to implement plans as intended. This measurement of the training variables is referred to as implementation fidelity (Ledford & Gast, 2018), perhaps more easily thought of as training fidelity (see Box 16.2 for definitions of these three terms). In short, without it we cannot accurately determine if the intervention "worked" for the student. In this chapter, we focus on explaining why treatment integrity matters and how to measure it.

> **BOX 16.2. Types of Integrity**
>
> - Treatment integrity involves measuring how intervention (A-R-E) components are in place as planned.
> - Procedural integrity involves measuring how all conditions (e.g., baseline, intervention, withdrawal, generalization phases) are in place as planned.
> - Training fidelity involves measuring how the training of implementers was implemented as intended.

The Importance of Treatment Integrity Data

Through this book, we have discussed the value of designing, implementing, and evaluating interventions on the basis of the reasons why a given behavior (or set of behaviors) occurs. FABIs are often highly effective in skill building because they teach students' replacement behaviors that often serve the same function as the target behavior. FABIs are apt to work more effectively in positively changing behavior compared to interventions that focus only on the form (topography) of the behavior (Common et al., 2017; Mace, 1994; Newcomer & Lewis, 2004). Yet, there are times when even FABIs do not yield the desired outcomes, possibly because the functional assessment process described as part of Step 2 did not yield the correct function. Alternatively, perhaps the intervention did not fully address multiple functions (e.g., addressing attention, but not escape), or perhaps the intervention was not implemented as designed.

If the FABI team does not assess—and analyze—information about the degree to which specific A-R-E components were put in place, it is difficult (actually impossible!) to conclude that the introduction of the intervention was associated with changes in students' performance (Gresham et al., 1993). Maybe the intervention was designed to fully address the function(s) of the student's behavior, but some components were not fully implemented or were left out altogether. Or maybe the intervention was implemented as planned, but the intervention was not appropriately linked to maintaining functions. Or maybe the intervention was modified in some way that improved its effectiveness. Without treatment integrity data, it is impossible to discern between these various scenarios. Furthermore, it is also not possible to generalize from the intervention context to other contexts (e.g., is it likely to work with other students with similar target behaviors that serve similar functions). For researchers reading this book, the absence of treatment integrity data threatens the internal and external validity of a study (Ledford & Gast, 2018). Yet treatment integrity data are not just of interest to researchers. These data are needed by every educator to inform instruction (Lane, Oakes, et al., 2014).

Collecting and Using Treatment Integrity Data

Given that treatment integrity data are needed to accurately determine if an intervention "worked" to enhance student performance, educators ought to know how to (1) collect these data accurately and feasibly and (2) use these data to analyze intervention efforts and support implementation efforts.

There are different ways to measure treatment integrity, including direct observations, self-report, and permanent product techniques (Lane & Beebe-Frankenberger, 2004). Next, we describe these three ways to collect this vital information.

Direct-Observations Method

Direct observations can be thought of as the "gold standard." This approach involves having a member of the FABI team (e.g., behavior specialist or school psychologist) who is trained in the intervention procedures come into the classroom to observe implementation of the A-R-E components. This person might record the presence or absence of the intervention (e.g., 0 =

not in place, 1 = *in place*). Or they might measure the quality of implementation using a 3- or 5-point Likert-type scale. It is also possible to conduct a classroom recording using recording devices (e.g., swivel technology), and have the outside observer code these videos at a later date using the same recording sheets (see Figure 16.1). Before conducting these observations, this person—like the person who is implementing the intervention (e.g., the classroom teacher)—needs to be trained to criterion (implementation or training fidelity) to make sure that each person who is implementing the data and assessing the implementation has a common understanding of each intervention component.

To conduct these observations, first create the treatment integrity checklist that includes each A-R-E intervention component, with clear definitions of what each intervention component entails. Then determine if the intervention implementation will be assessed using either a present or absent (see Figure 16.2) or quality coding approach. In our work, we often build these treatment integrity forms in Excel to support scoring and interpretation. We also set a schedule to have the observers record one to two times per week (about 25% of the implementation sessions). After recording this information, they compute component and session integrity ratings.

To illustrate, in Figure 16.2, we present an example of a present versus absent treatment integrity form. This FABI intervention includes five antecedent adjustments, four reinforcement shifts, and three extinction tactics. In this case, the school psychologist indicated A5 was not in place on Tuesday and Wednesday, R4 was not in place on Thursday and Friday, and E1 was not in place on Tuesday. Component integrity suggested that most components were implemented with 100% integrity over the course of this week, with A5 and R4 implemented at 60% integrity and E1 at 80% integrity. When looking at session integrity for each day, the percentages were computed by dividing the number of components present by the total number of components (12), then multiplying the result by 100% to obtain a percentage. The treatment integrity levels for the intervention were 100% on Monday, 83% on Tuesday, and 92% for Wednesday through Friday.

It is also possible for the outside observer (e.g., a member of the FABI team) to watch the whole intervention take place and complete the scale at the end of the session or day (cf., Gresham, 1989; Gresham et al., 2000). In this case, you might use a 4-point Likert-type scale with anchors ranging from 1 (*not in place*) to 4 (*fully in place*) at the end of the session. In optimal conditions, this information will be filled in as soon as possible to make certain people's recollections are as accurate as possible.

Self-Report Method

An indirect method of collecting treatment integrity data is to use self-report techniques (Gresham et al., 2000). For example, it is possible for the teacher who is using the intervention to monitor their own treatment integrity—often using the same forms completed by the outside observers. The teacher might fill out a daily form and the outside observer might observe once per week as a reliability check to make sure that both people are interpreting the same intervention components in the same way.

There are concerns about having people self-report, such as the concern that either intentional or unintentional inaccuracies may occur (Cooper et al., 2020). Yet self-report techniques

Week of: _____   0 = never   1 = sometimes   2 = always

		Monday	Tuesday	Wednesday	Thursday	Friday
Adjust the Antecedents						
A1	Behavior contract was in place.	0 1 2	0 1 2	0 1 2	0 1 2	0 1 2
A2	Self-monitoring checklist was completed.	0 1 2	0 1 2	0 1 2	0 1 2	0 1 2
A3	State how to appropriately access attention.	0 1 2	0 1 2	0 1 2	0 1 2	0 1 2
A4	Student is in the proper seat.	0 1 2	0 1 2	0 1 2	0 1 2	0 1 2
A5	Increase circulation around the room.	0 1 2	0 1 2	0 1 2	0 1 2	0 1 2
Adjust the Reinforcement						
R1	Teacher-specific praise contingent on appropriate on-task behavior.	0 1 2	0 1 2	0 1 2	0 1 2	0 1 2
R2	Provide access to daily rewards contingent on appropriate on-task behavior.	0 1 2	0 1 2	0 1 2	0 1 2	0 1 2
R3	Provide access to weekly rewards contingent on appropriate on-task behavior.	0 1 N/A	0 1 2 N/A	0 1 2 N/A	0 1 2 N/A	0 1 2 N/A
R4	Use PBIS tickets.	0 1 2	0 1 2	0 1 2	0 1 2	0 1 2
Extinction Components						
E1	Withhold attention for off-task behavior, except for a short redirection, and praise immediately upon onset of on-task behavior.	0 1 2	0 1 2	0 1 2	0 1 2	0 1 2
E2	Specific praise for others in close proximity for on-task behavior.	0 1 2	0 1 2	0 1 2	0 1 2	0 1 2
E3	Used brief if/then redirections.	0 1 2	0 1 2	0 1 2	0 1 2	0 1 2
Totals:		___/	___/	___/	___/	___/

FIGURE 16.1. Treatment integrity form. From Majeika, C. E., Walder, J. Pl, Hubbard, J. P, Steeb, K. M., Ferris, G. J, Oakes, W. P, & Lane, K. L. (2011). Improving on-task behavior using a functional assessment-based intervention in an inclusive high school setting. *Beyond Behavior*, 20, 55–66. Reprinted by permission of Sage Publications.

Antecedent Adjustments	Component	Monday	Tuesday	Wednesday	Thursday	Friday	Component Integrity
A1		1	1	1	1	1	100%
A2		1	1	1	1	1	100%
A3		1	1	1	1	1	100%
A4		1	1	1	1	1	100%
A5		1	0	0	1	1	60%
Reinforcement Shifts							
R1		1	1	1	1	1	100%
R2		1	1	1	1	1	100%
R3		1	1	1	1	1	100%
R4		1	1	1	0	0	60%
Extinction Tactics							
E1		1	0	1	1	1	80%
E2		1	1	1	1	1	100%
E3		1	1	1	1	1	100%
Session Integrity		100%	83%	92%	92%	92%	

FIGURE 16.2. Illustration of a present versus absent treatment integrity form. A "1" indicates the intervention component was implemented as planned. A "0" indicates the intervention component was not in place as planned. Adapted from Lane, K. L., & Beebe-Frankenberger, M. E. (2004). *School-based interventions: The tools you need to succeed.* Allyn & Bacon. Reprinted by permission.

are very practical within the classroom context and can be helpful if the treatment integrity form itself serves as a reminder (discriminative stimulus) for the intervention components that need to be used (Lane et al., 2003). If this method can be supplemented with direct observations by others, the information can even be used as "coachable moments." The outside observer can compare scores with the teacher, and then they can talk through any discrepancies and make adjustments to support high levels of implementation.

Permanent Products Method

Permanent products are another practical, effective way to monitor treatment integrity. This approach can be used if the intervention results in a specific "product." For example, the intervention might include completing tasks that are more challenging (Umbreit et al., 2004) or provide a choice of assignments (e.g., completing a writing assignment on the computer versus using pen and paper; Royer et al., 2017). In each instance, these products or outcomes could be measured as proxies for treatment integrity.

Using Treatment Integrity Data

When treatment integrity indicates that one or more of the intervention components are not implemented correctly, the most obvious use of the data is to retrain and/or coach the people involved in the implementation. However, this outcome also provides an opportunity to identify, with the teacher and classroom staff, why components are not being implemented. Sometimes this is a matter of forgetting or of not having sufficient training, both of which can be addressed. Moreover, additional training and/or coaching can be used to enhance treatment integrity, which can be especially salient at the beginning of implementation. However, once they begin implementation, classroom staff may identify one or more components that are more difficult or awkward to implement than they had anticipated. Training may also address these difficulties but, in some cases, minor adjustments in strategy may be necessary.

Summary

In this chapter, we explained what treatment integrity is, why it is important, and how to collect and use these data to inform implementation efforts. As we mentioned, information about the extent to which an intervention is implemented as planned is essential when determining intervention effectiveness. In short, we cannot accurately know if an intervention is working—or if parts of it are working—if we do not know the degree to which the intervention as a whole is actually implemented (or which parts are implemented). This information should be collected as accurately as possible, as you carefully consider the need for a collection method that is both rigorous and feasible. Ideally, we recommend using direct observations as well as self-report techniques to gain the benefits of both perspectives, with a goal of using this information in a nonevaluative manner. You might recall from Chapter 3 that this is the same approach used to monitor the treatment integrity of Tier 1 practices in Ci3T models of prevention. For purposes of collecting treatment integrity data as part of the manualized FABI process, review Box 11.1, Completion Checklist for Step 4: Designing the Intervention, and Box 11.2, Completion Checklist for Step 5: Testing the Intervention, for the time line of when to draft your treatment integrity form (see row 3 in Step 4) and collect treatment integrity data (see content beginning with row 2 in Step 5).

Next, in Chapter 17, we discuss social validity, another important source of information when building and evaluating interventions efforts.

CHAPTER 17

Social Validity

LEARNING OBJECTIVES

- Define social validity and explain its origin.
- Explain why it is important.
- Understand how to collect and use social validity data as part of the FABI process.

At this point in the process, you have conducted the FABI and developed the function-based intervention. Now you are ready to implement the intervention, provided baseline data are stable (see *Step 3: Collecting Baseline Data*). To ensure the best possible outcome, you will need to attend to three essential components—treatment integrity, social validity, and generalization and maintenance. You already learned about treatment integrity in Chapter 16 and learn about maintenance and generalization in Chapter 18. In this chapter, we address the concept of social validity.

In the early days of *applied* behavior analysis—from the late 1950s through the early 1970s—researchers produced a considerable amount of data that verified the improvements and benefits that ABA could provide. Much of this work was conducted in classrooms with teachers and students in local schools. The results were consistently positive and impressive.

Many reviews of this work were published. They were generally very positive but pointed out that researchers were collecting all of the data. Furthermore, the data only pertained to the period during which the intervention was being implemented. The question of whether or not teachers continued to use the successful intervention was seldom—if ever—addressed.

To address this issue of continued use (or not), researchers began to include maintenance data in their research; that is, they went back a few weeks later to observe what happened after they left. To their great dismay, they learned that the interventions they had created—no matter how successful they were—were hardly ever used by teachers after the researchers had left the school. It was as though they (the researchers) had never been there. The same pattern occurred in ABA research with parents.

Why would practitioners deliberately abandon interventions that had clearly been successful? Wolf, a leading authority on ABA, suggested there was likely a problem with what he termed *social validity* (Wolf, 1978). For example, it was possible that the intervention's goals were not viewed as important from the teacher's perspective or the intervention involved procedures they found objectionable. Or perhaps the intervention appeared to be a good fit, but the actual procedures were very time consuming. Maybe the benefit provided by the intervention simply did not justify all of the effort it required. Perhaps it called for the use of materials not typically found in a classroom setting. Or maybe the teacher simply did not think the intervention was likely to produce the desired outcomes (Baer et al., 1968, 1987). One way or another, there was something about the social value of the intervention that was unacceptable.

This chapter introduces the concept of social validity, its definition and importance, and different methods of measuring it. It also suggests guidelines about how and when to assess social validity when developing or monitoring a FABI—including when to assess social validity before the intervention begins and at the end of the process after the intervention has been

---

BOX 17.1. Ethical Considerations in Chapter 17: BACB Ethics Code for Behavior Analysts

1.07 Cultural Responsiveness and Diversity

As part of the FABI process, two social validity checks about the intervention are completed by the teacher, a family member, and the student. One check is completed before the intervention is implemented and one is completed after implementation. As noted in Chapter 17, social validity checks address three questions. Does the intervention address socially significant goals for those involved? Is it acceptable to those involved? Are the outcomes important to those involved? Input from those involved (i.e., teachers, families, students, school or program staff) is one avenue for identifying whether the intervention aligns with the family perspectives and values, the student's preferences and experiences, and the environmental context in which the intervention is implemented. They help answer the question: Is the intervention a contextual fit with the culture, perspectives, and values of the families, teachers, school staff, and support personnel? Being culturally responsive requires asking and considering this input during intervention development and implementation. Social validity checks are one important method for gathering this information that provides stakeholders with a broader perspective so they can evaluate whether the whole intervention maintains that cultural fit.

2.09 Involving Clients and Stakeholders

Social validity checks are one part of a multimethod approach for involving teachers, families, and students in selecting, developing, and implementing a behavioral intervention using the FABI process. As part of the FABI intervention team, teachers, family members, and students have multiple opportunities for input into the details of the intervention. The social validity check, completed after the intervention is developed but before it is implemented, conveys the entirety of the intervention and how the different strategies fit together.

tested (for details, see Box 11.1, Completion Checklist for Step 4: Designing the Intervention, and Box 11.2, Completion Checklist for Step 5: Testing the Intervention). Ethical considerations related to social validity are presented in Box 17.1.

Social Validity Defined

Social validity addresses three questions: Does (did) the intervention target socially significant goals? Are (were) the intervention procedures socially acceptable in the eyes of the consumers? Will (did) the intervention produce socially important outcomes? (Fawcett, 1991; Kazdin, 1977; Wolf, 1978). These three questions focus on whether the intervention considers the perspectives and values of the classroom staff, families, and students, that is, whether the intervention is responsive to the diversity and cultural uniqueness of the program, school, and classrooms in which it is implemented.

The Importance of Social Validity

As we discussed previously, information about social validity can be used to inform selection of A-R-E components, ensuring that the function-based interventions are acceptable or comfortable for all stakeholders. If teachers, families, students, and other stakeholders indicate high social validity before the intervention is put in place, it is far more likely it will be implemented as planned, sustained over time, and used in new settings and with people not directly involved in this particular intervention (Lane & Beebe-Frankenberger, 2004). We have also learned that social validity predicts the implementation of Tier 1 efforts in schools implementing Ci3T (Lane, Kalberg, Bruhn, et al., 2009) and PBIS (Vancel et al., 2016). This is excellent news. If social validity scores are low before beginning FABI implementation, the FABI team has an opportunity to refine the intervention before implementation to promote buy-in and enhance the likelihood of success.

Social validity can also be assessed after the intervention is under way. For example, teachers, families, and students can provide information on social validity after the intervention has been designed, implemented, withdrawn, and reintroduced (tested using an A-B-A-B or other design). This "post" social validity assessment can be used to determine if the FABI met expectations. In addition, information can also be used to make refinements as the plan moves into maintenance phases (Lane & Oakes, 2014).

Collecting and Using Social Validity Data

Given the multiple uses of social validity data, it is important for educators to know how to (1) collect these data accurately and feasibly and (2) use these data to inform intervention efforts (e.g., making revisions and shifts into maintenance phases). Fortunately, there are several methods you can use to assess social validity. Specifically, social validity can be assessed using rating scales, interviews, and social comparison techniques and indirectly via the future use of intervention procedures (Gresham & Lopez, 1996; Lane & Beebe-Frankenberger, 2004). Next, we describe these various approaches.

Rating Scales

Rating scales are the most common method of assessing social validity (Lane & Beebe-Frankenberger, 2004). The majority of commercially available rating scales focus on the acceptability of treatment procedures (Finn & Sladeczek, 2001). The earliest instruments were the Treatment Evaluation Inventory (TEI; Kazdin, 1980) and the Intervention Rating Profile–20 (IRP-20; Witt & Martens, 1983). Since the introduction of these two measures, a number of instruments have been developed based on them, some of which include the Treatment Evaluation Inventory—Short Form (TEI-SF; Kelley et al., 1989), the IRP-15 (Martens & Witt, 1982), the Children's Intervention Rating Profile (CIRP; Witt & Elliott, 1983), and the Treatment Acceptability Rating Form—Revised (TARF-R; Reimers & Wacker, 1988).

Perhaps the most user-friendly instruments for incorporating social validity into the FABI process are the materials adapted for use in schools implementing Ci3T models or other integrated tiered systems. They include the *pre*intervention forms for both the student and adult (see Figures 17.1 and 17.2) and the *post*intervention forms for both student and adult (Figures

Preintervention

Student: _____

Date: _____

	I agree. 1	2	3	4	5	6	I do not agree. 7
1. The program we will use sounds fair.							
2. I think my teacher will be too harsh on me.							
3. Being in this program may cause problems with my friends.							
4. There are better ways to teach me.							
5. This program will help other kids too.							
6. I think I will like being in this program.							
7. I think being in this program will help me do better in school.							

FIGURE 17.1. Children's Intervention Rating Profile (Preintervention). From Witt, J. C., & Elliott, S. N. (1983). *Children's Intervention Rating Profile.* University of Nebraska–Lincoln. Adapted by Ci3T (2015). Reprinted by permission.

The purpose of this questionnaire is to obtain information that will aid in the selection of future classroom interventions. These interventions will be used by teachers of children with identified needs. Please circle the number that best describes your agreement or disagreement with each statement.

	Strongly disagree	Disagree	Slightly disagree	Slightly agree	Agree	Strongly agree
1. This would be an acceptable intervention for the child's needs.	1	2	3	4	5	6
2. Most teachers would find this intervention appropriate for children with similar needs.	1	2	3	4	5	6
3. This intervention should prove effective in supporting the child's needs.	1	2	3	4	5	6
4. I would suggest the use of this intervention to other teachers.	1	2	3	4	5	6
5. The child's needs are severe enough to warrant use of this intervention.	1	2	3	4	5	6
6. Most teachers would find this intervention suitable for the needs of this child.	1	2	3	4	5	6
7. I would be willing to use this intervention in the classroom setting.	1	2	3	4	5	6
8. This intervention would *not* result in negative side effects for the child.	1	2	3	4	5	6
9. This intervention would be appropriate for a variety of children.	1	2	3	4	5	6
10. This intervention is consistent with those I have used in classroom settings.	1	2	3	4	5	6
11. The intervention is a fair way to handle the child's needs.	1	2	3	4	5	6
12. This intervention is reasonable for the needs of the child.	1	2	3	4	5	6
13. I like the procedures used in this intervention.	1	2	3	4	5	6
14. This intervention would be a good way to handle this child's needs.	1	2	3	4	5	6
15. Overall, this intervention would be beneficial for the child.	1	2	3	4	5	6

Total (sum all points circled; higher scores indicate higher acceptability; range = 15–90): _____

FIGURE 17.2. Adapted Preintervention IRP-15. From Martens, B. K., & Witt, J. C. (1982). *The Intervention Rating Profile.* University of Nebraska–Lincoln. Adapted by Ci3T. Reprinted by permission.

17.3 and 17.4). Preintervention instruments are used when developing the FABI. Postintervention instruments are used to evaluate and possibly fade the FABI.

Interviews

You can also conduct interviews to assess social validity. Gresham and Lopez (1996) designed a semistructured interview for use with classroom teachers. This interview contains three sections to address the three components of social validity: social significance of the goals, social acceptability of the procedures, and social importance of the effects.

Social Comparison Techniques

You can also assess social validity by making comparisons between the student participating in the FABI and a peer who is competent in the replacement behavior of interest. Consider a student who rarely regularly engages in on-task behavior. Instead, they talk out, get out of their seat, and talk with peers during class. Data for this student could be compared to the same measures for a student who regularly engages in appropriate on-task behavior (i.e., they remain in their seat, stay engaged in the assigned task, and raise their hand if they have a question or need help). If the participating student's behavior is substantially different from that of the

Postintervention

Student: _____

Date: _____

	I agree. 1	2	3	4	5	6	I do not agree. 7
1. The program we used was fair.							
2. I think my teacher was too harsh on me.							
3. Being in this program caused problems with my friends.							
4. There were better ways to teach me.							
5. This program could help other kids too.							
6. I liked the program we used.							
7. Being in this program helped me do better in school.							

FIGURE 17.3. Adapted Children's Intervention Rating Profile (Postintervention). From Witt, J. C., & Elliott, S. N. (1983). *Children's Intervention Rating Profile.* University of Nebraska–Lincoln. Adapted by Ci3T (2015). Reprinted by permission.

The purpose of this questionnaire is to obtain information that will aid in the selection of future classroom interventions. These interventions will be used by teachers of children with identified needs. Please circle the number that best describes your agreement or disagreement with each statement.

	Strongly disagree	Disagree	Slightly disagree	Slightly agree	Agree	Strongly agree
1. This was an acceptable intervention for the child's needs.	1	2	3	4	5	6
2. Most teachers would find this intervention appropriate for children with similar needs.	1	2	3	4	5	6
3. This intervention proved effective in supporting the child's needs.	1	2	3	4	5	6
4. I would suggest the use of this intervention to other teachers.	1	2	3	4	5	6
5. The child's needs were severe enough to warrant use of this intervention.	1	2	3	4	5	6
6. Most teachers would find this intervention suitable for the needs of this child.	1	2	3	4	5	6
7. I would be willing to use this intervention in the classroom setting.	1	2	3	4	5	6
8. This intervention did *not* result in negative side effects for the child.	1	2	3	4	5	6
9. This intervention would be appropriate for a variety of children.	1	2	3	4	5	6
10. This intervention was consistent with those I have used in classroom settings.	1	2	3	4	5	6
11. The intervention was a fair way to handle the child's needs.	1	2	3	4	5	6
12. This intervention was reasonable for the needs of the child.	1	2	3	4	5	6
13. I liked the procedures used in this intervention.	1	2	3	4	5	6
14. This intervention was a good way to handle this child's needs.	1	2	3	4	5	6
15. Overall, this intervention was beneficial for the child.	1	2	3	4	5	6

Total (sum all points circled; higher scores indicate higher acceptability; range = 15–90): _____

FIGURE 17.4. Adapted Postintervention IRP-15. From Martens, B. K., & Witt, J. C. (1982). *The Intervention Rating Profile.* University of Nebraska–Lincoln. Adapted by Ci3T. Reprinted by permission.

typical peer, it might suggest the need for a FABI. If not, then an individualized intervention may not be warranted. Social comparison techniques can also be used again at the conclusion of the intervention to see if the performance levels are more parallel.

Future Use

A final mechanism you can use to assess social validity is monitoring the extent to which the teacher (or other treatment adult) actually uses the intervention with subsequent students who present similar concerns. Gresham and Lopez (1996) contend that *use* serves as a behavioral marker for treatment acceptability. Namely, if teachers independently use the intervention in the future, then, by definition, the intervention was socially valid or acceptable.

Use of Social Validity Data

Social validity should be assessed before *and* at the conclusion of intervention. Preintervention assessment enables teachers, students, and/or parents to identify potential social validity concerns prior to implementation. Adopting this process also makes it possible to incorporate individualized and culturally appropriate adjustments that improve the FABI before social validity concerns arise.

If social validity is high at the onset of the intervention, then the treatment agents (teachers, parents, and/or students) may be more likely to implement the intervention as intended (e.g., with integrity). If the intervention is empirically sound, culturally appropriate, and accurately designed to teach an appropriate replacement behavior, and implemented with fidelity, then the intervention is likely to produce the desired outcomes. Postintervention assessment can confirm improvements in social validity, as well in intervention outcomes. Without this information, social validity problems and disappointing intervention outcomes may become unavoidable.

Summary

This chapter has described the concept of social validity, its definition and importance, and different methods of measuring it. It has also provided guidelines about how and when to assess social validity when developing or monitoring a FABI. For purposes of collecting social validity as part of the manualized FABI process, review Box 11.1, Completion Checklist for Step 4: Designing the Intervention, and Box 11.2, Completion Checklist for Step 5: Testing the Intervention, for the time line of when the FABI team selects and reviews social validity forms (see row four in Step 4) prior to the intervention and at the end of the process, after the intervention has been tested (see second to last row in Step 5).

Chapter 18 introduces generalization and maintenance. For each concept, we explain what it is, why it is important, and how to collect and use these data to inform implementation efforts.

CHAPTER 18

Generalization and Maintenance

LEARNING OBJECTIVES

○ Define generalization and maintenance in the context of an individualized intervention.

○ Describe why generalization and maintenance are important.

○ Collect and use generalization and maintenance data to inform implementation efforts.

Just as it is important to plan for and assess treatment integrity (Chapter 16) and social validity (Chapter 17), it is also essential to plan for and assess generalization and maintenance of the new skills acquired: the replacement behavior. The planned outcome of an individualized intervention is a replacement behavior that is more effective and efficient than the target behavior. The intervention is designed so the student *acquires* a new replacement behavior or becomes more *fluent* in a replacement behavior that is in their repertoire, responds to environmental stimuli designed to evoke the replacement behavior, and responds to contingencies that increase the replacement behavior. Of course, we also want the target behavior to decrease so that it is no longer a problem. The target behavior is what triggered the FABI process. But once the target behavior is no longer a problem, we want the student to have a skill that makes them more effective in their environment for the long term—across settings with everyone and over time (e.g., across grade levels). So, we repeat: The planned outcome of an individualized intervention is a replacement behavior that is more effective and efficient than the target behavior (Horner & Billingsley, 1988; Horner & Day, 1991).

When we have identified an appropriate replacement behavior and designed an effective intervention, we want that behavior change to have some generality in the student's life after we have completed training. We want that replacement behavior to continue to be effective and efficient so the student does not need the intervention repeated in the next month, or quarter, or year. For each of the intervention methods (see Chapters 12–15), you may have noticed that the FABI Planning Form features a section called "Data to be collected." These data include students' outcomes, treatment integrity, and social validity, as well as fading and generalization (noting that maintenance over time is one type of generalization).

You cannot simply hope the replacement behavior will be maintained and be used in all environments; you must plan for it. The plan for generalization and maintenance should ensure that the behaviors can generalize across time (maintenance), settings, and people, so that stimulus generalization and response generalization can occur. You plan for this ongoing effectiveness by using strategies that address generalization and maintenance at the outset of the intervention design. The FABI team identifies strategies during the intervention planning phase and uses data to test for generalization during intervention. After the intervention is successfully completed, the team uses data to probe for generalization and maintenance.

In this chapter, we introduce strategies to promote generalization and maintenance of the replacement behavior. Specifically, we define generalization and maintenance, identify why these concepts are important, and suggest ways to collect and use data to inform our intervention implementation efforts. Ethical considerations related to generalization and maintenance are presented in Box 18.1.

Generalization and Maintenance Defined

Baer and colleagues (1968) described generality of behavior change as a characteristic of behavior analysis. They identified generality as being demonstrated:

- when the behavior continues after the intervention has been implemented,
- when the behavior occurs in other settings without training, and
- when behaviors that are related to the replacement behavior occur.

Stokes and Baer (1977) reiterated this conception of generalization and further defined behaviors related to the replacement behavior as those that are functionally related.

The term *generalization* is sometimes used generically to refer to a specific behavioral process or behavior-change outcome. For example, we might say that the student generalized when using the replacement behavior in another setting and when responding to a new stimulus that is similar to a prior stimulus in which the student was trained for (stimulus generalization), as might be found in stimulus equivalence training. The term may also be used when referring to the maintenance of the replacement behavior over time (response maintenance) or to the student's use of a response that is untrained but functionally equivalent to the replacement behavior (response generalization). In this chapter, we are very specific in our use of terms and refer to the primary components of this generic term as (1) response maintenance, (2) stimulus generalization, and (3) response generalization. Keeping these three primary components in mind, in the next section we explore strategies to ensure maintenance and response generalization. We have included fading as a separate category because of its importance in both maintenance and stimulus generalization.

> **BOX 18.1. Ethical Considerations in Chapter 18:**
> **BACB Ethics Code for Behavior Analysts**
>
> Generalization and maintenance fall under the same ethical considerations identified for the intervention because they are a part of the intervention.
>
> ### 2.09 Involving Clients and Stakeholders
>
> In educational settings, the FABI team includes the teacher and other relevant service providers, family members, and the student, if possible. Members of the FABI team are kept apprised of outcome data throughout the maintenance and generalization phases of the intervention. The team provides input about strategies, including cultural practices that might affect generalization. During the generalization phase, the team might also consider addressing generalization in the home environment.
>
> ### 2.14 Selecting, Designing, and Implementing Behavior-Change Interventions
>
> The FABI team identifies and participates in decisions related to all relevant factors, including preferences for implementation in the classroom and at home. Maintenance and generalization strategies are individualized to take into account context or setting, preferences, and family values.
>
> ### 2.16 Describing Behavior-Change Interventions Before Implementation
>
> Generalization and maintenance strategies are developed and included in the FABI from the outset and are described along with the rest of the intervention procedures.
>
> ### 2.17 Collecting and Using Data
>
> Data are collected during the generalization and maintenance phase in the same manner as occurred during full intervention. These data are used to make decisions about which intervention strategies are to be changed, when to continue or modify maintenance strategies so the student continues the replacement behavior, and whether the replacement behavior is generalizing to untrained settings or whether the full intervention needs to be implemented again.
>
> ### 2.18 Continual Evaluation of the Behavior-Change Intervention
>
> Continual evaluation applies during the maintenance and generalization phases. As data collection is gradually reduced, the team monitors data to ensure that the replacement behavior continues at the same level it did during intervention. If data show a countertherapeutic trend for the replacement and/or target behaviors (meaning that the behavior is going in the opposite of the desired direction), the FABI team develops and implements corrections to the procedures until the student is successful. This may include reimplementation of the full intervention.

Strategies to Explore

Fading

Fading in the context of behavioral intervention means that stimuli and procedures are gradually changed so that the replacement behavior continues to occur. As we noted in our discussion of generalization, fading is often misunderstood to mean gradually decreasing or eliminating a strategy or procedure, but it may also refer to increasing something in the intervention. The illustration in Chapter 14 provides a good example. The intervention for Claire included gradually increasing the number of times Claire was required to respond before she could ask for a break. Additional responses were "faded in" to the procedure. The introduction of additional required responses also resulted in a decrease in the amount of time Claire was on a break. So the procedure also faded out reinforcement.

Fading is considered at the time the intervention is developed—not after the intervention is under way. In developing procedures for changing behavior, the team may identify some extraordinary measures. For example, reinforcement may be delivered at a very high and/or frequent rate or delivered over a lengthy period of time (e.g., the student gets a long break from work). Specialized materials, instructions, or other stimuli may be introduced as part of antecedent adjustments. As the FABI team develops the intervention, they evaluate which of the strategies are to remain in place and which they will fade (i.e., reduce or eliminate) once the student has met the intervention's final goal—when the student's replacement behavior occurs at a level sufficient for them to be successful, such as being on task for 85% of intervals. In this example, the FABI team may decide to reduce reinforcement to the level that is usual in the classroom but will maintain specialized instructions and materials that are effective teaching practices, which are expected in the learning environment. Self-monitoring may be continued. However, reminders or checks by the teacher, special materials, or high levels of reinforcing self-monitoring may be reduced or become more intermittent so the student is more independent.

Fading reinforcement does not mean that reinforcement for the replacement behavior is eliminated. Students should receive feedback and reinforcement for expected behavior in the classroom. However, reinforcement of replacement behaviors may be reduced from every occurrence to a more intermittent schedule that is natural in the environment. It should be noted that the schedule of reinforcement in a classroom should be sufficient to ensure that all students maintain a level of responding. Classrooms with minimal levels of positive feedback (e.g., noting a correct response) or reinforcement may need additional support to increase to a level of responding sufficient to maintain all students' behavior.

In summary, fading is gradually changing stimuli and procedures so the replacement behavior continues to occur at or near the same rate. Fading refers to both decreasing *and* increasing procedures. For intervention purposes, the important point to remember is that the FABI team should review their procedures and identify those that will continue after the formal intervention has ended and those that will be faded. Fading strategies identified by the FABI team are successful if data show that the replacement behavior continues to occur. Therefore, developing strategies that promote response maintenance will also assist the team in successfully fading an intervention.

Response Maintenance

Response maintenance refers to the reliable occurrence of the replacement behavior over time even in the absence of the intervention procedures. You want the student to continue to raise their hand, ask for help, use calming or problem-solving strategies, or talk rather than fight after the formal intervention procedures are no longer in place, and you want this behavior to be long-lasting. In other words, it is a behavior you want to see the student use well into the future (e.g., self-monitoring, making needs known, or politely greeting friends or adults).

Figure 18.1 on pages 251–252 lists some strategies that have been identified as successful in promoting response maintenance. These may be the most common strategies but they are not the only ones. The decision about what to do to enhance maintenance depends on the circumstances and the setting in which the intervention occurs. The strategy must fit the context, such that the student is able to function as the other students do in the environment. For instance, raising a hand may work perfectly for a classroom, but not so well on the playground.

Some strategies for response maintenance include the following:

- Select a behavior, often called a *behavioral trap*, that is naturally reinforced in the environment. When the behavior produces reinforcement for the student outside of the intervention environment, it is more likely to maintain and generalize to other, similar stimuli and environments. This category includes instruction-related behaviors, such as the student raising their hand or asking for help, as well as social skills, such as the student learning to ask if they can join a group or responding to questions. The natural reinforcement would be the student being called on, receiving help, joining the group, and interacting with their peers.

- Once the intervention has been shown to be effective, implement the intervention in multiple settings to increase the number of opportunities for the student to practice and to encounter minor variations in the stimulus. For example, implement during different subjects or in different classrooms, such as in reading during reading instruction and in reading during social studies. Implement the instruction in a large and small group.

- Change the reinforcement schedule. When you learned about reinforcement schedules in Chapter 4, you learned that intermittent schedules of reinforcement are more effective in maintaining behavior. Your intervention procedures may begin with a fixed schedule of frequent reinforcement but should include a procedure for decreasing the amount of reinforcement and delivering it intermittently, so it mimics the way the reinforcement occurs in the natural environment. Just a note here that reinforcement naturally occurs at a very low rate in some classrooms. In these cases, it may be helpful to work with the teacher to increase their overall rate of reinforcement for all students.

- Use a conditioned reinforcer to help keep reinforcement effective so the student does not become satiated. For example, a conditioned reinforcer might be a universal ticket, such as those used by adults in schools implementing tiered systems (e.g., Ci3T, PBIS), that the student can use to access a menu of preferred items or activities. A schoolwide reinforcer, such as tickets used in systems of support, not only provides choices for the student, but also supports generalization because the same reinforcement occurs across the school environment. In short, all adults share common expectations, use a universal reinforcement system (e.g., tickets), and communicate the outcomes of Tier 2 and Tier 3 interventions (see Chapter 3) to ensure consistency for all stakeholders. If the FABI is conducted in a school implementing a Ci3T model, the same universal reinforcer (e.g., ticket) should be used to program for generalization. Avoid introducing a competing reinforcer.

- Vary the stimulus dimensions. Broaden the antecedent conditions so the intervention setting includes multiple variations of the antecedents. For example, if there is a teacher and assistant in the classroom, both would be included in implementing the intervention so the student is more likely to continue to respond even as the antecedents are faded or there is an unexpected change in the conditions (e.g., change in teacher or instructions).

- Work with the teacher and student to identify different but functionally similar ways for the student to perform the replacement behavior so they can access reinforcement even if their response is a little different. For example, the student might get a teacher's attention by raising their hand, by placing an object on their desk (e.g., a yellow or red cup; see Lane, Eisner, et al., 2009) to signal the need for help or a break, or by going to the teacher's desk.

- Teach the student to solicit reinforcement or to manage their own behavior.

Stimulus Generalization

Stimulus generalization occurs when the student uses the replacement behavior under different stimulus conditions, such as in a setting that is different from the one in which the intervention occurred. Stimulus generalization may occur in a different environment, at a different time, or with a different person than in the intervention environment. For example, the student begins to raise their hand during instruction in a different subject (i.e., the intervention occurs during math and the student also begins to raise their hand during reading instruction) or during a different class in middle or high school. If stimulus generalization occurs in a different class, many dimensions of the setting may be different (e.g., different students and teacher, different class arrangement, different instructional strategies). For example, the student whose intervention teaches them to calm themselves when interacting with Joel during lunch may achieve stimulus generalization if they also use their calming techniques when confronted by Gabby during music.

Some strategies identified for response maintenance are also useful for stimulus generalization. If a behavior is naturally reinforced in a school environment, it is likely that the behavior will be reinforced in other subjects and classes or in other environments throughout the school. In addition, using the schoolwide reinforcement system, such as a ticket system, supports generalization and increases the opportunity for adults to provide feedback throughout the day by acknowledging the student using the ticket system and pairing it with behavior-specific praise. Other strategies include:

- Prompt the student to try out the replacement behavior in environments where the behavior may be reinforced.
- Ask teachers and other people on the staff to reinforce a student when they exhibit the replacement behavior.

- Implement the intervention in the natural environment or in a setting as close to the natural environment as possible. The natural environment provides stimuli across similar settings that will be conducive to setting generalization. In schools, this means implementing in classrooms or other school areas where the behavior occurs rather than moving the student to a separate room for training and then reintroducing the student into the natural environment.
- Purposefully plan to include a stimulus that is in place across multiple environments. For example, desks are set up in a semicircle in multiple classrooms or the student sits in a similar place in all classrooms or always sits near the same two peers.
- Use self-management strategies and materials that the student can implement in multiple settings in the school.

Response Generalization

Response generalization is the occurrence of untrained responses that are functionally equivalent to the replacement behavior. A functionally equivalent response generates the same reinforcement as the original response. For example, a student might use different techniques for calming themselves during stressful interactions (e.g., taking deep breaths may be the replacement behavior, but the student also closes their eyes and counts to 10) or use different ways to request assistance (e.g., raising their hand may be the replacement behavior but the student also stands a book on their desk to get the teacher's attention). The new response may be subtler. For example, the student may begin by holding their hand high to get the teacher's attention but may gradually change it to raising their hand at shoulder level. As long as the teacher finds the altered response acceptable and continues to provide attention, the generalized response works.

Strategies to encourage response generalization include some that were already listed, such as the behavioral trap. Other strategies include:

- Teaching and reinforcing different response examples. Identify different responses for the replacement behavior that will be effective and teach them to the student. Ensure that the teacher honors those different responses.
- Having the teacher reinforce various responses that they consider appropriate (e.g., the student can sign as well as ask for something verbally). In a bilingual classroom, the student can ask or respond in more than one language.

Collecting and Using Generalization and Maintenance Data

You begin to fade intervention components when the behavioral data are stable and at the level identified in the intervention goal (Common et al., 2015). For example, if you have a goal for the student to be on task 85% of intervals for 10 consecutive sessions, you begin fading once the student had successfully met all parts of that goal: (1) they were on task for 85% of intervals and (2) they continued to be on task for 10 consecutive sessions. During fading, you gradually change any strategies the FABI team has identified for reduction or removal. For example, you might gradually reduce the amount of reinforcement for the replacement behavior and/or how often it is delivered.

During fading, you will continue collecting student outcome data in the same manner as it was collected during the full intervention phase. In most cases, this is a daily direct observation but may also include permanent products (e.g., a self-monitoring checklist). Analyzing graphed data weekly will help the team determine whether behaviors continue to occur at levels seen during full implementation of the intervention. In some cases, you may have to temporarily reintroduce the full intervention to counteract deterioration of the behavior (i.e., behaviors change in the wrong direction, with the replacement behavior decreasing and/or the target behavior increasing). In some cases, there might be a decrease in stability (i.e., the replacement and/or target behaviors bounce, sometimes occurring as expected and sometimes less or more than expected). Before reintroducing the intervention, the FABI team will determine how the fading plan failed and will revise the plan accordingly.

Fading often fails because it occurs too quickly, in which case it can be implemented at a slower pace. Sometimes fading fails because a strategy that was identified to be withdrawn is, in fact, essential for the replacement behavior to occur. In this case, the team will devise a plan for accommodating that essential strategy. When fading fails, it is best to reimplement the original plan and get the replacement behavior back to goal levels. When data show that the behavior has returned to goal levels, you can begin the revised plan for fading. Throughout the fading process, you should continue to collect student outcome data as you did during intervention.

Once you have successfully completed the fading procedure, you want the replacement response to continue (response maintenance). You should continue to collect student outcome data during the response maintenance phase, but the frequency of data collection can be gradually reduced. Rather than collecting data every day, as you did when using the intervention, you could reduce data collection to twice a week, then to once a week, then three times in 2 weeks, and so on until you feel confident the student will continue to exhibit the replacement behavior. How quickly you reduce data collection will depend on your analysis of graphed data. As long as the behavior remains stable and at or near the level identified in the goal, you can feel confident in the maintenance of the student's behavior changes.

One way to check the success of the behavior plan is to do another social validity check-in with the rest of the team and especially with the teacher and family (see Box 11.2, FABI Step 5: Testing the Intervention). As we discussed in Chapter 17, you should have had the teacher and family complete a social validity survey at the end of the intervention. You could do that again or do something more informal as the student completes the response maintenance phase. You might ask whether they think the intervention was effective and the student was successful. We have had teachers respond that they think the student continues to be successful even after the replacement behavior has slightly deteriorated.

Stimulus generalization data can be collected throughout the intervention, fading, and maintenance phases. However, you may not observe the replacement behavior in another setting until the student's replacement behavior demonstrates improvement. We suggest probing for generalization in other settings as the student nears goal completion. Data collection can be scheduled once per week and continue during maintenance. If stimulus generalization does not occur, the FABI team can identify whether the full intervention needs to be implemented in the new setting(s) or conditions or whether less intense strategies will suffice, such as those identified in Figure 18.1.

Response Maintenance	Stimulus Generalization	Response Generalization
Select useful behaviors to teach that will be naturally reinforced in the environment.	Specify environments and settings where the behavior should occur and where it should not. Tell the student to try out the replacement behavior in the new setting.	
Once the intervention is successful in the primary setting, implement it in multiple settings.	Informally implement the intervention in more than one setting (e.g., in different classrooms, with different subjects in the same classroom, or in different ways of instructing, such as in small and large groups).	Teach different response examples. This might include teaching different ways to get teacher attention, different ways to request reinforcement, different ways to communicate a request, and different ways to complete an assignment.
Change the reinforcement schedule. • Gradually reduce high rates of reinforcement to the level naturally occurring in the environment. • Switch to intermittent reinforcement (variable schedule) as the replacement behavior gains fluency (occurs more frequently).	Randomly select times in other settings to reinforce the student for exhibiting the replacement behavior (e.g., another classroom or subject, such as math or reading).	Reinforce response variability. Reinforce replacement responses that are similar and functionally the same as the identified replacement behavior. For example, if the replacement behavior is communicating wants and needs, reinforce it with oral requests, signing, pointing, or use of the Picture Exchange Communication System (PECS), and so forth.
Use a conditioned reinforcer such as points, stickers, and tokens that provide both immediate reinforcement and can be accumulated for use later in the day or week. In schools implementing Ci3T model, use the universal reinforcer—the ticket to program for generalization.	Implement the intervention in the natural environment (e.g., classroom) rather than in a clinical setting. The similarity of stimuli across classrooms will help with setting generalization.	
Vary the stimulus dimensions. For example, if the stimulus is an instruction, vary other elements, such as tone of voice, type of paper, or who gives the instruction so the student perceives other settings as being similar.	Ask people in other classrooms to reinforce the replacement behavior. Or, if the student is in the same classroom all day, reinforce the behavior during a different subject. In schools not implementing a multi-tiered system, be certain to use the same universal reinforcer (e.g., ticket) to program for generalization. Avoid introducing a competing reinforcer.	

(continued)

FIGURE 18.1. Some common strategies to improve maintenance and generalization.

Response Maintenance	Stimulus Generalization	Response Generalization
Use best-practice instructional strategies and continue these after the intervention is finished.	Identify an object that occurs in both the setting in which you began the intervention and a setting in which you want generalization. For example, a timer or teacher visual cue for breaks.	
Teach self-management strategies. —Teach the student to go to the teacher or other staff to show finished products or after a specified period of time. —Teach the student to monitor their replacement behavior and request reinforcement or self-reinforce.	Use self-management strategies across settings (e.g., train other teachers to respond to requests for reinforcement, instruct the student to use the replacement behavior in other settings).	
	Use similar stimuli in other settings. For example, using a timer for breaks or using the same visual cues across settings.	
	Implement the intervention in the generalization setting.	

FIGURE 18.1. *(continued)*

In classrooms, data on response generalization are not usually collected. However, you may observe response generalization during an intervention observation, or it may be observed by others working in the primary or generalization settings. Remember that to be considered response generalization, the new response must be functionally related to the identified replacement behavior. That means you should consider whether the new response leads to the same outcome (consequence) as the original replacement behavior. Note these observations so that all members of the team are aware that they should also be reinforcing these functional topographies of the replacement behavior.

Summary

In this chapter, we identified three behavior-change outcomes: response maintenance, stimulus generalization, and response generalization. We defined and described the importance of each outcome to an effective and successful intervention. We also described fading procedures as they relate to response maintenance. Finally, we described how maintenance and generalization data might be collected and used to ensure the continued effectiveness of the behavioral intervention. Figure 18.1 provides some strategies for developing and supporting each of these outcomes.

Treatment integrity, social validity, and generalization and maintenance are not just incidental elements to be included in an intervention when possible. They are essential components or factors that influence the success of the intervention. If we do not assess whether the teaching staff and family support the intervention (social validity), whether the intervention is implemented accurately (treatment integrity), and whether the student maintains responding over time or generalizes to other pertinent settings, we are inhibiting the success of the intervention. We may also find ourselves repeatedly working to change a student's behavior. Be certain to review the information in Box 11.2, FABI Step 5: Testing the Intervention, to learn more about the timing of collecting these data.

In Chapter 19, the final chapter of Part V, we provide explicit directions for designing interventions. We summarize and synthesize intervention design components across the four intervention options (Method 1, 2, or 3, or the combination of Methods 1 and 2) explaining how to draft A-R-E components that link each intervention tactic to the hypothesized function of the challenging behavior. We also provide guidance for introducing the intervention to the teacher and students, including checks for understanding before beginning implementation of the FABI.

CHAPTER 19

Designing Your Intervention

LEARNING OBJECTIVES

- Describe how to draft A-R-E components (antecedent adjustments, reinforcement procedures, and extinction procedures), linking each intervention tactic to the hypothesized function.
- Explain tips for introducing the intervention to the teacher and students, including checks for understanding before implementation begins.

At this point, you have had an opportunity to read through the illustrations of Intervention Method 1: Teach the Replacement Behavior, Intervention Method 2: Adjust the Environment, Intervention Method 3: Shift the Contingencies, and the combination of Methods 1 and 2. In addition, you have also learned more about the core concepts needed to draw accurate conclusions about intervention outcomes: treatment integrity, social validity, and generalization and maintenance.

In each chapter, we described how to use the Function-Based Intervention Decision Model to select the intervention method as well as how to draft proposed antecedent adjustments, reinforcement procedures, and extinction procedures (A-R-E components) that constitute the FABI to be tested. A keystone skill in designing the A-R-E components is linking each intervention tactic to the hypothesized function(s) of the target behavior we would like to see less (or none!) of going forward. As such, in this chapter, we provide a more detailed description of how to design A-R-E components linked to the reasons the target behavior is occurring. In addition, we provide guidance for making sure that the teachers and others responsible for implementing the intervention have been trained and clearly understand the specific details. Ethical considerations in implementation design are presented in Box 19.1.

> **BOX 19.1. Ethical Considerations in Chapter 19:
> BACB Ethics Code for Behavior Analysts**
>
> **2.09 Involving Clients and Stakeholders**
>
> This chapter reminds you that in addition to the teacher, family members and the student should be part of selecting and designing the intervention.
>
> **2.14 Selecting, Designing, and Implementing Behavior-Change Interventions**
>
> This chapter provides additional detail on how to use the decision model to select and design the A-R-E components for an intervention. Ideas for additional assessment and observation to answer the questions in the decision model that were suggested in Chapters 12 and 13 are emphasized. Examples for each intervention method were included. The chapter also repeated the emphasis on considering feedback from family members and teachers to ensure that the intervention meets their diverse needs and perspectives and fits the context in which it will be implemented. The reinforcement component of the intervention was clearly linked to the function of the target behavior identified through the FBA. There was a reminder that *both* functions must be addressed in cases in which there is more than one. The extinction procedure was also emphasized as an essential component of the FABI.
>
> **2.16 Describing Behavior-Change Interventions Before Implementation**
>
> The last half of this chapter provides guidance and strategies for thoroughly training teachers implementing the intervention and for training family members who are implementing it in the home environment.

Drafting A-R-E Components: Linking to Hypothesized Functions

As we discussed previously, each intervention method includes <u>a</u>ntecedent adjustments (A), shifts in rates of <u>r</u>einforcement (R), and <u>e</u>xtinction procedures (E). More specifically,

1. Eliminate antecedent variables that set the stage for the target behavior and establish new conditions in which the replacement behavior is more likely to occur.
2. Provide needed positive reinforcement for the replacement behavior.
3. Withhold the consequence that previously reinforced the target behavior.

Each of the three components is important. It is essential that the specific tactics for each component address all the reasons that have been identified for the occurrence of the target behavior (i.e., the function of the behavior). If the FBA indicates that the target behavior is serving more than one function (e.g., accessing teacher and peer attention *and* escaping too-difficult tasks), then the A-R-E components need to address *both* maintaining functions, as addressing only one function would be far less likely to achieve the desired outcomes.

Developing the Antecedent (A) Component

When you answer the two questions in the Function-Based Intervention Decision Model, you are focused on the antecedents. Chapter 11 describes this model and how to make the distinction between a student who has not acquired or cannot fluently perform the replacement behavior and one who can perform the replacement behavior but does not do so under the conditions in which the problem behavior occurs. Chapter 12 describes how to identify or adjust antecedents when it has been determined that the student cannot perform the replacement behavior.

Once a skill deficit has been identified, Chapter 12 further identifies common deficits in social, communication, academic, or self-management skills that frequently result in problem behavior and suggests assessment and observation tools that probe more deeply to identify the specific skill deficit and possible antecedent modifications to address it. The intervention includes using validated tools, such as the SSiS-RS (Gresham & Elliott, 2008a), or reviewing the student's academic performance, especially in the subject area in which the problem behavior occurs. The illustration in Chapter 12 (Reeves et al., 2017) provided an example of one strategy that might be used to determine antecedent adjustments when the student cannot perform the replacement behavior. After reviewing data from the FBA interviews and A-B-C observations, the authors completed a task analysis of the replacement behavior to determine the specific skills the student needed to successfully perform the behavior.

As illustrated in Chapter 12, if the student cannot perform the replacement behavior, antecedent adjustments must include (1) training or instruction in the behavior, (2) adjusting stimuli and environmental conditions so that they prompt and support the replacement behavior, and (3) eliminating or adjusting stimuli that trigger the target behavior or prevent the student from performing the replacement behavior.

Let us briefly illustrate choosing antecedents for a Method 1 intervention. In this case, a student is aggressive (B) in math class. The target behavior is triggered when the teacher gives the student a math assignment (A). This results in the teacher removing the assignment and letting the student sit quietly (C). Additional assessments and task analyses determine that the student cannot complete the assignment because they are missing the necessary math skills. But the student also has a skill deficit in how to appropriately communicate to the teacher that they cannot complete the assignment. Both deficits must be addressed. Antecedent strategies will teach the math skill and how to request a break or how to ask for help, thus resolving the communication deficit and addressing the escape function of the behavior. Because the assignment has triggered the behavior, antecedent strategies might also adjust the assignment itself (Umbreit et al., 2004). For example, there may be fewer problems to complete, or the problems may be adjusted to the student's skill level. Another strategy is to offer the student additional help; for example, a peer buddy might work with the student as they both complete the assignment, or the teacher may take a few minutes to make sure the student understands the assignment and how to get started.

In summary, when determining antecedent adjustments for teaching the replacement behavior, you:

1. Review the interviews and observations to determine whether the student has a skill deficit.
2. Identify and use additional data sources to pinpoint the skill deficit (e.g., with validated tools such as the SSiS-RS (Gresham & Elliott, 2008a), academic data, task analysis).

3. Solicit family input about their values and goals and the student's preferences and perspective that might impact the selection of the replacement behavior or antecedents.
4. Identify a replacement behavior that addresses the function of the target behavior and the skill deficit.
5. Identify antecedents that trigger the target behavior, as illustrated in Chapters 12–15.
6. Design an antecedent adjustment for training the replacement behavior.
7. Design antecedent adjustments to prevent the target behavior and support the replacement behavior.

In Chapter 13, we described how to answer the second question: Do the antecedent conditions represent effective practices for the student? The answer to this question can be found broadly by reviewing all available implementation data for the classroom, the entire school, or the programwide system for supporting behavior. These data will give you the information you need to determine what support the environment already provides and what additional antecedent strategies are needed to best address the requirements of the intervention. If you are in a school or program implementing a tiered system of support such as Ci3T, the first part of the review would include data detailing whether Tier 1 is being implemented as intended in the classroom (e.g., expectations are posted) and in the school or program (e.g., there is a schoolwide reinforcement system). Examples of Tier 1 checklists are available on the Ci3T and PBIS websites, or your school may have its own tool. In your review, it will also help to identify what Tier 2 supports are available, whether a previous intervention for the student included their use, and what the data show about their effectiveness. For example, in schools implementing Ci3T, their Ci3T Implementation Manual includes secondary (Tier 2) and tertiary (Tier 3) intervention grids delineating all available interventions for students needing more than Tier 1 has to offer—including a FABI (Lane, Buckman, et al., 2020).

If you are not in a school or program implementing a tiered system of supports, it is still important to identify what schoolwide and classroom systems of behavioral support exist (e.g., discipline procedures, intervention teams, classroom feedback systems) and whether they are being implemented correctly (i.e., implementation fidelity). If your school evaluates the implementation fidelity of these systems, you can review the data. If not, observations are necessary to identify what practices are in place.

As noted in Chapter 13, the second question should also lead to an examination of whether best practices are implemented in the instructional environment. The chapter includes checklists and ideas for best instructional practice, including checklists to identify low-intensity strategies to increase engagement (Table 13.1) and considerations for differentiating instructional delivery (Table 13.2). The case illustration of David, an adapted version of Germer and colleagues (2011), provides an account of the team process for answering the second question. It includes a review of Tier 1 practices, observations of classroom academic instruction during the time David's target behavior occurred, and asking David's parents and teacher to complete the SSiS-RS.

When determining antecedent adjustments for implementing best practices, you:

1. Review interviews and observations to determine the specific antecedents that trigger the target behavior as described in Chapter 13.
2. Review additional data sources, such as a Tier 1 checklist, to evaluate the current

environment. Check for implementation of universal practices to prevent problem behavior (e.g., expectations, room arrangement, organized materials, a system of positive descriptive feedback) and use of less intensive interventions (e.g., Tier 2).
3. Observe to determine whether the teacher is using best practices related to instruction and task demands.
4. Review previous interventions to determine what has been ineffective.
5. Review the student's social, communication, and self-management skills to identify any that might be taught to support the replacement behavior.
6. Solicit input from family members and the classroom teacher to ensure a cultural and contextual fit for the antecedent adjustments.
7. Identify antecedent adjustments using effective behavioral and instructional practices (see Table 13.3 for some examples).

When the answer to both questions in the Function-Based Intervention Decision Model is negative (i.e., you find that the student needs instruction and that effective practices need to be added to the setting), you must identify antecedent strategies that address both training and effective practice. This process is clearly illustrated in Chapter 15, which discusses the use of Intervention Methods 1 and 2.

It can also happen that the antecedents for the target behavior are different in different settings, so accurately identifying the antecedents is key. That is to say, the target behavior may be the same in both settings and the function of the behavior may be the same, but the trigger may be different. As an example, you may identify a target behavior of noncompliance that includes verbal aggression with the function of task escape. During social studies, the behavior occurs when group activities are initiated, but during math it occurs during the teacher's instruction. When you ask the two questions, you find that math instruction does not represent best practice (Question 2), but in social studies, you identify a reading comprehension deficit. In this scenario, antecedent adjustments will necessarily be different in the different settings.

Developing the Reinforcement (R) Component

The reinforcement component is developed by identifying the function of the target behavior. The intervention almost always provides the same reinforcement for the replacement behavior that had been identified as reinforcing the target behavior. For example, if the reinforcement for the target behavior was gaining attention, the reinforcement for the replacement behavior would most likely be gaining attention. There is one exception. If the student is engaged in task escape because they cannot perform the behavior fluently, the instruction will likely be adjusted to a proper instructional level at which the student can learn. When this happens, essentially, the need to escape is no longer present. In this case, providing task escape as a reinforcer for learning is inadvisable. It would be preferable to positively reinforce the student's learning.

The illustrations in Chapters 12 through 15, based on interventions in tiered systems and other contexts, provide good examples of both positive and negative reinforcement functions for the target behavior and how to develop that reinforcement component. Interestingly, the illustrations in Chapters 13 and 15 provide examples of the dual functions of the target behavior. In the Chapter 13 illustration, David accessed attention and avoided instruction when the target behavior occurred. The dual functions were positive reinforcement: attention and negative reinforcement: activity. Both functions were addressed in the intervention. David received positive reinforcement for the replacement behavior in the form of tickets (the schoolwide reinforcer) and behavior-specific praise. He received negative reinforcement for the replacement behavior in the form of a brief break when he had finished a task.

The illustration of Saida in Chapter 15 provides an example of how to combine intervention strategies when both Method 1 and Method 2 are identified. Even though both methods were implemented in the intervention, the reinforcement component was the same for both. In this illustration, the dual functions of the target behavior were positive reinforcement: attention and negative reinforcement: activity (Turton et al., 2007). The reinforcement component of the intervention was designed so any appropriate responding resulted in Saida receiving many different kinds of attention from the staff (e.g., thumbs-up and praise) and allowed her to escape from further classwork once she had completed her activity.

The illustration in Chapter 14 is a little different. The function of Claire's behavior was identified as negative reinforcement: attention that occurred when she gave an incorrect response. The intervention developed by the team allowed her to escape attention when she completed her daily goal for participation, which was the replacement behavior. This reinforcement strategy addressed the function of the behavior. The team could have stopped there. However, they also added positive reinforcement to the intervention. The addition of positive reinforcement was due to input from the student, a family member, and her teacher, all of whom were part of the interview and teaming process for designing the intervention. Positive reinforcement serves several important purposes. First, students need feedback about how they are doing. Forms of attention, such as praise (e.g., high-five, verbal praise, or stickers), and tickets, used in a schoolwide system for following expectations, provide feedback when they are given and when they are exchanged. Because attention is so often used in the classroom, it provides continuity for the student and a longer-term support if positive reinforcement can be added to the intervention. Second, a break is a strategy that should be faded as the student becomes more fluent in the replacement behavior. Part of that fading and generalization procedure is to find another way to reinforce the replacement behavior. Interviews confirmed that the student responded to positive reinforcement under other circumstances, making this a viable reinforcement strategy.

Developing the Extinction (E) Component

The extinction procedure is an essential component of the FABI (Janney et al., 2013). Extinction means that the stimulus that previously reinforced the target behavior is no longer provided, and the behavior becomes weaker. The student must no longer be able to avoid a task or gain attention or participate in an activity if they exhibit the problem behavior. It's important to understand the behavioral principle of extinction so that you can accurately include it as part of a behavior-change plan. In Chapter 2, we define extinction, identify the key conditions that must be met for an extinction procedure, and recognize some challenges when extinction procedures are implemented. This information can be supplemented with more detailed descriptions in the behavioral literature. When designing an extinction procedure, first ensure that the key elements of extinction are in place: The behavior must have a history of reinforcement and the reinforcer that maintains the behavior must be eliminated. This should weaken the target behavior. In a FABI, the specific reinforcement that is maintaining the target behavior is identified during the FBA and eliminated as part of the intervention.

Extinction is more effective and leads to fewer challenges if both the other intervention components of antecedent adjustments and reinforcement for the replacement behavior are in place. This means adjusting the antecedents so that whatever triggered the problem behavior is eliminated or is modified sufficiently so that the problem behavior is less likely to occur. For example, if being given a math assignment consistently results in Angel's aggressive behavior, adjusting math assignments or adjusting the way they are presented should make it less likely that aggression is triggered. Even more important, the intervention must ensure that a more acceptable behavior—the replacement behavior in the FABI—receives the reinforcement that previously maintained the problem behavior. When reinforcement of the replacement behavior addresses the function of the problem behavior and the rates of reinforcement are sufficient, using a function-matched extinction procedure for the problem behavior should result in it weakening quickly with no spontaneous recovery or other side effects (e.g., anxiety or aggression).

The illustrations in Chapters 12 through 15 provide some interesting examples of extinction procedures. For example, in the illustration in Chapter 12, the authors identified an extinction procedure for two functions of the target behavior. The first extinction procedure withheld attention, but included a strategy for brief redirection, minimizing rather than eliminating attention, because completely eliminating reinforcement of the target behavior may not be possible. Continuing to question a student until she meets a response goal in the Chapter 14 illustration demonstrated the extinction of a problem behavior maintained by negative reinforcement (i.e., task escape).

The Ci3T system provides a planning form for the FABI that features a section for summarizing data gathered during the FABI process, including a section for documenting information from the interviews and observations, a section for information gleaned from rating scales, and a section for determining the intervention method. Summarizing this information makes it easier for the team to identify and design all intervention components.

Preparing for Intervention Implementation: Checking for Understanding

To set the stage for successful implementation, it is important to ensure that the team who put the intervention in place and the students themselves are comfortable with the proposed intervention plans (e.g., A-R-E components). Everyone must have a common understanding of how these plans will be implemented. We emphasize the importance of reviewing the finalized intervention plans with the teacher and students, including checking for understanding before implementation begins.

During the A-R-E planning process, several ideas may be generated for each A-R-E component. As the FABI team works through these ideas, some may be eliminated immediately because they are viewed as too cumbersome in terms of the time, effort, and/or materials needed. Others may not be included because they are not in line with Tier 1 efforts. For example, introducing a reinforcer other than the schoolwide reinforcer (ticket) is not advisable as it does not support generalization. It also limits the number of adults who can provide acknowledgments paired with behavior-specific praise.

After the A-R-E components are drafted, it is again important to revisit each specific tactic to determine how well it addresses the hypothesized function. For example, if the student's target behavior is maintained by accessing teacher and peer attention as well as escaping a nonpreferred (e.g., too-difficult or too-easy) task, each function will need to be addressed. For example, the plan might include working on the following:

- Complete the first five questions and then check them with your teacher (teacher attention).
- Complete the next five questions and then check them with your learning partner (peer attention).
- Take a brief break contingent on completing the work (escape task).

Review the strategies that have been eliminated to ensure that they are not essential for addressing the function. If they are essential but there are difficulties with implementation, work with the teacher and parent to find a way to modify them so the function is successfully addressed. Review the strategies that have been modified to ensure that the modification continues to sufficiently address the function of the behavior. If the function is carefully considered during the planning process, this review usually can be done quickly.

Once the final set of A-R-E components addressing the full scope of maintaining functions is finalized, the next step is to formally assess social validity from the adult and student perspectives. The goal is to be certain that people are comfortable with the goals, procedures, and intended outcomes. As we mentioned in earlier chapters, assessment can be done by using validated rating-skills tools such as the IRP-15 (Martens & Witt, 1982) for adults and the CIRP (Witt & Elliott, 1983) for children. You could also use semistructured interviews (see Gresham & Lopez, 1996; *www.ci3t.org* for illustrations) to gain stakeholders' perspectives. The point is to confirm that people are comfortable with the specifics of the intervention before taking the time to teach them how to implement them. If during this social validity assessment phase, it is determined that people are uncomfortable with one or more components, it may be necessary to revisit the A-R-E components as a FABI team. However, if people are comfortable with the full set of procedures, the next step is to make sure that they are comfortable in knowing how to implement them as planned (i.e., with treatment integrity).

There are a number of ways to check for understanding, for example, demonstrations and role plays, as well as brief written checks. The team might walk through specific steps with the teacher (who is also a member of the team) to first ensure that the adult components are clear, and then have the teacher walk through and role-play relevant components with the student. For example, return to Figure 16.1 (p. 232), for which the role play might sound like this: "Let's practice. After you finish your first five problems, you will raise your hand and wait for me to acknowledge you. Then, you can come over and show me the fine work you just did! This way, you can get a short break and we can share your success together." On the other hand, written checks of understanding might ask relevant adults to review the sequencing of steps or even answer multiple-choice questions just to make certain that everyone agrees about what implementation will look like. You might consider reviewing published works that have several practical illustrations of how to use checks for understanding (e.g., Aitken et al., 2011; Cox et al., 2011; Germer et al., 2011; Majeika et al., 2011).

Although doing formal checks for understanding may seem silly or unnecessary at the beginning, we actually think this step is important. People often think they are describing the same tactics when, in reality, the words on the page can mean different things to different people. For example, when a plan includes the tactic of a brief break, "brief" may mean 2 minutes to the student, but it might mean 30 seconds to the teacher. Clarity on implementation procedures should facilitate treatment integrity, which in turn will foster meaningful and lasting change for students.

Summary

In this chapter, we offered additional illustrations of how to design A-R-E components that are clearly linked to the reasons why the target behavior occurs. We included information to help you create interventions that properly address situations where there are multiple maintaining functions. We reiterated the need to include family members in the process of selecting intervention strategies and designing the intervention. We also provided guidance for ensuring the teacher and other agents are clear about the specific intervention details, so they can put the plan in place with treatment integrity. This chapter concludes Part V.

After designing an intervention based on the maintaining function(s) of the target behavior, the next task is to implement the intervention and conduct a "test" to determine if the introduction of the intervention yields systematic changes in the student's behavior. This step includes multiple components. Part VI introduces *Step 5: Testing the Intervention* and includes two chapters that introduce the process of determining the extent to which there is a functional relation between implementing the intervention with integrity and changes in student performance. In Chapter 20, we address three key questions in testing the intervention: (1) Is the intervention being implemented as planned (i.e., treatment integrity)?, (2) How is it working (i.e., functional relation)?, and (3) What do stakeholders think (i.e., social validity)? We also discuss monitoring factors that enhance an intervention's success.

PART VI
Step 5: Testing the Intervention

STEP #	FUNCTIONAL ASSESSMENT-BASED INTERVENTION STEPS
1	Identifying Students Who May Need a Functional Assessment-Based Intervention
2	Conducting the Functional Assessment
3	Collecting Baseline Data
4	Designing the Functional Assessment-Based Intervention
5	Testing the Intervention

After designing an intervention based on the maintaining function(s) in Step 4, the next task is to put the intervention in place and conduct a "test" to determine if the introduction of the intervention yields systematic changes in the student's behavior in Step 5—the final step. As you might expect, this step has multiple components. Part VI includes two chapters that introduce the process of determining the extent to which there is a functional relation between the introduction of the intervention, when implemented with integrity, and changes in student performance.

In Chapter 20, Determining Intervention Outcomes, we introduce three key questions to address when testing the intervention: (1) Is the intervention being implemented as planned (i.e., treatment integrity)?, (2) How is it working (i.e., functional relation)?, and (3) What do stakeholders think (i.e., social validity)? We also discuss monitoring factors that enhance an intervention's success.

In Chapter 21, Wrapping It Up: Ending with a Defensible Functional Assessment-Based Intervention, we explore how to prepare a practical report of intervention outcomes. We discuss finalizing the behavior intervention plan, having the proper documentation, and transitioning the plan and documents across time and settings.

CHAPTER 20

Determining Intervention Outcomes

LEARNING OBJECTIVES

- Determine how stakeholders view intervention goals, procedures, and outcomes (social validity).
- Determine whether the intervention is being implemented as designed (treatment integrity).
- Determine whether the intervention "works" to change student performance (functional relation).

At this point in in the process of designing, implementing, and evaluating FABIs, you have completed the following steps:

- Step 1: Identifying Students Who May Need a FABI
- Step 2: Conducting the Functional Assessment
- Step 3: Collecting Baseline Data
- Step 4: Designing the Intervention

To briefly summarize, in Step 1, you determined which student(s) needed a FABI: students receiving special education services, with an FBA and BIP specified in their IEP, and general education students whose behavior screening data suggest they require intensive intervention efforts to meet their multiple needs. In Step 2, you conducted an FBA, which involved using interviews, rating scales, and direct observations to determine why the target (undesirable) behaviors were occurring (e.g., to access and/or avoid attention, tangibles, tasks, and/or sensory experiences). In this step, you also identified a replacement behavior, which is often functionally equivalent to the target behaviors. In Step 3, you collected baseline data on the replacement and/or target behavior. In Step 4, you designed the intervention using the Function-Based Intervention Decision Model to select an appropriate intervention method and then developed A-R-E components based on the hypothesized function(s) of the target behavior.

At this point, we are ready to move on to the final step. In *Step 5: Testing the Intervention*, we engage in activities to ensure that the intervention is working for the student and other stakeholders. Specifically, we monitor the intervention and collect data to answer three questions:

1. Is the intervention happening as planned (treatment integrity)?
2. How well is the intervention working (functional relation)?
3. What do stakeholders think about the intervention goals, procedures, and outcomes (social validity)?

In this chapter, we provide an overview of Step 5. Then we offer suggestions on how practitioners and researchers can answer these three important questions. See Box 20.1 to review ethical considerations.

BOX 20.1. Ethical Considerations in Chapter 20: BACB Ethics Code for Behavior Analysts

2.17 Collecting and Using Data

This chapter outlines the treatment integrity, social validity, and behavior-change data that are collected during implementation of the FABI. Treatment integrity data are collected during each phase of the intervention, including maintenance and generalization. As part of the FABI process, you use treatment integrity data to tell you whether the intervention is being implemented as planned and ensures that data are measured accurately. Social validity data provide information about the stakeholders' (teachers', family members', and students') views of the goals, procedures, and outcomes. Before the intervention, social validity data are used to refine and individualize the intervention's "fit" within the environment. After the intervention, social validity data are used to evaluate whether the stakeholders feel the intervention met their goals and whether the outcomes were acceptable. When procedures and outcomes are acceptable, the intervention is more likely to be implemented as it was written and to be continued as needed. Data on the extent to which the behavior changes and the outcomes of intervention are used to demonstrate the effectiveness of the intervention.

2.18 Continual Evaluation of the Behavior-Change Intervention

Data are collected and monitored throughout all phases of the intervention. Part of the beauty of using single-case design methodology is that if data show less-than-successful implementation, a phase change can be implemented and a modified intervention can be introduced. In addition, if treatment integrity does not meet the criterion, training for people involved in implementation may address the issue. Review the data and talk to the stakeholders to assess the reasons for low treatment integrity. Lower social validity scores require a discussion with stakeholders about their reasons so their concerns can be addressed. If the behavior-change data show the intervention is not as successful as expected, intervention strategies should be reevaluated. Ongoing monitoring is needed so the goal of intervention, meaningful and lasting behavior change, can be realized.

Treatment Integrity: Is the Intervention Happening as Planned?

As we discussed in Chapter 16, it is important to collect information on the extent to which the A-R-E intervention components are implemented as planned. We encourage you to collect treatment integrity data during each phase to the extent possible (e.g., during later stages of the first baseline condition A_1 and the withdrawal phase A_2 as well as during both introductions of the intervention: B_1 and B_2).

This information needs to be collected each time the intervention is implemented (B_1 and B_2). For example, if you are using an A_1-B_1-A_2-B_2 withdrawal design to determine if there is a functional relation between the introduction of the intervention and changes in the student behavior being measured (e.g., engagement and positive social interactions), then the team would collect treatment integrity data during both B phases (B_1 and B_2). As noted previously, FABI teams analyze treatment integrity data so they can accurately determine if an intervention is producing the desired changes in student performance.

In addition to collecting information during each introduction of the intervention, information also should be collected during both A phases (A_1 and A_2) to see if any A-R-E components were present during the baseline or withdrawal phases. This information helps in accurately interpreting intervention outcomes lest they can be thought of as "contamination."

Given that treatment integrity data are important to accurately determine if the intervention results in the desired changes in student performance, FABI teams need to monitor whether the intervention components are being properly applied when the intervention is in effect. However, you might not also realize that teams also need to monitor for the use of the intervention components when the intervention is not in effect.

For example, if a FABI team is using an A_1-B_1-A_2-B_2 withdrawal design to determine if there is a functional relation between the introduction of the intervention and changes in the student behavior being measured, then the team would obviously want to collect treatment integrity data during both intervention phases (B_1 and B_2). But the team will also want to collect treatment integrity data during both baseline phases (A_1 and A_2). This helps the team understand which elements of the intervention are truly responsible for the changes in behavior and ensures that the intervention elements actually are being withdrawn during the return to baseline (A_2).

Student Performance: How Well Is the FABI Working?

The next question we want to ask in testing the intervention is: How well is the FABI working? Or more technically: Is there a functional relation between the introduction of the FABI when implemented with integrity and changes in student behavior? In Chapter 11, we discussed the basics of creating an experimental design to "test" the intervention. You might recall you selected a practical design, such as an A_1-B_1-A_2-B_2 withdrawal design, or a multiple baseline design (e.g., multiple baseline designs across behaviors or settings), that allows for one demonstration and two replications for a student.

Formal tests, such as an A_1-B_1-A_2-B_2 withdrawal design to assess whether a FABI addresses a performance deficit, or a multiple baselines design to assess a FABI addressing an acquisition deficit are important for practitioners and researchers alike. As practitioners, FABI teams will want to be certain they have clearly demonstrated the impact of the intervention to ensure that the FABI and not some other factor (e.g., serving blueberry pie after lunch) is producing the changes in student performance. Similarly, for researchers partnering with practitioners to study how well FABIs work with preschool, elementary, middle, and high school students (see Common et al., 2017), they also want to be confident in the experience for the student at hand (internal validity) so they can build an evidence base to support using FABIs with other students (external validity). In addition to needing to measure the integrity of the intervention (reliability of the independent variable) and the accuracy with which a student's behavior is measured (reliability of the dependent variable), it is also important to assess social validity.

Social Validity: What Do Stakeholders Think about the Goals, Procedures, and Outcomes?

As we discussed in Chapter 17, social validity refers to the social significance of the intervention goals, the social acceptability of the intervention procedures, and the social importance of the intervention effects. Wolf (1978) suggested that social validity is how applied behavior analysis found its heart. We have learned that social validity plays an important role in the intervention experience, influencing treatment integrity and intervention outcomes—including generalization and maintenance (Lane & Beebe-Frankenberger, 2004).

Thus, the next and final question to address is: What do stakeholders such as teachers, families, and the student themself think about the goals, procedures, and outcomes? This question is asked during *Step 4: Designing the Intervention* (see Box 11.1) and again after the intervention "test" has been conducted as detailed in *Step 5: Testing the Intervention* (see Box 11.2). Prior to implementation, this information is used to refine the intervention to increase the likelihood it will be delivered as designed (treatment integrity) and—if the intervention aligns with the target behaviors' maintaining function(s)—lead to the desired changes in student performance and generalize to other settings, with other individuals, and over time (maintenance). After the intervention occurs, social validity data can also be used to interpret intervention outcomes. For example, the data can be used to determine if various A-R-E components fell short of meeting teacher, family, and/or student expectations and whether the eventual outcomes are seen by stakeholders as socially valid.

The Logistics of Testing the FABI

In Box 11.2, *Step 5: Testing the Intervention*, we provide step-by-step guidelines for applying the specific lessons learned from earlier chapters in this book (e.g., how to measure behavior, assess reliability, and graph data). As you read through these logistics, note we include a step to ensure ethical, equitable conduct. In the beginning chapters of this book, we focused on meeting students' multiple needs in a respectful, positive, effective, and equitable manner. By referring to this ethical checklist, we can support adherence to core ethical principles, such as doing no harm and providing an intervention of benefit. The goal of FABI—actually of all interventions—is meaningful, lasting change (Baer et al., 1968, 1987). We emphasize this goal, but with an eye toward equity and ethical conduct.

Summary

In this chapter we introduced three key questions to address when testing the intervention: Is it happening (treatment integrity)? How is it working (functional relation)? What do stakeholders think (social validity)? We provided guidance to enhance the intervention's success, including steps and activities required in monitoring intervention efforts.

In Chapter 21, we provide guidance for preparing a practical report of intervention outcomes. We discuss finalizing the BIP, proper documentation, and transitioning the plan and documents across time and settings.

CHAPTER 21

Wrapping It Up
Ending with a Defensible Functional Assessment-Based Intervention

---

LEARNING OBJECTIVES

- Synthesize the FABI process.
- Describe the methods and procedures used within each step.
- Explain the connections between each step in the overall FABI process.

FABI is not a particular method or particular set of techniques. It is a process that includes many different methods and techniques aligned so that each one, in sequence, leads to the next. Some would say that each step "informs" the next one. The purpose of a FABI is not to identify the function of a target behavior. Identifying this behavior's function(s) is merely a means to an end—a key step in the process. The purpose of a FABI is to develop and implement an intervention that diminishes inappropriate or undesirable behavior, while simultaneously teaching and/or strengthening more appropriate, adaptive, and successful behavior in its place. Identifying the likely function of the target behavior is an essential piece in this process, but it is not the end goal.

Our goal is to apply this process in the natural setting rather than under highly controlled laboratory conditions to teach students behaviors that can help them to enjoy positive, productive experiences and interactions with others (see Lane, Oakes, et al., 2014; Umbreit & Ferro, 2022). Natural settings can include schools and classrooms and a wide variety of community-based settings, including homes and the workplace. Although the specific details of each situation may differ, the process remains the same. Ethical considerations for documenting and tying together all the information related to the FABI are presented in Box 21.1.

> **BOX 21.1. Ethical Considerations in Chapter 21: BACB Ethics Code for Behavior Analysts**
>
> **2.08 Communicating About Services**
>
> As part of the FABI process, the BIP communicates the intended intervention plan. As revisions are made and/or data are collected, the actual plan becomes a summary report meant for all the parties involved in the intervention, including current teachers, family members, the student, other service providers, future teachers, and school or program administrators. The BIP provides a historical record of the FBA and the subsequent individualized intervention (i.e., strategies, data, and outcomes).
>
> **2.14 Selecting, Designing, and Implementing Behavior-Change Interventions**
>
> The BIP described in Chapter 21 provides a written summary of the behavior-change interventions. This chapter also emphasizes that the goal of the FABI process is to apply it in natural settings to enhance the likelihood that the outcomes will be maintained and generalized in naturalistic conditions.
>
> **3.11 Documenting Professional Activity; 3.14 Facilitating Continuity of Services; 3.16 Appropriately Transitioning Services**
>
> The BIP coupled with the FABI Planning Form provide important documentation of all parts of the individualized intervention process. When used as intended, these forms facilitate communication among stakeholders. They document the services provided; describe and clarify all steps taken during the intervention process; list the intervention strategies; and provide data on intervention outcomes, treatment integrity, and social validity. Although the information in these forms covers a specific intervention and process, it will also be useful should there be an interruption in services or in the event the student is transitioned to another setting.

The Process

As you have read, the FABI process has five steps, with each step including multiple elements. These steps include:

- Step 1: Identifying Students Who May Need a Functional Assessment-Based Intervention
- Step 2: Conducting the Functional Assessment
- Step 3: Collecting Baseline Data
- Step 4: Designing the Functional Assessment-Based Intervention
- Step 5: Testing the Intervention

The FABI Planning Form and Behavior Intervention Plan (Lane, Menzies, et al., 2011), which has been presented repeatedly in this book, is an excellent tool for developing, managing, and implementing a FABI. At the end of this process, the FABI team reviews the completed the Functional Assessment and Behavior Intervention Plan: Planning Form to complete the BIP and/or school district standard forms after completing *Step 5: Testing the Intervention* (Handout 6.1 on *www.ci3t.org/FABI*). This BIP includes a brief summary of how the intervention was designed, implemented, and evaluated. Typically, this report also includes a graph summarizing the results, which can be used to determine if a functional relation was established between the introduction of the intervention and changes in student performance. In addition, information regarding the integrity with which the intervention was implemented as planned is also presented. The BIP also communicates the intended and actual plans with all involved parties: teachers, family members, and the students. It provides a fully defensible intervention plan that meets the highest professional standards and can be shared confidently with other professionals (e.g., those involved in due process hearings), families, and the student because it is based on the reasons why the target behavior occurred. In Form 21.1 (at the end of this chapter), we provide an illustration of how the team can extract information from the FABI planning form from Chapter 13 (Form 13.1) to prepare the BIP.

This FABI BIP document summarizes the entire process and becomes part of the student's educational records. In addition, this concise summary is shared with students' families so they will have a copy for their records and be able to share it with other professionals (e.g., future teachers) as they support their child navigating the PreK–12 education system. One benefit of having this concise FABI BIP is that it facilitates communication among all stakeholders. Another benefit is that it provides a historical record of the design, implementation, and evaluation of this evidence-based practice that serves a student's individualized needs through this intensive Tier 3 intervention. This information may be useful to other people in the child's life who want to learn more about what worked, for whom, and under what conditions.

Summary

In this chapter, we discussed preparing a practical report of intervention outcomes to facilitate communication and provide a historical record of the design, implementation, and evaluation of this intensive, tertiary Tier 3 intervention (see Form 21.1 at the end of this chapter). We discussed finalizing the BIP, having the proper documentation, and transitioning the plan and documents across time and settings.

Part VII, Getting Started in Your Own Context, provides considerations for getting started with the FABI process in various systems. In Chapter 22, we discuss ways to move forward with the FABI process, either in a tiered system or as an individual working on your own. We include considerations for implementation through school teams or a coaching model and offer general tips for collaboration, with a special emphasis on the influence of culture and community.

FORM 21.1

Behavior Intervention Plan

Directions: Review the completed the Functional Assessment and Behavior Intervention Plan: Planning Form to complete the Behavior Intervention Plan (BIP) and/or school district standard forms after completing *Step 5: Testing the Intervention* (Handout 6.1 on www.ci3t.org/FABI).

Student Name: David | **Student ID:** 138599

School: MLK Elementary School | **Date of Birth:** 1/30/2015

Current Grade Level: 2 | **Special Education:** ☐ Yes ☒ No

Gender: male | **Disability Eligibility:** NA

Parent(s): Bob and Tamekia | **Parent(s) Contact Number:** 555-867-5309

Date of Assessment: 9/15/2022 | **Classroom Teacher:** Ms. Jones

Persons Conducting the Assessment:

Role: ☒ Classroom Teacher ☐ SPED Teacher ☐ Teacher (Other) ☐ Teacher (Other)
☐ School Psychologist ☐ Counselor ☐ Behavior Specialist ☐ Intern
☐ University Student ☐ BCBA/ABA ☒ Other: Liaisons Kathryn & Eric

---

Behavioral Definitions

Target Behavior: Off-task behavior referred to engaging in behaviors or making verbal comments unrelated to instructional tasks. Examples include leaving the assigned instructional area without permission from teachers or adult; making inappropriate comments to others not related to instruction, engaged in activities other than the assigned activities, using instructional materials in ways not related to assigned activities, taking more than 30 seconds to get started on assigned activities. Non-examples include remaining in the assigned instructional area, making comments to others appropriately related to instruction, attending to or engaged in the assigned tasks, using instructional materials as intended, and getting started on assigned activities within 30 seconds.

Replacement Behavior: On-task behavior referred to engaging in behaviors or making verbal comments unrelated to instructional tasks. Examples include remaining in the assigned instructional area, making comments to others appropriately related to instruction, attending to or engaged in the assigned tasks, using instructional materials as intended, and getting started on assigned activities within 30 seconds. Non-examples include leaving the assigned instructional area without permission from teachers or adult; making inappropriate comments to others not related to instruction, engaged in activities other than the assigned activities, using instructional materials in ways not related to assigned activities, taking more than 30 seconds to get started on assigned activities.

Rationale for Replacement Behavior: We decided to focus on on-task behavior, because we wanted to make sure David was engaged constructively in the assigned tasks so that he could benefit from instruction academically as well as interact more easily with others in ways that protected his peers' learning opportunities and enhanced his social standing by limiting off-task and disruptive behaviors.

Baseline Statement: During the baseline condition, David's on-task behavior was variable (range 23.24% to 52.00%, M = 34.79%). An initial low level of on-task behavior was followed by a sharp increase in on-task behavior during the second observation (David spent part of this time working 1:1 with Ms. Jones). Between the second and fourth observation probes, a downward trend was noted.

(continued)

Form adapted from Lane, K. L., Menzies, H., Bruhn, A., & Crnobori, M. (2011). *Managing challenging behaviors in schools: Research-based strategies that work.* Guilford Press. Reprinted by permission. Graph from Germer, K. A., Kaplan, L. M., Giroux, L. N., Markham, E. H., Ferris, G. J., Oakes, W. P., & Lane, K. L. (2011). A function-based intervention to increase a second-grade student's on-task behavior in a general education classroom. *Beyond Behavior, 20,* 19–30. Reprinted by permission of Sage Publications.

Behavior Intervention Plan *(page 2 of 5)*

	Positive Reinforcement (Access Something)	**Negative Reinforcement (Avoid Something)**
Attention	Student interview: "They be falling on the floor on purpose . . . so people look at them and the teacher gets annoying [sic] . . . to get the teacher's attention." Direct observation A-B-C data: 97 incidences during morning work time: 1.1, 1.2, 1.3, 1.6, 1.8, 1.10, 1.15, 1.16, 1.17, 1.18, 1.20, 1.21, 1.22, 1.23, 1.24, 1.25, 1.26, 1.27, 1.30a, 1.31, 1.34a, 1.37, 1.38a, 1.40a, 1.41a, 1.42, 1.43, 1.46a, 1.48a, 1.50, 1.51, 1.53, 1.54a, 1.55, 1.56a, 1.58, 1.59a, 1.60, 1.61a, 1.62a, 1.63a, 1.64a, 1.66a, 1.67a, 1.68, 2.2a, 2.5a, 2.6a, 2.7, 2.9, 2.12, 2.13a, 2.14a, 2.15a, 2.16, 2.18, 2.19a, 2.20a, 2.21, 2.22, 2.23, 2.24, 2.25a, 2.27a, 2.28a, 2.29a, 2.30a, 2.32a, 2.33, 2.34, 2.35a, 2.37, 2.38a, 2.39, 2.41a, 2.42a, 2.43a, 2.44a, 3.1a, 3.3, 3.4a, 3.5a, 3.7, 3.8, 3.9, 3.10, 3.11a, 3.12, 3.15c, 3.18a, 3.19, 3.20, 3.23, 3.24a, 3.25, 3.26, 3.28	
Tangibles/ Activities	Teacher interview: Motivated to finish morning math work but does not complete during assigned time; finishes by copying during review of work; likes to turn it in. Direct observation A-B-C data: three incidences during morning work time: 1.4b, 2.8, 3.6b	Teacher interview: "He never finishes an assignment." It typically happens during independent work, "when I'm not directing it . . . he takes advantage of the freedom." The second-grade-level work might be too hard, but he has average math and reading ability compared to class. There's "nothing that interests him enough." Sometimes he will start an activity OK, but often he's not interested enough to stop engaging in off-task behavior. Direct observation A-B-C data: 84 incidences during morning work time: 1.4b, 1.5, 1.7, 1.9, 1.11, 1.12, 1.13, 1.14, 1.19, 1.28, 1.29, 1.30a, 1.32, 1.33, 1.34a, 1.35, 1.36, 1.38a, 1.39, 1.40a, 1.41a, 1.44, 1.45, 1.46a, 1.47, 1.48a, 1.49, 1.52, 1.54a, 1.56a, 1.57, 1.59a, 1.61a, 1.62a, 1.63a, 1.64a, 1.65, 1.66a, 1.67a, 1.69, 2.1, 2.2a, 2.3, 2.4, 2.5a, 2.6a, 2.10, 2.11, 2.13a, 2.14a, 2.15a, 2.17, 2.19a, 2.20a, 2.25a, 2.26, 2.27a, 2.28a, 2.29a, 2.30a, 2.32a, 2.35a, 2.36, 2.38a, 2.40, 2.41a, 2.42a, 2.43a, 2.44a, 3.1a, 3.2, 3.4a, 3.5a, 3.6b, 3.11a, 3.13, 3.14, 3.16, 3.17, 3.18a, 3.21d, 3.22, 3.24a, 3.27

(continued)

Behavior Intervention Plan *(page 3 of 5)*

	Positive Reinforcement (Access Something)	**Negative Reinforcement (Avoid Something)**
Sensory	Teacher interview: "He's not an unreasonable child . . . he intends to behave, but can't. He's not physically able to sit still." Student interview: Tends to be off-task "when I feel ticklish" Direct Observation A-B-C data: two incidences during morning work time: 3.15c, 3.21d	

Note.
a. Behaviors maintained by access to attention and avoidance of activities/tangibles.
b. Behaviors maintained by access to and escape from activities/tangibles.
c. Behaviors maintained by access to attention and sensory.
d. Behaviors maintained by access to sensory and escape from activities/tangibles.
Source: Umbreit, Ferro, Liaupsin, and Lane (2007).

Rating Scales Summary Statement:

Ms. Jones (teacher): below average in social skills (standard score of 73) and academic competence (75); above average for problem behaviors (130). Guardian: average social skills (91); problem behaviors were well above average (149).

Performance deficits:
—cooperation in class
—following directions
—respecting others' property

Acquisition deficits:
completing tasks without bothering or getting help

Outcome of Function Matrix: Hypothesized Function:

When given assignments or tasks to do, David engages in off-task behavior (e.g., leaving assigned area, doing things other than the assigned task, making inappropriate comments to others) to access attention from his teacher and peers and escape completing assigned tasks (positive reinforcement in the form of attention and negative reinforcement: activity).

Functional Behavioral Assessment:
Determining the Intervention Procedure

☐ Method 1: Teach the Replacement Behavior

☐ Method 2: Adjust the Environment

☐ Method 3: Shift the Contingencies

☐ Methods 1 & 2: Teach the Replacement Behavior and Adjust the Environment

(continued)

Behavior Intervention Plan *(page 4 of 5)*

Adjust Antecedents

A1 Student seated alongside designated peer and facing the board (access peer attention).

A2 Stop light system (access attention; brief escapes from tasks).

A3 Self-monitoring form for use during independent work time (access attention, brief break from task).

A4 Review picture schedule on the board prior to independent work time (access attention).

A5 Individual check for understanding after general instructions were provided to class (access teacher attention).

Reinforcement Rates

R1 Provide behavior-specific praise when David was on task (access attention).

R2 Acknowledge David when his stoplight was on red and assist him as soon as possible (access attention, briefly escape too-difficult task).

R3 Check David's work when he signaled "I'm finished!" with his stoplight and provide him with a brief break (access attention; brief escapes from tasks).

R4 Check David's self-monitoring form at the end of independent work time and write one thing that he did well on his self-monitoring form (access attention).

Extinguish Target Behavior

E1 Provide no praise or attention when David was off task with the exception of one verbal or gestural redirect per minute (remove attention for off-task behavior).

E2 Provide assistance without praise and provide the most minimal instruction possible when his stoplight was on red (remove attention for off-task behavior).

E3 Provide praise to other students who were on task when David was off task (remove attention for off-task behavior).

(continued)

Behavior Intervention Plan *(page 5 of 5)*

Data to be collected:

Student Outcome (What behavior(s) is (are) being measured? What measurement system? When/Where?)

Target Behavior: *Off task*

Replacement Behavior: *On task—measured using total duration recording procedures; during independent work time.*

Treatment Integrity (e.g., Checklist)

Treatment Integrity: *Component checklist; with each intervention component phrased as a question and assessed using a three-point Likert-type scale: 0 = never; 1 = sometimes; 2 = always*

Social Validity (e.g., IRP-15, CIRP)

Social Validity: *Adapted Version of the Intervention Rating Profile-15 (IRP-15) - Teacher; Children's Intervention Rating Profile (CIRP)*

Supporting Success (e.g., Evaluating the intervention)

Fading and Generalization: *Generalization data (20-minute probes) to be collected during afternoon instructional periods during both intervention phases. Maintenance was assessed at the completion of the intervention.*

Program Review Date: *1 week after intervention was under way*

Personnel and Roles: *teacher and liaisons*

Emergency Procedures: *schoolwide crisis plan*

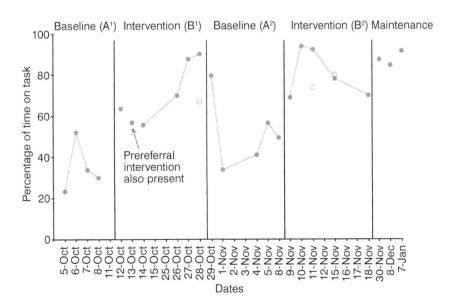

David's intervention outcomes (closed circles denote percentage of on-task behavior; open circles denote percentage of on-task behavior during generalization probes in the afternoon).

PART VII
Getting Started in Your Own Context

STEP #	FUNCTIONAL ASSESSMENT-BASED INTERVENTION STEPS
1	Identifying Students Who May Need a Functional Assessment-Based Intervention
2	Conducting the Functional Assessment
3	Collecting Baseline Data
4	Designing the Functional Assessment-Based Intervention
5	Testing the Intervention

Part VII provides considerations for getting started with the FABI process in various systems. Here we offer two final chapters.

In Chapter 22, Implementation Considerations, we discuss ways to move forward with the FABI process, either in a tiered system or as individuals working on their own. We include considerations for implementation through school teams and a coaching model and offer general tips for collaboration, with a special emphasis on the influence of culture and community.

In Chapter 23, A Step-by-Step Training Model: One Approach to Building Capacity, we summarize a series of studies and lessons learned from professional learning projects, in which the manualized FABI process has been tested at school district sites and in technical assistance projects. Specifically, we describe how various schools, districts, states, and technical assistance teams have taught school-site teams this systematic approach to designing, implementing, and evaluating FABIs. Finally, we provide suggestions for how to pace teaching FABI for instructors at the university level.

CHAPTER 22

Implementation Considerations

LEARNING OBJECTIVES

- Describe issues that may arise from working on a FABI as an individual or as a member of a team.
- Describe issues that may arise when taking a leadership role in developing a FABI using consultation and coaching models.
- Describe some general tips for successful collaboration on a FABI.
- Describe some of the broad FABI development considerations related to culture, community, equity, and ethics.

In this book, we have taken a step-by-step approach to developing a FABI, particularly through an integrated tiered system (Gandhi et al., in press) like the comprehensive, integrated, three-tiered (Ci3T) model. This model was designed, implemented, and evaluated in partnership with a range of school, district, state, and technical assistance partners in the United States from Hawaii to Vermont (Lane, Menzies, et al., 2020). We presented a five-step approach to creating a FABI that includes:

- Step 1: Identifying Students Who May Need a Functional Assessment-Based Intervention
- Step 2: Conducting the Functional Assessment
- Step 3: Collecting Baseline Data
- Step 4: Designing the Functional Assessment-Based Intervention
- Step 5: Testing the Intervention

Within each step of the process, we have drawn attention to some considerations specific to each step. For instance, in Step 2, we not only described how to conduct interviews and observations, we also pointed out the importance of considering the context of the environment. In Step 3, we not only reviewed the dimensions of data and how to select a data collection system, we also considered contextual issues that might impact data collection. We also included contextual concerns and other tips when we laid out the specific procedures for Steps 4 and 5.

Now that we have reviewed the procedures and specific issues related to the individual steps in the manualized five-step process, we provide some considerations that will arise as you engage in the steps as an *integrated* process. For instance, you may be engaging in this work as an individual or through a team model. We describe issues related to taking a leadership role in FABI development through consultation or coaching models and provide some general tips for successful collaboration. We also provide some final thoughts on issues of culture, community, equity, and ethics in the FABI process.

Working Individually or as Part of a Team

A FABI can be developed and implemented by individuals or teams, yet most often is conducted as a team-based process. A person who implements a FABI alone may be the classroom teacher, a counselor, a board-certified behavior analyst (BCBA), a school psychologist, a graduate student, or a person who has some combination of those roles. However, no one can really engage in the FABI process alone. Throughout the manualized five-step FABI process parents, students, teachers, and other professionals work collaboratively as described in this book. Working as an individual on a FABI usually means you are taking responsibility for implementing every step in the process. If you are implementing the FABI in this way, keep a few things in mind.

Depending on who you work for (e.g., a school district) and your reasons for engaging in the FABI (e.g., contract work, academic research, class project), be sure you obtain the permissions required to be engaged in the context or setting and with the student (see Chapter 4). If you are new to developing and implementing a FABI, find someone to review your work every step of the way. This person might be your supervisor, your instructor, or another individual who has successfully engaged in the FABI process. It can be particularly helpful to have someone with experience who can confirm your interpretations of interviews, observations, and functions.

Throughout this book, we have focused on implementing the FABI process as part of a team. FABI is one example of an evidence-based practice that is detailed as a tertiary (Tier 3) intervention in the Ci3T Implementation Manuals that are used to guide implementation for schools and districts implementing their Ci3T model. There are clearly benefits that come from including the FABI process as part of a comprehensive, tiered system of support (Markle et al., 2014). For example, it is a structured system with guidelines for prevention and intervention procedures at Tier 1 and Tier 2. Implementation data document which Tier 2 procedures were implemented for the target student, whether the practices were implemented accurately, and what the data show about their effectiveness. Although it is not necessary for students to progress from Tier 1 through Tier 2 to Tier 3, often that is the path. In other instances, students who are exposed to multiple risk factors may progress directly from Tier 1 to Tier 3. The

Ci3T Implementation Manuals and the manualized FABI process have clear procedures for teaming and developing an individualized intervention (Lane, Menzies, et al., 2020).

However, teams that work on FABIs are not always part of a tiered system (e.g., MTSS, Ci3T, PBIS). Some schools and districts assign this task to other teams, such as multiple disciplinary teams that support students receiving special education services, or teams established to support the prereferral intervention process (e.g., a general education intervention team, student study team, child study team). Prereferral intervention teams are problem-solving teams that assist general education teachers who have exhausted their ideas and options for meeting students' individualized needs. With parental permission, general education teachers may receive assistance in designing and implementing behavioral interventions for a student with academic, behavioral, and/or social problem behaviors,

In the FABI process we have described, the intervention team is encouraged to always include the teacher, a family member, and the student. Teams must make a sincere and concerted effort to include the family and student, who are able to provide input about the differences in student behavior in other environments, and about cultural perspectives and goals, preferences, and the acceptability of the intervention and implementation. The team also includes individuals with the range of expertise and insight needed for a successful FABI, such as an intervention expert, other school personnel working with the student, a school psychologist, or the school's behavior specialist. Team members share responsibility and make joint decisions about the intervention's design, implementation, and evaluation. Relationships among team members are equitable, recognizing that each member may have important information to contribute about the student's behavior. Team members use information and objective data to understand key concepts and procedures: determining the maintaining function of the target behavior, designing an intervention based on the function of the target behavior, monitoring intervention implementation, and analyzing data frequently to ensure the intervention is being implemented correctly and the strategies are successful. A team facilitator is needed to ensure that the FABI process and all steps of its development are completed correctly. The team may also include individuals, such as a note taker and timekeeper, who can help the team run smoothly.

Consultation and Coaching Models

FABIs are often implemented through consultation models. Consultation has a long history in the implementation of behavioral interventions. Behavioral consultation as a model generally evolved from medical and mental health consultation models. The most common is the *triadic model* of consultation, which consists of a consultant who works with a teacher or other implementer who delivers the intervention to the child (Bergan & Kratochwill, 1990; Friend & Cook, 2010; Tharp & Wetzel, 1969). In this consultation model, the expert consultant has little direct contact with the student receiving the intervention. There are many formats for consultation, such as conjoint behavioral consultation that focuses on connections between home and school (Sheridan et al., 2014) or collaborative consultation in which there is mutual participation in problem solving (Idol et al., 2010)

Coaching models can be considered as a form of consultation; it is still a three-part model that involves a person with intervention expertise, an individual or team who develops and implements an intervention, and a student who receives the intervention. However, coaching is usually considered to consist of an ongoing cycle in which the coach provides instruction, observation, modeling, and performance feedback (Kretlow & Bartholomew, 2010). Researchers have found that this explicit format of assistance is effective at producing successful results when social behavioral interventions are implemented (Stormont et al., 2015). Coaches engaged in the FABI process generally work with the person implementing the intervention (teacher or parent) to ensure they are well trained in all strategies and in how to implement the intervention correctly. The coach might also train the IOA data collector and monitor treatment integrity to ensure that implementation is accurate throughout all phases of the intervention.

Tips for Successful Collaboration

Consultation and coaching are both models that can produce better outcomes by organizing the quality and consistency of intervention efforts. In contrast, collaboration is usually considered as a set of shared ideals or a "style" of professional interaction that can also improve intervention results. Friend and Cook (2010) stated these ideals as mutual goals, parity, shared responsibility for key decisions, shared accountability for outcomes, and the development of trust, respect, and sense of community. These ideals can be critical to the implementation of a FABI whether the FABI is implemented by an individual or a team or through a consultation, coaching, or other behavioral-intervention model.

Considerations Related to Culture, Community, Equity, and Ethics

Throughout this book, we have considered the ways that the cultural and linguistic context of the family, the student, and the environment are integrated into the FABI process. In Chapter 1, we identified broad considerations for integrating and understanding the diversity of students and families that include increasing the cultural knowledge and self-awareness of the school staff through training and coaching, recognizing the strengths of students and families from different cultures, and validating the perspectives and experiences of families and students.

In our description of the steps in the FABI process, the selection and design of the intervention strategies are explained so families can understand them and give relevant input. Families and students are key participants on the intervention team. Along with the teacher and other school professionals, family members are sources of information about their experiences and goals. They provide input about the student's behavior during the FABI interview. They complete a social validity check before the intervention is conducted to ensure they understand and accept the goals, procedures, and intended outcomes. A second social validity check after implementation provides feedback about whether their expectations for goals and outcomes were met. As part of the FABI team, they monitor and review implementation data. Throughout the process, family members and students also have opportunities to question procedures and resolve any conflicts.

Each chapter also included a box or boxes with ethical considerations that identified how the FABI process addressed a specific BACB *Ethics Code for Behavior Analysts*. These codes included those related to each step of selecting, designing, implementing, and monitoring a

> **BOX 22.1. Ethical Considerations in Chapter 22: BACB Ethics Code for Behavior Analysts**
>
> **2.10 Collaborating with Colleagues**
>
> This chapter explores the different contexts in which the FABI might be conducted, the type of teaming, and the need to identify who should be included in the FABI process. Team members include those family members and colleagues who work with the student or client, provide services, and have knowledge of the behavior of interest. For example, depending on the context, the team might include a teacher; a teacher assistant; a group home caregiver; a clinical therapist; a psychologist; a therapy aide; or someone providing special services, such as speech and language, mental health or trauma care, or social work services. Although we have described collaboration with colleagues in a school or education program throughout this book, the process is applicable to other contexts and to colleagues in other environments.

behavioral intervention. Additional codes addressed cultural responsiveness and diversity, effective treatment, and involving stakeholders in the process. Box 22.1 provides ethical information for this chapter related to collaboration with colleagues. These cultural and ethical considerations are highlighted to emphasize their importance in implementing an effective intervention. They are as integral to the intervention process as assessment, treatment integrity, and data collection and analysis.

Summary

In this chapter, we discussed ways to move forward with the FABI process typically in a tiered system working as team members or as individuals. We included considerations for implementation through school teams and through working within a coaching model and offered general tips for collaboration, with a special emphasis on the influence of culture and community. We also reiterated cultural and ethical considerations that have been emphasized throughout this book.

In Chapter 23, we summarize a series of studies and the lessons learned from professional learning projects, in which the manualized FABI process has been tested at school sites in districts and in technical assistance projects. Specifically, we describe how various schools, districts, states, and technical assistance teams have taught school-site teams this systematic approach to designing, implementing, and evaluating FABIs.

CHAPTER 23

A Step-by-Step Training Model
One Approach to Building Capacity

LEARNING OBJECTIVES

- Describe learning outcomes for adults using this manualized approach to designing, implementing, and evaluating a FABI.
- Describe how this manualized approach to designing, implementing, and evaluating a FABI can be taught at the university level.

Throughout this book, we have focused on providing you with the knowledge and skills you need to design, implement, and evaluate a FABI using this manualized process (Umbreit et al., 2007). We have aimed to maintain a focus on individual students, whether we serve them through a direct intervention model, a coaching model, or an integrated tiered system of support, using Ci3T as an exemplar. See the Appendix (pp. 293–294) for a comprehensive list of research articles published in peer-reviewed journals, depicting the feasibility and effectiveness of this manualized approached in a range of settings (e.g., early childhood centers; elementary, middle, and high schools; and general and special education classrooms), with a host of children and students (PreK–12), to address a range of target behaviors, such as those that are off-task and disruptive (Common et al., 2017).

However, the FABI process we have taught in this book can be scaled up to provide broader access to services for students who need them. The process has been scaled to meet students' needs across schools, districts, and even states. It has also been incorporated into large-scale technical assistance projects and taught in university courses in several U.S. states.

In this final chapter, we summarize a series of studies and the lessons learned from professional learning projects in which the manualized FABI process has been taught and tested at school district sites and in technical assistance projects. Specifically, we describe how various school, district, state, and technical assistance teams have taught school-site teams to use this systematic approach to designing, implementing, and evaluating FABIs. Finally, we provide suggested pacing for people teaching this systematic approach at the university level.

Lessons Learned with Inservice Educators

As the number of studies conducted on the FABI process continued to grow, these peer-reviewed results consistently demonstrated the feasibility of using this intensive intervention in authentic school settings to meet the multiple needs of students exposed to multiple risk factors (Common et al., 2017; Hirsch et al., 2020; Lane, Bruhn, et al., 2009). As such, practitioners and researchers began to ask many questions, such as: How can we scale up the use of FABI with—and without—university support? How can we support teachers in becoming knowledgeable and confident in designing, implementing, and evaluating FABIs?

To answer these and other questions, collaborative studies were conducted with practitioners, technical assistance providers, and researchers. The goal was to explore how to best empower school-site teams through the use of practice-based professional learning (PBPL) opportunities (Ball et al., 2009; Desimone, 2009). First, Lane, Barton-Arwood, and colleagues (2007) offered a professional learning series, featuring three 6-hour sessions and 1-hour on-site meetings twice per month (ranging 28–30 hours) to assist four school-site teams in learning this manualized process. The series focused on teaching these teams how to design, implement, and evaluate a FABI while supporting students at their respective schools. In this study, the authors featured two students' outcomes, including information on the extent to which the interventions were implemented as planned (treatment integrity) and on stakeholders' views of the goals, procedures, and outcomes (social validity). Results demonstrated a functional relation between the introduction of the intervention and changes in the students' performance. In short, this first study demonstrated that school-site FABI teams were able to learn how to design, implement, and evaluate FABIs in their own context, benefiting from the manualized FABI process.

Next, Lane, Oakes, Powers, and colleagues (2015) conducted a study with 48 inservice educators teaching K–12 students to explore the effectiveness of a yearlong professional development training series designed to teach the five-step systematic approach to FABI described in our first textbook (Umbreit et al., 2007). Participants engaged in a 4-day, practice-based professional development series that also included coaching support and applied practice between sessions (see Lane, Oakes, et al., 2015, for an overview of the professional learning series content). To determine the adult learning outcomes, the 48 participants, constituting 19 FABI school-site teams, completed pre- and posttraining surveys. The surveys provided information about their perceived knowledge, confidence, and usefulness, as well as their actual knowledge, of 15 concepts and strategies addressed over the course of the yearlong training. Findings showed that participants reported statistically significant improvements in the levels of perceived knowledge, confidence, and usefulness of the FABI concepts and strategies presented in the professional learning series. In addition, participants also demonstrated statistically significant increases in their actual knowledge, with mean scores increasing threefold from pre- to posttraining.

Oakes and colleagues (2018) replicated and extended the Lane, Oakes, Powers, and colleagues (2015) study, confirming similar changes reported by 148 educator participants' perceived and actual knowledge, perceived confidence, and perceived usefulness of the concepts and strategies taught. In addition, they provided information on the levels of completion of the five-step FABI process across the 29 school-site teams from 15 districts.

These descriptive studies of educators' learning outcomes are encouraging. They suggest that using this five-step approach to scale up the use of this manualized process for teaching inservice educators the FABI process is both effective and feasible. Yet a question remained: To what extent can other professional learning providers, beyond the developers of the manualized process, use this process and achieve similar outcomes?

To answer this question, Common and colleagues (2022) conducted a large-scale randomized control trial to explore the impact of 342 educators' participation in PBPL settings to design, implement, and evaluate FABIs. Sixty-nine FABI teams were randomly assigned to one of three training cohorts to learn the FABI process using the five-step process featured in this book. Training cohorts were led by either university or state technical assistance providers. Results of this randomized cluster design trial provided additional evidence that this PBPL FABI training process is effective in improving school-site teams' knowledge, confidence, and use. In addition, the study produced initial evidence that the process was indeed scalable since state technical assistance providers demonstrated high implementation levels comparable with university trainers.

Collectively, these studies provide important evidence that school-site teams are able to learn and implement this manualized FABI process with integrity. Furthermore, this process is viewed as feasible.

Suggested Pacing for Teaching FABI at the University Level

For those readers who plan to use this manualized FABI training process as part of an undergraduate- or graduate-level course, we provide free-access resources on *www.ci3t.org/FABI*, as well as considerations for how to pace teaching the content covered in 7-, 10-, and 15-week course sequences. These pacing guidelines are presented in Figure 23.1.

Summary

In this final chapter, we summarized a series of studies and the lessons learned from professional learning projects in which the manualized FABI process has been tested at school district sites and in technical assistance projects. Specifically, we described how various school-site teams have been taught this systematic approach to designing, implementing, and evaluating FABIs. Finally, we offered pacing guidelines for those teaching this systematic approach at the university level.

As researchers, we have a combined total of more than 100 years invested in designing, implementing, and evaluating the FABI process thanks to the generosity and commitment of our school and district partners (Lane, 2017). We have conducted a series of studies approved

7-WEEK TOPIC AND CHAPTER RECOMMENDATIONS		
Week	Topic	Chapter(s)
1	Introduction and Overview	• Chapter 1. An Introduction to Functional Assessment-Based Interventions • Chapter 2. Primer on Behavior Analysis
2	Step 1: Identifying Students Who May Need a Functional Assessment-Based Intervention	• Chapter 3. Working in Tiered Systems of Support: A Focus on Tier 3 Considerations • Chapter 4. Identifying Students Who May Benefit from a Functional Assessment-Based Intervention
3	Step 2: Conducting the Functional Assessment	• Chapter 5. Getting Started: Understanding the Context • Chapter 6. Functional Assessment Interviews: Identifying the Problem and Establishing the Target Behaviors • Chapter 7. Functional Assessment: Direct Observation • Chapter 8. Determining the Function of the Behavior: The Function Matrix
4	Step 3: Collecting Baseline Data	• Chapter 9. Identifying the Dimension of Interest and Selecting an Appropriate Measurement System • Chapter 10. Getting Started: Collecting Baseline Data
5	Step 4: Designing the Functional Assessment-Based Intervention	• Chapter 11. Designing and Testing the Intervention • Chapter 12. Intervention Method 1: Teach the Replacement Behavior • Chapter 13. Intervention Method 2: Adjust the Environment • Chapter 14. Intervention Method 3: Shift the Contingencies • Chapter 15. Intervention Methods 1 and 2: Teach the Replacement Behavior and Adjust the Environment • Chapter 16. Treatment Integrity • Chapter 17. Social Validity • Chapter 18. Generalization and Maintenance • Chapter 19. Designing Your Intervention
6	Step 5: Testing the Intervention	• Chapter 20. Determining Intervention Outcomes • Chapter 21. Wrapping It Up: Ending with a Defensible Functional Assessment-Based Intervention
7	Getting Started in Your Own Context	• Chapter 22. Implementation Considerations • Chapter 23. A Step-by-Step Training Model: One Approach to Building Capacity
10-WEEK TOPIC AND CHAPTER RECOMMENDATIONS		
Week	Topic	Chapter(s)
1	Introduction and Overview	• Chapter 1. An Introduction to Functional Assessment-Based Interventions • Chapter 2. Primer on Behavior Analysis
2	Step 1: Identifying Students Who May Need a Functional Assessment-Based Intervention	• Chapter 3 Working in Tiered Systems of Support: A Focus on Tier 3 Considerations • Chapter 4. Identifying Students Who May Benefit from a Functional Assessment-Based Intervention

(continued)

FIGURE 23.1. FABI syllabi: Considerations for pacing.

Week	Topic	Chapter(s)
3	Step 2: Conducting the Functional Assessment (Part 1)	• Chapter 5. Getting Started: Understanding the Context • Chapter 6. Functional Assessment Interviews: Identifying the Problem and Establishing the Target Behaviors
4	Step 2: Conducting the Functional Assessment (Part 2)	• Chapter 7. Functional Assessment: Direct Observation • Chapter 8. Determining the Function of the Behavior: The Function Matrix
5	Step 3: Collecting Baseline Data	• Chapter 9. Identifying the Dimension of Interest and Selecting an Appropriate Measurement System • Chapter 10. Getting Started: Collecting Baseline Data
6	Step 4: Designing the Functional Assessment-Based Intervention (Part 1)	• Chapter 11. Designing and Testing the Intervention • Chapter 12. Intervention Method 1: Teach the Replacement Behavior • Chapter 13. Intervention Method 2: Adjust the Environment • Chapter 14. Intervention Method 3: Shift the Contingencies • Chapter 15. Intervention Methods 1 and 2: Teach the Replacement Behavior and Adjust the Environment
7	Step 4: Designing the Functional Assessment-Based Intervention (Part 2)	• Chapter 16. Treatment Integrity • Chapter 17. Social Validity • Chapter 18. Generalization and Maintenance
8	Step 4: Designing the Functional Assessment-Based Intervention (Part 3)	• Chapter 19. Designing Your Intervention
9	Step 5: Testing the Intervention	• Chapter 20. Determining Intervention Outcomes • Chapter 21. Wrapping It Up: Ending with a Defensible Functional Assessment-Based Intervention
10	Getting Started in Your Own Context	• Chapter 22. Implementation Considerations • Chapter 23. A Step-by-Step Training Model: One Approach to Building Capacity

15-WEEK TOPIC AND CHAPTER RECOMMENDATIONS

Week	Topic	Chapter(s)
1	Introduction and Overview	• Chapter 1. An Introduction to Functional Assessment-Based Interventions • Chapter 2. Primer on Behavior Analysis
2	Step 1: Identifying Students Who May Need a Functional Assessment-Based Intervention	• Chapter 3. Working in Tiered Systems of Support: A Focus on Tier 3 Considerations • Chapter 4. Identifying Students Who May Benefit from a Functional Assessment-Based Intervention
3	Step 2: Conducting the Functional Assessment (Part 1)	• Chapter 5. Getting Started: Understanding the Context • Chapter 6. Functional Assessment Interviews: Identifying the Problem and Establishing the Target Behaviors

(continued)

FIGURE 23.1. *(continued)*

Week	Topic	Chapter(s)
4	Step 2: Conducting the Functional Assessment (Part 2)	• Chapter 7. Functional Assessment: Direct Observation
5	Step 2: Conducting the Functional Assessment (Part 3)	• Chapter 8. Determining the Function of the Behavior: The Function Matrix
6	Step 3: Collecting Baseline Data	• Chapter 9. Identifying the Dimension of Interest and Selecting an Appropriate Measurement System • Chapter 10. Getting Started: Collecting Baseline Data
7	Step 4: Designing the Functional Assessment-Based Intervention (Part 1)	• Chapter 11. Designing and Testing the Intervention
8	Step 4: Designing the Functional Assessment-Based Intervention (Part 2)	• Chapter 12. Intervention Method 1: Teach the Replacement Behavior
9	Step 4: Designing the Functional Assessment-Based Intervention (Part 3)	• Chapter 13. Intervention Method 2: Adjust the Environment
10	Step 4: Designing the Functional Assessment-Based Intervention (Part 4)	• Chapter 14. Intervention Method 3: Shift the Contingencies
11	Step 4: Designing the Functional Assessment-Based Intervention (Part 5)	• Chapter 15. Intervention Methods 1 and 2: Teach the Replacement Behavior and Adjust the Environment
12	Step 4: Designing the Functional Assessment-Based Intervention (Part 6)	• Chapter 16. Treatment Integrity • Chapter 17. Social Validity • Chapter 18. Generalization and Maintenance
13	Step 4: Designing the Functional Assessment-Based Intervention (Part 7)	• Chapter 19. Designing Your Intervention
14	Step 5: Testing the Intervention	• Chapter 20. Determining Intervention Outcomes • Chapter 21. Wrapping It Up: Ending with a Defensible Functional Assessment-Based Intervention
15	Getting Started in Your Own Context	• Chapter 22. Implementation Considerations • Chapter 23. A Step-by-Step Training Model: One Approach to Building Capacity

FIGURE 23.1. *(continued)*

through various universities, taught this process to many exceptional scholars at the undergraduate and graduate levels, and supported local communities in learning this process as part of technical assistance projects and service activities. We are deeply thankful for the opportunity to learn with and from our students and district partners.

We hope you have found this book to be useful as you support children and youth with the most intensive intervention needs within integrated tiered systems, such as comprehensive, integrated, three-tiered (Ci3T) models of prevention as well as in (1) schools not yet implementing such tiered systems and in (2) other places, such as residential facilities, homes, and other community settings (Common et al., 2017). Our hope is that sharing the findings of our research and our lessons on capacity building supports others as they design, implement, and evaluate the FABI process, making this intensive intervention widely available to benefit an even greater number of children and youth.

APPENDIX

Published Research on the Functional Assessment-Based Intervention Model

(Publications are listed in chronological order.)

Umbreit, J., Lane, K. L., & Dejud, C. (2004). Improving classroom behavior by modifying task difficulty: Effects of increasing the difficulty of too-easy tasks. *Journal of Positive Behavior Interventions, 6*, 13–20.

Lane, K. L., Weisenbach, J. L., Little, M. A., Phillips, A., & Wehby, J. (2006). Illustrations of function-based interventions implemented by general education teachers: Building capacity at the school site. *Education & Treatment of Children, 29*, 549–571.

Liaupsin, C. J., Umbreit, J., Ferro, J. B., Urso, A., & Upreti, G. (2006). Improving academic engagement through systematic, function-based intervention. *Education & Treatment of Children, 29*, 573–591.

Stahr, B., Cushing, D., Lane, K., & Fox, J. (2006). Efficacy of a function-based intervention in decreasing off-task behavior exhibited by a student with ADHD. *Journal of Positive Behavior Interventions, 8*, 201–211.

Lane, K. L., Rogers, L. A., Parks, R. J., Weisenbach, J. L., Mau, A. C., Merwin, M. T., & Bergman, W. A. (2007). Function-based interventions for students who are nonresponsive to primary and secondary prevention efforts: Illustrations at the elementary and middle school levels. *Journal of Emotional and Behavioral Disorders, 15*, 169–183.

Lane, K. L., Smither, R., Huseman, R., Guffey, J., & Fox, J. (2007). A function-based intervention to decrease disruptive behavior and increase academic engagement. *Journal of Early and Intensive Behavior Intervention, 41*(1), 348–364.

Lane, K. L., Weisenbach, J. L., Phillips, A., & Wehby, J. H. (2007). Designing, implementing, and evaluating function-based interventions using a systematic, feasible approach. *Behavioral Disorders, 32*, 122–139.

Turton, A. M., Umbreit, J., Liaupsin, C. J., & Bartley, J. (2007). Function-based intervention for an adolescent with emotional and behavioral disorders in Bermuda: Moving across culture. *Behavioral Disorders, 33*, 23–32.

Wood, B. K., Umbreit, J., Liaupsin, C. J., & Gresham, F. M. (2007). A treatment integrity analysis of function-based intervention. *Education & Treatment of Children, 30*, 105–120.

Lane, K. L., Eisner, S. L., Kretzer, J. K., Bruhn, A. L., Crnobori, M., Funke, L., . . . Casey, A. (2009). Outcomes of functional assessment-based interventions for students with and at risk for emotional and behavioral disorders in a job-share setting. *Education & Treatment of Children, 32*, 573–604.

Underwood, M. A., Umbreit, J., & Liaupsin, C. J. (2009). Efficacy of a systematic process for designing function-based interventions for adults in a community setting. *Education and Training in Developmental Disabilities, 44*, 25–38.

Nahgahgwon, K. N., Umbreit, J., Liaupsin, C. J., & Turton, A. M. (2010). Function-based planning for young children at risk for emotional and behavioral disorders. *Education & Treatment of Children, 33*, 537–559.

Aitken, A., Harlan, A., Hankins, K., Michels, J., Moore, T. C., Oakes, W. P., & Lane, K. L. (2011). Increasing academic engagement during writing activities in an urban elementary classroom. *Beyond Behavior, 20*, 31–43.

Cox, M., Griffin, M. M., Hall, R., Oakes, W. P., & Lane, K. L. (2011). Using a functional assessment-based intervention to increase academic engaged time in an inclusive middle school setting. *Beyond Behavior, 20*, 44–54.

Germer, K. A., Kaplan, L. M., Giroux, L. N., Markham, E. H., Ferris, G. J., Oakes, W. P., & Lane, K. L. (2011). A function-based intervention to increase a second-grade student's on-task behavior in a general education classroom. *Beyond Behavior, 20*, 19–30.

Majeika, C. E., Walder, J. P., Hubbard, J. P., Steeb, K. M., Ferris, G. J., Oakes, W. P., & Lane, K. L. (2011). Improving on-task behavior using a functional assessment-based intervention in an inclusive high school setting. *Beyond Behavior, 20*, 55–66.

Turton, A. M., Umbreit, J., & Mathur, S. R. (2011). Systematic function-based intervention for adolescents with emotional and behavioral disorders in an alternative setting: Broadening the context. *Behavioral Disorders, 36*, 117–128.

Wood, B. K., Ferro, J. B., Umbreit, J., & Liaupsin, C. J. (2011). Addressing the challenging behavior of young children through systematic function-based intervention. *Topics in Early Childhood Special Education, 30*, 221–232.

Janney, D. M., Umbreit, J., Ferro, J. B., Liaupsin, C. J., & Lane, K. L. (2013). The effect of the extinction procedure in function-based intervention. *Journal of Positive Behavior Interventions, 15*, 113–123.

Reeves, L. M., Umbreit, J., Ferro, J. B., & Liaupsin, C. J. (2013). Function-based intervention to support the inclusion of students with autism. *Education and Training in Autism and Developmental Disabilities, 48*, 379–391.

Whitford, D. K., Liaupsin, C. J., Umbreit, J., & Ferro, J. B. (2013). Implementation of a single comprehensive function-based intervention across multiple classrooms for a high school student. *Education and Treatment of Children, 36*, 147–167.

Gann, C. J., Ferro, J. B., Umbreit, J., & Liaupsin, C. J. (2014). Effects of a comprehensive function-based intervention applied across multiple educational settings. *Remedial and Special Education, 35*, 50–60.

Gann, C. J., Gaines, S., Antia, S. D., Umbreit, J., & Liaupsin, C. J. (2015). Evaluating the effects of function-based interventions with deaf or hard-of-hearing students. *Journal of Deaf Studies and Deaf Education, 20*, 252–265.

Aldosari, M. S. (2016). Efficacy of a systematic process for developing function-based treatment for young children with disabilities. *Education and Training in Autism and Developmental Disabilities, 51*, 391–403.

Gann, C, J., & Kunnavatana, S. (2016). A preliminary study in applying the Function-Based Intervention Decision Model in consultation to increase treatment integrity. *Education and Treatment of Children, 39*, 445–466.

Reeves, L. M., Umbreit, J., Ferro, J. B., & Liaupsin, C. J. (2017). The role of the replacement behavior in function-based intervention. *Education and Training in Autism and Developmental Disabilities, 52*, 305–316.

Lansey, K. R., Antia, S., MacFarland, S. Z., & Umbreit, J. (2021). Training and coaching: Impact on peer mentor fidelity and behavior of postsecondary students with autism and intellectual disability. *Education and Training in Autism and Developmental Disabilities, 56*, 328–340.

FABI Completion Checklists

COMPLETION CHECKLIST

Step 1: Identifying Students Who May Need a Functional Assessment-Based Intervention

School: _____ District: _____ Date: _____

Team Members:

1. _____ 5. _____
2. _____ 6. _____
3. _____ 7. _____
4. _____ 8. _____

Coach: _____

Step 1: Identifying Students Who May Need a Functional Assessment-Based Intervention

	Check when completed	Item
Estimated Time: 1 week Start Date: ____ End Date: ____	☐	Communicate with parents and secure permission to conduct the functional assessment-based intervention. (Use your district procedures and forms for subsequent students.)
	☐	Talk to the student to answer questions. (Obtain assent according to your district procedures.)
	☐	Complete, confirm, and turn in the **Referral Checklist: Functional Assessment-Based Interventions** (Handout 1 [HO1] on *www.ci3t.org/fabi*).

Considerations for need:

1. ☐ Does the student's behavior impede their learning or the learning of others? Or does the student pose a threat to themself or others (Drasgow & Yell, 2001)?

2. ☐ Has the student been nonresponsive to other intervention efforts?

3. ☐ Does the student have multiple risk factors (e.g., harsh and inconsistent parenting or high mobility) making them more susceptible to school failure and/or dangerous behavior?

4. ☐ Has the student been (1) placed in an alternative setting for behavior dangerous to themself or others or (2) placed in an alternative setting for 45 days due to drug or weapons violations? Or (3), has the student been suspended from school for more than 10 days or has that suspension resulted in a change in placement (Drasgow & Yell, 2001)?

*If you answered yes to the first three questions, a FABI may be warranted. If you answered yes to the fourth question, a FABI is mandated by the Individuals with Disabilities Education Improvement Act (IDEIA, 2004).

(continued)

From *www.ci3t.org*. Lane, K. L., & Oakes, W. P. (2014). *Functional assessment-based interventions (FABI): Training materials—Step-by-step checklists.* Copyright © 2015 by Kathleen Lynne Lane. Reprinted by permission in *Functional Assessment-Based Intervention: Effective Individualized Support for Students* by John Umbreit, Jolenea B. Ferro, Kathleen Lynne Lane, and Carl J. Liaupsin (The Guilford Press, 2024). Permission to photocopy this material, or to download and print additional copies (*www.guilford.com/umbreit-forms*), is granted to purchasers of this book for personal use or use with students; see copyright page for details.

Step 1: Identifying Students Who May Need a Functional Assessment-Based Intervention *(page 2 of 2)*

Suggested Readings

1. In the *Beyond Behavior* Special Issue (2011, Vol. 20, No. 3), read the Method section of articles 2–4 to see how these elementary, middle, and high school students were identified as potentially benefiting from a Tier 3 functional assessment-based intervention (FABI).

2. Read Chapter 3 in the following book to learn about a functional approach to problem behavior: Umbreit, J., Ferro, J. B., Lane, K. L., & Liaupsin, C. J. (2024). *Functional assessment-based intervention: Effective individualized support for students.* Guilford Press.

3. In the following book, consider reading more about the various systematic screening tools: Lane, K. L., Menzies, H. M., Oakes, W. P., & Kalberg, J. R. (2012). *Systematic screenings of behavior to support instruction: From preschool to high school.* Guilford Press.

Step 1 Tips:

1. Make certain Tier 1 efforts are being implemented as planned (with treatment integrity).

2. Consider Tier 2 supports prior to beginning with a FABI.

3. Ensure a systematic approach is used to detect which students may benefit from a FABI to make certain students have equal access to this support.

4. Obtain permission from the parent or guardian as well as the student before beginning this process.

COMPLETION CHECKLIST

Step 2: Conducting the Functional Assessment

School: _____ District: _____ Date: _____

Team Members:

1. _____ 5. _____
2. _____ 6. _____
3. _____ 7. _____
4. _____ 8. _____

Coach: _____

Step 2: Conducting the Functional Assessment

Check when completed	Item
☐	Complete, confirm, and turn in **data collected from Informal Observation: classroom map; copy of PBIS plan; instructional schedule; classwide system for behavior management.**
☐	Complete, confirm, and turn in the **Universal Checklist** (Handout A [HOA] on *www.ci3t.org/fabi*).
☐	**Step 2.1 Records Review** Complete **School Archival Record Search (SARS) Forms** (Handouts 2 [HO2] and 3 [HO3])
☐	**Step 2.2 Interviews** Complete, confirm, and turn in the **Teacher Interview**, including the **operational definition of target behavior** (Handout 4 [HO4] on *www.ci3t.org/fabi*).
☐	Complete and confirm **FABI Planning** for **Target Behavior** with operational definition (Handout 6 [HO6] on *www.ci3t.org/fabi*).
☐	Complete, confirm, and turn in **Parent Interview** (Handout 4 [HO4] on *www.ci3t.org/fabi*).
☐	Complete, confirm, and turn in **Student Interview** (Handout 7 [HO7] on *www.ci3t.org/fabi*).
☐	**Step 2.3 Rating Scales** Review, confirm, and turn in **Social Skills Improvement System—Rating Scale (Teacher Version)**.
☐	Review, confirm, and turn in **Social Skills Improvement System—Rating Scale (Parent Version)**.
☐ ___/hours ___/instances	**Step 2.4 Direct Observation (A-B-C data collection)** Review, confirm, and turn in **A-B-C data (Data Collection Form)**; write in the number of hours (*N* = 3) you collected A-B-C data and the number of instances (*N* = 8 minimum) you saw the target behavior occur (check that data and time are recorded) (Handout 8 [HO8] on *www.ci3t.org/fabi*).

(continued)

From *www.ci3t.org*. Lane, K. L., & Oakes, W. P. (2014). *Functional assessment-based interventions (FABI): Training materials—Step-by-step checklists.* Copyright © 2015 by Kathleen Lynne Lane. Reprinted by permission in *Functional Assessment-Based Intervention: Effective Individualized Support for Students* by John Umbreit, Jolenea B. Ferro, Kathleen Lynne Lane, and Carl J. Liaupsin (The Guilford Press, 2024). Permission to photocopy this material, or to download and print additional copies (*www.guilford.com/umbreit-forms*), is granted to purchasers of this book for personal use or use with students; see copyright page for details.

Step 2: Conducting the Functional Assessment *(page 2 of 2)*

Check when completed	Item
☐	**Step 2.5 Identify the Function** Write and confirm **FABI Planning**; for **Function Matrix,** include a **hypothesis statement** as to what is maintaining the behavior (Handout 6 [HO6] on *www.ci3t.org/fabi*).
☐	Complete, confirm, and turn in **FABI Planning** for **Replacement Behavior** with operational definitions (Handout 6 [HO6] on *www.ci3t.org/fabi*).
☐	Complete and turn in this checklist to your coach. (To clarify: Complete HO6 FABI Planning up to Function Matrix and hypothesis.)

Suggested Readings

1. In the *Beyond Behavior* Special Issue (2011, Vol. 20, No. 3):
   a. Read the first article to learn more about the tools and overall process.
   b. Read the Method section of articles 2–4 to see how the functional assessment process was conducted and to learn how to complete the function matrix.

2. Read the following chapters in Umbreit, J., Ferro, J. B., Lane, K. L., & Liaupsin, C. J. (2024). *Functional assessment-based intervention: Effective individualized support for students.* Guilford Press.
   a. Chapter 6 to learn how to identify the target and replacement behaviors
   b. Chapter 6 to learn more about teacher, parent, and student interviews
   c. Chapter 7 to learn more about how to collect A-B-C data

Step 2 Tips:

1. When defining the target behavior, make certain to include a label, definition, examples, and non-examples. Also remember to observe the "dead man's rule."

2. A-B-C data (3 hours; 8–10 instances) are analyzed using the Function Matrix to determine the reasons why the target behavior occurs. These data are not graphed.

COMPLETION CHECKLIST

Step 3: Collecting Baseline Data

School: _____ District: _____ Date: _____

Team Members:

1. _____ 5. _____
2. _____ 6. _____
3. _____ 7. _____
4. _____ 8. _____

Coach: _____

Step 3: Collecting Baseline Data

Check when completed	Item
☐	Complete and confirm through **Determining the Function of the Behavior: Using the Function Matrix** on **Planning Sheet** (Handout 6 [HO6] on *www.ci3t.org/fabi*).
☐	What is the behavioral dimension you are focusing on? (in **Planning Sheet**) (Handout 6 [HO6] on *www.ci3t.org/fabi*). Explain here:
☐	What measurement system did you select to measure behavior? (in **Planning Sheet**) (Handout 6 [HO6] on *www.ci3t.org/fabi*). Explain here:
☐	Describe the data collection procedures you will use to measure the behavior: materials needed, data collection sheet, and scheduled observation times. Explain here:

(continued)

From *www.ci3t.org*. Lane, K. L., & Oakes, W. P. (2014). *Functional assessment-based interventions (FABI): Training materials—Step-by-step checklists.* Copyright © 2015 by Kathleen Lynne Lane. Reprinted by permission in *Functional Assessment-Based Intervention: Effective Individualized Support for Students* by John Umbreit, Jolenea B. Ferro, Kathleen Lynne Lane, and Carl J. Liaupsin (The Guilford Press, 2024). Permission to photocopy this material, or to download and print additional copies (*www.guilford.com/umbreit-forms*), is granted to purchasers of this book for personal use or use with students; see copyright page for details.

Step 3: Collecting Baseline Data *(page 2 of 2)*

Check when completed	Item
☐	How did your team become reliable in data collection? Explain here:
☐ ___ sessions	How many reliability data observations were completed?
☐ ___ %	What was the percent of agreement between observers (interobserver agreement [IOA]) on the data collection training (reliability training)?
☐ ___ data points	How many baseline data points did you collect?
☐ ___ points with IOA	How many baseline data points included IOA (at least 25% of observations)?
☐ ___ %	What was your IOA for baseline?
☐	Graph your baseline data.
☐	Complete and turn in this checklist to your coach.

Suggested Readings

1. In the *Beyond Behavior* Special Issue (2011, Vol. 20, No. 3):
   a. Read the Method section of articles 2–4 to see how the behavior was measured (e.g., What dimension? What recording system? How often was reliability assessed?) and how people became reliable in the measurement system.
   b. In these same articles, review the graphs to see how the data are displayed.

2. In the following book, read Chapter 9 to learn how to identify an appropriate measurement system and Chapter 10 to learn about the practicalities of collecting baseline data: Umbreit, J., Ferro, J. B., Lane, K. L., & Liaupsin, C. J. (2024). *Functional assessment-based intervention: Effective individualized support for students.* Guilford Press.

Step 3 Tips:

1. Make sure you pick a measurement system that allows you to capture the dimension of interest.

2. Be certain to pick a recording system that is feasible, reliable, and uses the same data collection system in each intervention phase.

3. Train with other data collectors before you begin collecting baseline data to be certain the data you are graphing and interpret is truly measuring student performance.

4. You will be measuring and graphing the target and/or replacement behavior.

COMPLETION CHECKLIST

Step 4: Designing the Intervention

School: _____ District: _____ Date: _____

Team Members:

1. _____ 5. _____
2. _____ 6. _____
3. _____ 7. _____
4. _____ 8. _____

Coach: _____

Step 4: Designing the Intervention

Check when completed	Item
☐	**Step 4.1 Select an Intervention Method** Select intervention method and confirm with teacher—**FABI Planning** (Handout 6 [HO6] on *www.ci3t.org/fabi*).
☐	**Step 4.2 Develop Intervention Components** Draft A-R-E components (**A**ntecedent adjustments, **R**einforcement adjustments, and **E**xtinction components). Link each intervention tactic to the hypothesized function on the planning sheet (*depending on the method* you selected according to the Function-Based Intervention Decision Model).
☐	**Step 4.3 Components Related to Valid Inference Making** Draft treatment integrity form, including the quality rubric **Treatment Integrity Checklist** (Handout 11 [HO11] on *www.ci3t.org/fabi*).
☐	Select and review social validity forms **Adapted-IRP-15 and Adapted-CIRP**.
☐	Prepare a plan for introducing the intervention to the teacher—include a check for understanding. Describe how it was done here:

(continued)

From *www.ci3t.org*. Lane, K. L., & Oakes, W. P. (2014). *Functional assessment-based interventions (FABI): Training materials—Step-by-step checklists*. Copyright © 2015 by Kathleen Lynne Lane. Reprinted by permission in *Functional Assessment-Based Intervention: Effective Individualized Support for Students* by John Umbreit, Jolenea B. Ferro, Kathleen Lynne Lane, and Carl J. Liaupsin (The Guilford Press, 2024). Permission to photocopy this material, or to download and print additional copies (*www.guilford.com/umbreit-forms*), is granted to purchasers of this book for personal use or use with students; see copyright page for details.

Step 4: Designing the Intervention *(page 2 of 2)*

Check when completed	Item
☐	Prepare a plan for introducing the intervention to the student—include a check for understanding. Describe how it was done here:
☐	Revise and finalize A-R-E intervention components, using feedback from the teacher, and draft the final Treatment Integrity Form (Handout 11 [HO11] on *www.ci3t.org/fabi*).
☐	Prepare intervention materials.
☐	Collect additional baseline data after any school breaks (3 data points) with at least 1 IOA.
☐	Complete and turn in this checklist to your coach.

Suggested Readings

1. In the *Beyond Behavior* Special Issue (2011, Vol. 20, No. 3):
   a. Read the first article to learn more about how to use the Function-Based Intervention Decision Model to select an intervention method.
   b. Read the Method section of articles 2–4 to see how the Function-Based Intervention Decision Model was used to identify an intervention method and how the A-R-E tactics were linked back to the student's maintaining function of their target behavior.

2. Read the following chapters in Umbreit, J., Ferro, J. B., Lane, K. L., & Liaupsin, C. J. (2024). *Functional assessment-based intervention: Effective individualized support for students.* Guilford Press.
   a. Chapter 11 to learn about the Function-Based Intervention Decision Model
   b. Chapter 12 to learn about Method 1: Teach the Replacement Behavior
   c. Chapter 13 to learn about Method 2: Adjust the Environment
   d. Chapter 14 to learn about Method 3: Shift the Contingencies
   e. Chapter 15 to learn about Methods 1 and 2: Teach the Replacement Behavior and Adjust the Environment
   f. Chapters 16–18 to learn about more factors that impact success: treatment integrity, social validity, and generalization and maintenance

Step 4 Tips:

1. Make sure you have sufficient evidence to answer the two questions constituting the Function-Based Intervention Decision Model.

2. Align the A-R-E intervention tactics with the maintaining functions determined using the Function Matrix.

3. Make certain all stakeholders are comfortable with the specific A-R-E tactics and have sufficient training and support to put them in place as designed.

COMPLETION CHECKLIST

Step 5: Testing the Intervention

School: _____ District: _____ Date: _____

Team Members:

1. _____ 5. _____
2. _____ 6. _____
3. _____ 7. _____
4. _____ 8. _____

Coach: _____

Step 5: Testing the Intervention

Check when completed	Item
☐	Implement intervention.
☐	Collect treatment integrity data daily (teacher perspective) with IOA for 25% of sessions (outside team observer).
☐	Collect a minimum of 5 data points (behavior measurement—same behavior and measurement system as baseline) with 25% IOA [Report as number of sessions, % of sessions, and actual IOA %].
☐ ___ data points	How many intervention data points did you collect?
☐ ___ points with IOA	How many intervention data points included IOA?
☐ ___ %	What was your IOA for intervention?
☐	Graph your intervention data. *(Coaches' review for support for deciding when to withdraw the intervention.)*
☐	Withdrawal of the intervention with at least 3 data points (1 IOA). ***Note phase-change decisions for each phase are guided by student performance on the variables measured.**
☐	Complete Treatment Integrity Form (daily by interventionist [teacher] with 25% IOA).
☐	Graph withdrawal data. *(Coaches' review for support for deciding when to reintroduce the intervention.)*
☐	Reintroduce the intervention. ***Note phase-change decisions for each phase are guided by student performance on the variables measured.**

(continued)

From *www.ci3t.org*. Lane, K. L., & Oakes, W. P. (2014). *Functional assessment-based interventions (FABI): Training materials—Step-by-step checklists*. Copyright © 2015 by Kathleen Lynne Lane. Reprinted by permission in *Functional Assessment-Based Intervention: Effective Individualized Support for Students* by John Umbreit, Jolenea B. Ferro, Kathleen Lynne Lane, and Carl J. Liaupsin (The Guilford Press, 2024). Permission to photocopy this material, or to download and print additional copies (*www.guilford.com/umbreit-forms*), is granted to purchasers of this book for personal use or use with students; see copyright page for details.

Step 5: Testing the Intervention *(page 2 of 2)*

Check when completed	Item
☐	Collect treatment integrity data daily (teacher perspective) with IOA for 25% of sessions (outside team observer).
☐	Collect a minimum of 3 data points (behavior measurement—same behavior and measurement system throughout all phases) with 25% IOA. [Report as number of sessions, % of sessions, and actual IOA %]
☐	Plan for follow-up data collection to assess maintenance. **FABI Planning** and **Behavior Intervention Plan (BIP)** (Handout 6.0 [HO6.0] and 6.1 [HO6.1] on *www.ci3t.org/fabi*).
☐	Work with your coaches to complete the BIP and the graphed data to share with teacher and parents.
☐	Conduct a final check of ethical considerations: **Ethics Checklist** (Handout 14 [HO14] on *www.ci3t.org/fabi*).
☐	After reviewing final graph, assess POST social validity (**Adapted-IRP-15** and **Adapted-CIRP**).
☐	Complete and turn in this checklist to your coach.

Suggested Readings

1. In the *Beyond Behavior* Special Issue (2011, Vol. 20, No. 3), read the Method, Results, and Discussion sections of articles 2–4 to see how the intervention was design, implemented, and evaluated.

2. In the following book, read Chapter 20 to learn how to test the intervention: Umbreit, J., Ferro, J. B., Lane, K. L., & Liaupsin, C. J. (2024). *Functional assessment-based intervention: Effective individualized support for students*. Guilford Press.

Step 5 Tips:

1. Be sure you use an experimental design to make certain you can actually demonstrate a function relation between the introduction of the intervention and changes in student performance.

2. Phase changes are determined by examining data (e.g., its stability, level, and trend) and are not determined by the amount of time a student spends in each phase.

3. Phase changes should not occur before or after breaks in the school year calendar.

4. Be certain to collect treatment integrity data with each introduction of the intervention.

5. The postintervention social validity measures are completed by stakeholders after the intervention has been tested and the outcomes (e.g., graphed and other data) have been shared with and explained to the stakeholders.

6. When you complete HO 6.1, remember it will be used by the current and future teachers. Be certain to include a blank copy of the Treatment Integrity Form for future use as well as a completed graph showing the complete intervention outcomes.

References

Achenbach, T. M. (1991a). *Integrative guide for the 1991 CBCL/4–18, YRS, & TRF profiles.* University of Vermont Department of Psychiatry.

Achenbach, T. M. (1991b). *Manual for the teacher's report form and 1991 profile.* University of Vermont Department of Psychiatry.

Aitken, A., Harlan, A., Hankins, K., Michels, J., Moore, T. C., Oakes, W. P., & Lane, K. L. (2011). Increasing academic engagement during writing activities in an urban elementary classroom. *Beyond Behavior, 20,* 31–43.

Alberto, P. A., & Troutman, A. C. (2016). *Applied behavior analysis to teachers* (9th ed.). Pearson.

Algozzine, B., Barrett, S., Eber, L., George, H., Horner, R., Lewis, T., . . . Sugai, G. (2014). *School-wide PBIS Tiered Fidelity Inventory.* OSEP Technical Assistance Center on Positive Behavioral Interventions and Supports. www.pbis.org

Baer, D., Wolf, M., & Risley, T. (1968). Some current dimensions of applied behavior analysis. *Journal of Applied Behavior Analysis, 1,* 91–97.

Baer, D. M., Wolf, M. M., & Risley, T. R. (1987). Some still-current dimensions of applied behavior analysis. *Journal of Applied Behavior Analysis, 20,* 313–327.

Bal, A., Afacan, K., & Cakir, H. I. (2018). Culturally responsive school discipline: Implementing Learning Lab at a high school for systemic transformation. *American Educational Research Journal, 55*(5), 1007–1050.

Bal, A., & Perzigian, A. (2013). Evidence-based interventions for immigrant students experiencing behavioral and academic problems: A systematic review of the literature. *Education and Treatment of Children, 36*(4), 5–28.

Ball, D. L., Sleep, L., Boerst, T. A., & Bass, H. (2009). Combining the development of practice and the practice of development in teacher education. *Elementary School Journal, 109,* 458–474.

Bambara, L., Janney, R., & Snell, M. (2005). *Behavior support* (3rd ed.). Brookes.

Banks, T., & Obiakor, F. E. (2015). Culturally responsive positive behavior supports: Considerations for practice. *Journal of Education and Training Studies, 3,* 83–90.

Barrett, S., Eber, L., & Weist, M. (Eds.). (2013). *Advancing education effectiveness: Interconnecting school mental health and school-wide positive behavior support.* Center for School Mental Health.

Behavior Analyst Certification Board. (2022). *Ethics code for behavior analysts.* www.bacb.com/wp-content/uploads/2022/01/Ethics-Code-for-Behavior-Analysts-220316-2.pdf

Bergan, J. R., & Kratochwill, T. R. (1990). *Behavioral consultation and therapy*. Plenum Press.

Bijou, S. W. (1970). What psychology has to offer education—now. *Journal of Applied Behavior Analysis, 3*, 65–71.

Bijou, S. W., & Baer, D. M. (1961). *Child development: Vol. 1. A systematic and empirical theory*. Appleton-Century-Crofts.

Bijou, S. W., Peterson, R. F., & Ault, M. H. (1968). A method to integrate descriptive and experimental field studies at the level of data and empirical concepts. *Journal of Applied Behavior Analysis, 1*, 175–191.

Billingsley, F. F., White, O. R., & Munson, R. (1980). Procedural reliability: A rationale and an example. *Behavioral Assessment, 2*, 229–241.

Briesch, A. M., & Chafouleas, S. M. (2009). Review and analysis of literature on self-management interventions to promote appropriate classroom behaviors (1988–2008). *School Psychology Quarterly, 24*(2), 106–118.

Buckman, M. M., Lane, K. L., Common, E. A., Royer, D. J., Oakes, W. P., Allen, G. E., . . . Brunsting, N. (2021). Treatment integrity of primary (tier 1) prevention efforts in tiered systems: Mapping the literature. *Education and Treatment of Children, 44*, 145–168.

Carr, E. G. (1977). The motivation of self-injurious behavior: A review of some hypotheses. *Psychological Bulletin, 84*(4), 800–816.

Carr, E. G., & Durand, V. M. (1985). Reducing behavior problems through functional communication training. *Journal of Applied Behavior Analysis, 18*(2), 111–126.

Carr, E. G., Levin, L., McConnachie, G., Carlson, J. I., Kemp, D. C., & Smith, C. E. (1994). *Communication based intervention for problem behavior: A users guide for producing positive change*. Brookes.

Chafouleas, S. M., Volpe, R. J., Gresham, F. M., & Cook, C. (2010). School-based behavioral assessment within problem-solving models: Current status and future directions. *School Psychology Review, 34*, 343–349.

Children's Defense Fund (1975). *School suspensions: Are they helping children?* U.S. Department of Health and Human Services, National Institute of Education. https://files.eric.ed.gov/fulltext/ED113797.pdf

Committee for Children. (2002). *Second Step: A violence prevention curriculum*. Author.

Common, E. A., Lane, K. L., Cantwell, E. D., Brunsting, N. C., Oakes, W. P., Germer, K. A., & Bross, L. A. (2020). Teacher-delivered strategies to increase students' opportunities to respond: A systematic methodological review. *Behavioral Disorders, 45*(2), 67–84.

Common, E. A., Lane, K. L., Oakes, W. P., Schellman, L. E., Shogren, K., Germer, K. A., . . . Lane, N. A. (2022). Building site–level capacity for functional assessment-based interventions: Outcomes of a professional learning series. *Behavioral Disorders, 48*(1), 44–61.

Common, E. A., Lane, K. L., Pustejovsky, J. E., Johnson, A. H., & Johl, L. E. (2017). Functional assessment-based interventions for students with or at-risk for high-incidence disabilities: Field-testing single-case synthesis methods. *Remedial and Special Education, 38*(6), 331–352.

Common, E. A., Oakes, W. P., & Lane, K. L. (2015). *Functional assessment-based intervention process guide: Component checklist visual analysis: Guiding questions for phase change decision making*. Unpublished tool. http://www.ci3t.org/fabi

Cooper, J. O., Heron, T. E., & Heward, W. L. (2020). *Applied behavior analysis* (3rd ed.). Pearson.

Cox, M., Griffin, M. M., Hall, R., Oakes, W. P., & Lane, K. L. (2011). Using a functional assessment-based intervention to increase academic engaged time in an inclusive middle school setting. *Beyond Behavior, 20*, 44–54.

Desimone, L. M. (2009). Improving impact studies of teachers' professional development: Toward better conceptualizations and measures. *Educational Researcher, 38*, 181–199.

Drasgow, E., & Yell, M. L. (2001). Functional behavioral assessments: Legal requirements and challenges. *School Psychology Review, 30*(2), 239–251.

Drummond, T. (1994). *The Student Risk Screening Scale (SRSS)*. Josephine County Mental Health Program.

Dunlap, G., Kern-Dunlap, L., Clarke, S., & Robbins, F. R. (1991). Functional assessment, curricular revision, and severe behavior problems. *Journal of Applied Behavior Analysis, 24*, 387–397.

Dunlap, G., Kern, L., dePerczel, M., Clarke, S., Wilson, D., Childs, K. E., . . . Falk, G. (1993). *Preliminary functional assessment survey*. Unpublished document, Division of Applied Research and Educational Services, University of South Florida, Tampa.

Durand, V. M. (1990). *Severe behavior problems: A functional communication training approach.* Guilford Press.

Erdy, L., & Zakszeski, B. N. (2021, March). *Train and coach: Supporting educators' implementation of trauma-informed practices.* Paper presented at the 18th International Conference on Positive Behavior Support, Virtual.

Fawcett, S. (1991). Social validity: A note on methodology. *Journal of Applied Behavior Analysis, 24,* 235–239.

Ferro, J. B., Umbreit, J., & Liaupsin, C. J. (2008). *Assessing the classroom environment checklist.* Unpublished document, Special Education Program, University of Arizona, Tucson.

Finn, C. A., & Sladeczek, I. E. (2001). Assessing the social validity of behavior interventions: A review of treatment acceptability measures. *School Psychology Quarterly, 16,* 176–206.

Forness, S. R., Freeman, S. F. N., Paparella, T., Kauffman, J. M., & Walker, H. M. (2012). Special education implications of point and cumulative prevalence for children with emotional or behavioral disorders. *Journal of Emotional and Behavioral Disorders, 20,* 4–18.

Freeman, R., Miller, D., & Newcomer, L. (2015). Integration of academic and behavioral MTSS at the district level using implementation science. *Learning Disabilities: A Contemporary Journal, 13,* 59–72.

Friedman-Krauss, A. H., Raver, C. C., Morris, P. A., & Jones, S. M. (2014). The role of classroom level child behavior problems in predicting preschool teacher stress and classroom emotional climate. *Early Education and Development, 25,* 530–552.

Friend, M. M., & Cook, L. (2010). *Interactions: Collaboration skills for school professionals.* Longman.

Fuchs, D., & Fuchs, L. S. (2017). Critique of the national evaluation of response to intervention: A case for simpler frameworks. *Exceptional Children, 83,* 255–268.

Fuchs, D., Fuchs, L. S., & Compton, D. L. (2012). Smart RTI: A next-generation approach to multilevel prevention. *Exceptional Children, 78,* 263–279.

Gandhi, A. G., Clemens, N., Coyne, M., Goodman, S., Lane, K. L., Lembke, E., & Simonsen, B. (in press). Integrated multi-tiered systems of support (I-MTSS): New directions for supporting students with or at risk for learning disabilities. In C. M. Okolo, N. Patton Terry, & L. E. Cutting (Eds.), *Handbook of learning disabilities* (3rd ed.). Guilford Press.

Gann, C. J., Ferro, J. B., Umbreit, J., & Liaupsin, C. J. (2014). Effects of a comprehensive function-based intervention applied across multiple educational settings. *Remedial and Special Education, 35,* 50–60.

Gann, C. J., Gaines, S., Antia, S. D., Umbreit, J., & Liaupsin, C. J. (2015). Evaluating the effects of function-based interventions with D/HH students. *Journal of Deaf Studies and Deaf Education, 20,* 252–265.

Gast, D. L., & Hammond, D. (2010). Withdrawal and reversal designs. In D. L. Gast, *Single subject research methodology in behavioral sciences.* Routledge.

Germer, K. A., Kaplan, L. M., Giroux, L. N., Markham, E. H., Ferris, G. J., Oakes, W. P., & Lane, K. L. (2011). A function-based intervention to increase a second-grade student's on-task behavior in a general education classroom. *Beyond Behavior, 20,* 19–30.

Gilliam, W. (2005). *Prekindergartners left behind: Expulsion rates in state pre-kindergarten systems.* Foundation for Child Development.

Good, R. H., & Kaminski, R. A. (Eds.). (2002). *Dynamic Indicators of Basic Early Literacy Skills* (6th ed.). Institute for the Development of Educational Achievement.

Gresham, F. M. (1989). Assessment of treatment integrity in school consultation and prereferral intervention. *School Psychology Review, 18,* 37–50.

Gresham, F. M., & Elliott, S. N. (1990). *Social Skills Rating System.* American Guidance Service.

Gresham, F., & Elliott, S. N. (2008a). *Social Skills Improvement System (SSIS) Rating Scale.* Pearson.

Gresham, F. M., & Elliott, S. N. (2008b). *Social Skills Improvement System Rating Scales manual.* Pearson.

Gresham, F. M., Gansle, K. A., & Noell, G. H. (1993). Treatment integrity in applied behavior analysis with children. *Journal of Applied Behavioral Analysis, 26,* 257–263.

Gresham, F. M., & Lopez, M. F. (1996). Social validation: A unifying construct for school-based consultation research and practice. *School Psychology Quarterly, 11,* 204–227.

Gresham, F. M., MacMillan, D. L., Beebe-Frankenberger, M. E., & Bocian, K. M. (2000). Treatment integrity in learning disabilities intervention research: Do we really know how treatments are implemented? *Learning Disabilities Research & Practice, 15,* 198–205.

Grove, R. D., & Hetzel, A. M. (1968). *Vital statistics rates in the United States, 1940–1960* (Public Health Services Publ. No. 1677). U.S. Department of Health, Education, and Welfare.

Hawken, L. S., Vincent, C. G., & Schumann, J. (2008). Response to intervention for social behavior: Challenges and opportunities. *Journal of Emotional and Behavioral Disorders, 16*(4), 213–225.

Heath, A. K., Ganz, J. B., Parker, R., Burke, M., & Ninci, J. (2015). A meta-analytic review of functional communication training across mode of communication, age, and disability. *Review Journal of Autism and Developmental Disorders, 2*(2), 155–166.

Hirsch, S. E., Randall, K. N., Common, E. A., & Lane, K. L. (2020). Results of practice-based professional development for supporting special educators in learning how to design functional assessment-based interventions. *Teacher Education and Special Education, 43*(4), 281–295.

Horner, R. H., & Billingsley, F. F. (1988). The effect of competing behavior on the generalization and maintenance of adaptive behavior in applied settings. In R. H. Horner, G. Dunlap, & R. L. Koegel (Eds.), *Generalization and maintenance: Lifestyle changes in applied settings* (pp. 197–220). Brookes.

Horner, R. H., & Day, H. M. (1991). The effects of response efficiency on functionally equivalent competing behaviors. *Journal of Applied Behavior Analysis, 24*(4), 719–732.

Horner, R. H., & Sugai, G. (2015). School-wide PBIS: An example of applied behavior analysis implemented at a scale of social importance. *Behavior Analysis in Practice, 8*, 80–85.

Idol, L., Paolucci-Whitcomb, P., & Nevin, A. (2010). The collaborative consultation model, *Journal of Educational and Psychological Consultation, 6*(4), 329–346.

Individuals with Disabilities Education Improvement Act of 2004, Public Law 20 U.S.C. 1400 et seq. (2004).

Institute of Education Sciences. (2017). *Request for applications: Research networks focused on critical problems of policy and practice in special education* (CFDA No. 84.324N). Author.

Iwata, B. A., Dorsey, M., Slifer, K., Bauman, K., & Richman, G. (1982). Toward a functional analysis of self-injury. *Analysis and Intervention in Developmental Disabilities, 2*, 3–20.

Janney, D. M., Umbreit, J., Ferro, J. B., Liaupsin, C. J., & Lane, K. L. (2013). The effect of the extinction procedure in function-based intervention. *Journal of Positive Behavior Intervention, 15*, 113–123.

Kantor, J. R. (1959). *Interbehavioral psychology*. Principia Press.

Kazdin, A. E. (1977). Assessing the clinical or applied significance of behavior change through social validation. *Behaviour Modification, 1*, 427–452.

Kazdin, A. E. (1980). Acceptability of alternative treatments for deviant child behavior. *Journal of Applied Behavior Analysis, 13*, 259–273.

Kazdin, A. E. (1982). *Behavior modification in applied settings*. Oxford University Press.

Kelley, M. J., Heffer, R. W., Gresham, F. M., & Elliott, S. N. (1989). Development of a modified Treatment Evaluation Inventory. *Journal of Psychopathology & Behavioral Assessment, 11*, 235–247.

Kern, L., Childs, K. E., Dunlap, G., Clarke, S., & Falk, G. D. (1994). Using assessment-based curricular intervention to improve the classroom behavior of a student with emotional and behavioral challenges. *Journal of Applied Behavior Analysis, 27*, 7–19.

Kern, L., Dunlap, G., Clarke, S., & Childs, K. (1994). Student-Assisted Functional Assessment Interview. *Diagnostic, 19*, 20–39.

Kerr, M. M., & Nelson, C. M. (2010). *Strategies for addressing behavior problems in the classroom* (6th ed.). Pearson.

Kretlow, A. G., & Bartholomew, C. C. (2010). Using coaching to improve the fidelity of evidence-based practices: A review of studies. *Teacher Education and Special Education, 33*(4), 279–299.

Lane, K. L. (2009a). *Comprehensive, integrated three-tiered model of prevention: Treatment Integrity Direct Observation Tool (Ci3T TI: DO)*. www.ci3t.org/measures

Lane, K. L. (2009b). *Comprehensive, integrated three-tiered model of prevention: Treatment Integrity Teacher Self-Report Form (Ci3T TI: TSR)*. www.ci3t.org/measures

Lane, K. L. (2013). *Functional assessment-based intervention (FABI): Training materials—Step-by-step checklists*. www.ci3t.org/fabi

Lane, K. L. (2017). Building strong partnerships: Responsible inquiry to learn and grow together: TECBD-CCBD keynote address. *Education and Treatment of Children, 40*, 597–617.

Lane, K. L., Barton-Arwood, S. M., Spencer, J. L., & Kalberg, J. R. (2007). Teaching elementary school educators to design, implement, and evaluate functional assessment-based interventions: Successes and challenges. *Preventing School Failure, 51*(4), 35–46.

Lane, K. L., & Beebe-Frankenberger, M. E. (2004). *School-based interventions: The tools you need to succeed*. Allyn & Bacon.

Lane, K. L., Bocian, K. M., MacMillan, D. L., & Gresham, F. M. (2004). Treatment integrity: An essential—but not forgotten—component of school-based intervention. *Preventing School Failure: Alternative Education for Children and Youth, 48*, 36–43.

Lane, K. L., Bruhn, A. L., Crnobori, M. L., & Sewell, A. L. (2009). Designing functional assessment-based interventions using a systematic approach: A promising practice for supporting challenging behavior. In T. E. Scruggs & M. A. Mastropieri (Eds.), *Policy and practice: Advances in learning and behavioral disabilities* (Vol. 22, pp. 341–370). Emerald.

Lane, K. L., Buckman, M. M., Oakes, W. P., & Menzies, H. M. (2020). Tiered systems and inclusion: Potential benefits, clarifications, and considerations. In J. M. Kauffman (Ed.), *On educational inclusion: Meanings, history, issues, and international perspectives* (pp. 85–106). Routledge/Taylor & Francis Group.

Lane, K. L., Eisner, S. L., Kretzer, J. M., Bruhn, A. L., Crnobori, M. E., Funke, L. M., . . . Casey, A. M. (2009). Outcomes of functional assessment-based interventions for students with and at risk for emotional and behavioral disorders in a job-share setting. *Education and Treatment of Children, 32*, 573–604.

Lane, K. L., Kalberg, J. R., Bruhn, A. L., Driscoll, S. A., Wehby, J. H., & Elliott, S. N. (2009). Assessing social validity of school-wide positive behavior support plans: Evidence for the reliability and structure of the Primary Intervention Rating Scale. *School Psychology Review, 38*(1), 135–144.

Lane, K. L., Kalberg, J. R., & Menzies, H. M. (2009). *Developing schoolwide programs to prevent and manage problem behaviors: A step-by-step approach*. Guilford Press.

Lane, K. L., & Menzies, H. M. (2009). *Student Risk Screening Scale for Internalizing and Externalizing (SRSS-IE)*. www.ci3t.org/screening

Lane, K. L., Menzies, H., Bruhn, A., & Crnobori, M. (2011). *Managing challenging behaviors in schools: Research-based strategies that work*. Guilford Press.

Lane, K. L., Menzies, H. M., Ennis, R. P., & Oakes, W. P. (2015). *Supporting behavior for school success: A step-by-step guide to key strategies*. Guilford Press.

Lane, K. L., Menzies, H. M., Oakes, W. P., & Kalberg, J. R. (2020). *Developing a schoolwide framework to prevent and manage learning and behavior problems* (2nd ed.). Guilford Press.

Lane, K. L., & Oakes, W. P. (2014). *Functional assessment-based interventions (FABI): Training materials—Step-by-step checklists*. Form updated May 18, 2016. www.ci3t.org/FABI

Lane, K. L., Oakes, W. P., Buckman, M. M., & Menzies, H. M. (2019). Comprehensive, integrated, three-tiered (Ci3T) models of prevention: Considerations for the field. In D. Bateman, J. Cline, & M. Yell (Eds.), *Current trends and legal issues in special education* (pp. 22–36). Corwin Press.

Lane, K. L., Oakes, W. P., Cantwell, E. D., & Royer, D. J. (2019). *Building and installing comprehensive, integrated, three-tiered (Ci3T) models of prevention: A practical guide to supporting school success* (Vol. 3). KOI Education.

Lane, K. L., Oakes, W. P., & Cox, M. (2011). Functional assessment-based interventions: A university–district partnership to promote learning and success. *Beyond Behavior, 20*, 3–18.

Lane, K. L., Oakes, W. P., & Menzies, H. M. (2010). *Schoolwide Expectations Survey for Specific Settings*. ci3t.org/pdf/SESSS_large.pdf

Lane, K. L., Oakes, W. P., & Menzies, H. M. (2014). Comprehensive, integrated, three-tiered models of prevention: Why does my school—and district—need an integrated approach to meet students' academic, behavioral, and social needs? *Preventing School Failure: Alternative Education for Children and Youth, 58*, 121–128.

Lane, K. L., Oakes, W. P., & Menzies, H. M. (2021). Considerations for systematic screening PK–12: Universal screening for internalizing and externalizing behaviors in the COVID-19 era. *Preventing School Failure: Alternative Education for Children and Youth, 65*(3), 275–281.

Lane, K. L., Oakes, W. P., Powers, L., Diebold, T., Germer, K., Common, E. A., & Brunsting, N. (2015). Improving teachers' knowledge of functional assessment-based interventions: Outcomes of a professional development series. *Education and Treatment of Children, 38*, 93–120.

Lane, K. L., Rogers, L. A., Parks, R. J., Weisenbach, J. L., Mau, A. C., Merwin, M. T., & Bergman, W. A. (2007). Function-based interventions for students who are nonresponsive to primary and secondary prevention efforts: Illustrations at the elementary and middle school levels. *Journal of Emotional and Behavioral Disorders, 15*(3), 169–183.

Lane, K. L., & Walker, H. M. (2015). The connection between assessment and intervention: How does screening lead to better interventions? In B. Bateman, M. Tankersley, & J. Lloyd (Eds.), *Enduring issues in special education: Personal perspectives* (pp. 283–301). Routledge.

Lane, K. L., Wehby, J., Menzies, H. M., Doukas, G. L., Munton, S. M., & Gregg, R. M. (2003). Social skills instruction for students at risk for antisocial behavior: The effects of small-group instruction. *Behavioral Disorders, 28*, 229–248.

Lane, K. L., Weisenbach, J. L., Little, M. A., Phillips, A., & Wehby, J. (2006). Illustrations of function-based interventions implemented by general education teachers: Building capacity at the school site. *Education and Treatment of Children, 29*, 549–571.

Lane, K. L., Weisenbach, J. L., Phillips, A., & Wehby, J. H. (2007). Designing, implementing, and evaluating function-based interventions using a systematic, feasible approach. *Behavioral Disorders, 32*(2), 122–129.

Lansey, K. R., Antia, S., MacFarland, S. Z., & Umbreit, J. (2021). Training and coaching: Impact on peer mentor fidelity and behavior of postsecondary students with autism and intellectual disability. *Education and Training in Autism and Developmental Disabilities, 56*, 328–340.

Laraway, S., Snycerski, S., Michael, J., & Poling, A. (2003). Motivating operations and terms to describe them: Some further refinements. *Journal of Applied Behavior Analysis, 36*(3), 407–414.

Ledford, J. R., Ayres, K. M., Lane, J. D., & Lam, M. F. (2015). Identifying issues and concerns with the use of interval-based systems in single case research using a pilot simulation study. *The Journal of Special Education, 49*(2), 104–117.

Ledford, J. R., & Gast, D. L. (2018). *Single case research methodology: Applications in special education and behavioral sciences* (3rd ed.). Routledge/Taylor & Francis Group.

Liaupsin, C. J., Umbreit, J., Ferro, J. B., Urso, A., & Upreti, G. (2006). Improving academic engagement through systematic, function-based intervention. *Education and Treatment of Children, 29*, 573–591.

Lund, K., Schnaps, L., & Bijou, S. W. (1983). Let's take another look at record keeping. *Teaching Exceptional Children, 15*, 155–159.

Maag, J. (2005). Social skills training for students with emotional and behavioral disorders and learning disabilities: Problems, conclusions, and suggestions. *Exceptionality, 13*, 155–172.

Maag, J. (2006). Social skills training for students with emotional and behavioral disorders: A review of reviews. *Behavioral Disorders, 32*, 5–17.

Mace, F. C. (1994). The significance and future of functional analysis methodologies. *Journal of Applied Behavior Analysis, 27*, 385–392.

Majeika, C. E., Walder, J. P., Hubbard, J. P., Steeb, K. M., Ferris, G. J., Oakes, W. P., & Lane, K. L. (2011). Improving on-task behavior using a functional assessment-based intervention in an inclusive high school setting. *Beyond Behavior, 20*, 55–66.

Markle, R. S., Splett, J. W., Maras, M. A., & Weston, K. J. (2014). Effective school teams: Benefits, barriers, and best practices. In M. Weist, N. Lever, C. Bradshaw, & J. Owens (Eds.), *Handbook of school mental health: Issues in clinical child psychology* (pp. 59–73). Springer.

Martens, B. K., & Witt, J. C. (1982). *The Intervention Rating Profile*. University of Nebraska–Lincoln.

Martin, G., & Pear, J. (2019). *Behavior modification: What it is and how to do it* (11th ed.). Routledge.

Mathur, S. K., & Rodriguez, K. A. (2022). Cultural responsiveness curriculum for behavior analysts: A meaningful step toward social justice. *Behavior Analysis in Practice, 15*, 1023–1031.

Mayer, R. G., Sulzer-Azaroff, B., & Wallace, M. (2018). *Behavior analysis for lasting change* (3rd ed.). Sloan.

McIntosh, K., Borgmeier, C., Anderson, C. M., Horner, R. H., Rodriguez, B. J., & Tobin, T. J. (2008). Technical adequacy of the Functional Assessment Checklist Teachers and Staff (FACTS) FBA interview measure. *Journal of Positive Behavior Intervention, 10*(1), 33–45.

McIntosh, K., & Goodman, S. (2016). *Integrated multi-tiered systems of support: Blending RTI and PBIS*. Guilford Press.

McIntosh, K., Sugai, G., & Simonsen, B. (2020, February). *Ditch the clip!: Why clip charts are not a PBIS practice and what to do instead*. Center on PBIS, University of Oregon; www.pbis.org

Michael, J. (1982). Distinguishing between discriminative and motivational functions of stimuli. *Journal of the Experimental Analysis of Behavior, 37*, 149–155.

Michael, J. (1993). Establishing operations. *The Behavior Analyst, 16*, 191–206.

Miller, L. K. (2006). *Principles of everyday behavior analysis* (4th ed.). Brooks/Cole.

Moll, L. C., Amanti, C., Neff, D., & Gonzalez, N. (1992). Funds of knowledge for teaching: Using a qualitative approach to connect homes and classrooms. *Theory into Practice, 31*(2), 132–141.

Nahgahgwon, K. N., Umbreit, J., Liaupsin, C. J., & Turton, A. M. (2010). Function-based planning for young children at risk for emotional and behavioral disorders. *Education and Treatment of Children, 33*, 537–559.

National Center for Pyramid Model Innovations. (2022). *Functional Assessment Interview—Teacher Form.* Author.

National Association of School Psychologists. (2020). *NASP 2020 professional standards.* Author.

National Association of Social Workers. (2021). *Code of ethics of the NASW.* Author.

Nelson, J. R., Benner, G. J., Lane, K., & Smith, B. W. (2004). Academic achievement of K–12 students with emotional and behavioral disorders. *Exceptional Children, 71*(1), 59–73.

Newcomer, L. L., & Lewis, T. J. (2004). Functional behavioral assessment: An investigation of assessment reliability and effectiveness of function-based interventions. *Journal of Emotional and Behavioral Disorders, 12*(3), 168–181.

Northup J., Wacker, D., Sasso, G., Steege, M., Cigrand, K., Cook, J., & DeRaad, A. (1991). A brief functional analysis of aggressive and alternative behavior in an outclinic setting. *Journal of Applied Behavior Analysis, 24*, 509–522.

Oakes, W. P., Lane, K. L., & Germer, K. (2014). Developing the capacity to implement Tier 2 and Tier 3 supports: How do we support our faculty and staff in preparing for sustainability? *Preventing School Failure, 58*, 183–190.

Oakes, W. P., Schellman, L. E., Lane, K. L., Common, E. A., Powers, L., Diebold, T., & Gaskill, T. (2018). Improving educators' knowledge, confidence, and usefulness of functional assessment-based interventions: Outcomes of professional learning. *Education and Treatment of Children, 41*, 533–565.

O'Neill, R., Albin, R., Storey, K., Horner, R., & Sprague, J. (2015). *Functional assessment and program development for problem behavior: A practical handbook* (3rd ed.). Cengage Learning.

Peterson, L., Homer, A. L., & Wonderlich, S. A. (1982). The integrity of independent variables in behavior analysis. *Journal of Applied Behavior Analysis, 15*, 477–492.

Positive Action. (2008). *Positive action: Positive development for schools, families and communities.* Author.

Preciado, J. A., Horner, R. H., & Baker, S. K. (2009). Using a function-based approach to decrease problem behaviors and increase academic engagement for Latino English language learners. *The Journal of Special Education, 42*(4), 227–240.

Premack, D. (1959). Toward empirical behavior laws: I. Positive reinforcement. *Psychological Review, 66*(4), 219.

Reeves, L. M., Umbreit, J., Ferro, J. B., & Liaupsin, C. J. (2013). Function-based intervention to support the inclusion of students with autism. *Education and Training in Autism and Developmental Disabilities, 48*, 379–391.

Reeves, L. M., Umbreit, J., Ferro, J. B., & Liaupsin, C. J. (2017). The role of the replacement behavior in function-based intervention. *Education and Training in Autism and Developmental Disabilities, 52*, 305–316.

Reichle, J., & Wacker, D. P. (2017). *Functional communication training for problem behavior.* Guilford Press.

Reimers, T. M., & Wacker, D. P. (1988). Parents' ratings of the acceptability of behavioral treatment recommendations made in an outpatient clinic: A preliminary analysis of the influence of treatment effectiveness. *Behavioral Disorders, 14*(1), 7–15.

Repp, A. C., Felce, D., & Barton, L. E. (1988). Basing the treatment of stereotypic and self-injurious behaviors on hypotheses of their causes. *Journal of Applied Behavior Analysis, 21*(3), 281–289.

Royer, D. J., Lane, K. L., Cantwell, E. D., & Messenger, M. L. (2017). A systematic review of the evidence base for instructional choice in K–12 settings. *Behavioral Disorders, 42*(3), 89–107.

Shaw, D. (2013). Future directions for research on the development and prevention of early conduct problems. *Journal of Clinical Child & Adolescent Psychology, 42*(3), 418–428.

Sheridan, S. M., Clarke, B. L., & Ransom, K. A. (2014). The past, present, and future of conjoint behavioral consultation research. In W. P. Erchul & S. M. Sheridan (Eds.), *Handbook of research in school consultation* (pp. 210–247). Routledge/Taylor & Francis Group.

Sidman, M. (1989). *Coercion and its fallout.* Authors Cooperative.

Skinner, B. F. (1938). *The behavior of organisms: An experimental analysis.* Appleton-Century.

States, J., Detrich, R., & Keyworth, R. (2017). *Overview of multitiered system of support.* Wing Institute. www.winginstitute.org/school-programs-multi-tiered-systems

Stewart, R. M., Benner, G. J., Martella, R. C., & Marchand-Martella, N. E. (2007). Three-tier models of reading and behavior: A research review. *Journal of Positive Behavior Interventions, 9*(4), 239–253.

Stokes, T., & Baer, D. (1977). An implicit technology of generalization. *Journal of Applied Behavior Analysis, 10,* 349–367.

Stormont, M., Reinke, W. M., Newcomer, L., Marchese, D., & Lewis, C. (2015). Coaching teachers' use of social behavior interventions to improve children's outcomes: A review of the literature. *Journal of Positive Behavior Interventions, 17*(2), 69–82.

Sugai, G., & Horner, R. H. (2009). Defining and describing schoolwide positive behavior support. In W. Sailor, G. Dunlap, G. Sugai, & R. Horner (Eds.), *Handbook of positive behavior support* (pp. 307–326). Springer.

Sugai, G., Lewis-Palmer, T., Todd, A., & Horner, R. H. (2001). *School-wide evaluation tool.* University of Oregon.

Tharp, R. G., & Wetzel, R. J. (1969). *Behavior modification in the natural environment.* Academic Press.

Thomas, D. E., Bierman, K. L., Thompson, C., & Powers, C. J. (2008). Double jeopardy: Child and school characteristics that predict aggressive-disruptive behavior in first grade. *School Psychology Review, 37*(4), 516–532.

Turton, A. M., Umbreit, J., Liaupsin, C. J., & Bartley, J. (2007). Function-based intervention for an adolescent with emotional and behavioral disorders in Bermuda: Moving across culture. *Behavioral Disorders, 33,* 23–32.

Turton, A. M., Umbreit, J., & Mathur, S. R. (2011). Systematic function-based intervention for adolescents with emotional and behavioral disorders in an alternative setting: Broadening the context. *Behavioral Disorders, 36,* 117–128.

Umbreit, J. (1995). Functional assessment and intervention in a regular classroom setting for the disruptive behavior of a student with attention deficit hyperactivity disorder. *Behavioral Disorders, 20,* 267–278.

Umbreit, J., & Ferro, J. B. (2022). The role of function in behavioral intervention. In M. Tankersley, T. J. Landrum, & B. G. Cook (Eds.), *Designing intensive, individualized interventions for children and youth with learning and behavioral disabilities: Advances in learning and behavioral disabilities* (Vol. 32, pp. 67–83). Emerald.

Umbreit, J., Ferro, J. B., Liaupsin, C. J., & Lane, K. L. (2007). *Functional behavioral assessment and function-based intervention: An effective, practical approach.* Pearson.

Umbreit, J., Lane, K. L., & Dejud, C. (2004). Improving classroom behavior by modifying task difficulty: Effects of increasing the difficulty of too easy tasks. *Journal of Positive Behavior Interventions, 6*(1), 13–20.

Underwood, M. A., Umbreit, J., & Liaupsin, C. J. (2009). Efficacy of a systematic process for designing function-based interventions for adults in a community setting. *Education and Training in Developmental Disabilities, 44,* 25–38.

U.S. Department of Education and Office for Civil Rights. (2012). *Helping to ensure equal access to education.* Author.

U.S. Government Accountability Office. (2018). *K–12 education: Discipline disparities for black students, boys, and students with disabilities.* www.gao.gov/products/gao-18-258

Utley, C., & Obiakor, F. (2015). Special issue: Research perspectives on multi-tiered system of support. *Learning Disabilities: A Contemporary Journal, 13*(1), 1–2.

Vancel, S. M., Missall, K. N., & Bruhn, A. L. (2016). Teacher ratings of the social validity of schoolwide positive behavior interventions and supports: A comparison of school groups. *Preventing School Failure: Alternative Education for Children and Youth, 60*(4), 320–328.

Walker, H. M., Block-Pedego, A., Todis, B., & Severson, H. (1991). *School archival records search.* Sopris West.

Walker, H. M., Forness, S. R., & Lane, K. L. (2014). Design and management of scientific research in applied school settings. In B. Cook, M. Tankersley, & T. Landrum (Eds.), *Advances in learning and behavioral disabilities* (Vol. 27, pp. 141–169). Emerald.

Walker, H. M., Horner, R. H., Sugai, G., Bullis, M., Spragues, J. R., Bricker, D., & Kaufman, M. J. (1996).

Integrated approaches to preventing antisocial behavior patterns among school-age children and youth. *Journal of Emotional and Behavioral Disorders, 4,* 194–209.

Walker, H., Ramsey, E., & Gresham, G. (2004). *Antisocial behavior in schools: Evidence-based practices.* Cengage.

Walker, H. M., & Severson, H. (1992). *Systematic screening for behavior disorders: Technical manual.* Sopris West.

Wallace, J. M., Goodkind, S., Wallace, C. M., & Bachman, J. G. (2008). Racial, ethnic, and gender difference in school discipline among U.S. high school students: 1991–2005. *The Negro Educational Review, 59,* 47–62.

Wetzel, R. J., & Hoschouer, R. L. (1984). *Residential teaching communities: Program development and staff training for developmentally disabled persons.* Addison Wesley.

Whitford, D. K. (2017). School discipline disproportionality: American Indian students in special education. *Urban Review, 49,* 693–706.

Whitford, D. K., Liaupsin, C. J., Umbreit, J. & Ferro, J. B. (2013). Implementation of a single comprehensive function-based intervention across multiple classrooms for a high school student. *Education and Treatment of Children, 36,* 147–167.

Will, M., & Najarro, I. (2022, April 18). What is culturally responsive teaching? *Education Week.* https://www.edweek.org/teaching-learning/culturally-responsive-teaching-culturally-responsive-pedagogy/2022/04

Witt, J. C., & Elliott, S. N. (1983). *Children's Intervention Rating Profile.* University of Nebraska–Lincoln.

Witt, J. C., & Martens, B. (1983). Assessing the acceptability of behavioral interventions used in classrooms. *Psychology in the Schools, 20,* 510–517.

Wolery, M., Lane, K., & Common, E. A. (2018). Writing tasks: Literature reviews, research proposals, and final reports. In D. L. Gast & J. Ledford (Ed.), *Single case research methodology: Applications in special education and behavioral sciences* (3rd ed., pp. 43– 76). Routledge.

Wolf, M. M. (1978). Social validity: The case for subjective measurement or how applied behavior analysis is finding its heart. *Journal of Applied Behavior Analysis, 11,* 203–214.

Wood, B. K., Ferro, J. B., Umbreit, J., & Liaupsin, C. J. (2011). Addressing the challenging behavior of young children through systematic function-based intervention. *Topics in Early Childhood Special Education, 30,* 221–232.

Wood, B. K., Oakes, W. P., Fettig, A., & Lane, K. L. (2015). A review of the evidence base of functional assessment-based interventions for young students using one systematic approach. *Behavioral Disorders, 40,* 230–250.

Woodcock, R. W., McGrew, K. S., & Mather, N. (2001). *Woodcock–Johnson III Tests of Cognitive Abilities.* Riverside.

Yeaton, W., & Sechrest, L. (1981). Critical dimensions in the choice and maintenance of successful treatments: Strength, integrity, and effectiveness. *Journal of Consulting and Clinical Psychology, 49,* 156–167.

Yell, M. L. (2019). *Endrew F. v. Douglas County School District* (2017): Implications for educating students with emotional and behavioral disorders. *Behavioral Disorders, 45*(1), 53–62.

Zirpoli, T. J. (2016). *Behavior management: Positive applications for teachers* (7th ed.). Pearson.

Index

Note. *f* or *t* following a page number indicates a figure or a table.

A_1-B_1-A_2-B_2 withdrawal design, 267–268
A-B-A-B reversal design, 219
A-B-C (antecedent–behavior–consequence) model. *See* Antecedent–behavior–consequence (A-B-C) model
A-B-C data and recording
   adjusting the environment and, 179–180
   data collection and, 76–82, 80*f*
   direct observations and, 73–75
   example of, 201, 202, 204
   Function Matrix tool and, 91–92
   functional assessment interviews and, 63, 66
   overview, 49–50
   See also Antecedent–behavior–consequence (A-B-C) model; Baseline data; Contextual variables; Data collection; Direct observations; Environmental factors; Function of behaviors
A-B-C Data Collection Form, 79, 80*f*, 83–84, 90, 91, 92*f*
Academic factors, 31, 160
Acquisition deficits, 49–50, 157–158, 167
Activity reinforcers, 20, 21*f*. *See also* Reinforcers
Adjust the Environment (Method 2)
   ethical standards and, 176
   example of, 182–189, 186*f*, 187*f*, 188*f*
   Functional Assessment and Behavior Intervention Plan: Planning Form and, 190–197
   overview, 12, 129, 138*f*, 139, 155, 175, 180–181
   understanding the current environment, 175–180, 177*t*, 178*t*, 179*t*
   See also Combining Method 1 and Method 2; Environmental factors; Intervention grids
Aggressive behaviors, 3, 24, 60–62
Agreement, interobserver. *See* Interobserver agreement (IOA)

Antecedent, reinforcement, and extinction (A-R-E) components. *See* A-R-E (antecedent, reinforcement, and extinction) components
Antecedent–behavior–consequence (A-B-C) model, 10, 11, 16–17, 17*f*, 65–66, 75–76. *See also* A-B-C data and recording; Antecedents; Behavior; Consequences
Antecedents
   adjusting the environment and, 177, 179–180, 179*t*, 181, 187–188, 187*f*
   adjustments to, 139
   drafting A-R-E components and, 255–258
   functional assessment interviews and, 65–66
   identifying, 5
   overview, 17–18, 17*f*, 24–25, 75
   selecting an intervention method and, 135, 136–137
   shifting contingencies and, 199
   teaching the replacement behavior and, 161
   See also A-B-C data and recording; Antecedent–behavior–consequence (A-B-C) model; A-R-E (antecedent, reinforcement, and extinction) components; Contextual variables; Function of behaviors; Stimulus
Anxiety, 3
Applied behavior analysis (ABA) principles, 4
A-R-E (antecedent, reinforcement, and extinction) components
   adjusting the environment and, 181
   combining Method 1 and Method 2, 215–216
   designing interventions and, 255–260, 262
   developing, 139–141
   example of, 187–188, 187*f*
   Function-Based Intervention Decision Model and, 133–134

A-R-E (antecedent, reinforcement, and extinction) components *(cont.)*
  overview, 9, 129–130, 133, 143–144, 155, 254
  preparing for intervention implementation and, 260–262
  shifting contingencies and, 199, 207
  social validity and, 237
  Teach the Replacement Behavior (Method 1) and, 161–162
  treatment integrity and, 229, 230–231, 267
  See also Antecedents; Extinction; Reinforcement
Assessment, 6, 39, 158. *See also* Conducting the functional assessment; Direct observations; Functional assessment interviews; Functional assessments; Identifying students in need of services; Measurement methods
Avoidance behaviors, 24

B

Baseline data
  collecting additional baseline data, 141
  data collection procedures and, 119–123
  data reliability and, 126–127
  ethical standards and, 127
  example of, 163, 185, 218
  interobserver agreement (IOA) and, 123–126, 125*f*
  overview, 11, 117–119, 128, 265–266
  See also A-B-C data and recording; Data collection
Behavior
  categories of, 87–88
  extinction of, 20, 22
  overview, 16–17, 17*f*, 24–25
  punishment and, 22–24
  reinforcement of, 18–20
  See also Antecedent–behavior–consequence (A-B-C) model; Behavioral challenges; Function of behaviors
Behavior analysis, 1, 10, 25
Behavior Analyst Certification Board (BACB)
  ethical standards of, 15, 36, 39, 52, 75, 87
  identifying students in need of services and, 39
  involving clients and stakeholders in the intervention process and, 36
  overview, 6, 7
Behavior Intervention Plan (BIP), 37, 142, 144, 271–272, 273–277. *See also* Functional Assessment and Behavior Intervention Plan: Planning Form; Intervention grids
Behavior Intervention Rating Profile (BIRP), 219
Behavioral challenges, 3–4, 31, 32*t*, 60–63, 105–107. *See also* A-B-C data and recording; Behavior; Replacement behaviors; Target behaviors
Behavioral trap, 247
Behavior-change interventions, 156–157
Board-certified behavior analyst (BCBA), 9, 282

C

Children's Intervention Rating Profile (CIRP)
  example of, 188, 204, 219
  family involvement and, 35
  overview, 140–141
  social validity and, 238, 238*f*, 240*f*

Ci3T Implementation Manual
  identifying students in need of services and, 40
  implementing interventions and, 282–283
  informal observations and, 50–51
  overview, 31
  selecting an intervention method and, 136
  See also Comprehensive, integrated, three-tiered (Ci3T) model of prevention
Classroom environments
  informal observations and, 50–53
  social skills and, 159–160
  understanding the current environment, 175–180, 177*t*, 178*t*, 179*t*
  See also Adjust the Environment (Method 2)
Client involvement
  ethical standards and, 52, 58, 143, 156, 176, 206, 255
  maintenance and generalization and, 245
  social validity and, 236
Coaching models, 283–284
Collaboration, 284, 285. *See also* FABI teams
Collecting baseline data. *See* Baseline data; Data collection
Combining Method 1 and Method 2
  example of, 216–220, 220*f*
  Functional Assessment and Behavior Intervention Plan: Planning Form and, 221–227
  overview, 12, 129, 215–216, 220
  See also Adjust the Environment (Method 2); Intervention grids; Teach the Replacement Behavior (Method 1)
Communicating about services. *See* Describing interventions
Communication skills, 159
Community, 284–285
Competence, 15
Completion Checklist, 37
Completion Checklists, 42–43, 142, 295–306. *See also* Functional Assessment and Behavior Intervention Plan: Planning Form
Comprehensive, integrated, three-tiered (Ci3T) model of prevention
  adjusting the environment and, 178–179
  defining and prioritizing problem behaviors and, 60
  functional assessment-based interventions (FABIs) and, 7–8
  identifying students in need of services and, 39–43, 41*f*–42*f*
  implementing interventions and, 282–283
  overview, 1, 4, 9, 10, 13, 25, 30–36, 32*t*, 33*f*, 34*f*, 37
  reinforcers and, 20
  selecting an intervention method and, 136
  social skills and, 159
  teaching the replacement behavior and, 161–162
  treatment integrity and, 234
  See also Tier 3 interventions; Tiered approaches
Conducting the functional assessment
  A-B-C model and, 75–76
  example of, 163, 164*f*, 183–184, 200–201, 217–218
  overview, 47–48, 265
  See also Assessment; Contextual variables; Direct observations; Function Matrix; Function of behaviors; Functional assessment interviews
Consequences
  adjusting the environment and, 181
  functional assessment interviews and, 65–66

overview, 16, 17f, 75
shifting contingencies and, 199
See also A-B-C data and recording; Antecedent–behavior–consequence (A-B-C) model; Reinforcement; Reinforcers
Consulting models, 283–284
Consumable reinforcers, 20, 21f. *See also* Reinforcers
Contextual variables
functional assessment interviews and, 65
overview, 8–9, 47, 49–50, 75
statement of function and, 93–94
See also A-B-C data and recording; Antecedents; Conducting the functional assessment; Cultural context
Contingency, 12, 16, 187–188, 187f. *See also* Shift the Contingencies (Method 3)
Continuity of services, 271
Covert behaviors, 61. *See also* Behavioral challenges
Cultural context
cultural responsivity, 142, 236, 237
family interviews and, 64
implementing interventions and, 284–285
informal observations and, 53
overview, 8–9
reinforcers and, 19
See also Contextual variables

D

Data, 33, 34f, 41f–42f. *See also* Data collection; Data-informed practices
Data collection
A-B-C data and recording and, 76–82, 80f
data reliability and, 126–127
dimensions of behaviors and, 106–107
ethical standards and, 127, 266
example of, 163, 185, 201, 202, 204, 218
Function Matrix tool and, 90, 93, 99
interobserver agreement (IOA) and, 123–126, 125f
maintenance and generalization and, 245, 249–252, 251f–252f
methods and considerations in, 112–115, 114f
overview, 11, 101–102, 116, 117, 128, 265–266
procedures for, 119–123
social validity and, 237–242, 238f, 239f, 240f, 241f
treatment integrity and, 230–234, 232f, 233f, 267
why measure behaviors, 105–106
See also A-B-C data and recording; Baseline data; Direct observations
Data collectors, 119–121
Data-informed practices
baseline data collection and, 127
collecting and using generalization and maintenance data, 249–252, 251f–252f
combining Method 1 and Method 2 and, 229
ethical standards and, 266
maintenance and generalization and, 245
overview, 35, 105
teaching the replacement behavior and, 156
See also Data collection
Decision making. *See* Function-Based Intervention Decision Model

Describing interventions, 176, 206, 207, 245, 255
Designing assessments, 39, 58, 156, 176. *See also* Assessment
Designing interventions
combining Method 1 and Method 2 and, 216
drafting A-R-E components and, 255–260
ethical standards and, 52, 75, 142–143, 156, 176, 207, 255, 271
example of, 164–165, 165f, 185–188, 186f, 187f, 202–204, 203f, 218–219
identifying functions of behaviors and, 87
maintenance and generalization and, 243–244, 245
manualized approach to, 286–292, 289f–291f
overview, 11–12, 129–130, 131–134, 143–144, 254, 262
preparing for intervention implementation and, 260–262
purpose of, 133
selecting an intervention method and, 134–141, 138f
See also Adjust the Environment (Method 2); Intervention; Shift the Contingencies (Method 3); Teach the Replacement Behavior (Method 1)
Direct observations
data collection and, 76–82, 80f, 119–123
data reliability and, 126–127
ethical standards and, 75
example of, 200–201, 202–203, 218
Function Matrix tool and, 90, 93
how much to observe, 79, 81–82, 115
how to observe, 78–79, 80f, 115
overview, 11, 48, 49–50, 73–75, 82
scheduling, 121–123
steps and activities in, 81
treatment integrity and, 230–231, 232f, 233f
when to observe, 77–78, 115
See also A-B-C data and recording; Assessment; Conducting the functional assessment; Informal observations
Disruptive behaviors, 3, 177, 177t. *See also* Behavioral challenges
Diversity, 142, 236, 237. *See also* Cultural context
Documentation, 36, 271. *See also* Ethical considerations; Functional Assessment and Behavior Intervention Plan: Planning Form
Dual language learners, 97
Duration of behaviors, 106, 110, 113, 114f, 125. *See also* Behavioral challenges

E

Early childhood, 65–66
Educational records, 49, 53–54
Elementary school intervention grids. *See* Intervention grids
Emotional and/or behavioral disorders (EBD), 3–4
Engagement, 177, 177t
Entry criteria, 33, 34f, 41f–42f
Environmental factors
data collection procedures and, 122
designing FABIs and, 12
replacement behaviors and, 97–98
understanding the current environment, 175–180, 177t, 178t, 179t
See also A-B-C data and recording; Adjust the Environment (Method 2)

Equity, 284–285
Escape behaviors, 24. *See also* Behavioral challenges
Ethical considerations
    adjusting the environment and, 176
    BACB ethics code and, 15
    data collection and, 127
    designing and testing the intervention and, 142–143
    designing interventions and, 255
    determining intervention outcomes, 266
    direct observations and, 75
    documentation and, 271
    functional assessment interviews and, 58
    identifying functions of behaviors and, 87
    identifying students in need of services and, 39
    implementing interventions and, 284–285
    informal observations and, 52
    involving clients and stakeholders in the intervention process, 35, 36
    maintenance and generalization and, 245
    overview, 6–7, 271
    shifting contingencies and, 206–207
    social validity and, 236
    teaching the replacement behavior and, 155–157
    treatment integrity and, 229
Evaluation of interventions, 266, 286–292, 289*f*–291*f*. *See also* Outcomes
Event-based measurement, 108–110, 109*f*, 114*f*, 115, 202, 204. *See also* Measurement methods
Exchangeable reinforcers, 20, 21*f*. *See also* Reinforcers
Exit criteria, 33, 34*f*, 41*f*–42*f*
Externalizing behavior patterns, 3. *See also* Behavioral challenges
Extinction
    adjusting the environment and, 187–188, 187*f*
    combining Method 1 and Method 2 and, 216
    drafting A-R-E components and, 255, 259–260
    example of, 204, 219
    overview, 20, 22, 24–25
    of target behavior, 140
    teaching the replacement behavior and, 162
    See also A-R-E (antecedent, reinforcement, and extinction) components

F

FABI Behavior Intervention Plan. *See* Behavior Intervention Plan (BIP); Functional Assessment and Behavior Intervention Plan: Planning Form
FABI Completion Checklists 1–5. *See* Completion Checklists
FABI Grid. *See* Intervention grids
FABI teams
    adjusting the environment and, 179–180
    ethical standards and, 36
    functional assessment interviews and, 58
    implementing interventions and, 282–285
    informal observations and, 52–53
    measurement methods and, 103
    reviewing cumulative files by, 53–54
    treatment integrity and, 230
Fading, 246, 249–250. *See also* Generalization and maintenance

Family involvement
    Ci3T model of prevention and, 35
    ethical standards and, 36
    functional assessment interviews and, 64, 65–66
    identifying students in need of services and, 39
    informal observations and, 53
Fidelity, training, 229. *See also* Treatment integrity
Fluency, 158, 167
Force of behaviors, 107. *See also* Behavioral challenges
Frequency of behaviors, 106, 108, 109*f*, 114*f*, 124. *See also* Behavioral challenges
Function Matrix
    example of, 163, 164*f*, 184
    overview, 6, 11, 50, 87–93, 89*t*, 90*t*, 92*f*, 93*f*, 98–99
    replacement behaviors and, 95–98, 96*t*
    statement of function and, 93–95, 94*t*
    See also Function of behaviors
Function of behaviors
    data collection and, 76
    ethical standards and, 87
    identifying, 5, 11
    overview, 48, 85–87
    reinforcement and, 87
    See also A-B-C data and recording; Antecedents; Conducting the functional assessment; Function Matrix
Function statement, 93–95, 94*t*, 98. *See also* Function Matrix
Functional Assessment and Behavior Intervention Plan: Planning Form
    Adjust the Environment (Method 2) and, 190–197
    combining Method 1 and Method 2 and, 221–227
    ethical standards and, 271
    example of, 273–277
    overview, 99, 132, 145–154, 271–273, 279
    Shift the Contingencies (Method 3) and, 208–214
    Teach the Replacement Behavior (Method 1) and, 168–174
    See also Completion Checklists
Functional assessment, conducting. *See* Conducting the functional assessment
Functional assessment interviews
    A-B-C data and recording and, 75–76
    combining Method 1 and Method 2 and, 217
    data collection procedures and, 121
    defining and prioritizing problem behaviors and, 60–63
    Function Matrix tool and, 90, 93
    overview, 11, 47, 57–59, 66
    Preliminary Functional Assessment Survey (PFAS), 68–70
    recommendations for, 63–66
    Student-Assisted Functional Assessment Interview (FASAI), 71–72
    with teachers, parents and the student, 49
    See also Assessment; Conducting the functional assessment; Functional assessments
Functional assessment-based interventions (FABIs) in general
    conducting, 14–15
    data collection and, 106
    drafting A-R-E components and, 255–260
    ethical standards and, 271
    extinction and, 140

identifying students in need of services and, 39
levels of prevention and, 34f
manualized approach to, 286–292, 289f–291f
overview, 1–2, 4–6, 10, 13, 270
research on, 293–294
teaching at the university level, 288, 289f–291f
testing the FABI and, 268–269
in tiered systems, 6–8
treatment integrity and, 229
See also Conducting the functional assessment; Testing the interventions
Functional assessments, 10–11. *See also* Assessment; Identifying students in need of services; Measurement methods
Functional behavior assessments (FBAs), 5, 10–11, 64
Function-based intervention. *See* Functional assessment-based interventions (FABIs) in general; Intervention
Function-Based Intervention Decision Model
designing and testing the intervention and, 143–144, 258
ethical standards and, 142
overview, 6, 133–134, 138f
selecting an intervention method and, 134–141, 138f

G

Generalization and maintenance
collecting and using generalization and maintenance data, 249–252, 251f–252f
ethical standards and, 245
overview, 12, 141, 243–244, 252–253
strategies for, 246–249
Goals, 268. *See also* Outcomes

H

High school intervention grids. *See* Intervention grids

I

Identifying students in need of services
checklist for, 42–43
example of, 162–163, 182–183, 199–200, 216–217
overview, 9, 10, 27, 38–43, 41f–42f, 44, 265
See also Assessment
Identifying the function of behavior(s). *See* Function Matrix; Function of behaviors
Implementation fidelity, 257
Implementing assessments
ethical standards and, 58, 75, 143, 156, 176, 207, 271
identifying students in need of services and, 39
See also Assessment
Implementing interventions
ethical standards and, 52, 156, 176, 255
identifying functions of behaviors and, 87
individual or team implementation, 282–285
maintenance and generalization and, 245
manualized approach to, 286–292, 289f–291f
overview, 281–282, 285
preparing for, 260–262

Individuals with Disabilities Education Improvement Act (IDEIA), 3–4, 37
Inferences, 134, 140–141
Informal observations, 49–53, 54. *See also* Direct observations
Informed consent, 39
Instructional delivery, 177, 178t, 179t
Integrated tiered systems, 9, 13, 30. *See also* Tiered approaches
Integrity, treatment. *See* Treatment integrity
Intensity of behaviors, 107, 109–110, 114f, 124–125. *See also* Behavioral challenges; Magnitude
Interconnected systems framework (ISF), 4, 30. *See also* Tiered approaches
Internalizing behavior patterns, 3. *See also* Behavioral challenges; Emotional and/or behavioral disorders (EBD)
Interobserver agreement (IOA)
calculating, 124–126, 125f
ethical standards and, 127
example of, 166, 185, 202, 218, 219
overview, 123–126, 125f, 128
Interval recording methods, 110–111, 112f, 115, 123. *See also* Measurement methods
Intervention
informal observations and, 50–53
levels of prevention and, 32–35, 33f, 34f
See also Adjust the Environment (Method 2); Designing interventions; Functional assessment-based interventions (FABIs) in general; Implementing interventions; Prevention; Shift the Contingencies (Method 3); Teach the Replacement Behavior (Method 1); Testing the interventions
Intervention grids
creating transparency and, 35, 36–37
identifying students in need of services and, 40, 41f–42f
informal observations and, 50
levels of prevention and, 32–35, 33f–34f
overview, 7–8, 10, 25, 27, 30, 31
See also Adjust the Environment (Method 2); Behavior Intervention Plan (BIP); Combining Method 1 and Method 2; Shift the Contingencies (Method 3); Teach the Replacement Behavior (Method 1)
Intervention implementation. *See* Implementing interventions
Intervention outcomes. *See* Outcomes
Intervention Rating Profile–15 (IRP-15)
example of, 188, 204
family involvement and, 35
preparing for intervention implementation and, 261
social validity and, 238, 239f, 240f
Intervention Rating Profile–20 (IRP-20), 238
Intervention team. *See* FABI teams
Interviews, 240. *See also* Functional assessment interviews
Introducing punishment, 22–23

L

Latency of behaviors, 106, 110, 114f, 125. *See also* Behavioral challenges

M

Magnitude, 20, 109–110, 114f, 124–125. *See also* Intensity of behaviors; Reinforcers
Maintenance and generalization. *See* Generalization and maintenance
Measurement methods
  data collection procedures and, 119, 122
  data reliability and, 126–127
  dimensions of behaviors and, 106–107
  event-based methods, 108–110, 109f
  identifying information, 114–115
  overview, 6, 103–105, 107–108, 116
  selecting, 112–114, 114f
  time-based methods, 110–112, 112f
  when and how often to observe, 115
  why measure behaviors, 105–106
  See also Assessment; Functional assessments
Methods of intervention. *See* Adjust the Environment (Method 2); Combining Method 1 and Method 2; Shift the Contingencies (Method 3); Teach the Replacement Behavior (Method 1)
Middle school intervention grids. *See* Intervention grids
Motivating operations (MOs), 19–20. *See also* Reinforcement
Multilanguage learners, 97
Multi-tiered systems of support (MTSS), 4, 7–8, 30

N

Negative punishment, 22–23
Negative reinforcement, 18–19, 88, 89t, 90t. *See also* Reinforcement
Noncompliance, 3
Nonuniform behaviors, 108. *See also* Behavioral challenges

O

Observations. *See* Direct observations; Informal observations
Office discipline referrals (ODRs), 40, 60
Operant behavior, 16. *See also* Behavior
Outcomes
  ethical standards and, 266
  overview, 12, 265–266
  social validity and, 268
  student performance and, 267–268
  testing the FABI, 268–269
  See also Evaluation of interventions; Testing the interventions; Treatment integrity

P

Parent involvement. *See* Family involvement
Partial-interval recording methods, 110–111, 112f, 114f, 125–126. *See also* Measurement methods
Performance deficits, 49–50, 158, 167
Permanent product recording, 108, 124, 233
Physiological factors, 179t
Positive behavioral interventions and supports (PBIS), 4
Positive punishment, 22–23
Positive reinforcement
  example of, 203–204
  functions and categories of reinforcers and, 88, 89t, 90t
  overview, 18–19
  See also Reinforcement
Postintervention instruments, 240, 240f, 241f
Preintervention instruments, 238, 238f, 239f, 240
Preliminary Functional Assessment Survey (PFAS), 63–64, 68–70, 217
Preschool intervention grids. *See* Intervention grids
Prevention, 32–35, 33f, 34f. *See also* Intervention
Prioritizing behaviors, 60–63. *See also* Behavioral challenges
Problem behaviors. *See* Behavioral challenges; Target behaviors
Procedural integrity, 229, 268. *See also* Treatment integrity
Professional learning, 286–292, 289f–291f
Progress monitoring, 33, 34f, 41f–42f, 266
Project PREVENT, 199–200
Punishment and punishers, 22–25, 75. *See also* Consequences
Pyramid Model, 66

R

Rate of behaviors, 108–109, 114f, 124
Rating scales, 238–240, 238f, 239f, 240f, 241f
Reactive approaches, 4, 5
Reactivity, 78, 126–127
Record reviews, 53–54
Referral Checklist: Functional Assessment–Based Interventions, 40, 43, 45
Reinforcement
  adjusting the environment and, 181, 187–188, 187f
  behavioral traps and, 247
  categories of behavior and, 87–88
  combining Method 1 and Method 2 and, 216
  drafting A-R-E components and, 255, 258–259
  example of, 203, 219
  extinction and, 22
  fading, 246
  functions of behavior and, 87
  informal observations and, 53
  overview, 18–20, 21f, 24–25
  punishment and, 23–24
  reinforcement shifts, 139–140
  schedules for, 247
  shifting contingencies and, 198–199
  teaching the replacement behavior and, 161
  See also A-R-E (antecedent, reinforcement, and extinction) components; Behavior; Consequences; Reinforcers
Reinforcers
  categories of behavior and, 87–88
  effectiveness of, 19–20, 21f
  functions and categories of, 88, 89t, 90t
  overview, 75
  types or classifications of, 20, 21f
  See also Consequences; Reinforcement
Reliability, 119–121, 126–127

Removing punishment, 22–23
Replacement behaviors
  ability to perform the replacement behavior and, 157–161
  adjusting the environment and, 181
  baseline data collection and, 118
  designing FABIs and, 12
  example of, 201, 202
  fading and, 246
  Function Matrix tool and, 95–98, 96t
  maintenance and generalization and, 243–244
  overview, 47, 95–98, 96t
  selecting an intervention method and, 135, 136
  shifting contingencies and, 199
  teaching the replacement behavior and, 157–161
  See also Behavioral challenges; Teach the Replacement Behavior (Method 1)
Response duration, 110. *See also* Duration of behaviors
Response generalization, 249, 251f–252f, 252. *See also* Generalization and maintenance
Response maintenance, 247–248, 251f–252f, 252. *See also* Generalization and maintenance
Response to intervention (RTI), 4, 30. *See also* Tiered approaches
Risk of interventions, 15, 156–157, 176, 207

S

Schedules of reinforcement, 247. *See also* Reinforcement
Scheduling, 121–123
School factors, 177
Schoolwide data, 33, 34f, 41f–42f
Screening, 39. *See also* Assessment; Identifying students in need of services
Selecting assessments, 39, 58, 143, 156, 176. *See also* Assessment
Selecting interventions
  ethical standards and, 52, 75, 156, 176, 207, 255, 271
  identifying functions of behaviors and, 87
  maintenance and generalization and, 245
  replacement behaviors and, 95–98, 96t
Self-management skills, 160–161
Self-regulation struggles, 3
Self-report methods, 231, 233
Sensory reinforcers, 20, 21f. *See also* Reinforcers
Shift the Contingencies (Method 3)
  ethical standards and, 206–207
  example of, 199–205, 203f, 205f, 206f
  Functional Assessment and Behavior Intervention Plan: Planning Form and, 208–214
  overview, 12, 129, 137–138, 138f, 155, 198–199
  See also Contingency; Intervention grids
Shyness, 3
Social and emotional well-being needs, 31
Social comparison techniques, 240, 242
Social factors, 3, 159–160, 179t
Social reinforcers, 20, 21f. *See also* Reinforcers
Social Skills Improvement System—Rating Scale (SSiS-RS)
  example of, 184
  overview, 58, 66
  performance, fluency, and skill deficits and, 158
  performance of the replacement behaviors and, 160

Social validity
  collecting and using social validity data, 237–242, 238f, 239f, 240f, 241f
  ethical standards and, 236
  example of, 204, 219
  generalization and maintenance and, 250
  importance of, 237
  informal observations and, 53
  overview, 6, 12, 140–141, 235–237, 242, 253, 268
Special education services, 3–4, 38
Staff, 36
Stakeholder involvement
  ethical standards and, 36, 52, 58, 143, 156, 176, 206, 255
  identifying students in need of services and, 39
  maintenance and generalization and, 245
  perspective of stakeholders, 8–9
  social validity and, 236, 268
Statement of function, 93–95, 94t, 98. *See also* Function Matrix
Step 1. *See* Identifying students in need of services
Step 2. *See* Conducting the functional assessment
Step 3. *See* Baseline data; Data collection
Step 4. *See* Designing interventions
Step 5. *See* Testing the interventions
Stimulus, 16, 17f, 20, 21f. *See also* Antecedent–behavior–consequence (A-B-C) model; Antecedents
Stimulus generalization, 248–249, 250, 251f–252f, 252. *See also* Generalization and maintenance
Structured interviews. *See* Functional assessment interviews
Student interview, 66. *See also* Functional assessment interviews
Student performance, 267–268. *See also* Outcomes
Student Risk Screening Scale for Internalizing and Externalizing (SRSS-IE), 40, 60
Student-Assisted Functional Assessment Interview (SAFAI), 63, 71–72, 183–184, 200, 217
Students, 53–54, 94
Supports, 32–35, 33f, 34f
Systematic Screening for Behavior Disorders (SSBD), 53, 182, 185, 200

T

Tangible reinforcers, 20, 21f. *See also* Reinforcers
Target Behavior Template, 60, 62, 67
Target behaviors
  adjusting the environment and, 181
  baseline data collection and, 118
  defining and prioritizing, 60–63
  direct observations and, 79, 81
  example of, 202
  extinction of, 140, 162
  Function Matrix tool and, 95, 96
  overview, 47
  statement of function and, 94
  See also Behavioral challenges
Task demands, 179t
Teach the Replacement Behavior (Method 1)
  ability to perform the replacement behavior, 157–161
  drafting A-R-E components and, 256–257

Teach the Replacement Behavior (Method 1) *(cont.)*
   example of, 162–167, 164*f*, 165*f*, 166*f*
   Functional Assessment and Behavior Intervention Plan: Planning Form and, 168–174
   overview, 12, 129, 137, 138*f*, 139, 155–157, 167
   A-R-E components for, 161–162
   See also Combining Method 1 and Method 2; Intervention grids; Replacement behaviors
Teacher Rating Form (TRF), 200
Teachers, 36
Teams. *See* FABI teams
Testing the interventions
   ethical standards and, 142–143, 266
   example of, 165–167, 166*f*, 188–189, 188*f*, 204–205, 204*f*, 206*f*, 219–220
   overview, 12, 131–133, 141–144, 263, 265–266
   purpose of, 133
   social validity and, 268
   testing the FABI and, 268–269
   treatment integrity and, 267
   See also Intervention; Outcomes
Three-term contingency, 16. *See also* Contingency
Tier 1 interventions
   adjusting the environment and, 175, 177–179, 178*t*
   contextual variables and, 49
   identifying students in need of services and, 40, 42
   implementing interventions and, 282–283
   informal observations and, 52, 53
   See also Comprehensive, integrated, three-tiered (Ci3T) model of prevention; Tiered approaches
Tier 2 interventions
   adjusting the environment and, 178–179
   generalization and maintenance and, 247–248
   identifying students in need of services and, 40, 42
   implementing interventions and, 282–283
   informal observations and, 52
   See also Comprehensive, integrated, three-tiered (Ci3T) model of prevention; Tiered approaches
Tier 3 interventions
   adjusting the environment and, 178–179
   creating transparency and, 36–37
   data collection and, 106
   defining and prioritizing problem behaviors and, 60
   generalization and maintenance and, 247–248
   identifying students in need of services and, 40, 42
   implementing interventions and, 282–283
   informal observations and, 52
   overview, 1, 9, 29–30, 37
   See also Comprehensive, integrated, three-tiered (Ci3T) model of prevention; Tiered approaches
Tiered approaches
   adjusting the environment and, 178–179
   generalization and maintenance and, 247–248
   identifying students in need of services and, 39, 40
   implementing interventions and, 282–283
   overview, 4, 9, 25, 29–30

   social skills and, 159
   See also Comprehensive, integrated, three-tiered (Ci3T) model of prevention; Integrated tiered systems; Tier 1 interventions; Tier 2 interventions; Tier 3 interventions
Tiered Fidelity Inventory (TFI), 52
Time-based measurement. *See also* Measurement methods
   data collection procedures and, 123
   interobserver agreement (IOA) and, 125–126
   overview, 110–112, 112*f*, 113, 114*f*, 115
Tokens, 20, 21*f*. *See also* Reinforcers
Topography of behaviors, 106–107. *See also* Behavioral challenges
Training, 229, 234, 286–292, 289*f*–291*f*. *See also* Treatment integrity
Transitioning services, 271
Transparency, 36–37
Treatment Acceptability Rating Form—Revised (TARF-R), 166, 238
Treatment Evaluation Inventory (TEI), 238
Treatment Evaluation Inventory—Short Form (TEI-SF), 238
Treatment integrity
   collecting and using treatment integrity data, 230–234, 232*f*, 233*f*
   ethical standards and, 229
   example of, 166, 205, 206*f*, 219
   importance of, 230
   overview, 6, 12, 228, 229, 234, 253, 267
   types of integrity, 229
   See also Outcomes
Treatment Integrity Checklists/Forms, 187–188, 187*f*, 205, 206*f*, 231, 232*f*, 233*f*
Triadic model of consultation, 283–284
Type I punishment, 23
Type II punishment, 23

U

Uniform behaviors, 107–108, 114*f*. *See also* Behavioral challenges
Universal Checklist, 53, 55–56
Using data. *See* Data-informed practices

V

Valid inference making, 134, 140–141
Validity, social. *See* Social validity
Verbal behavior, 61. *See also* Behavioral challenges

W

Whole-interval recording methods, 110–111, 113, 114*f*, 125–126. *See also* Measurement methods
Withdrawal, 3